Zion in the Courts

Zion in the Courts

—

*A Legal History of the Church
of Jesus Christ of Latter-day Saints,
1830–1900*

—

Edwin Brown Firmage
and
Richard Collin Mangrum

University of Illinois Press
Urbana and Chicago

© 1988 by the Board of Trustees of the University of Illinois
Manufactured in the United States of America
C 5 4 3 2 1

This book is printed on acid-free paper.

Library of Congress Cataloging-in-Publication Data

Firmage, Edwin Brown.
  Zion in the courts.

  Bibliography: p.
  Includes index.
    1. Mormons—Legal status, laws, etc.—United States—
History.   2. Ecclesiastical courts—United States—
History.   3. Church of Jesus Christ of Latter-Day Saints
—History.   4. Mormon Church—History.   I. Mangrum,
Richard Collin.   II. Title.
KF4869.M6F57   1988   262.9'89373   87-30171
ISBN 0-252-01498-7

Contents

Acknowledgments

Our students and colleagues in the law contributed substantially to the research represented in many of the chapters in this book: Michael Later, Richard Van Wagoner, and Paul Simmons deserve special thanks for their contributions to the chapters dealing with polygamy. Blake Ostler, Steve Clark, Mark Nelson, Jeffrey Robinson, David Scofield, Julie Lund, David D. Peck, Russell Cline, Kedric A. Bassett, Doyle Buchanan, Kevin Holderness, Guy Price, Thomas A. Blakely, Scott Hagen, and William Richards all enriched several chapters. Blake Ostler deserves special recognition for his reviewing our material on the concept of Zion and providing substantial historical enrichment.

Professors Davis Bitton and Dean May read our entire manuscript and provided criticism that has substantially improved the quality of our book. Of course we are responsible for the errors, misperceptions, and misinterpretations that remain.

Lora Lee Petersen, Mary Hoban, Carol Jo Cameron, Cary McBreen, Karen Duffy, Eileen Leuschen, and Vicki Simants typed interminable drafts of major sections of this work over a four-year period, sometimes rescuing whole chapters from memory tracts of computers which, periodically and inexplicably, consumed our work. Elizabeth Kirschen and Barbara McFarlane also gave valuable help that is sincerely appreciated.

We are grateful especially to our editors, Lavina Fielding Andersen, Paul Simmons, and Ron Bitton, who made us look better in print than we are. We also appreciate Becky Staples's work as copyeditor.

The financial assistance of the University of Utah and Creighton University Research Committees made our research possible.

Finally, and most important, following seven years of work, we are deeply in debt to our dearest friends, Gloria Paramore Firmage, Barbara Isaac Mangrum (deceased), and Ann Walton Mangrum for their encouragement, for their love, and for their tolerating long absences, interspersed with increasingly cranky reappearances, as this book neared completion.

Introduction

Our study of nineteenth-century Mormon legal history follows a somewhat different path from most general Mormon histories. It examines Mormon experiences with the civil law and Mormon attempts to implement a church court system. We conclude that Mormonism was devoted to the ideal of Zion, a perfected community of Saints organized in economic, political, and social affairs by priesthood direction and united by love of God and expectation of his Second Coming. This theological commitment decisively influenced Mormon legal conflicts with the state and Mormon efforts to operate a church court system with broad jurisdictional powers. This vision of Zion explains Mormon legal history in a way that purely materialistic explanations cannot. Radical change and assimilation occurred only when priesthood leadership decided to abandon, for a time, the here-and-now concept of Zion. Although social and economic considerations certainly influenced that vision of Zion, Mormonism's resistance to economic pressures depended on the strength of that theological commitment.[1]

At present, Mormons have lost much of the sense of the ideal of Zion that earlier Mormons felt. Nibley correctly interprets Joseph Smith's (1833) statement "We will still weep for Zion" (HC 1:317) as prophetic "because the Zion he has so clearly in mind has not been realized" (Nibley 1972–73). (For HC and other abbreviations, consult the list following the Epilogue.) The early Mormon Saints wept because they had failed to implement an attainable Zion, complete with radical social relations characteristic of the eternal order of the perfected community. Thus when Jedediah M. Grant challenged in 1854, "If you want a heaven, go to and make it" (JD 3:66), he was urging them to do the difficult, but not the impossible. Modern scripture and prophetic utterance had provided a map. Brigham Young enunciated the same idea in 1862: "I have Zion in my view constantly. We are not going to wait for angels, or for Enoch and his company to come and build Zion, but we are going to build it" (JD 9:284). Mormon theology translated directly into social responsibility.

In many ways, Mormonism is heir to the American quest for religious freedom and holy commonwealth. The heart of the early Puritan attempt to order society according to scriptural mandate was the "covenant theology" that had been propounded by Calvin, Zwingli, Heinrich, Bullinger, and their successors (Ahlstrom, 1:176–78). Covenant theology premised social relationships and governmental legitimacy on an elaborate system of personal and social covenants (Simpson, 17–28; Miller 1933, 676–715). The Puritans who colonized New England used this covenant theology to give economic, social, and political order to their communities. They entered into "holy commonwealths" that were incipient governments. These commonwealths were founded on principles embodied in the articles of agreement of individual covenants. The famous Mayflower Compact is an example of such a political theory:

> In ye name of God, Amen. We whose names are underwritten . . . doe by these presents solemnly & mutualy in ye presence of God, and one of another, covenant and combine our selves togeather into a civill body politick, for our better ordering & preservation, & furtherance of ye ends aforesaid; and by vertue hereof to enacte constitute, and frame such just & equall lawes, ordinances, acts, constitutions, & offices, from time to time, as shall be thought most meete and convenient for ye generall good of ye Colonie, unto which we promise all due submission and obedience. . . . (Miller and Johnson 1963, 198–99)

The first colonies were indeed corporate bodies bonded together by "contractual" agreements, but the ideal of the social contract extended to every phase of life. Formation of a Holy Commonwealth was thought to embody responsibility not only among persons, but between the community and God. John Winthrop, first governor of Massachusetts, reflected on the relationship between covenants with God and with society while still aboard the *Arbella*:

> It is of the nature and essence of every society to be knit together by some covenant, either expressed or implied. . . . Thus stands the cause between God and us: we are entered into a covenant with Him for this work; we have taken out a commission, the Lord hath given us leave to draw our articles. . . . For we must consider that we shall be as a city upon a hill, the eyes of all people are upon us. (Ahlstrom, 1:195)

The covenant society was a balance between the desires of the individual and the demands of the community, for the well-being of society depended upon individual acceptance and performance of the covenant obligations rather than legal coercion. Thus the New England colonies utilized covenantal ideas to curb purely individual endeavors, while the underlying political theory of social compact gave a feeling of solidarity and calling from God (Miller 1939, 430–40). Eventually, the political theories implicit in the Puritan covenant theology were embodied in the Declaration of Independence and the more conservative United States Constitution (Andrus 1973, 96–105; Ahlstrom, 1:437–70). Mormons expressed great respect for the principles underlying the Constitution, and they emulated them in their own quest for a more just society.

The early nineteenth century gave rise to numerous utopian aspirants: Jemima Wilkinson, Robert Owen, John Noyes, the Shakers, and the followers of George Rapp all founded utopian communities in the northeastern United States. Sidney Rigdon, who joined the Mormon Church in late 1830 and had considerable influence on Joseph Smith after February 1831, was familiar with the communitarian efforts of Robert Owen, the Rappites, and the German Separatists at Zoar, Ohio.

Yet it would be a mistake to conclude that Joseph Smith simply derived his ideas from these movements. Indeed, in many ways Mormonism is closer to the sixteenth-century Anabaptists whose communal and polygamous theocracy gave rise to the "radical reformation," than to the nineteenth-century descendants of the radical reformation such as the Quakers, Unitarians, and Campbellites (Arrington, Fox, and May, 3–4). As Richard Bushman has explained, Joseph's radicalism both absorbed and transcended the socioreligious living attempts and ideas with which he had contact (Bushman, 184–88).

The communitarian utopias generally shared a number of characteristics. All were formed by innovative and charismatic leaders who rejected codes and statutes and traditions and customs (Backman 1965, 237ff). Most embraced what they considered to be a vision of primitive, first-century Christianity and expected the restoration of the untainted primitive church to be followed by the renewal of the spiritual gifts enjoyed by the original apostles (Bedell, Sandon, and Wellborn, 189–91). Most communities were motivated by Christian perfectionism and a conviction that attaining such perfection required a conducive social order (Ahlstrom, 1:593–94; Foster, 15). Most also were motivated by a millennarian belief in the Second Coming of Christ (Foster, 15–18). The new communitarian orders usually practiced non-traditional kinship and marriage patterns ranging from celibacy to complex marriage (Foster, 10–12). Some adopted strict and abstemious new health codes (Bush, 46–65). All of the orders rejected the holding of private property and adopted new forms of ownership including communal living and the owning of common stock in cooperative businesses (Nordhoff 1875; Egbert and Persons 1952). Early Mormons went out of their way to distinguish their vision of the United Order from other communitarian societies; yet Mormonism shared all of these characteristics, albeit in a distinctive synthesis that was unique in both its expectations and its degree of fulfillment.

One communitarian attempt that was particularly important in Mormon history was "The Family," the group founded by Sidney Rigdon after he broke with Alexander Campbell over doctrinal issues. Rigdon embraced Christian primitivism and believed that the Christian church should be organized precisely as it was portrayed in the New Testament. He attempted to duplicate the early Christian practice described in Acts 4:32–35, "And the multitude of them that believed were of one heart and of one soul: neither said any of them that ought of the things which he possessed was his own; but they had all things in common." Rigdon's flock of believers settled on a farm owned by Isaac Morley near Kirtland, Ohio. The members of Rigdon's community owned all goods through a common-stock arrangement, including clothes and other personal items. As Hyrum Andrus noted, "the first one up in the morning was often the best dressed that day" (Andrus 1973, 7). The unity the group sought through common ownership proved difficult to obtain. Discord arising from a sense of private ownership constantly threatened the community; it was abandoned in February 1831 after Sidney Rigdon and many of his followers were converted to Mormonism (Arrington, Fox, and May, 19).

Some have characterized attempts at socioreligious orders as "experiments." As Sterling M. McMurrin has noted,

> This is like calling marriage an experiment in the case of people who are genuinely in love and expect to stay married. . . . However others may regard it, those who follow a course in the belief that they are dedicating themselves to the will of God are not experimenting. This manner in which scholars so frequently look back over the serious living of those generations tends sometimes to rob those generations of their sincerity and purpose and of the degree of their commitment. (McMurrin, 18)

For early Mormons, Zion was a fulfillment and culmination of this Judeo-Christian heritage. Zion was the ideal of a more just society predicated on a new economic order, social equality, and sacred covenants. Zion was the New Jerusalem that would prepare the earth for the imminent Second Coming. Zion was the hope for a new social relationship of which the family, as redefined under a patriarchal system, was a microcosm. Zion was thus a rejection of existing social and economic mores because these defined Babylon, the society that Mormonism was called to transform, or at least live apart from. Only after the imminence of Zion had been explained away did Mormon leadership abandon the distinctive practices that made coexistence with Babylon impossible.

Perhaps the most significant influence on the Mormon hope for Zion was a belief in the literal fulfillment of biblical prophecies regarding Zion in both the Old and New Testaments. The Old Testament speaks of Zion as an eschatological society where the Lord himself would dwell in his tabernacle (Pss. 9:11; 76:2; Isa. 24:23; 59:20; 60:14). Zion was the mountain of Yahweh that came to be associated with Jerusalem. In latter days, the law would go forth from Zion, and scattered Israel would return there (Isa. 2:3; Micah 4:2; 2 Neh. 12:2). In the Book of Revelation the eschatological dwelling place of God was described as Zion, the New Jerusalem. It was God's kingdom on earth during his millennial reign (Rev. 21:1–3). Like many in early nineteenth-century America, indeed in Christianity in general, the Mormon community looked forward to the fulfillment of biblical prophecies and reinterpreted and applied them to their own situation. Mormonism appropriated the practices of the Hebrew culture represented in the Old Testament to a remarkable degree because it expected the "restoration of all things" (D&C 27:6; 77:7; 86:10; 132:40, 45). It looked not only to the Sinai covenant as a basis for social order, but to the patriarchal practice of plural marriage and the covenant of a promised land to give meaning to its own "new and everlasting covenant." The Book of Mormon is one of the best examples of the reinterpretation of Israel and its fulfillment in Mormon history. Through the Book of Mormon, Mormonism was imbued with a providential sense of history that allowed it to see purpose in its persecutions and trials. Through the Book of Mormon, Mormonism gained immediate identity with ancient Israel and the Chosen People of God.

The Saints thus possessed an explanatory paradigm that could account for misunderstanding and abuse from Babylon, the larger unregenerated society. Indeed, it would have been surprising had their radical theological beliefs and practices not caused a stir. Persistent legal and extralegal persecution signified that the Saints were on the right track; indeed such obstacles were deemed part of the process of sanctification. Babylon would not yet receive the eternal order, but God would intercede once a proper purity amongst his people was achieved. Conversely, to purchase peace with Babylon by capitulation (lowering standards to accommodate the world) meant postponing the cause of Zion. "If this people neglect their duty, turn away from the holy commandments which God has given us, seek for their own individual wealth, and neglect the interests of the Kingdom of God," warned Brigham Young in 1865, "We may expect to be here quite a while—perhaps a period that will be far longer than we anticipated" (JD 11:102).

That postponement came but Mormons resisted Babylon longer than materialistic historiography can explain, refusing to assimilate long after any economic watershed had passed. Evidence of the persistent orientation toward Zion is manifest in the continuation of distinctive Mormon social, political, and juridical practices into the last decade of the nineteenth century. Despite intense persecution and deprivation, the priesthood tenaciously held onto polygamy until 1890 when President Woodruff issued the Manifesto. Indeed, many leaders and members regarded the Manifesto as an unrighteous capitulation to Babylon, an abandonment of the cause of Zion (Quinn 1985). Similarly, Mormons retained elevated political ambitions for some time; they, at a minimum, remained politically isolated until 1891 when their People's Party was dissolved and members were encouraged to align themselves evenly with the national parties. The church court records also show the priesthood retained exclusive jurisdiction over secular as well as religious cases throughout the 1890s.

By the second decade of the twentieth century, assimilation had been adopted as a social objective in place of the immediacy of a here-and-now Zion. For a time the Second Coming and the attainment of Zion was thought to be close at hand. Repeated delays and setbacks contributed to a revised view of Zion as the familiar heavenly city of Christianity: a community too perfect for this life, but an ideal that would be realized in the eternities. This revised vision made more sense to the second generation of Mormons, who were taking over church leadership in increasing numbers. Perhaps they would have to wait for angels after all. Once the sense of the imminence of Zion was lost, assimilation naturally followed.

While the Mormon view of Zion endured in nineteenth-century America, legal pressure and harassment were predictable. The story of the persecution Mormons suffered through the institutions of the legal system, and of their efforts to establish their own legal system—one appropriate to Zion—throws into high relief a number of important historical concepts: (1) it illustrates democracy's potential to oppress an insular, minority community; (2) it demonstrates the difficulty of establishing and maintaining a distinctive socioeconomic structure in a hostile legal environment; (3) it reveals an ambitious attempt by a religious community to preempt the state's role in mediating conflicts among believers; (4) it depicts the central place of religious objectives in the processes of history, objectives that have sometimes been ignored or slighted in favor of economic factors; (5) it presents an alternative to the Anglo-American system of adversarial justice; and (6) it dramatizes religiously motivated cooperation as an alternative to coercion in encouraging obedience to a community's normative standards. Mormon legal history, in brief, considers the critical role of law, both civil and religious, in either building and maintaining or dismantling and suppressing any community's normative structure.

Part I of this volume describes the interaction between what the early Saints interpreted as legal persecution and the rise of a church court system based on Mormon theology and experience. Mormon beliefs about the proper ordering of church and state relations are considered. Persistent problems with "vexatious" lawsuits and the inadequacy of the courts in shielding the Saints from open conflict with their neighbors as they actively pursued Zion in New York, Ohio, Missouri, and Illinois are recounted.

Part II reviews the constitutional crisis the Mormons faced in the Great Basin as they worked to establish their Zion with distinctive political, social, and economic practices. The unwillingness or inability of American society to tolerate the peculiar institutions embraced by Mormons was one of the major events in the nineteenth-century religious history of this country. The Mormon struggle against the attempts of the larger society to dominate or to absorb their culture became the first great precedent in determining the scope of the "free exercise of religion" clause of the First Amendment to the Constitution. The first response of the United States Supreme Court to this crisis, the *Reynolds* case, recognized an unworkable distinction between religious belief and religious practice. While *Reynolds* accorded absolute protection to belief, it provided little protection for religiously inspired conduct. Mormons tested the limits of American pluralism: the courts consistently ruled that group idiosyncrasy remained beyond the social contract. Indeed, from a modern perspective it would seem that the state cut constitutional corners in response to the stubbornness of Mormon leaders in repudiating community mores.

Part III analyzes how the church court system operated for internal purposes as an alternative to the civil system. The Mormon ecclesiastical system played a critical role in furthering the cause of Zion: church courts simply translated the theological basis of Mormon distinctiveness into practical terms.

Analyses of the church court system are relatively few and incomplete. None deal with the central role of church courts in the religious objective of building Zion. These unsatisfactory treatments probably reflect simply the dearth of available resource material. Part III, which benefits from an exhaustive investigation of original materials, provides the most complete analysis of the Mormon ecclesiastical court system attempted to date. In doing so it clears up some misconceptions and offers an alternative view of the courts.

The few existing analyses of the Mormon court system contradict each other. Raymond Swenson (1978, 587–88), in "Resolution of Civil Disputes by Mormon Ecclesiastical Courts," calls the ecclesiastical courts

> generally scrupulous in obeying the statutory law and basic principles of court-made law. The high council cited decisions of the territorial and United States Supreme Courts, and rulings were made on the basis of the predicted outcome in civil courts. . . . Probably the only instance of noncompliance with a clearly applicable statute was the failure to observe the anti-polygamy laws.

Swenson argues that by 1886 attorneys practiced in many church courts, suggesting "that their decisions should be legally accurate as well as roughly equitable. Their judgments began to be viewed as illegitimate if they did not conform to the legally-defined rights and obligations of the parties." He attributes this situation to the adoption of a capitalist economy in the Great Basin by the late 1880s that "moved the Church courts away from establishing a separate body of 'Mormon law.' They avoided placing Mormons in the anomalous position of living under two competing standards of legal behavior" (Swenson, 593). He concludes his study by denying any distinctive importance to the Mormon courts: "In reality, the Church courts sought to follow the accepted law of American society, rejecting only those precedents which they considered unsuited to their unique social environment" (Swenson, 594).

Mark Leone (1979) derived his radically different perspective on church courts from a limited study of cases between 1884 and 1896 in eastern Arizona. He argues that the church courts, unlike their civil counterparts, relied entirely on inspiration in resolving disputes, thereby rejecting any reference to rules, legal or otherwise:

> Inspiration, however, required a short memory, of the sort the Mormons guaranteed themselves by not using precedent, or not considering the context of any past event used as a citation, or not having lawyers. There is no hint that any councillor ever consulted the council's minutes for precedent or guidance. The result, consequently, was that a govern-

ment that used sanctity to rule forgot its own history. In being flexible, avoiding conflict, remaining pragmatic, and requiring consensus, such a government divorced itself from its own past. (Leone, 146)

Leone further suggests that the power of both church courts and high councils diminished, at least in eastern Arizona, after about 1890 with the rise of civil courts and secular government. "Neither courts nor council disappeared, but both became limited solely to affairs internal to the church" (Leone, 120). Unlike Swenson, Leone argues that the church and civil systems did not converge, but that the church system gave way to the civil system as soon as it reached the Mormon hinterland.

Both analyses miss the essence of the church court system in the nineteenth century. The church courts did not adopt civil law procedures or rules of decision as Swenson suggests, nor did church courts ignore their own history in making decisions as Leone argues. Furthermore, both are mistaken in believing that the absorption of the Mormon markets into the national economy and the extension of the federal court system into the far reaches of the Great Basin immediately affected the Mormon ecclesiastical courts.

In reality, Mormons adopted distinctive normative standards in some areas and followed the civil law in a limited sense in others. Unusual social practices ranging from natural resource policies to plural marriage created conscious deviations from civil law rules. In other areas, such as those affecting commercial transactions, the church courts looked to their civil counterparts in resolving disputes, a process that accelerated as the Mormon community meshed with the national economy. Even in these cases, however, the church courts did not feel any moral obligation to follow the civil law and sought unconventional resolutions in many cases.

The church courts continued to exercise jurisdiction over temporal as well as spiritual matters well after alternative adjudicative forums were available. They had arisen as part of a distinctive view of society and continued to provide an orderly defense of that religious vision until the Mormons abandoned any immediate commitment to it. Unquestionably, economic and political factors constrained many of the distinctive Mormon concepts. Nonetheless, as long as the Mormons held themselves responsible for building Zion, the church courts flourished, despite secular alternatives, much longer than any materialistic historical model would have predicted.

PART I

Early Mormon Legal Experience

―――

While Mormon theology posited the possibility of Zion's peaceful co-existence with the constitutional state, Mormon history catalogs a long list of negative experiences with gentile law, lawyers, and legal institutions that ensured continued hostility between the Saints and the state. The Mormon exodus into the uninhabited Great Basin was a direct result of the state's lack of interest or ability to protect the Saints' constitutional (inalienable) rights to freedom of conscience and religious practice. Mormons protested on constitutional grounds against persecutors who used civil law to assail them and ultimately lost confidence in civil law and government when they were unable to obtain legal redress from the state for mob attacks on their persons and property. Similarly Mormons condemned pettifogging lawyers, the technical, inefficient, and divisive nature of the adversarial system of justice, and the injustice manifest in the inflexible application of the common law. For these reasons, they rejected gentile law and turned to their own church court system.

The perceived deficiencies of civil law, lawyers, and legal institutions no doubt hastened church court development, but these courts would have grown up anyway. Mormon theology taught the Saints that it was their special responsibility to build a distinctive religious community, unified in purpose and conduct. Achieving oneness in the community of Zion would prepare for the impending millennial reign of Christ. The church courts enforced church discipline in the pursuit of unity; the resulting religious conformity was to replace the chaos of pluralistic American society with the oneness of Zion.

Ecclesiastical courts served the cause of Zion in many ways. They legitimized religious discipline among leadership and membership alike. They kept the community from fragmenting into disparate parts by removing those who refused to conform to religious norms or priesthood directives. The civil courts, of course, were not competent to hear matters of religious discipline; Zion's courts provided the only forum for spiritual offenses. Applied to temporal disputes, the church courts provided cost-free and trusted forums, eliminated the divisive influence of lawyers, and removed the church's dependence on the state as a competing source of authority in the community. Ecclesiastical priesthood leaders were aware of community conflict and involved themselves in its resolution, through applying religious considerations. For the Mormons, these benefits justified the "exclusive jurisdiction" rule adopted in Utah: willingly suing another member before "the ungodly" constituted "unChristianlike conduct." For the remainder of the nineteenth century, Mormons relied almost exclusively on their own courts and institutions to resolve disputes in a community imbued with the vision of Zion.

1

Zion and the State

Mormons, like other Christians, accepted Jesus' instruction to render unto Caesar the things which are Caesar's and unto God the things which are God's. But, as the history of church-state relations amply demonstrates, it is easier to say this than to draw a clear line of demarcation. Mormons thought that God, not Caesar, had the final authority to make the division of responsibility. Moreover, the expansive vision of Zion seemingly left a grudgingly small allocation of authority to the state. Not surprisingly, gentiles who controlled the state sometimes found the Mormon view of the division unsatisfactory; they denied Mormon revelatory claims any effect in resolving jurisdictional boundaries. The history of the Mormon legal experience in the nineteenth century provides a case study of the tension likely to arise in a liberal state whenever a distinct group with its own normative, economic, and social bases aspire to dominance, even over its own institutions and members (Mangrum 1988).

The preeminent social obligation to build Zion necessarily called into question the controversial boundaries between church and state: a political question that has perplexed this country and its people from the pilgrims forward. Where secular laws varied from religious rules in economic or social relations, which should prevail? For Mormons in the nineteenth century this question entailed more than hypothetical significance. When the highest ecclesiastical authorities directed certain believers to enter polygamous marriages, what effect should legal sanctions have on individuals faced with a choice between obedience to God or the state? Where public land laws permitted homesteading a quarter-section of federal lands, what difference should it make to a Mormon who had been allocated only a fraction of that acreage as his inheritance in Zion? In those instances where a successful farmer had a valid contractual claim against a less fortunate widow, should he forbear when a church court required him to abandon it? The Saints faced these and other conflicts between the normative orders of the state and Zion throughout the nineteenth century. Many deferred to Zion. Their obedience sometimes conflicted with their own secular interest; at times members concluded that the church asked too much. Deference to the state's conflicting norms, however, often resulted in excommunication and social ostracism: severe costs to religious people.

Some viewed Mormon disregard for the laws of the state that conflicted with religious obligations as evidence of sedition and totalitarianism. Priesthood leaders countered with the argument that conflict was not inevitable, but followed from the state's encroachment of natural rights or proper principles that formed the basis of constitutional government (Firmage 1976, 11; Firmage 1981, 37–39; Mangrum 1988).

While "governments were instituted of God for the benefit of men" (D&C 134:1; 98:5–6), their justification came from preserving the "inherent and inalienable rights" of man (D&C 134:5). In a very Lockean sense, the Mormons ranked religious liberty highest amongst those rights worthy of the state's protection (Mangrum 1988). For Joseph Smith religious liberty meant more than the Puritans' view that each has a right to practice true religion, but encompassed freedom of conscience for all, even those in error:

> We deem it a just principle, . . . that all men are created equal, and they all have the privilege of thinking for themselves upon all matters relative to conscience. Consequently, then, we are not disposed, had we the power, to deprive any one of exercising that free independence of mind which heaven has so graciously bestowed upon the human family as one of its choicest gifts. (Smith 1940, 49)

Granted Smith did not address the issue of religious beliefs, say human sacrifice, which conflicted with other human values. John Stuart Mill had not yet written *On Liberty*, wherein he introduced the liberal principle (although from the perspective of a utilitarian) of "harm to others" as a limiting constraint. Indeed Mill in his famous treatise would rely on the Mormon polygamy example as an instance where the state had unfairly encroached upon personal liberty. In any event, Smith undoubtedly felt that whatever limits religious liberty necessarily entailed, Mormon beliefs and practices did not exceed them.

Thus if the state would respect the inalienable rights of Mormons, they would dwell peacefully within its borders, practicing such religiously ordained principles as polygamous marriage and communitarian economic relationships.

Indeed, Mormon leaders, especially Joseph Smith, explained that providential history had been at work for the very purpose of preparing the way for the building up of the kingdom of God. "[F]or this purpose" the Lord "raised up" the "wise men" who framed the United States Constitution with its Bill of Rights (D&C 101:80; Mangrum 1988). Undoubtedly the Saints were naive in their belief that a radical Zion could peaceably coexist within the state. They certainly did not expect the turbulent interaction that became their history.

INSPIRED CONSTITUTIONAL PRINCIPLES AND THEIR LIMITS

The belief that American constitutional principles were divinely inspired placed Mormons in an anomalous situation when they were interpreted against the Saints. Many viewed the anomaly as evidence of insincerity; despite public respect for constitutional government, Mormons were really secessionists who longed to supplant democratic institutions with dictatorial priesthood control. But the affection Mormons held for the principles of the American constitution, even while condemning its officials, belies this view and requires a more persuasive explanation of Mormon ideas of the relation between church and state.

Prior to their exodus from the Midwest to the Great Basin, the Mormons looked to the federal government for vindication of their rights against local encroachment. Joseph Smith's major criticism of the Constitution was that its civil libertarian provisions did not extend to state and local government, a condition remedied after the Civil War with the passage of the Fourteenth Amendment and the gradual inclusion of most protections of the Bill of Rights within its due process clause. Smith made one of his most comprehensive statements on the subject in Nauvoo in 1843, when he said:

> I am the greatest advocate of the constitution of the United States there is on the earth. In my feelings I am always ready to die for the protection of the weak and the oppressed in their just rights. The only fault I find with the Constitution is, it is not broad enough to cover the whole ground.
>
> Although it provides that all men shall enjoy religious freedom, yet it does not provide the manner by which that freedom can be preserved, nor for the punishment of Government officers who refuse to protect the people in their religious rights, or punish those mobs, state, or communities who interfere with the rights of the people on account of their religion. Its sentiments are good but it provides no means of enforcing them. It has but this one fault. Under its provision, a man or a people who are able to protect themselves can get along well enough; but

those who have the misfortune to be weak or unpopular are left to the merciless rage of popular fury. (Smith 1940, 326–27; HC 6:56–57)

Any talk about Joseph Smith's views about the federal constitution would not be complete, however, without reference to the Council of Fifty.

Available references to Joseph Smith's teachings about the Constitution are limited. The 1844 minutes of the meetings of the Council of Fifty are said to contain literally hundreds of pages of Smith's teachings about the meaning of the federal constitution and its application to the Saints in the world and during the millennium, but these are not generally available at this time (Quinn 1980, 163–64, 192).

Joseph Smith stated that, in accordance with a revelation received 7 April 1842, he was to set up an organization whose formal name was "[t]he Kingdom of God and His Laws with the Keys and Power[s] thereof, and Judgment in the Hands of His Servants, Ahman Christ," and whose more popular (and much shorter) name was "The Kingdom of God" or, as it shall be referred to herein, "The Council of Fifty." The organization was not established until 10 March 1844, when the first people were called to positions in the group.

The purpose of the Council of Fifty is outlined in a revelation dated 27 June 1882:

> Thus saith the Lord God who rules in the heavens above and in the earth beneath, I have introduced my kingdom and my Government, even the Kingdom of God, that my servants have heretofore prophesied of and that I taught to my disciples to pray for, saying "Thy Kingdom come, thy will be done on earth as it is in heaven," for the establishment of my rule, for the introduction of my law, for the protection of my Church, and for the maintenance, promulgation and protection of civil and religious liberty in this nation and throughout the world; and all men of every nation, color and creed shall yet be protected and shielded thereby; and every nation and kindred, and people, and tongue shall yet bow the knee to me, and acknowledge me to be Ahman Christ, to the glory of God the Father. (Quinn 1980, 170)

There were two parliamentary rules to the Council: it could not convene without a quorum (defined as being 50 percent of the membership), and it only existed officially when convened to conduct business. The group had its own constitution that was largely based on the United States Constitution, a document that was perceived as inspired, or close to it.

There has been quite a bit of speculation about the role the Council of Fifty played in Mormon history. Klaus Hansen has taken the position that the Council played a dynamic role in the building of Brigham Young's Utah theocracy (Hansen 1967, 190). But a more persuasive view is taken by Michael Quinn, who wrote that the Council, in reality, was only a formality, in that it functioned infrequently, and then only ratified decisions made by church leaders (Quinn 1980).

In relation to Mormon legal history, the Council of Fifty was analogous to a government-in-exile. The Council was to be the political arm of the Kingdom of God when the Lord finally established his kingdom on the earth. It was formed in anticipation of an imminent Second Coming, and as long as the belief in that was preached and believed, there existed a need for at least a skeletal framework of a political system that could step in when all of earth's governments were wiped out. This is indicated in a talk given by Heber C. Kimball:

> "The Church and the Kingdom to which we belong will become the kingdom of our God and his Christ, and brother Brigham Young will become President of the United States."
>
> (Voices responded, "Amen.")
>
> "And I will tell you he will be something more; but we do not now want to give him that name; but he is called and ordained to a far greater station than that, and he is foreordained to take that station, and he has got it." (JD 5:219)

Like a government-in-exile, the Council had no real political power, and as the belief in an imminent millennium faded, so too did the Council. The last member of the Council of Fifty, Heber J. Grant, died in 1944.

Joseph Smith's views on the American Constitution, federalism, and the proper relation between church and state were affected, of course, by the needs of the Mormon people as a tiny and defenseless minority. Smith's pronounced nationalistic views, favoring a strong federal government that could override the state to protect the civil rights and civil liberties of its citizens, were appropriate to the needs of his people.

After they arrived in Utah and became a local majority, Mormon leaders predictably supported states' rights that would allow them nearly total control over local legislation. Their critics warned that if the Saints ever received statehood they would quickly install a coercive theocratic state. The aura of a shadow government and the Mormon Council of Fifty did little to allay these fears. It is true that Mormons relied upon theocratic institutions when dealing with members. It is also true the Saints were not beyond legitimating their peculiar social practices by local legislation. But there is less evidence that the brethren extolled the virtues of constitutional government as a thinly veiled screen for autocratic government. While the Saints conducted their affairs apart from the gentiles who shared the geography occupied by their kingdom, coercion of outsiders was the stuff of sensational headlines rather than everyday occurrence.

Nor did the acclaim afforded constitutional government waiver during times of persecution. Even after weathering a threatened military assault during the winter of 1857–58, suffering their third rejected bid for statehood in 1862, and submitting to the ignominy of a federal army stationed within the corporate limits of Salt Lake City during the Civil War to suppress perceived secessionist tendencies among the Mormons (JD 10:107), Brigham Young on 8 March 1863 rhetorically asked: "have we not shown to the world that we love the Constitution of our country and its institutions better than do those who have been or are now distracting the nation?" Young denied secessionist and dictatorial accusations, explaining that while they occasionally criticized corrupt administration, Mormons were religiously committed to constitutional government: "There is not another people upon the face of the earth that could have borne what we have, and still remain loyal to our brethren as we have been and are. They might be displeased with some of the acts of the administrators of the law," he admitted, "but not with the Constitutional laws and institutions of Government . . ." (JD 10:108).

Two decades and countless polygamy convictions later Apostle Erastus Snow affirmed on 6 April 1883 the principles of human rights contained in the Constitution as part of the Mormon view of providential history:

> I deem it of much importance that these principles should be well understood and thoroughly impressed upon the minds of the Latter-day Saints throughout the world, and especially those dwelling upon this American Continent and within the pale of this government, that they may implant in the hearts of our children a love of freedom and human rights, and a desire to preserve them, and to aid in maintaining and defending them in all lawful and proper ways; . . . study them that we may also learn how to use them in suppressing tyranny, misrule and other evils that affect mankind; for God has ordained this form of government in this age of the world, and has chosen His own instruments to further His great purposes on the earth. (JD 24:67)

The press, Congress, the federal judiciary, the "Gentile League of Utah," the Liberal Party, and other critics would continue to read Mormon affirmation of the principles of constitutional government as insincerity, pointing to Mormon lawless polygamous practices, block voting, church courts, and hierarchical leadership as inconsistent with American pluralistic democracy and mainstream Christianity. Mormons, in turn, came to recognize the limits of constitutional principles filtered through the lenses of unsympathetic officials. Polygamy seemed sufficiently perverted to justify concerted attacks on Mormondom. This blight, second only to slavery, impugned the moral integrity of a whole nation and demanded, especially after the slavery issue had been resolved by a bloody civil war, immediate repudiation. The Saints remained able to voice commitment to constitutional principles in the midst of the onslaught, by blaming officials, rather than principles, for the Mormon predicament.

Apostle Orson Hyde made a typical differentiation between inspired constitutional principles and corrupt administration in January 1858 as a federal army was en route to put down supposed insurrection in Utah and the Mormons were preparing to abandon their homes and to burn everything that would be of use to the approaching army. Members of the Utah legislature had prepared a memorial to the president and Congress pleading with them to respect their constitutional rights. Under these dangerous circumstances, Hyde stated in a sermon in the Salt Lake Tabernacle that ". . . the Almighty saw fit to bring forth His work under this Constitution. . . . Now, look at the disgraceful roguery practiced under that Constitution. . . . The Constitution now serves but little purpose other than a cloak for political gamblers, merchants, and hucksters" (JD 6:153).

The Supreme Court's decision in the *Reynolds* case, which formally determined the constitutionality of the antipolygamy Morrill statute, exacerbated the Mormon perceived discrepancies between principles and practice. At a general conference held in April 1879 John Taylor warned that "it is true that the founders of this nation, as a preliminary step for the introduction of more correct principles and that liberty and the rights of man might be recognized . . . had that great palladium of liberty, the Constitution of the United States, framed. . . ." He also noted that Mormon experience had amply demonstrated that "good, virtuous and holy principles may be perverted by corrupt and wicked men" (JD 21:31).

Mormons were sensitive to their persecutors' charges that their intentional violation of anti-polygamy statutes placed them in the same category as thieves and murderers. Angrily they pointed out that polygamy presented a conflict of constitutionally protected rights absent from other crimes. Mormons felt that the state's demand that they forsake polygamy contradicted a divine command that it be practiced.

The Mormon doctrine of civil disobedience or conscientious refusal[1] was consistent with their beliefs regarding the legitimate bounds of government. Scripture spoke clearly on this point:

> We believe that no government can exist in peace, except such laws are framed and held inviolate as will secure to each individual the free exercise of conscience, the right and control of property, and the protection of life.
>
> We believe that religion is instituted of God; and that men are amenable to him, and him only, for the exercise of it, unless their religious opinions prompt them to infringe upon the rights and liberties of others; but we do not believe that human law has a right to interfere in prescribing rules of worship to bind the consciences of men, nor dictate forms for public or private devotion; that the civil magistrate should restrain crime, but never control conscience; should punish guilt, but never suppress the freedom of the soul. (D&C 134:2, 4)

The vengeance of a state repudiated in every measure of governance by a recalcitrant people ensured that no stone would remain unturned in the process of demanding compliance. Incarcerating practicing polygamists was not enough. The Poland Act of 1874 disqualified Mormon jurors and restricted the jurisdiction of Mormon-controlled probate courts. The Edmunds Act of 1882 disfranchised many Mormons. Federal judges refused to naturalize Mormon immigrants. The Edmunds-Tucker Act of 1887 dissolved the church corporation and the Perpetual Emigration Fund (appropriated church property to the state), further limited the jurisdiction of the probate courts, and gave the President of the United States the power to appoint probate judges, thus ensuring that territorially appointed Mormon judges could not influence policy through the judiciary. Mormons felt that these laws, enacted and applied by those unsympathetic with their predicament, violated inalienable constitutional rights of self-governance and religious freedom. They would deny their political as well as religious heritage if they submitted to unconstitutional subjugation. If they remained loyal to the dictates of God, on the other hand, not only the Saints but all freedom-loving people would eventually be grateful for their saving the constitution.

In the April general conference of 1884, the year prosecutions under the Edmunds Act commenced, Apostle Moses Thatcher articulated the Mormon position, saying:

> I was born in this country. I can trace my lineage to the revolutionary fathers. I love the institutions of my country; I love and venerate the Constitution. But I am not so ignorant, I am not so blind that I cannot see that anything which you or I may do may be made contrary to law, and may be called unconstitutional; but I hold that the Constitution was

made broad enough, high enough and deep enough to enable us to practice our religion and be free before God and man.

Thatcher further insisted that ". . . [i]n the due time of the Lord, there will grow up in these mountains a race of people that will not only defend the Constitution, but defend the flag of the nation, and at the same time be willing to extend the principles of freedom to all who desire to receive them" (JD 25:115).

Out of Zion Shall Go Forth The Law

Mormon respect for constitutional principles never meant that the Saints would stay out of politics. Joseph instituted the Council of Fifty for purposes of coordinating church efforts in political affairs. The Council of Fifty's more formal name, "The Kingdom of God and His Laws," would likely trouble any nonmember who potentially would be subject to its jurisdiction. Whether the Council of Fifty would have enshrined constitutional principles or dictatorial practices had it ever had the opportunity to control the state cannot be determined. Certainly the rhetoric associated with the Council of Fifty respected the inalienable rights of all. Indeed had extant civil government protected the Saints more fully, Joseph likely would have been less inclined to consider alternative governmental forms. Nonetheless Mormon eschatological beliefs encouraged the Saints to see themselves as the embodiment of John Winthrop's City on a Hill, unto whom all righteous people would ultimately turn for safety and security. Thus the "Kingdom of God and His Laws" would supersede the imperfections of American constitutional government. Doubting nonmembers questioned whether their safety and security stood any chance in a theocratic state controlled by priesthood authoritarianism.

Orson Pratt in an 8 July 1855 discourse, while explaining Mormon respect for the existing constitutional government, expressed his millenarian expectations of better things to come: "The day will come," he predicted, "when the United States government, and all others, will be uprooted, and the kingdoms of this world will be united in one, and the kingdom of our God will govern the whole earth, and bear universal sway; and no power beneath the heavens can prevent this taking place. . . ." He concluded, "Consequently, we respect the government of the United States, because it has good principles in it, and not that we think it will endure forever" (JD 3:7).

The perfected form of government favored by the Mormons for the governance of Zion has been characterized as theo-democracy (Hansen 1967; Jensen 1938), a system that would be adopted voluntarily by the pure in heart, member and nonmember alike. John Taylor described its political theory in a 6 April 1861 discourse, in which he said,

> The government of God is not a species of priest craft . . . where one man dictates and everybody obeys without having a voice in it. We have our voice and agency, and act with the most perfect freedom; still we believe there is a correct order—some wisdom and knowledge somewhere that is superior to ours; that wisdom and knowledge proceeds from God through the medium of the holy Priesthood. (JD 9:10)

Not surprisingly, gentiles condemned the Mormon vision of theo-democracy as dictatorial. For Mormons it was the Lord's right to rule through his priesthood leaders and the believer's right to accept or reject that divine guidance. Within the religious community, members pursued this ideal by deferring to priesthood direction in all matters. Thus economic relations, domestic affairs, and social conflict would all be mediated and directed under the auspices of religious institutions. Beyond the religious community many nonmembers would be so impressed with the righteousness and prosperity of the Saints that they would seek them out for guidance and association even in the operation of secular institutions: hence the significance of the Council of Fifty. Those unimpressed would retain inalienable (constitutional) rights to march to the beat of different drummers; so much their loss, but free agency required that they be allowed to exercise their choice.

Mormon belief in the literal establishment of the Kingdom of God and his laws on this earth received much attention when the Civil War presented the real threat of an end to traditional governance and the imminence of mobocracy. When the Union survived, the immediacy of the Kingdom of God taking over control of government receded, but the inevitability remained.

In an April 1879 discourse, for instance, Taylor confidently told the Saints that "these things that are spoken of will assuredly come to pass when 'out of Zion shall go forth law, and the word of the Lord from Jerusalem'" (JD 21:32). Mormons took their obligation to fulfill prophecy seriously; in the interim they would voluntarily defer to religious dictates regardless of choices made by others.

SUING BEFORE THE UNGODLY

Holy writ and social history are replete with warnings against substituting the intricacies of law for real justice. Certainly any community based on spiritual and humanitarian values will try to replace legalism with a caring, personalistic blend of justice and mercy. Not surprisingly the priesthood repudiated any reliance on gentile legal institutions in the settling of internal disputes between members. The injunction against "suing before the ungodly" expressed this sentiment for many years.

Mormon mistrust of the strictures of the law, especially as interpreted by the uninspired, follows a long-standing tradition in Christian history. Jesus had strongly condemned lawyers who neglected the compassion underlying the law in favor of casuistry. His condemnation grew from the overriding theme he preached in the gospels: love of God and neighbor, self and enemy. In his Sermon on the Mount, Christ offered his doctrine of love in substitution for the propitiational Mosaic law of retribution. He rejected suing for justice's sake saying: "And if any man will sue thee at the law and take away thy coat, let him have thy cloak also . . . But I say unto you, love your enemies, bless them that curse you, do good to them that hate you, and pray from them which despitefully use you, and persecute you" (Matt. 5:40, 44).

Paul warned of the threat to the community of saints presented by those who would rely on "outsider" legalism in place of "insider" reconciliation. In Corinthians, he urged the early Christian community in Corinth not to go to nonChristians to resolve their conflicts.

> Dare any of you, having a matter against another, go to law before the unjust, and not before the saints?
>
> Do ye not know that the saints shall judge the world? And if the world shall be judged by you, are ye unworthy to judge the smallest matters?
>
> Know ye not that we shall judge angels? How much more things that pertain to this life?
>
> If then ye have judgments of things pertaining to this life, set them to judge who are least esteemed in the church.
>
> I speak to your shame. Is it so, that there is not a wise man among you? No, not one that shall be able to judge between his brethren?
>
> But brother goeth to law with brother, and that before the unbelievers.
>
> Now therefore there is utterly a fault among you, because you go to law one with another. Why do ye not rather suffer yourselves to be defrauded?
>
> Nay, ye do wrong, and defraud, and that your brethren. (1 Cor. 6:1–8)

The Mormons drew on this early Christian prohibition for an important aspect of Zion. Priesthood leaders taught the Saints, consistent with Pauline counsel, that it was their religious responsibility to resolve disputes between members in a brotherly fashion; therefore they regarded one Mormon suing another before "the ungodly" as unChristianlike conduct. For example, on 24 February 1865, Brigham

Young rebuked those who loved litigation before gentile courts, asserting:

> There is not a righteous person in this community who will have difficulties that cannot be settled by arbitrators, the Bishop's Court, the High Council, or by the 12 Referees . . . far better and more satisfactorily than to contend with each other in law courts, which directly tends to destroy the best interests of the community, and to lead scores of men away from their duties, as good and industrious citizens. . . . (JD 3:238)

John Taylor, as presiding authority of the church in 1878 the year following Brigham Young's death, continued the same prohibition against suing before gentile courts:

> Whenever a man would attempt to 'pop' you through the courts of the law of the land, you should 'pop' him through the courts of our Church; you should bring him up for violating the laws of the church, for going to law before the ungodly, instead of using the means that God has appointed. (JD 20:104–5)

This religious aversion paralleled frontier hostility to adversarial justice: lawyers had suffered condemnation for being conniving, unprincipled, and dilatory since the colonial period. Colonists protested the gauntlet of technicalities and quibbles justice had to run in America's early courts and despised the delays, confusion, and unnecessary expense legal systems represented to most Americans. "Some Observations on the Pernicious Practice of the Law," a 1786 series of articles published in a Boston newspaper under the pseudonym of "Honestus,"[2] argued that while laws were necessary "for the safety and good order of society," shyster lawyers

> are endeavoring to perplex and embarrass every judicial proceeding; who are rendering intricate even the most simple principles of law; who are involving individuals, applying for advice, in the most distressing difficulties; who are practicing the greatest art in order to delay every process; who are taking the advantage of every accidental circumstance which an unprincipled person might have, by the lenity and indulgence of an honest creditor; who stand ready to strike up a bargain, (after rendering the property in a precarious state) to throw an honest man out of three quarters of his property.

His not-surprising conclusion was that "when such men pretend to cloak themselves under the sacredness of law, it is full time the people should inquire, 'by what authority they do these things.'"

On the frontier, homemade, inexpensive, popular law seemed preferable to the archaic English common law. One historian, in considering public criticism of lawyers in the nineteenth century, comments:

> The American people have at all times distrusted attorneys. The roots of popular suspicion perhaps inhere in the very structure of common-law justice—a system that places a premium upon aggressive individualism, pitting the self-interest of the client against that of his legal representative in matters of cost and efficiency. Throughout the nineteenth century, at any rate, anti-lawyer protest is overwhelmingly a middle-class protest that centers upon demands for cheaper and speedier justice. (Bloomfield 1971, 269–70)

The Mormons shared this general antipathy, but theirs was exacerbated by their communitarian tendencies, their treatment at the hands of those they perceived as unsympathetic lawyers, jurors, and judges in New York, Ohio, Missouri, and Illinois, and their experiences of persecution in Utah associated with the practice of polygamy.

Relying on Mormon courts in the development of Zion had practical advantages. Ecclesiastically based rules of evidence and judicial practices sought reconciliation rather than mere formal resolution of legal issues. The courts were essentially cost-free, and lawyers were, for the most part, excluded. Church court proceedings were not adversarial. Ecclesiastical officers charged all participants to pursue truth and accommodate the individual with community interests. The proceedings were confidential except where the conflict involved the larger community, and the courts adapted the decisions to the particular needs of the litigants. The church thus attempted (although not always successfully) simultaneously to achieve justice and protect rights by enforcing the values of the community and accommodating the rights of the disputants. Mormon institutions, whether domestic (polygamy) or economic (law of consecration), were also preserved and defended in the Mormon courts. In civil courts, they were tolerated at best and frequently became the objects of attack.

Of course, by tying membership to faithful acceptance of priesthood directives in secular affairs, the church ran the risk of alienating members who doubted the inspiration of local leaders or preferred to rely on legal rights. Certainly not everyone came away happy from church court proceedings. Those who had had enough frequently condemned a church hierarchy who presumed so much control over the total lives of church members. They would often highlight the dictatorial tendencies of a church that attempted to control so much. Nonetheless the vast majority of the Saints seemingly, whether out of fear of excommunication, social ostracism, or true acceptance, adhered to the rule forbidding members to sue other members in secular courts.

The Corrupt Influence of Gentile Lawyering

Latter-day Saint condemnation of gentile lawyering (as well as members suing each other before gentiles) dated from the inception of the church. Joseph Smith complained bitterly of lawyers who aided his persecutors by means of vexatious lawsuits that plagued him personally and contributed to dissension among the members. In 1838 Oliver Cowdery, a member of the First Presidency, and Apostle Lyman Johnson were excommunicated for, among other reasons (undoubtedly more significant), "urging vexatious law suits" and forsaking church responsibilities "for the sake of filthy lucre, and turning to the practice of law" (Far West Record, 118–190; Gunn, 146–163). When the Saints migrated to Utah, they found a wilderness that the lawyers had not yet reached. Even with the establishment of territorial government and the opening of the federal court's doors, Mormon reliance on church courts generated little work for lawyers. C. C. Goodwin summarized the predicament:

> In those early days there was really very little litigation and even less crime. The Bishops took it upon themselves to settle all ordinary civil and criminal cases through their system of arbitration. Those who wanted to go to court were not denied that privilege, for the federal government kept open house for that very purpose. But it must be admitted that the Bench of Utah in the early territorial days served more as an ornament than a utility. (Goodwin, 21–22)

In a statement delivered 24 February 1856, Brigham Young insisted that in an honest community there would be no need for lawyers; consequently Mormons committed to building an honest community should neither participate in the practice of law nor patronize those who did. "I would like to see a strictly honest community, if we can have one," he said, "and then there would be no differences of opinion brought before a Gentile court—never, never! Every difficulty would be settled amicably, without ever calling upon a court." He continued "I am ashamed of many of you; it is a disgrace for men who profess to be men of dignity and character to condescend to the mean, low-lived calling of a pettifogger, and miserable tools at that. I am ashamed for such persons, their conduct is a disgrace to them and to the name of 'Mormon'" (JD 3:240). Young left little doubt as to his feelings toward those who would create divisions among the Saints: "To observe such conduct as many lawyers are guilty of," he thundered, "stirring up strife among peaceable men, is an outrage upon the feelings of every honest, law abiding man. To sit among them is like sitting in the depths of hell, for they are as corrupt as the bowels of hell, and their hearts are as black as the ace of spades." After continuing in this vein for some time, Young concluded by asking that "God Almighty curse them from this time henceforth, and let all the Saints in this house say, Amen, [a unanimous Amen from 3,000 persons resounded through the house] for they are a stink in the nostrils of God and angels, and in the nostrils of every Latter-Day Saint in this Territory" (JD 3:240).

The proper mode of settling disputes via negotiation, mediation, arbitration, and above all, loving kindness was available to all; the legal profession obscured this truth by urging casuistry in place of common sense. A righteous lawyer (somewhat a contradiction in terms) would urge forbearance rather than encourage litigation. Like Jesus' admonition in the Great Sermon, Brigham counseled:

> What is the advice of an honorable gentleman in the profession of the law? "Do not go to law with your neighbor; do not be coaxed into a lawsuit, for you will not be benefitted by it. If you do go to law, you will hate your neighbor, . . ." Why not . . . say we will arbitrate this case, and we will have no lawsuit, and no difficulty with our neighbor, to alienate our feelings one from another? This is the way we should do as a community. (JD 15:224–25)

In later years, as the gentile presence in Utah increased, Brigham came to realize that honest Mormon lawyers were needed to defend polygamy cases and Mormons against other constitutional deprivations, as well as to facilitate honestly commercial contracts with the non-Mormon community. In an 1873 conference address he expressed, in what appeared as a radical shift in attitude, the wish "for from one to five thousand of our young and middle-aged men to turn their attention to the study of law." He accompanied this recommendation with an almost-ritual denunciation of lawyers "who spend their time from morning till night in thinking and planning how they can get up a lawsuit against this or that man . . ." (JD 16:9). Young went on to define the conduct of a righteous lawyer: "If you draw up a will, deed, mortgage or contract," he urged, "do not study to deceive the man who pays you for this, but make out a writing or instrument as strong and firm as the hills, that no man can tear to pieces, and do your business honestly and uprightly, in the fear of God and with the love of truth in your heart." He concluded: "We live by law, and I only condemn those among the lawyers who are eternally seeking to take advantage of their neighbors" (JD 16:11–12).

The line between eschewing pettifogging lawyers and embracing righteous lawyers who could plead the cause of Zion and presumably influence the profession was sometimes less than clear. Members who joined the legal profession had to be continually on the defensive in justification of their services. However, Brigham Young's encouragement of would-be Mormon lawyers struck a responsive chord with Apostle Franklin D. Richards. His sons Charles Comestock Richards and Franklin S. Richards had each chosen law as a profession. Franklin S. Richards served as general counsel for the church for over thirty years and represented it during the controversy over polygamy. In a sermon on 18 January 1885, Apostle Richards, responding to the criticism of a bishop who had questioned the propriety of his sons' choice of profession, observed that "once in a while that same Bishop wants my son or someone else's son to help defend them before the courts [Laughter]. . . ." Richards assured his audience that "we do not want men to become lawyers, turn infidels, and live for nothing but the little money they can make." Instead, he asserted, "We want to raise up a corps of young men armed with the Spirit of the Gospel, clothed with the Holy Priesthood, who can tell the judges in high places what the law is, and what equity is, and can plead for the cause of Zion, and help maintain the rights of God's people. . . . Our rights are infringed," Richards concluded, "and we have got to defend ourselves as best we can" (JD 26:102–3).

This qualified tolerance regarding the moral worthiness of Mormon lawyers did not cause the church to abandon its own courts. For strictly internal disputes lawyers continued to be considered excess baggage, regardless of their competence or honesty. However, the need for righteous lawyers to defend polygamy cases and Mormon economic interests was an ever-increasing necessity in dealing with the gentile world.

Gentile Legal Proceedings

Brigham Young chastised any Mormon who voluntarily placed himself in the environment of gentile legal processes, warning on 24 February 1851 that "court watchers" were subjecting themselves to seductive influences. He even advised those called for jury service to "tell them to judge the case themselves, and you keep away and mind your own business." He accused those who willingly served on jury duty of "lov[ing] to be there. You suck down the drink that is there, eat the food that is there, and sup the broth that is there, because it is of hell and you like it better than you do the Saints, and the sustenance of the Saints" (JD 3:241). Brigham urged members to limit their involvement with civil courts to protecting the innocent. "There is not an honest man in this community would go there merely for money, or would plead law unless it was demanded at his hands," he counseled, "by the principles of justice to prevent the innocent from being wronged and abused" (JD 3:239).

Priesthood leaders counseled against the waste associated with civil litigation because it seemed closely related to the vice of dissension. Brigham Young, speaking 9 April 1871, was especially critical of the social costs of litigation:

> Do not go to law at all; it does you no good and only wastes your substance. It causes idleness, waste, wickedness, vice, and immorality. Do not go to law. You cannot find a court room without a great number of spectators in it; what are they doing? Idling away their time to no profit whatever. As for lawyers, if they will put their brains to work and learn how to raise potatoes, wheat, cattle, build factories, be merchants or tradesmen, it will be a great deal better for them than trying to take the property of others from them through litigation. (JD 14:82)

A decade later on 27 June 1881 President John Taylor ridiculed the divisiveness of lawyers and urged members to resolve disputes with the admonition in mind that we should love our neighbors as ourselves:

> I remember when a little boy, seeing a somewhat curious picture. Two farmers were quarreling over or disputing the ownership of a cow, and one had her by the horns, the other had her by the tail. In order to settle the difficulty, they secured the services of one of the peace-makers of the law, and his love for his fellowman was so great that while they pulled at either end of the cow, he sat between them quietly milking her. [Laughter] In case of difficulty, for difficulties will arise sometimes, would it not be better for us to attend to the milking of the cow ourselves, and go to the Lord for His guidance and manifest feelings of liberality and kindness towards our fellowmen, towards all men? (JD 22:221)

Many priesthood leaders attributed the unity of the Saints in part to their willingness to settle their differences amicably rather than pursuing every possible claim through litigation. On 24 July 1881, George Q. Cannon of the First Presidency commented on the unity of the Saints as evidenced by their disinclination to sue one another. Even though they might come from Danish, French, German, Italian, and English backgrounds as well as all parts of the United States, "They have been patient, long suffering, forbearing, and averse to quarrels and litigation. There is no disposition to go to law and quarrel with one another, and yet every man is tenacious of his rights . . . .

Who ever hears of 'Mormons' going to law with one another?" he asked. "It is a rare thing. They have a way of settling their differences as brothers and sisters should and as all Christian men and women should" (JD 22:366).

In short, priesthood leaders consistently opposed the use of gentile courts for Latter-day Saints and also consistently challenged gentile lawyering and legal processes for their inherent enmity to the cause of Zion. This evaluation carried great weight with pioneer immigrants who had suffered persecution for their religious beliefs. Throughout the nineteenth century, as later chapters will illustrate, Mormons resolved conflict within the religious community by reference to religious norms and institutions in place of their secular counterparts.

ECCLESIASTICAL FORUMS FOR DISPUTES AMONG MEMBERS

Mormon leaders were not so naive as to suppose that simply banning lawyers and civil action would make conflict disappear. They did assume that they could significantly reduce the level of animosity in the community by controlling the forum used to resolve disputes, its procedure, and its underlying objectives. The church courts emerged to hear charges on spiritual matters, matters that fell outside the competence of civil courts. The success of the ecclesiastical courts led to an extension of their jurisdiction to any non-criminal dispute between members. Criminal jurisdiction remained vested in the state (unless the state demonstrated an inability to honestly handle such matters), since only the state could apply coercive sanctions such as imprisonment or the death penalty. This trend toward expanding church court jurisdiction beyond religious matters to include secular disputes might have occurred anyway as part of the developing concept of Zion, but the hostility of the civil courts made it inevitable. The concept of Zion —a unified and sanctified community—shaped the philosophy of the courts. Any type of conflict among members threatened the unity of Zion, and reconciliation, not simply equity, became the goal of the ecclesiastical courts.

As a practical matter, such distinctive social practices as the law of consecration, polygamy, or the allocation of community resources such as land and water could be heard within a religious perspective only in Mormon courts. Even though Mormon rules regarding contracts, for instance, were almost identical to secular norms, the church forums allowed leaders to reconcile members rather than merely to decide cases. They reduced costs, expedited the resolution of conflict, gave Zion greater autonomy and elevated the law of God over the law of man. For these reasons, the priesthood required the Saints as a matter of duty to defer to the church's courts in all civil disputes between Mormons. This deference provided the basis of the "exclusive jurisdiction" rule that prevailed throughout the nineteenth century. The church courts provided the exclusive forum within which the Saints could resolve disputes with their brethren.

Brigham Young encouraged adherence to the exclusive jurisdiction of church courts for the thirty years he led the church. Failure to abide by this counsel could cost a Saint his or her membership in the church. In 1852, celebrating the anniversary of the organization of the church, Young counseled members in disagreement to lay "themselves down in the cradle of humility, and say 'Brother, (or sister) I want to do right; yea, I will even wrong myself, to make you right.' Do you not think that a man or woman, acting in that manner towards his or her neighbor, would be justified by the law of righteousness?" But, he warned, "for those who bear the name of Saints to go into a Gentile court to settle their differences is a stink in the nostrils of the Almighty. To me it is disgusting, filthy and loathsome" (JD 6:319).

Under threat of ecclesiastical sanction, the Saints referred disputes to their own courts despite available alternatives, and the preference did not wane with Brigham's death. His successor, John Taylor, reiterated the anti-litigation theme in an 1878 sermon, claiming that ". . . it is not an infrequent thing for men not belonging to our Church to express themselves desirous to bring their cases for trial before our High Council, believing they could get better justice than they could before the courts of the world" (JD 20:104). In this sermon, Taylor explained at length the proper procedure a Saint should follow in pursuing a claim against another member. If an attempt to settle the matter privately fails, then the injured party should make another attempt with the aid of "another brother." The matter should then be called to the attention of "the Teachers or the Priest," then a case should be preferred before the man's bishop and his counselors, who "should hear and decide the case according to the evidence, with all long-suffering and humility and justice and prayer before God, to guide him in his decision. And when they operate together in this way, such things will be disposed of aright." A high council appeal would bring either reconciliation or excommunication. If a member was excommunicated for his failure to abide a church court disposition of a case, then the offended party could legitimately "pop him through by the law, if that be the term you use." If an offended party tried to "pop" another member through the civil courts before exhausting all church court remedies then the complainant would properly become the accused in a church action for unChristianlike conduct. Taylor quoted Paul's admonition against the Saints suing one another before the "unjust" (1 Cor. 6:1–7), then concluded by his own admonition against suing before the ungodly:

> And I will give you fair warning, to carry it out, that when he finds any Latter-day Saint under his jurisdiction going to law with his brother before the ungodly, to bring him up and deal with him for his fellowship. This is a correct principle before God and as Saints of God we should be governed by his laws, and not by the laws of the world. But these laws are made and provided for our protection, and when it is proper and right we can make use of them in common with other citizens. But we have laws among ourselves, and all honorable men among us will submit to the decision of our Church authorities, and those who are not honorable we do not want, and we will cut them off. (JD 20:106)

In response to the familiar charge of theocratic domination leveled against church court jurisdiction over nonreligious matters, priesthood leaders stressed voluntariness and the elaborate efforts to ensure fairness. No effort was made to imply infallibility. The very fact that appeals were possible implied that even priesthood leaders could be mistaken on any particular issue. On 21 June 1883, Joseph F. Smith asserted that "God has given to us the broadest latitude peacefully to defend our individual rights, agreeably to just and righteous laws." After reviewing the entire judicial process from individual reconciliation to First Presidency appeals, Smith concluded that

> He permits us first to be tried by the Bishop and his Counsellors; and even before that we have the opportunity to settle our difficulties amicably without going to trial; or if we cannot settle them amicably among ourselves, we are permitted to call in our Teacher to assist us if possible to be reconciled to one another; and if that cannot be done we can then bring the matter before the Bishop to be formally tried. If we have reason to believe the decision to be unjust, we have the right then to appeal our case to the High Council, and then, if the First Presidency so decides, there may be a rehearing. So that the Lord has given unto us every possible chance to vindicate our rights, defend our causes, and maintain our standing in the Church. NO man is asked to bow to unrighteousness. (JD 24:193)

Of course the prospects of an erring First Presidency did not pose a real threat to the priesthood, if it did to skeptical members. From a Mormon perspective, the likelihood of an unrighteous result loomed much greater in the secular than the religious courts.

This raises again the issue of peaceful coexistence between Zion and the state, and members with disparate obligations to each. Mormon theology, at least, suggested that reconciliation was possible (Mangrum 1988). From an internal standpoint voluntary deference to priesthood directives required by the principle of agency was constitutive of church standing. One did not have to be a member of the church, but anyone choosing to become a member necessarily accepted priesthood control as long as membership continued. In theory, the obligations imposed within Zion had to be accepted by free choice and were a voluntary act, not a geographical coincidence. Inquisition, holy war, or any other coercive enforcement of the commandments on believers or nonbelievers would contradict this basic tenet. Persuasion, not coercion and long-suffering, was the required pattern (D&C 121; Firmage 1976, 11). Citizenship in Zion came from voluntary commitment to its principles. "Denaturalization" through a falling away, formalized by excommunication, was always a possible sanction, but the scriptures allowed no other.

Of course, in any community where a single belief system is accepted by a large majority, the minority faces a variety of practical problems. While in theory the Mormon concept of Zion precluded coercion and domination, in practice the "persuasion" exercised by priesthood directives would have been compulsive regardless of any contrary theory. Loss of membership could lead to loss of business, friendship, and even family ties, for the wayward soul. The threat of social ostracism must have loomed ominously for anyone who considered challenging priesthood authority or pervasive religious norms.

From an external perspective there is little evidence to suggest that the Mormon hierarchy aspired to political domination over nonmembers akin to the religious domination exercised over members. Even if the Saints had established substantial political independence in Deseret, either with early statehood or actual independence, the Council of Fifty likely would have preserved substantial separation of church and state.[3] Undoubtedly the church would have enjoyed more protection for its peculiar institutions, which would have been given constitutional protection. Further, the omnipresence of a religious community with distinctive norms would have appalled many. Still, the civil rights of other individuals and communities might have been preserved in the process.

A definition of religious freedom that permits social associations separate from, but not completely independent of, the state is at the core of the political theory of Zion. Orson Pratt, in his 8 July 1855 discourse on civil government, asserted that the constitution permitted any number of "theocractical" governments, but that such governments, even though emanating "from the throne of God," would not "make us independent of the laws of the United States." Pratt noted that in "keeping our covenants, and observing our religious laws and ceremonies, or the laws that God has given to the children of men, we are not required to violate the principles of right that are contained in the Constitution and laws of the United States" (JD 3:72).

In any event, priesthood leaders taught that in external affairs the Saints were subject only to the constitutional laws, while permitting civil disobedience to those that were unconstitutional.

Brigham Young, on 8 March 1863, claimed, "We have our Constitutional laws and our Territorial laws; we are subject to these laws, and always expect to be, for we love to be. . . . I stand for Constitutional law, and if any transgress, let them be tried by it, and, if guilty, suffer its penalty" (JD 10:109).

On 14 October 1860, he pointed out to those who "grumbled" about the law: "Our Legislature has never passed a law that infringed upon me, because I live above the law through honouring every particle of it. In this course the law is beneath my feet and is my servant, not my master. Thousands live in this way" (JD 8:208).

Thus Mormons deferred to secular courts in criminal affairs (D&C 42:79–88) and in civil disputes with nonmembers. Of course, Mormons preferred the probate courts, often presided over by members of the Council of Fifty, to the federal courts, which were staffed by gentile appointees. Mormon legislators under the Council of Fifty's model argued for local control over legislation, local courts and legal processes, but not at the expense of encroachment on the civil rights of nonmembers. Since Mormon political control remained precarious under federal governance, we cannot know whether the priesthood would have abused its sway over politics and the secular courts had it been given the opportunity. We can examine first, the actual exercise of political and judicial power of the state as applied to the Mormon experience and second, Mormon maintenance of their own church court system as an alternative to gentile justice.

2

The Mormon Ecclesiastical
Court System

The Mormon court system, which developed along priesthood lines, provided an institutional forum for authoritatively resolving issues ranging from petty quarrels to succession crises. Actions for denying the faith or unChristianlike conduct tried by local leaders (initially elders and later bishops) contributed to a congregational atmosphere where members largely controlled community standards. Adding appellate review permitted the monitoring of doctrinal controversies by hierarchical leaders, lest local church communities fragment into disparate groups. Formalization of an elaborate church court system introduced a legalistic overlay on a rapidly expanding religious body paradoxically known for its anti-legalistic sentiments. Respect for the authoritative pronouncements of these church courts reduced the necessity for charismatic leadership in times of transition and crisis. The church courts contributed to the stability of a church often under siege from outside opponents and inside dissenters.

EARLY CHURCH COURTS

Even before Joseph Smith formally organized the Mormon church on 6 April 1830, he announced in a revelation, known as the "law" of the Church, that "[a]ny member of the church of Christ transgressing, or being overtaken in fault, shall be dealt with as the scriptures direct" (D&C 20:80). The scriptures directed that elders—Joseph Smith and Oliver Cowdery were ordained as the church's first and second elders but soon ordained others to this Melchizedek priesthood office—should appoint a clerk to keep a record of church membership, "[a]nd also, if any have been expelled from the church, so that their names be blotted out of the general church record of names" (D&C 20:83).

The Elders' Council

Pursuant to these organizational directives, elders' conferences conducted the earliest church court proceedings. Typically a trial before an elders' council would open with prayer, followed by a hymn and scripture reading.[1] The transgressor or parties in dispute would be asked to make sufficient acknowledgment of their sins to avoid the necessity of a trial.[2] The elders always accepted back into the fold a penitent spirit. If the transgressor would not willingly reconcile himself to the church, a trial would follow. The trial had to be before at least two elders;[3] the charges were to be premised on infractions of the "Lords law" (D&C 42:59) or "the commandments and covenants of the church" (D&C 42:78) and supported by at least two Mormon witnesses;[4] and the elders separately had to cast their lots for guilt or innocence.[5] A majority vote carried the decision, but on most occasions the councils unanimously concurred.[6] If an elder cast a dissenting lot the council would hear additional testimony or would further discuss the case until it reached a unanimous decision. If the transgressions were a matter of public knowledge, these early trials were open to the entire branch on the authority of the revelation providing that where the offense was widely known, the offender was to be rebuked openly before the church (D&C 42:91).

These public trials contributed to group cohesiveness and provided important social experiences for a community of members with widely divergent backgrounds who were seeking the unity of Zion. Church court proceedings, in effect, helped create a common basis of shared expectation amongst a newly emerging religious community. The First Presidency stressed the importance of the priesthood exercising an active role in searching out and putting down iniquity in the church in a 2 July 1833 letter to the elders at Eugene, Ohio:

> We feel to rebuke the Elders of that branch of the Church of Christ, for not magnifying their office, and letting the transgression go unpunished. We, therefore, enjoin upon you, to be watchful on your part, and search out iniquity, and put it down wherever it may be found. You will see by this, brethren, that you have authority to sit on council on [those in transgression] and if found guilty, to deal with them accordingly. (HC 1:371)

Forging unity out of diversity, however, inevitably entails costs. The potential for unrighteous dominion loomed ominously. After all, excommunication represented a serious sanction to the believer; he or she not only lost present and eternal blessings tied to Church membership, but also suffered estrangement from the social community.

Mormonism thus developed an early track record for stifling radical individualism. The excommunicant did not always respect the inspiration that supposedly pervaded the church court experience. Some trials generated hostility by those excommunicated, who, on occasion, sensationalized Mormon intolerance and in turn encouraged the persecution of the Saints. Ezra Booth, for example, "silenced from preaching as an elder in this church" on 6 September 1831 at Nelson, Portage County, Ohio, by a council of elders that included Joseph Smith, Jr., Oliver Cowdery, and Sidney Rigdon,[7] shortly thereafter published a series of nine letters critical of the Mormons. Joseph Smith's *Church History* records that these letters first appeared in Ravenna's *Ohio Star*, which E. D. Howe later republished in his *Mormonism Unveiled* (HC 1:216n.).

The elders' conferences, initially organized to hear charges for members denying the faith, soon offered their courts as an alternative to the costly, dilatory, divisive, and prejudiced gentile courts that Mormons avoided in dealing with internal conflicts. On 7 December 1831, for example, two of the brethren, Walker and Hearty, brought a disagreement before an elders' conference for arbitration. After prayer, the singing of a hymn, and scripture reading, the elders asked the disputants to withdraw and attempt an amicable settlement. This effort to obtain a voluntary resolution of the dispute followed the scriptural injunction that "if thy brother or sister offend thee, thou shalt take him or her between him or her and thee alone; and if that he or she confess thou shalt be reconciled" (D&C 42:88). The scripture continues that if reconciliation proved impossible "thou shalt deliver him or her up unto the church, not to the members but to the elders, and it shall be done in a meeting, and that not before the world."[8] Since the two were unable to settle the matter between themselves, the council appointed, with the approval of the parties, two arbitrators, John Whitmer and Thomas Marsh, who fashioned an acceptable disposition of the matter. The church courts thereby involved the community in maintaining harmony within the group. In another 1831 case, an elders' conference asked a brother to give up his license as a teacher for misconduct in "whipping" his wife. Denying the faith extended to immoral conduct as well as profane beliefs.[9]

The conference's expansive jurisdiction over the conduct and beliefs of members undoubtedly led to abuse on various occasions. A conference of elders at Jackson County, Missouri, in March 1832, for example, chided Sidney Rigdon for imprudently filing charges against Bishop Edward Partridge:

> Resolved that Whereas the duty of the disciple of Christ is to promote union, harmony, and brotherly love and not at any time to imprudently prefer charges and demand confession and settlement of the same in the absence of a brother, after having had a privilege of doing the same face to face, and more especially after sitting in conference in the name of the Lord and communing together at sacrament. We do therefore after deliberately weighing the subject before us the cause in which we labor and for which we suffer persecutions do candidly reflect upon whether he was not actuated by his own hasty feelings rather than the Spirit of Christ when indicting the same.[10]

In this case the conference recommended that "the wounding in the church be healed and that they walk together as brothers" rather than involve the elders further in fault finding and excoriating local leadership.

While "[w]e do not know definitely when trials before a body of Elders were largely superseded by other courts,"[11] church court records demonstrate that elders' councils heard cases even after scripture designated the bishop as a "judge in Israel."[12] Indeed, the bishop initially sat as a judge with elders' councils and gave a joint decision with the council (D&C 42:81–82). There are several reasons explaining the continuation of elders' courts even after the establishment of the bishop's court. First, elders presided over scattered branches—where bishops were unavailable—and officiated in all their affairs. Second, as church membership increased, the task of judging every matter became too burdensome for Bishop Partridge in Missouri and Bishop Whitney in Ohio; moreover, delegating judging responsibilities followed the pattern set by ancient Israel; an effort that guided much of the Mormon experience during this period. Moses' father-in-law Jethro, for example, from whom he received the priesthood (D&C 84:6), counseled Moses as Judge of Israel to delegate judging responsibility to local leaders in all but the most difficult cases (Exodus 18:14, 26). Third, the elders' charge to watch over iniquity within the church undoubtedly predisposed them to hear cases until priesthood authorities clearly released them from responsibility. As a result elders' councils operated concurrently with bishops' courts for a few years. In Kirtland, Ohio, for example, councils of elders and bishops' courts separately heard cases 26 December 1833 (HC 1:469–70).

After Joseph Smith organized the high council on 17 February 1834 at Kirtland, he discouraged, then disapproved of, any further use of elders' councils as ecclesiastical forums. This organizational move reoriented the congregational structure of church court proceedings along hierarchical lines. It allowed Joseph to consolidate central control over a burgeoning church. He publicly announced the jurisdictional change in a June 1835 article in the *Messenger and Advocate*:

> According to the order of the kingdom begun in the last days, to prepare men for the rest of the Lord, the elders in Zion or in her immediate region, had no authority or right to meddle with her spiritual affairs, to regulate her concerns, or hold councils for the expulsion of members, in her unorganized condition. The High Council has been expressly organized to administer in all her spiritual affairs: and the Bishop and his council are set over her temporal matters; so that the Elders' acts are null and void. (HC 2:229)

The early elders' councils, however, during the church's early years contributed substantially to the emerging system of Mormon ecclesiastical justice. The successor bishop and high council courts adopted many of its practices, which soon became standardized for church court proceedings.

The Bishop's Court

A revelation on 1 August 1831 established the bishop's duties as a "judge in Israel, like it was in ancient days" (D&C 58:17). That revelation instructed Bishop Partridge, who had been ordained six months earlier as the church's first bishop, "to judge his people by the testimony of the just, and by the assistance of his counsellors, according to the laws of the kingdom which are given by the prophets of God" (D&C 58:18). On 4 December 1831, at Kirtland, the prophet called Newell K. Whitney as the church's second bishop, to preside over the eastern branches (D&C 72:2, 8).

Ever since the August 1831 revelation, the bishop's court has provided the basic ecclesiastical forum in the Mormon judicial system. While "[t]he proceedings in the Bishop's court have never been uniform in the Church" (Keeler, 5), general norms of procedure emerged out of the early courts. Written complaints, often a mere note on a scrap of paper, normally commenced an action, although the courts also received oral complaints. Any member acquainted directly or even indirectly with the offense could file a complaint, but teachers provided special services as complaining witnesses. Later, disputants would present their claims to teachers as a preliminary matter before bishop's courts would take jurisdiction. The brief complaint followed no technical form, although if written it had to be signed. After receiving the complaint the bishop generally had his clerk prepare and deliver a summons, giving notice to the person accused of the charges and the time appointed for the hearing. Later the practice developed of filing a return on notices served.

Bishops would occasionally hear disputes immediately upon receipt of the complaint where the parties and any necessary witnesses were present, but normally the notice set the hearing for a few days hence. The bishop and his two counselors presided over the trial. If a counselor was unavailable the bishop would appoint another priesthood bearer to assist in the trial. Following the pattern set by the elders' council, the trial commenced with prayer, song, and scripture reading, followed by an exhortation to the parties to repent and to seek forgiveness or reconciliation. If the conflict could not be settled amicably, or the parties were unwilling to repent fully, the trial commenced. The parties represented themselves throughout the proceedings; the absence of technical rules of evidence or pleading aided in the exclusion of attorneys. After hearing the testimony and any closing remarks the bishop would seek the advice of his counselors before rendering a decision. At least one counselor had to sustain the decision; otherwise either the court would hear additional evidence or refer the case to a higher court.

The High Council Court

The high council court also emerged early in the history of the church and soon provided the court system with an appellate level of review that became increasingly necessary if the Saints were to remain unified; like the bishop's court, the high council court continues to the present in much its original form. A council of high priests met for the first time as a quorum separate from the elders on 5 October 1832 at Independence, Missouri.[13] Shortly thereafter the high priests began meeting in council, much like the council of elders, to try cases. On 15 December 1832, for example, the high priests at Independence convened in council to try a member for teaching false doctrine.[14] In a similar fashion a council of high priests met on 13 February 1833, and again on 26 February 1833, in Kirtland, and excommunicated a high priest, Burr Riggs (HC 1:327).

The high council courts that initially exercised original jurisdiction primarily over spiritual, as compared with temporal, transgressions also heard cases on appeal. The case of "Doctor" Hurlburt, involving a charge of unChristianlike conduct with women while on a mission in the East, provides an example. A "conference of High Priests" initially heard the case with Bishop Whitney on June 3, 1833 in Kirtland, and excommunicated Hurlburt (HC 1:352). On June 21, 1833 he appealed from "the Bishop's council of High Priests" to the "President's council of high priests for a re-hearing, according to the privilege guaranteed to me in the laws of the Church. . . ."[15] The "President's" council affirmed the decision, but restored Hurlburt to fellowship after he made a liberal confession. His repentance was apparently insincere because he was again tried two days later on the same charges and cut off (HC 1:355). He thereafter became a bitter anti-Mormon; Joseph Smith later initiated criminal actions against him because the "Doctor" threatened Smith's life.

The Prophet Joseph considered the soberness of the councils, which under inspiration were responsible for accommodating both mercy and justice, of utmost importance to the well-being of the church. On 12 February 1834, just a few days before he formally organized the first high council, the Prophet addressed a council of high priests and elders on the significance of judging rightly:

> No man is capable of judging a matter in council unless his own heart is pure; and that we are frequently so filled with prejudice, or have a beam in our own eye, that we are not capable of passing right decisions.
>
> In ancient days councils were conducted with such strict propriety, that no one was allowed to whisper, be weary, leave the room, or get uneasy in the least, until the voice of the Lord, by revelation, or the voice of the council by the Spirit, was obtained, which has not been observed in this church to the present time. It was understood in ancient days, that if one man could stay in council, another could; and if the president could spend his time, the members could also; but in our councils generally, one will be uneasy, another asleep; one praying, another not; one's mind on the business of the council, and another thinking of something else.
>
> Our acts are recorded, and at a future day they will be laid before us, and if we should fail to judge right and injure our fellow-beings, they may then, perhaps, condemn us; there they are of great consequence, and to me the consequence appears to be of force, beyond anything which I am able to express. Ask yourselves, brethren, how much you have exercised yourselves in prayer since you heard of this council; and if you are now prepared to sit in council upon the soul of your brother. (HC 2:25–26)

After giving instructions on appropriately conducting these solemn church trials, the prophet Joseph organized the first high council at Kirtland on 17 February 1834 (D&C 102). In place of the bishop acting as moderator for the high priests, as had been the custom,[16] the revelation directed that the high council court be presided over by "one or three presidents as the case might require" (D&C 102:1). Also, in place of having the entire quorum of high priests, the high council was to consist of a standing body of twelve high priests called as high councillors.

High councils were responsible for the "settling of important difficulties which might arise in the church, which could not be settled by the Church or the bishop's council to the satisfaction of the parties" (D&C 102:2). Thus high councils ensured hierarchical control of local church courts. The significance of this control is illustrated by the fact that the church's First Presidency acted as presidents of the first council, namely, Joseph Smith, Jr., Sidney Rigdon, and Frederick G. Williams.

At this first organization those called to sit as councillors each agreed to "act in that office according to the law of heaven" (D&C 102:4) and in accordance with the scriptural directives specifying the procedure to govern the conduct of trials. Seven out of the twelve high priests on the council were required to be present at any hearing (D&C 102:6), but the presidency had authority to appoint other high priests to act for absent councillors (D&C 102:7). The president nominated prospective members for the approval of the entire council. The high council president, appointed by revelation (D&C 102:9), presided with two councillors whom he called; any two members of the presidency could hear cases (D&C 102:11). Up to three speakers on each side, chosen by numbered lot, presented the respective positions of the disputants after the parties had offered their evidence (D&C 102:12, 14). Both the accused and the complainant, in addition to having a proportionate number of councillors speaking on their behalf, also had "a right to one-half of the council, to prevent insult or injustice" (D&C 102:15). In practice the councillors were numbered from one to twelve in terms of seniority. The even-numbered councillors defended the interests of the accused; the odd-numbered represented the claims of the complainant. Later, the councillors chose lots for their numbers. Councillors on each side served not as advocates, but instead were "to speak according to equity and justice" (D&C 102:16). Once the speakers had completed their comments on the merits of the case then "the accuser and the accused shall have the privilege of speaking for themselves before the council . . ." (D&C 102:18). The president rather than the council rendered the decision, but a majority of the council had to sustain any decision (D&C 102:19, 22). Discovery of "an error in the decision of the president would require a rehearing, with the first decision standing unless additional light was given" (D&C 102:20, 22). Finally, the council was to submit a copy of the proceedings to the seat of the First Presidency of the church, who would, after reviewing the transcript, decide the case without regard to the previous high council decision (D&C 102:26–27).

The institutional structure of the high council court was designed to minimize the danger of unrighteous dominion. By dividing the council between the respective parties and assigning spokesmen for each side, heavy-handedness was discouraged. Nonetheless, if the sentiment of the entire council was arrayed against any party, institutional checks and balances had little effect.

With the formal organization of the high council, the council of high priests, similar to the council of elders, ceased to perform judicial functions other than quorum disfellowshipping. Revelation specified one exception for high priests abroad; in those areas where organized high councils do not exist, "traveling or high priests abroad" may organize ad hoc high councils, to hear "difficult" but not "ordinary" cases, with "the president being appointed from the council" (D&C 102:23).

Joseph Smith soon replicated the high council pattern established in Kirtland in other organized "stakes" of Zion. Thus in Clay County, Missouri, on 3 July 1834, under the direction of the Prophet Joseph, "the High priests of Zion assembled for the purpose of organizing a general council of high priests, agreeable to the revelation for the purposes of settling important business that might come before them which could not be settled by the Bishop and his council" (D&C 102:24–25, 28). This created a separate source of authority in parts of the church, but by retaining appellate jurisdiction in the First Presidency even these councils were relegated to subordinate status. The crucial matter recognized by Joseph was that a formal church court structure diminished any necessary dependency on the personal leadership of any individual. He expressed this realization in suggesting that with the establishment of these high councils

> if he should now be taken away that he had accomplished the great work which the Lord had laid before him, and that which he had desired of the Lord, and that he now had done his duty in organizing the High Council, through which Council the will of the Lord might be known on all important occasions in the building up of Zion, and establishing truth in the earth.[17]

Joseph transmitted his personal respect for the institution of the high council throughout the community, thereby enhancing its prestige and institutional legitimacy among the members. Local presidencies also internalized the reverence owed their council proceedings.

David Whitmer, as president of the Far West High Council,[18] for example, on 31 July 1834, just a few weeks after the council had been organized, instructed the council that "when there shall be any case brought forward all should be patient and attentive to what is passing for I know it is your duty to do so in all cases, and avoid confusion and contention which is offensive in the sight of the Lord."[19] The following week on 6 August 1834, when a case came before the council against an entire branch for failing to accept the instruction of priesthood leadership, President Whitmer addressed the members of the council as follows:

> in speaking [they] ought not to seek to excel but ought to speak according to truth and equity—saying that they should chase away darkness and have their minds exercised upon the subject upon which they are to speak in order that they might teach upon points and bring hidden things to light and make dark things clear."[20]

In the months and years that followed, continued reliance on the high council courts for dispute resolution enhanced their authority as final arbiters of church controversy. This institutional forum absorbed the legitimacy that previously had been reserved for charismatic leadership.

Final Courts of Appeal

The February 1834 revelation establishing the first high council also provided for courts of final appeal in the First Presidency (D&C 102:27), the Quorum of the Twelve, and the First Quorum of Seventy. Joseph Smith had organized the First Presidency 25 January 1832, having Sidney Rigdon ordain him as president. On 8 March 1832 Joseph called Sidney Rigdon and Jesse Gause as counselors; Gause's appointment was soon transferred to Frederick G. Williams upon Gause's disaffection (D&C 81). On 5 and 6 December 1834, Joseph called additional assistants, including Oliver Cowdery, Joseph Smith, Sr., and Hyrum Smith. Cowdery's call may have been to an "associate President" status with rights of succession (Quinn, 1976, 199 n.34), but his excommunication 12 April 1838 mooted the issue. Joseph Smith, Sr.'s initial call as church patriarch and Hyrum Smith's succeeding call as church patriarch may also have entailed rights of succession to church leadership upon Joseph's death. The death of these patriarchs left the claim to the discredited William Smith who was unable to convince many of his succession claims. Sidney Rigdon was also unsuccessful in establishing his claim to authority as the surviving member of the First Presidency. Thus tradition witnessed the dissolving of the

First Presidency upon the death of the president, and the transferal of authority to the Quorum of the Twelve Apostles.

The First Presidency during the early years occasionally sat in council with elders or high priests in their trials. Similarly, the First Presidency previously had sat on ad hoc appellate courts typically assisted by high priests called for that purpose.[22] The 17 February 1834 "high council revelation" therefore, effected a formal centralization of church authority in the First Presidency.

The amended "high council revelation" provides for an Apostle Court to sit as the final court of appeal in limited cases when the First Presidency is either not in existence or not available. Although initially established as a traveling presiding high council (D&C 107:33), the Quorum of the Twelve gradually acquired institutional authority subordinate only to the Quorum of the First Presidency. The three witnesses to the Book of Mormon (Oliver Cowdery, David Whitmer, and Martin Harris) were given responsibility to call twelve apostles as early as June 1829 (D&C 18:37), but they delayed calling the Twelve until 14 February 1835. At that time, they called Lyman E. Johnson, Brigham Young, Heber C. Kimball, Orson Hyde, David W. Patten, Luke S. Johnson, William E. McLellin, John F. Boynton, Orson Pratt, William Smith, Thomas B. Marsh, and Parley P. Pratt from among those who accompanied the Prophet on "Zion's Camp" to Missouri.

The alternative name for the court of the Quorum of the Twelve, the Court of the Traveling High Priests Abroad, designates a special case when such a court would properly be called: when the apostles as a quorum are abroad and an important matter requiring an immediate decision arises. This court is distinct from the ad hoc high council courts previously mentioned that can be established abroad when a standing high council is unavailable, because a decision from the Court of Apostles cannot be appealed; whereas a decision from any high council can be properly laid before the First Presidency (D&C 102:39, 31). The Court of Apostles also sits as the final court of appeals when the First Presidency has been dissolved following the death of a prophet.

Following the death of Joseph Smith, the Quorum of the Twelve constituted the presiding Council of the Church from June 1844 until December 1847. At that time, Brigham Young was sustained as president, and from his death in August 1877 until October 1880, the Quorum presided again. John Taylor then served as president until his death in July 1887. The Quorum then presided once more until Wilford Woodruff succeeded Taylor in April 1889. Thus the Quorum of the Twelve has had many opportunities to sit as the presiding authority at a final court of appeal. Following Woodruff's death, in September 1898, the Apostles adopted the practice of sustaining the senior member of the Quorum of the Twelve as President of the church as soon as possible; consequently the Quorum, except by assignment of the First Presidency, has not sat as a final court of appeals since that time.

According to revelation (D&C 107:22–30) the First Presidency, the Quorum of the Twelve, and the First Quorum of Seventy are equal in authority and represent the governing bodies of the church. As such the First Quorum of Seventy has authority to act as the final court of appeals for the church if both the First Presidency and the Quorum of the Twelve are not in existence. Circumstances have never required that this court be called into session as a final court of appeals, but the appellate provision provides institutional assurance that the church will never be without priesthood authority and a final court of appeals.

Scripture provides a final assurance that even these quorums will not misuse their authority with impunity by stating that if any of their decisions are made "in unrighteousness, it may be brought before a general assembly of the several quorums, which constitute the spiritual authorities of the church; otherwise there can be no appeal from their decision" (D&C 107:32). In this democratizing of church court proceedings, scripture has affirmed the ultimate control of the members over the church.

Presiding Bishop's Court

The Presiding Bishop's Court, which consists of the presiding bishop assisted by twelve high priests specifically chosen to sit as a court, completed the early church court system. This court has exclusive jurisdiction to try members of the First Presidency if it should become necessary; it has been called into session to excommunicate Oliver Cowdery and Sidney Rigdon (D&C 107:76, 82–83). With the provision for the trial of members of the First Presidency, "there is not any person belonging to the church who is exempt from this council of the church" (D&C 107:81, 84).

Thus the church courts provided an aura of the rule of church law and institutions as an alternative to total reliance on the personal magnetism of leaders that undoubtedly would be easier to assail at times of trouble and dissension. The formal structure of the church courts replicated, in part, the rule of law model of American constitutional democracy whereby checks and balances preserved the Union against the exercise of prerogative and unlawful excesses. As long as the institutions generally, and the members ultimately, reserved checks over leaders, uncontrolled excesses on the part of the priesthood could be sanctioned without undermining the sanctity of the church.

LEADERSHIP ON TRIAL

The status of the church courts as authoritative institutions for disciplining factious leaders served an important role in preserving the church in troubled times. Church courts, for example, excoriated dissenters who would challenge the prestige or authority of the Prophet Joseph during periods of personal crisis. Also, ecclesiastical forums assured the Saints that apostate leaders could be authoritatively removed by the congregation itself if necessary. More importantly, church courts provided the accepted forum for formally determining such critical issues as rights of succession at the death of the prophet. Of course, the personal authority of the priesthood leaders calling the court into session or defended by the court imbued specific courts with legitimacy; nonetheless, the courts accustomed the Saints to look for formal dispositions of church controversy.

Despite their aura of legitimacy, the church courts were not immune to injustice. Mormon theology made no claim to infallibility. Indeed, if the subsequent lives of the people tried were to be examined, they would possibly reveal great distress and unfairness in many cases. Of course, this is equally true of both secular courts and the church courts of other religious groups. But it would be grossly unfair and insensitive to the suffering of many individuals to ignore the fact that there must have been special sting to a wound inflicted, sometimes unfairly, in God's name.

Apart from the question of justice in the individual case, the question of individualistic dissent by those who saw a different vision than Joseph Smith must be addressed. Joseph was no tyrant. He appears to have been capable of absorbing within his vision of Zion the thinking of many others, Mormon and non-Mormons alike. But when the core was reached, when compromise was not possible without debasing the vision, the church hierarchy had to draw the line. Dissenting views, however noble in their own right, had to give way. And this had its cost in individual human suffering.

Apostasy, dissension, and fault-finding in Kirtland in 1837–1838 illustrate the operation of the church courts in times of leadership crisis. The failure of the Kirtland Safety Society prompted a spate of court actions that called many leaders to repentance (HC 2:485–86, 509–512) and resulted in the disfellowship of, among others, apostles Luke S. Johnson, Lyman E. Johnson, and John F. Boynton who split from Joseph's leadership and claimed authority to establish their own church according to the "old standard" (HC 2:528). Feelings of dissension ran so high that Smith and Rigdon left Kirtland for Far West, Missouri on 12 January 1838 to escape vexatious lawsuits and persecution.

The Far West High Council, sensitive to local apostasy during this same period, used church court proceedings to remove their own presidency (consisting of David Whitmer, president, W. W. Phelps and John Whitmer, assistants, and Oliver Cowdery, clerk) for improprieties in leadership and their refusal of Joseph's directives over temporal affairs.[23] The council, sustained by the Far West congregation, on 10 March 1838 also decided that W. W. Phelps and John Whitmer were "no longer members of the Church of Christ of Latter-Day Saints," and should be "given over to the buffetings of Satan, until they learn to blaspheme no more against the authorities of God, nor fleece the flock of Christ."[24] In a similar fashion the high council excommunicated David Whitmer on 14 April 1838.[25] Oliver's trial required special procedural attention because he had been sustained as an associate president to Joseph Smith on 3 September 1837 and never released (HC 2:509). Only the Presiding Bishop's Court, therefore, had jurisdiction over Oliver. Bishop Partridge, assisted by twelve high priests, heard the case against Oliver, who answered the charges by voluntarily "withdraw[ing] from a society assuming they have such a right" as to "control men in [their] temporal interest."[26] The court excommunicated Oliver, who had served only second to Joseph in importance in the Restoration movement.[27] Apostle William E. McLellin also repudiated Joseph's leadership and was excommunicated in May 1838 at Far West (HC 3:31). He thereafter joined Mormon persecutors (HC 3:215, 287).

These losses of close friends and early associates must have saddened many, including Joseph Smith, but the theology of a uniform vision of Zion would not permit toleration of persistent dissent. The vision came before the importance of the contribution of any individual member, including those who had publicly claimed to share in the miraculous beginnings of the early church. Joseph's detractors, who saw the Mormon church as a fraudulent conspiracy by a handful of men who claimed to have heavenly authority to restore the church, must have been surprised at Joseph's willingness to risk disclosure by excommunicating the alleged coconspirators.

These excommunication trials embittered the Whitmers, Phelps, Cowdery, and McLellin, who believed them to be abusive and unfair. The cathartic experience of excommunicating the Far West Presidency and several apostles polarized the Saints in Missouri. Persistent persecution by outsiders had made the Saints increasingly intolerant of internal dissent. By the summer of 1838 Sidney Rigdon decided it was time to purge the Saints internally. On 19 June 1838 Rigdon delivered his "Salt Sermon," taking Matthew 5:13 as his text. He suggested that the dissenters were no better than salt that had lost its savor and was good for nothing "but to be cast out, and to be trodden under foot of man." Shortly thereafter Sampson Avard organized a secret society, the Danites, to purge the community of dissenters. One of their first acts was to present a document signed by eighty-four members to the leading dissenters (Oliver Cowdery, David and John Whitmer, W. W. Phelps, and Lyman E. Johnson) ordering them to leave Far West or suffer dire consequences.[28] This intolerance for dissidents within the Mormon community provided much of the testimony upon which Circuit Judge Austin King would bind Joseph Smith and others over to Liberty Jail from December 1838 until April 1839, as we shall see in a subsequent chapter.

With persecution precipitating the expulsion of the Mormons from Missouri in the winter of 1838–39, issues of loyalty arose. When the exiled Mormons assembled as a conference in Quincy, Illinois, 17 March 1839, they considered charges against "those who had left us in the time of our perils, persecutions and dangers," and were acting against the interests of the church. Thomas B. Marsh, president of the Twelve was excommunicated for his 24 October 1838 affidavit at Richmond, condemning Joseph Smith as a "second Mahomet to this generation," which directly led to Joseph's arrest and subsequent Liberty jail incarceration. Frederick G. Williams, who had previously served as a member of the First Presidency, was also excommunicated for falling away.[29] George M. Hinkle, Sampson Avard, John Corrill, Reed Peck, and Burr Riggs, all of whom had testified against the Mormons at the November 1838 King hearing were excommunicated (HC 3:284). Orson Hyde and William Smith were also suspended from their apostleships on 4 May 1839 for misconduct in Missouri. Hyde had corroborated Marsh's October 24 affidavit. Hyde and Smith, however, were restored to their offices the following conference after confession and forgiveness (HC 3:345). Williams confessed and, though not restored to office, was received back in fellowship in Nauvoo, 8 April 1840 (HC 4:110).

Thus between 1837 and 1839, two members of the First Presidency and six apostles were excommunicated, and two other apostles were otherwise sanctioned in church courts. These leaders, in effect, had become sources of dissension from within that could not be tolerated if the vision of a unified religious community was to survive the persecution from without. Of those excommunicated, some were rebaptized and a few played an important role in the church. W. W. Phelps served faithfully in Nauvoo and afterward. Orson Hyde, suspended as an apostle for a few months, made important contributions later. William Smith served the church until shortly after Joseph Smith's death when he claimed authority to lead the church. He was rejected as an apostle and a patriarch and excommunicated in October 1845 (Jenson 1899, xii). A persistent issue in these trials was the requirement to submit to ecclesiastical authority in temporal affairs and to remain loyal in the face of persecution. Each case can thus be read as a test of the degree of deviance tolerated by the church. The loyalty and commitment of those who remained faithful were affirmed by their willingness to participate fully in the process and abide the consequences of these public trials. The dissident leaders who psychologically removed themselves from church affiliation were also excommunicated, a formal act of purifying and unifying the religious community that precluded any later claim for authority.

Following the Missouri purging, the Quorum of the Twelve stabilized under the direction of leaders who had suffered much for their religious belief and were willing to commit themselves to a concept of religion that touched every facet of one's life. Members of the Quorum experienced minimal sanctions in Nauvoo prior to Joseph Smith's martyrdom. The prophet publicly reproved apostles John E. Page and Orson Hyde in the Nauvoo newspaper on 15 January 1841 for delaying their appointed mission to Palestine (HC 4:274). No court proceedings formalized the reproof. Orson Hyde successfully completed the assignment, but John E. Page abandoned the project upon his arrival in Philadelphia. When the Quorum of the Twelve members returned from their missions in 1841 they were taught the doctrine of polygamy. Joseph apparently had understood the doctrine as early as 1831 and may have taken plural wives as early as 1835. He taught the principle to others in 1841, including the Twelve. All had problems accepting the doctrine. Orson Pratt's total rejection of it led to his excommunication in 1842. His later acceptance of it as a revelatory commandment led to his restoration to the Twelve on 20 January 1843; he later wrote much of the public literature for the church explaining the doctrine. This brief period, however, when he had questioned the most difficult of all Mormon doctrines cost him his seniority in the Quorum (HC 5:255–56).

Joseph Smith did encounter problems with new assistants in the First Presidency during the Nauvoo period. John C. Bennett's temporary appointment on 8 April 1841 as "assistant President until President Rigdon's health should be restored" was short-lived. Bennett, a quartermaster-general in the Illinois state militia at the time the Saints removed to Commerce in 1840, came to Nauvoo and aligned himself with the church. He became Nauvoo's first mayor on 1 February 1841 and a temporary assistant to the First Presidency a few months later, probably because of his political status in Nauvoo. On 11 May 1842 the First Presidency, the Quorum of the Twelve, and the presiding bishop meeting together disfellowshipped him for licentious conduct toward certain females in Nauvoo and for teaching spiritual wifery, a perversion of the increasingly practiced doctrine of polygamy (HC 5:18–19). No presiding bishop's court conducted the rather informal proceedings, possibly because his appointment had been temporary. Bennett confessed his sins, but soon became a bitter enemy of the church. He accused Joseph Smith of teaching that illicit intercourse was acceptable as long as it was kept secret, of directing secret Danite murders, and of plotting the overthrow by violence and plunder of the United States. He published these accusations in a series of newspaper articles, then republished them in August of 1842 in *The History of the Saints or an Expose of Joe Smith and Mormonism*. His accusations of illicit intercourse, of course, involved the emerging notion of polygamy, which was to become the prime source of persecution for the next fifty years. The Danite and insurrection charges were a repetition of accusations that had never been resolved in the courts of Missouri, and, while based primarily on factual events, they remained controversial at the time.

William Law, who replaced Hyrum Smith in the First Presidency on 19 January 1841, after Hyrum became church patriarch (HC 4:282; D&C 124), was excommunicated for unChristianlike conduct on 18 April 1844. William, along with Wilson and Jane Law, Robert S. Foster, and Howard Smith, was tried before a special council of church leaders including six apostles, five city council members, several Nauvoo High Council members and nineteen other prominent church leaders including Newell K. Whitney, who, although not sustained as presiding bishop until 7 October 1844, became the senior bishop of the church following Edward Partridge's death on 27 May 1840.

The defendants were alarmed by Joseph Smith extending his authority from religious to political matters, taking what they saw as control over the lives of the faithful. William Law was also fearful that the emerging practice of polygamy, while kept secret, was going to tear apart the church and the community. The defendants also accused

Smith of being a financial schemer who was defrauding faithful members. After their excommunication they organized a "New Church Movement." They were arrested and tried for causing disturbances, and thereafter retaliated by counterarrests for false imprisonment and defamation. William Law presented testimony before the Carthage grand jury in May of 1844. Law also published the *Nauvoo Expositor*, for the purpose of exposing the flaws he saw in the church and in Smith. The *Expositor* was especially controversial in focusing opposition to polygamy (Van Wagoner 1986, 67).

The first and only issue of the *Expositor* was published on 7 June 1844. The church leadership was having a hard enough time with criticism from outside the community and was not prepared to permit internal dissent. The apostate newspaper so enraged church leadership that the city council, under Joseph Smith's direction, declared the newspaper a public nuisance and ordered the destruction of the *Expositor* press. This precipitous action resulted in Joseph and Hyrum's incarceration in the Carthage jail, where they were murdered on 27 June 1844 (Oaks 1965b:862–903). It is relevant that one of the minor matters complained of in the *Expositor* (in addition to the adultery charges against Joseph Smith) was the irregularity of Law's 18 April 1844 excommunication trial; the argument was that the special council called to hear the case had no jurisdiction over William Law since, as a member of the First Presidency, he could only be tried by the presiding bishop assisted by twelve high priests especially chosen. It would appear that William Law had a legitimate complaint about the technical deficiencies of his excommunication trial. This procedural mistake would not be repeated in subsequent proceedings against members of the First Presidency.

The slaying of Joseph Smith prompted a whole slate of succession claims (Quinn 1976). Church leadership faced a dilemma of highest significance. From a sociological standpoint the problem of transferring Joseph's charismatic authority to another or to an institution posed a special problem that would never be satisfactorily resolved. Joseph could have assisted, but not removed, the succession crisis. Possessing the keys of revelation for the church, he could have definitively pronounced in scriptural form the Lord's directives on the transference of the mantle of authority. Many believed he did just this. Unfortunately, more than one claimant believed he had received Joseph's assurance of succession authority. Claimants and their supporters sought to persuade the body of the church that Joseph (and therefore the Lord) had chosen them as heirs. Because the issue had never previously arisen, custom could not give any direction—

although it would in future cases. Relying on Weberian typology, charismatic and legal alternatives remained. While the personal charisma of the claimants undoubtedly influenced the outcome, the availability of legal forums endowed with decisional authority shifted the focus to an institutional (legal) level. Not that any court had been vested with jurisdiction over succession issues; rather the court structure existed (independent of the authority of the First Presidency) for considering the standing of any member—including the president if necessary. By invoking the perceived legitimacy of ecclesiastical forums, church standing issues could indirectly resolve the succession issue; anyone improperly assuming the mantle of authority could be tried. If the appropriate forum deemed the assumption to be legitimate, a "no action" decision could be translated into institutional (legal) acceptance; otherwise, disfellowshipping or excommunication would jeopardize any succession claim.

The most significant succession claim came from one of the church's most prominent leaders, Sidney Rigdon. An associate of Joseph Smith since his conversion in 1830, Rigdon had become a member of the First Presidency on 18 May 1837, but his influence waned as the Saints moved to Nauvoo in 1840. His "Salt Sermon" in June of 1838, which implicitly threatened dissenters such as Cowdery and the Whitmers, together with his inflammatory Fourth of July oration in 1838 that threatened non-Mormon persecutors, may have provoked mob violence in Missouri, and a breach developed between him and Smith. On 13 August 1843, Smith accused Rigdon of attempting to betray him and asked that he be released as counsellor (HC 5:532). Rigdon's disfellowship was made the subject of a special conference on 6 October 1843. Joseph Smith expressed "his dissatisfaction with Elder Sidney Rigdon as a counsellor, not having received any material benefit from his labors or counsels since their escape from Missouri." Rigdon asked for forgiveness, and Patriarch Hyrum Smith, Joseph's brother, spoke in his behalf. The conference attenders displayed their affection for Rigdon, specifically rejecting the advice of Joseph Smith, by voting to retain him in his station as counsellor in the First Presidency. Joseph responded to this rebuke by his people, saying, "I have thrown him off my shoulders, and you have again put him on me. You may carry him, but I will not" (HC 5:532, 6:47–49). Smith more or less exiled Rigdon to Pittsburgh, where, after Smith's assassination, he claimed to have received a revelation that as the sole surviving member of the First Presidency he would be appointed "guardian" of the church.

Brigham Young, senior apostle, met in Boston with two other members of the Twelve, following the martyrdom of Joseph and Hyrum

Smith, and wrote to Rigdon at Pittsburgh instructing him to consult with the Quorum before taking any action. Assuming that, after Joseph's death, the Twelve had no jurisdiction over him, Rigdon returned to Nauvoo and attempted to persuade the Saints, still stunned by the martyrdom, to believe his "guardian" revelation. The apostles, scattered abroad on missions, were not able to return to Nauvoo before Rigdon had begun preaching his position.

At Rigdon's request, William Marks called a conference on 8 August 1844. At the conference, Rigdon spoke for ninety minutes, but had already disaffected many of the people by his speeches days before, in which he alluded to violence and bloodshed as being the future of the Saints (Newell & Avery, 202–3). Brigham Young (who, along with most of the other Apostles, had made it back to Nauvoo) also spoke to the conference crowd, and declared that "no man can put another between the Twelve and the Prophet Joseph" (Newell & Avery, 203). The majority of the Saints who attended the meeting voted to sustain Young and the Twelve as the leaders of the church, and to defeat Rigdon's motion for "guardianship" (HC 7:231–43). On 3 September 1844 the Twelve met with Rigdon and demanded he give up his license for having ordained men to unheard-of offices (Prophets, Priests, and Kings) and attempting to divide the church. Rigdon refused. As a result the Twelve "withdrew fellowship" from him and set a trial for Sunday, 8 September 1844, before the congregation.

Bishop Newell K. Whitney presided, assisted by the Nauvoo High Council, according to church law that required a member of the First Presidency be tried before the presiding bishop and twelve high priests (HC 7:268–69; D&C 107:82–84). The Quorum of Twelve appeared as witnesses against the accused. According to the minutes published in the church's paper, *Times and Seasons* (15 Sept. 1844, 18:660–67; 15 Oct. 1844, 19:685–87), the issue was legitimacy. Should Rigdon be excommunicated for teaching false doctrine, for ordaining individuals to unknown and unauthorized callings, and for attempting to set himself above the Twelve in authority and divide the church, or should he be followed as the proper guardian of the church? Brigham Young, at the commencement of the trial (which was presided over by Bishop Whitney), explained the organization of this special court:

> It is written in the book of the Doctrine and Covenants, that the president can be tried before a bishop and twelve high priests, or the high council of the church. . . . We have here this morning, the high council, and Bishop Whitney at their head, and we will try Sidney Rigdon before this council and let them take an action on his case this morning; and

then we will present it to the church, and let the church also take an action upon it.

Rigdon was absent. Young testified that he had been informed that Rigdon was sick but that he believed Rigdon and his followers had "concluded not to say anything in their own defense, thinking that would be best for them." Notice had been given to Rigdon five days earlier as well as being published in the *Nauvoo Neighbor*. "Was he sick he could have sent us word to have the case deferred." As senior apostle, Young preferred charges against Rigdon, adding that the Twelve were "witnesses in this trial, and not judges." By avoiding "judging" Rigdon, the Twelve sought institutional legitimacy for a decision that would likely leave them in control of the church. They avoided, however, an explicit claim to the charismatic authority of any apostle, including Brigham Young.

Apostles Orson Hyde, Parley P. Pratt, Amasa Lyman, John Taylor, and Heber C. Kimball each testified that Rigdon had attempted to divide the church and had acted contrary to Smith's direction, that he had threatened "to publish all your secret meetings and all that history of the secret works of this church, in the public journals," and to purge the church by mob violence if it refused his leadership. William Marks, president of the Nauvoo Stake and its high council, spoke in defense of the accused, less on the merits of the case than to fulfill the church's judicial requirements:

> It has always been the case before this High Council, that there are two sides to the question; there are some to speak in favor of the accused, but there seems to be only one side to this subject. There has been many things said which I know nothing about. But as it has always been the case before the High Council that some should speak in the defense of the accused, I feel to volunteer to speak on his behalf. It is no more than right that both sides should be represented. I don't wish to justify any man in an error but there is a trial before this church and council.

Mark's defense admitted the errors that Rigdon had been accused of but appealed for mercy on the grounds that the errors had been innocent.

Young submitted the case to Whitney and the high council. Members of the high council had additional discussion; then, without withdrawing for private deliberation, Whitney pronounced excommunication. He "then presented the motion to the High Council and the vote was unanimous in the affirmative." The motion was then sustained by those present in the congregation, with a few dissenting. The congregation thereby affirmed the institutional legitimacy of the church.

This issue was so critical that those who had dissented or who thereafter advocated Rigdon's position were suspended by a motion at the same meeting, until a trial for membership could be held before the Nauvoo High Council. William Marks was released as stake president on 7 October 1844, "because he did not acknowledge the authority of the Twelve, but the authority of Elder Rigdon" (HC 7:296).

Marks, like Rigdon and James J. Strang, did not recognize this decision, and each led a group of their followers away from Nauvoo. These groups had varying amounts of success on their own, and they united in 1859 under Joseph Smith's son and formed the Reorganized Church of Jesus Christ of Latter Day Saints. While Joseph Smith III undoubtedly had a stronger claim to succession than Rigdon, by the time he had matured sufficiently to be considered, Brigham Young's charismatic leadership had been consolidated sufficiently to remove any serious challenge from even Joseph Smith III, who had not followed the body of the Saints west. Marks assisted in Joseph Smith III's ordination in 1860 and served as a counsellor in the RLDS presidency from 1863 until his death in 1872. There is no record of Marks's excommunication, if it ever took place (Quinn 1976, 214 n. 72).

Other succession claims resulted in the excommunication of would-be successors. William Smith, an apostle and the only surviving brother of Joseph, claimed a right to presidency as a matter of succession after he had been ordained by the apostles to the office of presiding patriarch on 24 May 1845. As presiding patriarch his succession claim was not entirely without foundation. Had Hyrum survived, the pattern of succession may have been different. But William did not enjoy the charismatic authority of Hyrum. He was dropped from the Quorum and as patriarch to the church at general conference 6 October 1845 (HC 7:433, 458–59). On 19 October 1845 he was excommunicated for publishing a pamphlet challenging the authority of the Twelve Apostles to govern the church (HC 7:483). He then became a leader in the Strang group until he was excommunicated in 1847 for moral infractions. After being rebuffed for many years by Brigham Young, in an appeal to be restored to baptism and apostleship, on 9 April 1878, Smith aligned himself with his nephew, Joseph Smith III, who in the interim had become president of the Reorganized Church of Jesus Christ of Latter Day Saints (Quinn 1976, 205–6; Bates, 11; Gary Smith, 24).

Several claimants declared their right to succession by reason of appointment under the hand of Joseph Smith. James J. Strang, baptized on 25 February 1844, insisted that Joseph had designated him as the successor. When he announced his claim on 5 August 1844 at Florence,

Michigan, the branch at Florence excommunicated him, as did the apostles at Nauvoo. Nonetheless, many followed Strang, including John C. Bennett (who initially supported Rigdon's claims), Apostle John E. Page, and previous apostles William E. McLellin and (for a brief time) William Smith. John E. Page was disfellowshipped from the Quorum of the Twelve on 9 February 1846 and excommunicated on 27 June 1846 (Jenson 1899, 30; CHC 2:431, n.5). Apostle Lyman Wight was also excommunicated for his unwillingness to accept the Quorum of the Twelve as the presiding authority of the church. After supporting the succession claims of William Smith and Joseph Smith III, he proclaimed his own authority by virtue of a secret ordination in 1834 to the office of "Banamey" in the presence of an angel (Quinn 1976). His church standing came up at the April conference of 1845, but was continued for lack of information until 3 December 1848, when he was excommunicated (CHC 2:436, n.15). Alpheus Cutler, a member of the Nauvoo High Council and one of Joseph Smith's bodyguards, also claimed a right of succession by special ordination. He left the Saints at Winter Quarters in 1848, and established an Iowa colony. He was excommunicated on 20 April 1851 (Quinn 1976, 197–98).

Succession claims, therefore, resulted in the formal excommunication of three apostles, the sole surviving member of the First Presidency, and many other members.

The church court system had played an important role in disciplining church leaders. As an effective system for dealing with dissidents who refused to confess faults and conform, these courts helped forge a distinctive Mormon community. They lent formal authority to the Twelve's claim of succession rights by removing serious competitors and facilitated the orderly administration of church policy. Further, each case helped legitimize the authority of the courts to resolve important conflicts within the church.

3

Early Trials in New York
and Ohio

Mormon experiences with gentile litigation left an indelible mark on the collective memory of the early Saints, especially the priesthood leaders who often found themselves targets of what they perceived as vexatious lawsuits. Various factors contributed to the growing distrust of legal proceedings. The saints early determined, whether accurately or not, that they were a persecuted people; they came to believe that their enemies could and would use the law to harass and annoy the faithful. In addition, experience taught them the perils of relying on the fairness of frontier justice. During the nineteenth century Mormons continually were on the borders of settled communities. The few lawyers available were ill-trained and their library resources woefully limited. Even where early Mormons experienced as fair a trial as was reasonably possible at that place and time, injustices were readily apparent. In addition, litigation expenses frequently drained the limited financial resources of the church and its leaders; the expense of civil and criminal proceedings in Mormon eyes simply outstretched any good attributable to the outcome. As a result the Saints soon looked with discouragement at the prospect of repeatedly suing and being sued before the law.

LEGAL EXPERIENCES IN NEW YORK

Recent historical studies provide evidence that Joseph Smith on occasion used folk or white magic as a money-digger. Critics of Mormonism have long argued that such superstitious activities establish conclusively the fraudulent roots of the Mormon church. Mormon apologists, on the other hand, have either denied or downplayed the extent or significance of Joseph's mystical undertakings, explaining the emphasis given to them by contemporaries as evidence of the type of persecution that often accompanies efforts to establish true religion. The earliest trials involving Joseph Smith raised the twin issues of superstitious beginnings and religious persecution.

The trials occurred in 1826 and 1830. In each instance the charge related to Smith's money-digging activities. The vagrancy statute prohibited "pretending . . . to discover where lost goods may be found." The 20 March 1826 "glass looking" charges filed at South Bainbridge against the young Joseph (Walters 1974, 129) certainly would have fit the statutory offense. The bilkee, Josiah Stowell, apparently had expended money digging for hidden treasures of gold and silver. A. W. Benton in 1831 recounted Joseph's early "glass looking" enterprises, which prompted the prosecution (Benton, 120). William D. Purple, who claimed to have been present at the trial, recorded his reminiscences fifty-one years later in the local newspaper, *The Chenango Union* (May 2, 1877, xxx, 3). The actual trial record purportedly taken from Justice Albert Neely's docket book was published in *Fraser's Magazine* in 1873 (C.M., 225).

Surprisingly, the person supposedly defrauded, Josiah Stowell, served not as the complainant but as a defense witness. He later joined the church and was devoted to the prophet Joseph. Peter G. Bridgman, a nephew of Miriam Stowell (Josiah's wife), swore out the warrant. Wesley P. Walters speculates that his concern over the fortune of his aunt and cousins likely motivated his actions, but notes that within a month of the trial "he was licensed as an exhorter by the Methodists and within three years had helped establish the West Bainbridge Methodist Church" (Walters 1974, 141). Walters further notes that Bridgman was "an ardent Methodist" throughout his life who would have vigorously rejected any contrary doctrine. Bridgman's objections to Smith's religious claims, therefore, may well have been the motivation for the prosecution.

The trial's significance lies in Joseph's apparent reference to a seer stone he possessed that he occasionally used to determine where treasures in the earth were hidden. Joseph admitted that he had used the stone to look for treasures for Mr. Stowell, but added "that he did not solicit business of this kind, and had always rather declined having anything to do with this business" (reprinted in Walters 1974, 149). Joseph in his history admits participating in some money-digging for Josiah Stowell prior to 1826 (HC 1:17). Thus the fact that the trial records do not clearly specify a judgment or a sentence is of minor import.[1]

The religious significance of Joseph's money-digging experiences has generated a great deal of controversy. Brodie felt the evidence of Joseph's involvement with folk magic tainted his role as a prophet.

Marvin Hill's analysis suggests that imposing "twentieth century ratio-
nalistic assumptions" on "the nineteenth century situation" will likely
lead to misinterpretations of the sincerity and beliefs of people whose
outlook is unfamiliar to us (*Church History* 43 [March 1974]: 85–86).
Based on the evidence, Bushman acknowledges Smith's participation
in money-digging, but argues that following the Stowell incident and
the 1826 trial, Joseph began to heed Moroni's warnings against using
the gifts of God for ignoble purposes (Bushman, 75). Bushman urges
tolerance in the interpretation of these matters, suggesting that en-
lightenment rationalism had not entirely penetrated the thinking of
the common man during this period. Folk magic and religion blended
more naturally at that time than today (Quinn 1987).

The vagrancy charges associated with money-digging surfaced
again in 1830, almost certainly the result of religious curiosity, if
not persecution. Between the March 1826 and the June 1830 trials
Joseph's acquisition of the golden record and translating devices on 22
September 1827, his subsequent translation efforts, his claim to have
received the power of the priesthood by angelic visitation, and his
organization of a pretentious religion that claimed exclusive authority
to speak for God had caused much commotion. Joseph later recorded
that "severe persecution at the hands of all classes of men, both religious and irreligious" resulted from his announcing such religious
manifestations (HC 1:7–9). The translation of the Book of Mormon
was complete in 1829, and Joseph secured a copyright on 11 June 1829.
Abner Cole published derogatory remarks in his Palmyra newspaper,
The Reflector, about the "Golden Bible" that E. B. Grandin had agreed
to publish. When Cole began publishing excerpts of the Book of Mormon he had stolen from the printer's manuscript, Joseph enforced
the copyright to forbid him further publications. Publication of the
Book of Mormon was advertised 6 March 1830. The book immediately
"was seen as a blasphemous rival to orthodox Christianity," which
made Joseph Smith "a minor national figure" (Bushman, 109–11). The
church's organization the following month on 6 April 1830 attracted
attention to this "religious imposter."

This public notoriety undoubtedly prompted Joseph's arrest in June
1830 on charges of being a "disorderly person." The trial took place
in South Bainbridge, Chenango County, New York, before a Justice
Chamberlain (Walters 1974, 125). Smith's followers retained James
Davidson and John Reid to represent him in defense, both "well
versed in the laws though neither was a lawyer or a Mormon" (HC
1:89). Reid recorded later "[t]hose bigots soon made up a false accusation against him [Joseph]. . . . The prosecutors employed the best

counsel they could get, and ransacked the town of Bainbridge and county of Chenango for witnesses that would swear hard enough to convict the prisoner; but they entirely failed" (HC 1:89; Walters 1977, 124–25).

The trial commenced at 10:00 A.M. and closed at midnight. Smith was acquitted, but was seized immediately on similar charges filed in Boone County. The second trial commenced the next morning, lasted 23 hours, and involved 43 witnesses (Walters 1977, 135). The "vagrancy" charges ranged from "setting the country in an uproar by preaching the Book of Mormon," to using the pretense of having received angelic visitations to obtain money (the 1826 money-digging charges revisited), and the casting out of a devil; Joseph had cast out a devil from Newell Knight in April 1830 (HC 1:89–91). It is not clear why the money-digging charge arising out of the Stowell incident was not precluded by the prohibition against double jeopardy. Apparently he was acquitted (HC 1:96; Bushman, 162).

While Smith's fantastic claims would have appeared fraudulent to most, his personal account reflects dismay at what he considered unconstitutional harassment: "Thus were we persecuted on account of our religious faith—in a country the Constitution of which guarantees to every man the indefeasible right to worship God according to the dictates of his own conscience—and by men, too, who were professors of religion, and who were not backward to maintain the right of religious liberty for themselves, though they could wantonly deny it to us" (HC 1:97).

LEGAL EXPERIENCES IN OHIO

Perhaps the New York incidents contributed to Smith searching for a less hostile environment. Parley P. Pratt, an early convert and later an apostle, was proselytizing en route to Missouri in October 1830 when he stopped near Kirtland, Ohio to preach to his former minister, Sidney Rigdon. Rigdon not only joined the new church, but brought along most of his Campbellite congregation.[2] Smith arrived in Ohio in February 1831, two months after announcing a revelation designating Ohio as a temporary gathering place; the body of the remaining New York Saints followed within a few months[3] (D&C 37; HC 1:39–45; CHC 1:240). From then until the church's exodus from Kirtland seven years later for Far West, Missouri, the Mormons co-existed with their neighbors with minimal religiously dependent litigation. Although Joseph explained when he left in March of 1838 that "wicked and vexatious lawsuits for seven years past" (HC 3:11) had contributed to his financial disasters which compelled his departure, the Ohio litigation seems attributable more to self-inflicted commercial disasters than Mormon beliefs in the "Golden Bible" (Parkin 1966, 263–273).

The Mormons in Ohio occasionally sought redress for religious persecution in the courts. These cases are significant because within a few years Missourians would accuse the same Mormon leaders of taking the law into their own hands in punishing dissenters and enemies. In Ohio, at least, the Saints were willing to present their complaints before the gentile courts.

Joseph, for example, filed an assault complaint in April 1834 against Philastus Hurlburt. Hurlburt had joined the church in 1833, but had been excommunicated the same year for sexual misconduct (HC 1:352, 355). Following his excommunication, Hurlburt became a bitter enemy of the Prophet Joseph; he alleged that Joseph had stolen the Book of Mormon story from a "Spalding manuscript,"[4] and he apparently threatened Joseph's life.[5] A trial on the assault charge sensationalized by the religious overtones involved took place on 2 April 1834, in Chardon, Ohio. A newspaper account of the trial reported:

> On Tuesday last, the court-house was filled, almost to suffocation, with an eager and curious crowd of spectators, to hear the Mormon trial, as it was called. A great number of witnesses attended, and were examined, chiefly members of the Mormon society, among whom, was the renowned prophet himself. It appeared, that Hurlburt had been a disciple of Mormonism, and ordained an elder by Joe himself, but for misconduct, as the Mormon witnesses alleged, was excommunicated. After this, he discovered that Joe was a false prophet, and the Book of Mormon was taken from a manuscript romance, written by one Spalding. . . . Many witnesses testified to threats of revenge from Hurlburt. One witness who testified to threats of Hurlburt, on cross-examination, being asked the reason why she had not communicated these threats to Smith, answered that she did not believe that Hurlburt, or any other human being, had the power to hurt the prophet;—but Joe himself appears to have placed little reliance upon his divine invulnerability;—for he testified that he became afraid of bodily injury from the defendant.[6]

Following the trial, Joseph, pleased with the proceedings, wrote that "after an impartial trial, the court decided that Dr. Philastus Hurlburt be bound over, under two hundred dollar bonds, to keep the peace for six months, and pay the cost, which amounted to nearly three hundred dollars all of which was in answer to our prayer, for which I thank my Heavenly Father" (HC 2:49).

Parley P. Pratt similarly obtained legal redress for an assault prompted by adverse reaction to public preaching in an action filed before the 1835 October term of the Court of Common Pleas. The newspaper account of *Pratt v. Howell* reported:

> Pratt is a Mormon Preacher, and had determined to preach to the people of Mentor, whether they wished it or not. Having been warned not to do so, and refused admittance into their meeting-house, he mounted the steps of the same, and began to hold forth from the Book of Mormon. The defendant acted as captain of a company, who with drama, fifes, trumpets, etc., marched back and forth before the stand chosen by the preacher, and saluted him with music and bows; some, in the rear of the company pelted him with eggs until he was well hammered;—to recover damages for which, the suit was brought. It was proved that defendant issued orders to march, and halt, and keep time, but gave no orders to fire. The jury, however, came to the conclusion, that, holding them under military command, he was responsible for their acts, and returned a verdict against him for forty-seven dollars damages.[7]

For the time being, only a few isolated actions brought church leaders into court as defendants. One such action, filed against Joseph, raised the issue of compensation for services rendered for religious causes. During the winter of 1833–34 local citizens expelled the Mormons in Jackson County, Missouri from their lands and homes. In the Spring of 1831 Joseph Smith organized "Zion's camp" in Kirtland, Ohio, with the purpose of "redeeming" Jackson County, Missouri. On 24 June 1834, Zion's camp, which had fought no battles other than fatigue, disease, and inclement weather, was disbanded.[8] It was generally regarded as a failure due to its inability to put the Mormons back in possession of their lands in Jackson County. Mormons viewed this experience, however, as invaluable priesthood training. Upon return to Kirtland, one of the members of Zion's camp, Dennis Lake, sued to recover $200 for his services. The newspaper account reported:

> A trial was last week had before a magistrate in Kirtland township, involving some very intricate points of national as well as military law. A suit was brought against the Mormon prophet, Gen. Jo. Smith, by one of the men composing his military crusade to Missouri last May, to recover pay for his services. Judgment for the plaintiff. The case has been appealed to a higher tribunal, where it will be determined how far individuals are obliged to serve as soldiers, without pay, for an indefinite period, under a pretended revelation from God.[9]

Although Lake prevailed in the Justice of the Peace Court, Joseph won on appeal in the Court of Common Pleas.[10]

In another case tried in 1835 the state charged Sidney Rigdon with solemnizing marriages without a license. The court entered a dismissal nolle prosequi when Rigdon produced a valid license he had previously received from the court while serving as a Campbellite minister.[11]

In another action, Justice Miller arraigned Joseph Smith in April 1835 and then tried him 10 June 1835 for assault and battery on his brother-in-law, Calvin W. Stoddard. The trouble likely stemmed from Stoddard charging Joseph with being a false prophet. Witnesses testified that Stoddard had been the first aggressor. The court dismissed the case, stating that "there could be no cause for further prosecution; that the assault might perhaps be justified on the principle of self-defense."[12]

These cases suggest that the Saints generally received fair treatment in the Ohio courts. Although Joseph may have begrudged the expense of defending spurious claims, the courts could not be held responsible for his detractors. The level and type of litigation changed significantly with the failure of the Kirtland Safety Society. The Safety Society, however, did not fail as a result of religious prejudice; nor was most of the ensuing litigation religiously inspired. The bankruptcy of the church's "bank," however, convinced many that the Prophet Joseph was a fraud in religious as well as banking matters. Creditor suits, therefore, carried religious implications. These "vexatious lawsuits," as Smith would call them, forced his abandonment of Kirtland in 1838.

Church leaders, including the Prophet Joseph, had organized the "Kirtland Safety Society" on 2 November 1836. The Safety Society was to act as a bank for the church. There exists no evidence that the "bank" was part of any "scam" or get-rich scheme. Kirtland, Ohio, was one of hundreds of similar communities of the credit-starved frontier. Even specie was scarce. The attitude was, essentially, that "the East won't finance us and if they do, they will kill us with interest." The conclusion that frontier communities should finance themselves, whatever their hard equity, was not unique to Kirtland. Added to the economic condition of the western frontier was the Mormon impulse favoring self-sufficiency. The concept of a self-contained Zion was central to the Mormon view of a religious community.

Upon organization of the Society, the group sent Orson Hyde to Columbus, Ohio to apply to the Ohio state legislature for a bank charter—the bank to be known as the "Kirtland Safety Society Bank." Oliver Cowdery was also sent to Philadelphia to procure bank name plates from which to print the proposed currency. The application for the charter was denied by the Ohio state legislature. Unfortunately for the Saints, financial needs prevailed over discretion. Rather than scrapping the "bank" for lack of legislative authority, on 2 January

1837 the same group instead organized the "Kirtland Safety Society Anti-Banking Company."[13] An attempt was made to change the appearance of the notes by stamping them to read Anti-Banking Company instead of Bank. Because the society had no state charter, notes were consistently rejected by merchants in New York, Pittsburgh, and Cleveland, where large quantities of merchandise had been purchased on credit for use in Kirtland.[14] Newspapers of the day sensationalized the "worthless paper" that was being circulated by the Kirtland Safety Society.[15] Within six months the financial "panic of 1837" swept the entire nation taking down the Kirtland Society along with thousands of other over-subscribed banks and institutions.[16]

Nothing in Ohio injured the reputation of the Prophet Joseph more than the failure of the Society. Hostility often surfaced in the form of litigation. Grandison Newell, for example, commenced an action in May 1837 against Joseph Smith for attempted murder; Newell alleged that Joseph wanted him dead for Newell's impugning the integrity of the founders of the Kirtland Safety Society.

The preliminary hearing, held 3 June 1837 at the Painesville Methodist Church, was widely publicized and well attended. Newell, a resident of Mentor, located two miles from Kirtland, in May had filed the complaint in Painesville, located nine miles from Kirtland. There was speculation that his purpose in doing so was to harass the Mormons, as well as have the case tried before Painesville's Justice of the Peace Flint, whose political associations promised a favorable result.

At the commencement of the hearing, General Charles C. Paine, a leader of the Federalist Party in the county in which Painesville was located, sat next to Mr. Newell. He passed notes throughout the hearing suggesting questions to be put to the witnesses and occasionally made remarks favorable to the prosecution. Grandison Newell's allegations, taken from his letter to the editor, printed in the *Painesville Telegraph* May 26, were that

> two of the saints of the latter-day, by concert, and under the express direction of the prophet, this high priest of Satan, met in the night, at a little distance from my house, with loaded rifles, and pistols, with a determination to kill me. But as they drew near the spot where the bloody deed was to be performed, they trembled under the awful responsibility of committing a murder, a little cool reflection in darkness and silence, broke the spell of the false prophet—they were restored to their right minds, and are now rejoicing that they were not left to the power of the devil and co-adjuter Smith, to stain their souls with a crime so horrible.

Joseph's alleged coconspirators, according to Newell, were Solomon Denton and Mr. Davis.

During the hearing Luke Johnson, Mr. Whitney, Warren Parrish, Mr. Hyde, and Solomon Denton testified for the prosecution, while Hyrum Smith, Mr. Cahoun, and Sidney Rigdon, among others, testified for the defense. The hearing concluded with Justice Flint requiring Joseph Smith to post a $500 bond to keep the peace, pay Mr. Rigdon, Mr. Hyde, and Mr. Denton $50 witness fees, and appear for trial at the next term of the Court of Common Pleas.[17] On 9 June 1837 the case went to trial before Justice Humphrey of the Court of Common Pleas; the court discharged Joseph on the grounds of the insufficiency of the evidence.[18] Commenting on both proceedings, the *Painesville Republican* carried the following report:

> I attended the trial and took down the evidence, but was much surprised to find that no testimony appeared, on which, any reliance could be placed, that went in the least degree to crimination [*sic*] the respondent, but rather to raise him in the estimation of men and candor. But the Justice of the Peace who had been selected to try the question, decided otherwise, and Mr. Smith was held to bail in the sum of $500, to appear at the Court of Common Pleas, at the next term, which commenced the Monday following, being last week. The trial again came on before the County Court, on Friday last, and resulted in the entire acquittal of Joseph Smith, Jr. of the charges alleged against him. This is said to be the thirteenth prosecution which has been instituted against Joseph Smith, Jr. for the prejudice against him, he has never in a single instance been convicted, on a final trial. This fact shows on the one hand, that a spirit of persecution has existed, and on the other hand it certainly furnishes some evidence that he has for some reason, been falsely accused, and that he is indeed and in truth better than some of his accusers.[19]

This newspaper account suggests that Joseph by this time had defended a number of questionable claims. The fact he successfully prevailed and that the reporter was favorably impressed demonstrates that religious prejudice was not so pervasive as to make fair trials impossible.

Criminal actions stemming from violations of state banking laws presented the most serious threat to Joseph's status in Kirtland. In March 1837, Joseph Smith, as treasurer, and Sidney Rigdon, as secretary of the ill-fated "Kirtland Safety Society," were arrested on charges of violating the banking laws of Ohio. Samuel D. Rounds entered a suit on behalf of himself and the state of Ohio, demanding from each a penalty of one thousand dollars. Identical suits were also filed by Rounds against Warren Parrish, Frederick G. Williams, Newell K. Whitney, and H. Kingsbury in their capacities as officers in the Kirtland Safety Society. All six suits were originally scheduled to be heard

21 March 1837—at the March term of the Court of Common Pleas—but the suits were continued until the June term, apparently on the court's own motion.

At the June term, the six cases came before the court on a "demurrer to the declaration of the plaintiff," which was overruled by the court with costs to the plaintiff. However, on motion of the defendant, leave was given to amend, and it was ordered by the court that the cases be continued to the October term.[20] At the October term the suit against Warren Parrish was discontinued by the plaintiff, and the court nonsuited the plaintiff in the case against Frederick G. Williams, Newell K. Whitney, and H. Kingsbury for failure to prosecute the suit; in all four cases costs were awarded to the defendants. The suits against Joseph Smith and Sidney Rigdon, however, were tried before a twelve-person jury, which found them guilty. Although Joseph Smith and Sidney Rigdon appealed the decision, the case was never ruled on because both left the state before it could be heard.[21]

At the same term the court denied another case involving the Kirtland Safety Society. In that case, Joseph Smith had assigned a promissory note for $100 from Edson Barney, Royal Barney, Jr., and Truman O. Angell to Henry C. Skinner. When Skinner sued to enforce the note, the three signers defended on the grounds that the note was invalid for want of consideration because Joseph Smith had originally given Kirtland Safety Society bills in return for the promissory note. The court rejected that argument, holding that the promissory note was enforceable.[22] In a separate action, Sarah Cleveland was committed to Niagara jail for passing $390 in Kirtland Safety Society bills with intent to defraud. She was subsequently released on bail.[23]

Joseph Smith recorded the circumstances of a "vexatious lawsuit" initiated 27 July 1837:

> When we arrived at Painesville we were detained all day by malicious and vexatious law suits. About sunset I got into my carriage to return home to Kirtland; at this moment the sheriff sprang into the carriage, seized my lines, and served another writ on me, which was sworn out by a man who had a few weeks previously brought a new fashioned cooking stove to Kirtland, and prevailed on me to put it in my kitchen, saying it would give credit to his stove, wishing to have it tested by our people; and now he thought would be a good time to get pay for it. I gave my watch to the officer for security and we all returned home.[24]

The final days in Kirtland were colored by a constant flow of debt-collection litigation. For example, on 24 October 1837, Van R. Humphrey, president of the Court of Common Pleas in Geauga County,

Ohio, agreed to a stipulation to discontinue a suit for $295 against Sidney Rigdon, Joseph Smith, and Oliver Cowdery by John Newbold, awarding costs to the plaintiff.[25] On 7 December 1837 Joseph recorded that "one printing establishment was attached to satisfy an unjust judgment of the county court."[26] On 15 September 1838 the Geauga courthouse filed a statement that a $10,071.48 judgment against Joseph Smith and Reynolds Cahoon, in favor of Charles Holmes, had been satisfied.[27] And on 24 June 1839, the Kirtland sheriff returned the execution on a judgment for $1,186.66 against Joseph Smith in favor of Winthrop Eaton as "unsatisfied for want of property."[28] In this same vein the local newspapers recorded notice after notice of mortgage foreclosures entered against the Saints.[29]

From the June term of 1837 through the April term of 1839, seventeen lawsuits were brought against Joseph Smith in the Geauga County court for debt involving original claims of $30,206.44. Four of these suits were settled; three were discontinued voluntarily by the plaintiffs; and ten resulted in judgments; three were satisfied in full, three were satisfied in part; and four were wholly unsatisfied.[30]

One must conclude from a consideration of the failure of the Kirtland Safety Society that Mormon leadership exhibited extraordinarily bad judgment, and poor understanding or concern over the banking laws. But there is no evidence that this was a "scam." No self-enrichment was evident as a motivating factor. No subterfuge against would-be investors took place. Whether justified or not, the members of the priesthood leadership who suffered the brunt of the financial assault were convinced that they had been unfairly condemned.

The Saints left Ohio as a financially beaten community. The Society episode embarrassed Joseph Smith and cost him many of his closest supporters. The Saints had experienced a brief pinnacle of success and acceptance in Ohio; in the end, however, they departed in shame and disappointment. Although there is little evidence of unfairness or religious persecution in the judicial proceedings commenced against the Saints, persistent and expensive litigation must have frustrated many, especially Joseph Smith. With the exodus of 1838, church leadership and the majority of the Saints left financial disaster in Ohio only to face militant hostilities in Missouri.

4

Persecution in Missouri

Early Mormons regarded Missouri, specifically Jackson County, as the divinely revealed site for the establishment of Zion. The concept of a designated site for a holy city was an important part of Mormon theology from the very beginning. The Book of Mormon speaks prophetically of the New Jerusalem that will be built upon the American continent during the millennium (Esther 13:2–11). On 6 April 1830, the date the Mormon church was formally established, Joseph Smith received a revelation that confirmed his concept of Zion: "Him have I inspired to move the cause of Zion . . . yea, his weeping for Zion I have seen . . ." (D&C 21:7–8). In September 1830, Smith received the revelation that Zion would be located "near the borders by the Lamanites" and that the exact location would yet be revealed (D&C 28:9). From that time on, Smith's followers eagerly waited for God to fulfill His promise to reveal the location of the City of Zion (Book of Commandments, 68, 80, 82, 90, 92, 94). The significance of Zion as a concrete place can hardly be overstated. As William Mulder observed, "while other millenarians set a time [for the Second Coming], the Mormons appointed a place" (Mulder 1954, 23:252).

In December 1831 Joseph further defined the concept of Zion in his announced vision of Enoch. According to this vision, after the earthly Zion was established, the heavenly Zion would descend with Christ at his Second Coming to initiate the millennial reign. Thus Zion would not appear after the reign, as many believed in the early nineteenth century; the millennium would be ushered in by the establishment of Zion (Bushman, 170–71). Zion would be built up by gathering the people of Israel from the four quarters of the world. The sequence of events was preordained.

> In the last days . . . righteousness and truth will I cause to sweep the earth as with a flood, to gather out mine elect from the four quarters of the earth, unto a place which I shall prepare, an Holy City, that my people shall gird up their loins, and by looking forth for the time of my

coming, for there shall be my tabernacle, and it shall be called Zion, a
New Jerusalem.

And the Lord said unto Enoch: Then shalt thou and all thy city meet
them there, and we will receive them into our bosom, and they shall see
us. (Smith, *The Pearl of Great Price*; Moses 7:62–64)

The vision of Enoch also clarified the social order of Zion, which
after this vision was often called the Order of Enoch: "The Lord called
his people Zion because they were of one heart and one mind, and
dwelt in righteousness; and there was no poor among them" (Moses
7:18). The concept of Zion had begun to assume important territorial
and social dimensions by mid-1831.

Prophetic history and Mormon experience coalesced when Joseph
Smith sent Oliver Cowdery to the borders near the Indians on a mission to convert them and to discover the location of the city of Zion
(Bushman, 186–87). On 31 July 1831, Joseph identified Independence,
Missouri as the "center place; and a spot for the temple is lying westward" (D&C 57:3). The Saints thus entered sacred history as they
prepared to establish Zion. Zion had become the center place, the *cen-
trum mundi* where the four corners of the earth would be gathered and
heaven and earth would meet. The Mormons would become the new
Israel, the people of God, through building Zion. The symbolic power
of Zion and the sense of living out sacred history should not be over-
looked, for Joseph Smith had tapped into a view of reality common
to all significant religious movements (Shipps; Eliade, 367–87). Zion
endowed Mormonism with cosmic significance through its expression
of sacred space and time.

On 25 June 1833, Smith sent a "Plat of the City of Zion" to Church
leaders in Missouri (Andrus 1958, 300–304). The city was to be a classic
"hierocentric state," a concentric layout one mile square surrounding a
central temple complex that would house government and priesthood
buildings, meetinghouses, schools, and temples as well as the central
bishop's storehouses (Nibley 1951, 226–53; Eliade, supra). The city
was designed to be inhabited by ten to fifteen thousand people. Every
family would receive a lot within the city, and farmers would receive
an additional allotment of land outside the city. The city's plan thus
preserved the sense of sacred space.

In the June 1833 communication, Smith also introduced an important innovation in the geographic concept of Zion. Zion was not a
single city; it was a complex of cities that would be built around Zion
until the entire earth had become sacred space: "When this square
is thus laid off and supplied, lay off another in the same way, and
so fill up the world in these last days" (HC 1:358). Joseph Smith ap-

propriated the Old Testament vision of Zion as a tent with a center stake that would be supported by outlying "stakes, for the curtains are the strength of Zion." He took literally Yahweh's words to Isaiah, "[e]nlarge the place of thy tent, and let them stretch forth the curtains of thine habitations; spare not, lengthen the cord, and strengthen thy stakes" (Isa. 54:2; D&C 82:14). Thus, the outlying cities were designated "stakes of Zion," each built after a plan similar to that of the Plat of Zion.

The Mormon dreams of the church peacefully expanding from the center place never materialized. Instead the Saints were forced to flee from Jackson County, and later from the entire state of Missouri. Expulsion meant that for the time being Zion would have to be freed from its territorial moorings. Joseph Smith received just such a transforming revelation 23 July 1833 on the eve of the forced exodus from Jackson County: "Therefore, verily, thus saith the Lord, let Zion rejoice, for this is Zion—THE PURE IN HEART; therefore, let Zion rejoice" (D&C 97:21). Zion had become a sacred people; it was the identity as God's people that remained essential, not the land. Joseph thereafter subordinated the location of Zion to the identity of the covenant people.

The causes of the Missouri persecution are complex. E. E. Ericksen (1922) attributed them to Mormon group consciousness and group morality: communal identity discouraged Mormon assimilation into the larger Missouri community. The sheer number of Saints must have made the original settlers fear Mormon economic competition and political domination. The distinctive economic, social, and religious backgrounds of Mormons sparked legal and extralegal reaction from non-Mormon neighbors. When the Saints realized that gentile law would more often be used against them than in their defense, they became alienated from both civil law and legal processes. During this period the seed of mistrust of gentile law and legal institutions, which had been planted in New York and Ohio, began to germinate. It would flower in Utah.

THE LAW OF CONSECRATION

Early Mormonism closely identified Zion with an economic system called the law of consecration and stewardship. Under that system, each member consecrated or deeded all of his or her possessions to the bishop of the church by an irrevocable deed, then received back a limited estate in certain "steward" property (D&C 42:30–36). Basic theological principles lay behind this law: possessions belonged to the Lord; and spiritual commitment required the individual to give priority to the Kingdom of God over materialistic desires. But implementing these ideals in a legally enforceable arrangement proved more problematic; the law would not accommodate Zion.

Leonard J. Arrington, Feramorz Y. Fox, and Dean L. May (1976) have carefully traced the evolution of the law of consecration and the various attempts to implement it. Several of their observations bear on this legal analysis. They stress the critical significance Joseph Smith gave to the law of consecration and stewardship in the realization of Zion:

> It was to provide the model upon which all human society would be organized when the Savior returned to the latter-day Zion in Missouri. It would build unity among a people fragmented by their individualistic search for economic well-being. It would impose order upon the chaos of a society suffering from an excess of liberty. An ideal community of the Saints would be prepared to administer Christ's millennial reign. . . . Order, unity, and community were the supreme values of the Prophet's ideal society. (Arrington, Fox, and May 1976, 2–3)

The first effort to implement this law had been made by a group of converts who settled near Kirtland, Ohio, in May 1831. When dissatisfied wealthy members thwarted the effort by successfully suing in the civil courts for the return of their consecrated property, Smith directed the group to try again in Jackson County, Missouri, where they arrived in July 1831.

But legal problems reappeared in Missouri. Bishop Edward Partridge sought to make the "steward" interest tentative rather than vested. Each steward would be entitled to a right of use only, subject to cancellation by the bishop. A conditional title policy would have allowed the bishop to make future reapportionments of "steward" property if the number of newly arriving converts necessitated a reduction in the size of the "inheritance" awarded earlier stewards. It would also discourage the unfaithful member who might join the Saints solely to obtain an inheritance and then immediately withdraw. The policy would also strengthen the bishop's ability to enforce work standards, social behavior, and personal morality. Arrington, Fox, and May suggest that the conditional-title policy ensured that "the wealth of the community would never be lost to apostates, 'trouble-makers', or idlers." Of course, it also deprecated traditional notions of property rights. Not surprisingly, the "lease-and-loan" agreement initially adopted failed to hold up when "some apostates successfully sued in the courts for the return of their consecrated properties" (Arrington, Fox, and May, 23, 25).

As a result, "church authorities finally came to agree that a steward should hold legal rights to 'the Lord's property' placed in his charge," a modification Orson Pratt characterized "as an unavoidable concession to the property laws of 'Babylon'" (Arrington, Fox, and May, 26, 434 n. 41). The early revelation on consecration in the Book of Commandments was modified to conform with the laws of the land (Arrington, Fox, and May, 433–34 n. 39). The "laws of Babylon" thus constrained the implementation of the law of consecration.

CONFLICT IN JACKSON COUNTY

The first Mormon missionaries arrived at Independence, Jackson County, Missouri, on 13 January 1831 (JH, 13 Jan. 1831, p. 1). To counter the Mormons, a "secret constitution" or "Manifesto of the Mob" was entered into in July 1833 by many of the prominent men of the county (HC 1:374–76). By 7 November 1833, the Mormons began an exodus out of their beloved Zion (HC 1:426–37). The Mormons' ability to generate so much hostility in so little time merits investigation.

The "secret constitution" acknowledged that resolution of the Mormon situation lay outside civil law and asserted that the responsibility for action therefore devolved upon the citizenry. Vigilantism was not uncommon in nineteenth-century frontier communities. Typically these extralegal groups organized to redress violations of law that went unpunished by formal legal processes. In Jackson County, the vigilante group cited "self-preservation" as a justification for admittedly extralegal acts.

The grounds cited by the subscribers in justification for the expulsion of the Mormons included, first, the assertion that the Mormons were the dregs of society, for they brought "little or no property with them"; second, that Mormons were "inviting free negroes and mulattoes from other states to become 'Mormons,' and remove and settle among us," which would "corrupt our blacks, and instigate them to bloodshed"; third, that the Mormons pretended "to receive revelations direct from heaven"; fourth, that they claimed God had given them the county as an inheritance, implying that Mormons would use force if necessary to claim it; and finally, that since the number of Mormon immigrants was daily increasing, old settlers were in danger of losing control over local politics and community affairs.

Certainly Mormons acknowledged their differences and proselytized in an effort to convert others to their peculiar beliefs. They also acknowledged their general poverty but denied that they were, as a result, the dregs of society. Parley P. Pratt later challenged the persecutors "to produce the name of any individual of our society on the list of indictments, from the time of our first settlement in the county, to the time of our expulsion, a period of more than two years," as evidence that Mormons generally were criminals (HC 1:377). Mormon eschatology gave Missourians reason to fear dispossession of their lands even while the Saints denied any intention to possess their Zion by any method other than free purchase. Many Mormon settlers in Missouri were from eastern and New England states and shared anti-slavery views, contrary to many slave-owning Missourians. Their denial that they were stirring up insurrection with "free negroes and mulattoes" persuaded few when an article in the Mormon paper, the *Evening and the Morning Star* lent itself to this interpretation.[1] The Mormons could not deny their rapid influx into the county; 1,300 had immigrated to Jackson County in approximately eighteen months. Like any frontier community, Jackson County welcomed new growth; but not in these unprecedented numbers, and not where the newcomers, who always acted in concert, would likely alter political control of the community. Given these circumstances, the established settlers invoked the natural "law of self-preservation" to rid their community of the blight of religious zealots whom they could not understand and whom they therefore feared.

The pledgees of the "secret constitution" along with their friends and neighbors (between 400 and 500 citizens) gathered at the courthouse in Independence on 20 July 1833 to present certain "removal" propositions to the Mormons (HC 1:395–99). The leaders of the vigilante group included many leaders of the community: Samuel D. Lucas, judge of the county court; Samuel C. Owens, county clerk; Russell Hicks, deputy county clerk; John Smith and Samuel Weston, justices of the peace; William Brown, constable; and Thomas Pitcher, deputy constable (CHC 1:341). The Mormons declined to leave their appointed place of gathering, and violence soon followed.

The first action came the same day, in separate assaults on Bishop Partridge and W. W. Phelps, the proprietor of the *Evening and the Morning Star*. The vigilantes violently beat Bishop Partridge and then tarred and feathered him in the public square when he refused to commit to a Mormon evacuation. Next they tore down W. W. Phelp's house, where the church's printing office was located, and either destroyed or stole all the printing equipment.[2] The Saints later recorded that Lieutenant Governor Lilburn W. Boggs, who five years later as governor was to issue his infamous extermination order, witnessed these events with approval (HC 1:391–92).

The vigilantes reassembled on 23 July with further threats. Partridge, along with other ecclesiastical leaders, agreed that if their attackers would cease further assaults, they would persuade the Mormons to leave the county, half by 1 January and the remainder by 1 April 1834 (HC 1:394).

Although warned against pursuing legal redress, the Saints nonetheless sent a petition to Governor Daniel Dunklin on 28 September asking for military protection so that they might defend their rights by suing for "the loss of property, for abuse, for defamation, as to ourselves, and if advisable try for treason against the government; that the law of the land may not be defiled, or nullified, but peace be restored to our country" (HC 1:410–15). This petition, presented personally by Orson Hyde and W. W. Phelps, was the first of many unsuccessful efforts to secure redress and protection. The governor, in a response dated 19 October 1833, advised the Mormons to file civil actions before the local circuit judges and justices of the peace, expressing his confidence that the courts would readily grant relief (HC 1:423–24).

In response, the Mormons contacted attorneys William T. Wood, Amos Rees, Alexander W. Doniphan, and David R. Atchison of neighboring Clay County, and the four offered their services on 30 October for $250 each. Although their fees were high, they advised the Mormons that they could undoubtedly command a similar fee to represent the defense. The high fees were probably justified, since whatever side the four attorneys represented, they stood to lose the other side's future patronage. Newel Knight recorded in his journal that as soon as the Missourians heard the Saints had retained prominent legal counsel "they disregarded the compact and assembled together vowing vengeance on all the 'Mormons,' being determined that we should leave forthwith" (Knight, 80; HC 1:425).

John Corrill, second counselor to Bishop Partridge, wrote to Oliver Cowdery that on 1 November, when the Mormons sought a peace warrant from a local magistrate against certain mob leaders who had demolished ten houses west of the Big Blue River the night before, the magistrate refused, despite being shown the governor's letter (*Evening and Morning Star*, Jan. 1834). One assailant, Richard McCarty, "was caught in the act of throwing rocks and brickbats into the doors [of the retail store of Gilbert and Whitney], while the goods lay scattered around him in the streets." The Mormons immediately took him before Samuel Weston, justice of the peace, who refused to act. McCarty, on the other hand, had the complainants arrested and jailed for false imprisonment (HC 1:428 and note; *Evening and Morning Star*,

Jan. 1834). On 2 November a battle at the Big Blue River, six miles from Independence, resulted in injuries on both sides (HC 1:428–29).

On 3 November church members unsuccessfully sought a peace warrant from Justice Silvers in Independence (HC 1:429; Jennings 1962, 172), and dispatched four men to Lexington to see if Circuit Judge John F. Ryland would give them a peace warrant. According to Pratt, Ryland refused the warrant but "advised us to fight and kill the outlaws whenever they came upon us" (Pratt 1938, 98). The next day, another battle between opposing interests resulted in fatalities and injuries on both sides (HC 1:430–31). Colonel Thomas Pitcher, a pledgee of the "secret constitution," held the Mormons responsible for the trouble, assembled a militia and on 5 November and secured the surrender of all the Mormon arms in Jackson County upon his pledge to similarly disarm the mob. In fact, he made no such attempt, and according to Joseph Smith many of those known to have participated in assaults on the Mormons appear on Pitcher's militia rolls (HC 1:432–35). Pitcher also compelled the surrender of certain Mormons to stand trial for the murder of the non-Mormons killed during the previous night's battle. The men were detained one day and gave Pitcher a watch to cover "costs of court." They were taken to a cornfield and told to leave (HC 1:435–36).

Once the Mormons had been disarmed, their opponents freely attacked Mormon homes, driving women and children into the night and beating Mormon men wherever they could be found. On 7 and 8 November the Mormons escaped across the Missouri River by ferry (HC 1:437). The aims of the "secret constitution" had been achieved.

Outside Jackson County, the unlawful expulsion of the Mormons received sympathetic attention. The editor of the *Missouri Republican*, for example, commented:

> It is possible to foresee what is to be the result of this singular and outrageous violation of the laws. We fear that the party opposed to the Mormons will think themselves placed so far beyond the pale of the law as to continue utterly regardless of it. . . . There may be many worthless and intolerable members of the obnoxious sect; but the laws are equal to the punishment of all those who are guilty of violating them. The Mormons are as much protected in their religion, their property, and persons, as any other denomination of class of men. (Jennings, 205)

The Attorney General of Missouri, R. W. Wells, wrote to attorneys Doniphan and Atchinson on 21 November advising them that if the Mormons wished to regain their property in Jackson County an adequate military force would be made available to them. He advised the Mormons to organize themselves into a regular company of militia and make application for public arms (HC 1:444–45). About this time Wells met Doniphan in Saline County and informed him that the governor was willing to order a court of inquiry to consider the grievances of the Mormons, but first they must let the governor know of their plans (HC 1:446–47).

The next day Judge Ryland wrote to Amos Rees, attorney for the Fifth Judicial Circuit as well as counsel for the Mormons, asking whether the Saints intended to take legal action against their persecutors. After indicating his willingness to come to Jackson County to conduct a court of inquiry, he wrote, "It is a disgrace to the state for such acts to happen within its limits, and the disgrace will attach to our official characters, if we neglect to take proper means to insure the punishment due such offenders" (HC 1:445–46).

However, public indignation did not resolve the problem. During the latter part of December, Governor Dunklin directed a court of inquiry into the conduct of Colonel Pitcher; many members, however, felt that any criminal prosecution against their enemies was futile, and refused to return to Jackson County to testify for fear of their lives. At least ten leaders returned under a court-ordered guard on 24 February 1834, but their attorney, the district attorney, and the attorney general of Missouri informed them that criminal prosecution of their assailants was impossible given the anti-Mormon feeling in Jackson County. W. W. Phelps writing several days later to the church leadership at Kirtland lamented, "The bold front of the mob . . . was not to be penetrated by civil law, or awed by executive influence." Eager to avoid any confrontation, the court ordered the guard to disperse, "apparently, on account of the speedy gathering of the old mob . . . and their assuming such a boisterous and mobocratic appearance." The men who had gone to testify retreated with the guard, and the matter was dropped. Phelps concluded, "Thus ends all hope of 're-dress,' even with a guard ordered by the Governor for the protection of the court and witnesses" (HC 1:481–482; Jennings, 223–24).

Nevertheless, the Mormons did not give up. They turned to federal authority in their efforts to seek redress. A petition containing 114 signatures was sent to President Andrew Jackson on 10 April 1834 asking that federal troops restore the Saints to their homes and thereafter maintain peace until civil order could be restored (HC 1:483–85). Mormon leaders asked Governor Dunklin to join in their petition. Although he was hesitant to do so, doubting whether the President had authority in this case, he admitted that the "laws, both civil and military, seem deficient in affording your society proper protection" (HC 1:489). The church received its formal reply from the War Department on 2 May 1834. Secretary Lewis Cass, for President Jackson, instructed them that the President had no authority to call out the military to aid in the enforcement of state laws (HC 1:493).

Church leaders correctly anticipated that efforts to obtain legal redress at the state level were also doomed to failure. Dunklin apparently wanted to aid them but was unwilling to take the extreme measures required. He did sanction Pitcher on 5 November 1833 for having illegally assembled his troops, and on 2 May 1834 ordered the return of the Mormons' illegally seized arms (HC 1:491). The order went unheeded (HC 1:492–93). On 6 June, Dunklin appointed Colonel J. Thornton of the state militia as an "aid to the commander-in-chief" for the purpose of negotiating a compromise between the parties. In the appointment letter, the governor acknowledged: "A more clear and indisputable right does not exist, than that of the Mormon people, who were expelled from their homes in Jackson County, to return and live on their lands" (HC 2:85). Nonetheless, if the matter could be compromised, the state would benefit.

Judge Ryland also desired a compromise, and arranged for the parties to meet on 16 June at Liberty, the seat of Clay County. The Jackson County representatives proposed buying out the Mormons, or alternatively the Mormons buying them out. The apparent reasonableness of this proposal was vitiated by the plight of the Saints. The Mormons, who had suffered the loss of a crop and most of their houses and furnishings the previous winter, certainly could not finance the purchase of all the non-Mormon properties within the county. Nor did they wish to sell lands they believed had religious significance. They countered with an offer to buy out only those inhabitants who believed they could not live peaceably with them, with the damages they had previously sustained to be deducted from the settlement amount (HC 2:107, 113–14).

Jackson County citizens rejected the counterproposal, and the matter remained deadlocked. In November 1834, Dunklin expressed his frustration to the state legislature: "As yet none have been punished for these outrages, and it is believed that, under our present law, conviction for any violence committed upon a Mormon, cannot be had in Jackson County" (Jennings, 238). Thus ended the Mormon legal efforts to return to Jackson County.

Bishop Partridge and W. W. Phelps continued to retain Wood, Atchison, Doniphan, and Rees to represent them in a civil suit for damages connected with the 20 July 1833 assault. They paid the attorneys $600 to file the action and an additional $200 to have the venue changed to Ray County due to the involvement of many prominent citizens in Jackson County. Partridge claimed $50,000 in damages against known participants in the assault. Russell Hicks, the deputy county clerk for Jackson County who had signed the "secret constitution" and had played a prominent role in the expulsion effort (Partridge 1839), had his law firm of Reynolds, Birch, Burden, Young, Hicks, Chiles, and Wilson defend against both Partridge's and Phelp's complaints. Somewhat surprisingly, none of the defendants denied the charges. Instead they presented stock affirmative defenses. In answer to Partridge's complaint the forty or more defendants filed identical pleas of self-defense, alleging that Partridge single-handedly had threatened each man

> and would then and there have beat, bruised, and ill treated him and said defendant, if he had not immediately defended himself against the said plaintiff, wherefore, he the said defendant did then and there defend himself against the said plaintiff, as he lawfully might, for the cause aforesaid, and in so doing did necessarily and unavoidably, a little, pull and hawl about before a large concourse of people, and thereby, then and [there] in self defense, did indignantly treat the said plaintiff, by shaking, kicking, striking, throwing him upon the ground and did then and there for the cause aforesaid, a little, rend, tare and damage the clothes of the said plaintiff, and there being then and there upon the ground, where the said defendant was so compelled, in self defense as aforesaid, to throw down the body of the defendant [plaintiff?], as aforesaid, a large quantity of tar pitch and feathers, by means whereof, the said plaintiff became a little covered and besmeared with tar, pitch and feathers . . . doing no unnecessary damage to the plaintiff. (Ray County Circuit Court, July 1836, Book A, pp. 236–38)

In the July 1836 term, the Circuit Court for Ray County found the defendants culpable for the acts and awarded Bishop Partridge a peppercorn and one penny, known legally as nominal damages, for the assault.

W. W. Phelps similarly enjoyed less-than-adequate success in his cause of action. His complaint alleged damages in the amount of $3,000 for loss of building, $500 for loss of press, $2,000 for conversion of property, and $50,000 for loss of business. Again the defendants did not deny the allegations of violence, but explained that they had torn down the building at the request of the true owner. Interestingly, they did not even bother to agree on the identity of the actual owner of the premises. Phelps received $750 in damages (Ray County Circuit Court, July 1836, Book A, pp. 249–50). In short, Partridge and Phelps together recovered less in damages than their legal fees.

FURTHER CONFLICT IN CLAY, CALDWELL, AND DAVIESS COUNTIES

Many of the Mormons who fled Jackson County went to neighboring Clay County. Once again, the older settlers were initially receptive, but soon felt threatened. On 29 June 1836, Clay County residents presented a memorial admitting that they did not have "the least right, under the Constitution and laws of the country, to expel [the Mormons] by force," but warning them of war if the Mormons did not leave voluntarily (HC 2:451). Their grievances were that Mormons were "non-slaveholders; and opposed to slavery," that they believed "that the Indians are a part of God's chosen people," and that their religious tenets were so peculiar as to "excite deep prejudices against them" (HC 2:450).

On 1 July 1836 the Mormons agreed to leave "for the sake of friendship" (HC 2:453). With the assistance of state representative Alexander Doniphan, they petitioned for and received an enactment creating Caldwell County. Although the originally proposed boundaries were reduced in half by opponents south of Caldwell in Ray County and north in newly created Daviess County, the Saints anticipated peace if for no other reason than their isolation. The rapid influx of Saints from the East, however, resulted in the expansion of Mormon communities outside the boundaries of Caldwell County. Local settlers in adjoining Ray, Daviess, and Carroll counties interpreted Mormon encroachment on their lands as a breach of implied promise to stay exclusively within Caldwell. Agitation increased during the summer of 1838 when, after the failure of the Kirtland Safety Society, the number of recently arriving Mormons increased dramatically. Overreacting to internal dissension and bolstered by the apparent strength of the Mormon position in northern Missouri, Sidney Rigdon, delivered two speeches the summer of 1838 which contributed to the succeeding persecution. Rigdon's "Salt Sermon," delivered 19 June 1838, cited Matthew 5:13 as authority for castigating such dissenters as Cowdery and the Whitmers who were no better than salt that had lost its savor and was good for nothing "but to be cast out, and to be trodden under foot of man." Shortly thereafter Sampson Avard organized a secret society, the Danites, for the purpose of purging dissenters from the community. This highly publicized persecution of Mormon dissenters would provide partial justification for legal actions subsequently filed against Mormon leaders in connection with the extermination order.

Sidney Rigdon, in a second well-publicized address delivered 4 July 1838 warned future mobs and instigators of further "vexatious law suits against us," who would "cheat us out of our rights," that if they attempted to persecute the Saints, "we say woe unto them" (Roberts 1965a, 193). Non-Mormons interpreted this oration as treasonous, and further hostility resulted almost as a response to Rigdon's challenge (Union Historical Co., 266). A battle in neighboring Daviess County set in motion the final tragedy (LeSueur 1981).

The battle occurred on the county's first general election day, 6 August 1838. The Whig candidate for the state legislature, William Peniston, prompted the battle by rallying the non-Mormons at Gallatin, the county seat, to prevent the Mormons from voting, saying: "The Mormon leaders are a set of horse thieves, liars, counterfeiters. . . ." He told the voters that if they allowed the Mormons to vote, they would soon lose their suffrage. Addressing the Saints, he declared, "I headed a mob to drive you out of Clay county, and would not prevent your being mobbed now" (HC 3:57). A member of the mob concurred, saying, "The Mormons were not allowed to vote in Clay county no more than the negroes," and physically attacked the few Mormons who had come to vote. Joseph Smith's history records that "very few" voted (HC 3:58), but Reed C. Durham, who reviewed eighteen personal accounts of the incident, concludes that most of the Mormons voted before returning to their homes (Durham, 46). Joseph Smith recorded that John L. Butler gathered the Saints after the fray, exclaiming, "We are American citizens; our fathers fought for their liberty, and we will maintain the same principles." He further noted that the Mormons withdrew from the brawl at the request of the county authorities to avoid further conflict (HC 3:58).

The first excited reports received by the Saints at Far West had two or three Mormons dead, with the mob refusing to let them be buried. Joseph Smith rode from Far West in Caldwell County to Gallatin at the head of some twenty men "armed for their own protection." This group met with a local justice of the peace, Adam Black, to have him swear that he would not align himself with any mob to deprive Mormons of their constitutional rights. Adam Black refused to sign any prepared statement but under coercion drafted and signed the following statement:

> I, Adam Black, a Justice of the Peace of Daviess county, do hereby Sertify to the people, coled *Mormin*, that he is bound to support the

Constitution of this State, and of the United States, and he is not attached to any mob, nor will not attach himself to any such people, and so long as they will not molest me, I will not molest them. This the 8th day of August, 1838. (HC 3:59–60)

Although no civil officer ever filed charges against those who attempted to prevent the Mormons from voting, Joseph Smith was indicted. Peniston, who had instigated the election-day battle, filed an affidavit on 10 August before Judge Austin A. King of the Fifth Circuit, sitting in Ray County. Peniston alleged that Smith had led 120 armed men in an assault on Black and that they were in insurrection (HC 3:61). On the strength of Peniston's verified affidavit, King issued a writ to the Daviess County sheriff for the arrest of Smith and Lyman Wight for rioting (HC 3:63).

The Daviess County sheriff attempted to serve the writ at Far West on 16 August. Smith declined arrest claiming that the Daviess sheriff had no authority in Caldwell County. Smith informed the sheriff that he preferred to be tried in Caldwell County because of the prejudice against Mormons in Daviess County (HC 3:63). The sheriff withdrew to Richmond to be advised by King, who confirmed Smith's point. On 28 August Black kept the issue alive by filing a similar affidavit—this time with the number of armed Mormons inflated to 154—before William Dryden, a justice of the peace for Daviess County, against certain Mormons over the same incident (HC 3:64–65).

The legal stand-off between the anti-Mormons and the Mormons could not last forever. The anti-Mormon vigilantes used Smith's insistence on being tried in Caldwell County as evidence that the Mormons believed themselves above the law and spread this rumor to vigilante groups organizing in surrounding counties.

On 2 September Smith appealed to General David R. Atchison, commander of the local militia and former counsel for the Saints, to have the mobs in Daviess County dispersed; he also wrote Judge King for the same purpose and consulted Alexander Doniphan, General Atchison's partner, for legal advice. On 4 September he and Sidney Rigdon began to study law under the tutelage of Atchison and Doniphan with assurances of being admitted to the bar after a year's "diligent application" (HC 3:69). Smith and Lyman Wight were advised to submit themselves to trial over the Black incident in Daviess County, before Judge King of Ray County. This good faith act, it was suggested, would defuse the explosive atmosphere.

Their predicament appeared anomolous to the Mormons. Their leaders were to be tried before a prejudiced community for reacting to the assault on Mormons who merely wanted to vote, while settlers who illegally had assaulted the Mormons at Gallatin remained free to lead further attacks. One wonders what the reaction of the non-Mormons would have been if the Saints would have violently prevented others from voting. Smith's entreaties to King to remedy the insurrection exhibited by anti-Mormon vigilante groups who themselves were crossing county lines in armed force went unheeded even as these same persecutors demanded justice against the Mormons for similar conduct. Smith and Wight voluntarily appeared before Judge King in Daviess County on 7 September 1838.

William Peniston, who had incited the attack on the Mormons at Gallatin, prosecuted while Black served as the prosecution's only witness. King bound Wight and Smith over for rioting. The reasoning behind this ruling is unclear. Some have suggested that King was prejudiced against the Mormons, since his brother-in-law had died a few years earlier in vigilante violence against the Mormons. Smith suggested that it was done "to pacify, as much as possible, the feelings of the mobbers" (HC 3:73).

King may have determined in good faith that whatever the cause, Mormons could not arm themselves and threaten their enemies. In any event the defendants met the $500 bail King set and returned to Far West.

About this same time, Daviess County justice of the peace William Dryden issued a writ for the arrest of other Mormons named in Adam Black's affidavit. On 17 September some of these defendants appeared before a court of three magistrates at the state militia's camp in Daviess county for a court of inquiry concerning the Black incident and were acquitted (HC 3:81, 84; Gentry 1965, 192–93).

The next few months witnessed further armed assaults on Mormon settlements. Lilburn Boggs, who by this time had become governor, denied the Mormons any assistance from the state militia. On one occasion, Boggs responded to a petition from Mormons at Dewitt in Carroll County who were under siege by an organized vigilante group of as many as 300 men, with the callous statement that "the quarrel was between the Mormons and the mob" and that they could "fight it out" (HC 3:157). Unable to obtain civil relief, the Mormons evacuated Dewitt on 11 October. Several died of exposure occasioned by the siege (HC 3:158–60).

Following the evacuation of Dewitt, Mormons began to fight back, claiming that General H. G. Parks of the militia had authorized Lyman Wight to call out companies of Mormon militia with "full authority . . . to suppress all mob violence" (Roberts [1900] 1965a, 214). There is no official record of any Missouri general authorizing the Mormons to suppress mob violence. Mormon attacks were interpreted as aggressive rather than defensive or retaliatory measures. Many Danite assaults may have been unjustified and excessive. As soon as reports reached Boggs that the Mormons were arming themselves and committing acts of violence, he issued an order of extermination, which directed the state militia to treat the Mormons as enemies who *"must be exterminated* or driven from the state, if necessary for the public good."[3] Three days after this order was given, on 30 October 1838, eighteen or nineteen Mormons, including children (thirty-one according to another source) were massacred at Haun's Mill, Caldwell County (HC 3:183–86, 212). The following day a mob led by state militia surrounded the Mormons gathered at Far West, arrested and imprisoned their leaders, and forced the people to give up their arms.

Boggs had ordered General Samuel D. Lucas of the state militia, who previously as county judge had been one of the leaders to expel the Mormons from Jackson County, to arrest the Mormon leadership: "The ringleaders of this rebellion should be made an example of; and if it should become necessary for the public peace, the 'Mormons' should be exterminated, or expelled from the state" (HC 3:192). Those arrested included Joseph and Hyrum Smith, Sidney Rigdon, Lyman Wight, Parley P. Pratt, and George W. Robinson, as well as forty-seven others. Lucas apparently held a court-martial and sentenced the prisoners to be shot. General Doniphan, who previously had represented the Saints as their legal counsel, refused the order on the ground that it would be an act of "cold-blooded murder" (HC 3:190–91, note). Convinced of the illegality of the proposed execution, Lucas turned the prisoners over to Judge Austin A. King, circuit judge of the Fifth District, who commenced the preliminary examination on 13 November with Thomas C. Burch acting as prosecuting attorney. Joseph Smith records that both of these civil officers had also sat as members of the court-martial (HC 3:417) and were hardly impartial, but there is no other evidence of their attendance.

The Mormons viewed this court of inquiry as a further attempt to misuse the law. Joseph Smith characterized it as a "mock investigation," and Hyrum Smith spoke of it as a "pretended court" (HC 3:211, 418). Doniphan and Rees once again served as defense attorneys (HC 3:212). Sidney Rigdon, one of the accused, "requested that we might be tried separately; but this was refused, and we were all put on our trial together." Furthermore, he said, "No papers were read to us, no charges of any kind preferred, nor did we know against what we had to plead" (HC 3:463).

The prosecution's main witness was Sampson Avard, who testified that he had directed the Danite band as a counter-vigilante group at the direction of church leaders. Mormon leaders expressed dismay at Avard's testimony and testified that they had been unaware of the Danites (HC 3:192–93, 209–10; Gentry 1974, 433–34, 448–49). In return for turning state's evidence, Avard, the founder of the Danites, received immunity from prosecution.

According to the court record, non-Mormons and Mormons who had disaffiliated themselves testified that Joseph Smith held the civil law in contempt. John Corrill testified that Smith and Sidney Rigdon had once stated that they "would suffer vexatious lawsuits no longer" and would "resist an officer in the discharge of his duty." Reed Peck also stated that Joseph had commented that while he revered constitutional laws he was less likely to obey the local laws since "they were made by lawyers and blacklegs." The Caldwell County clerk, John Cleminson, stated that Smith had told him not to issue a writ against him because he "did not intend to submit to it [for] it was a vexatious thing." W. W. Phelps also offered evidence that Smith had decided that "the time had come when he should resist all law" (Document 1838, 111, 119, 114, 123).

Although the Mormons undoubtedly responded violently to attacks on their communities, the accused were critical of these criminal proceedings for several reasons. First, Joseph records that the testimony came from the persecutors against whom the Mormons had been defending themselves, dissenters who were seeking to protect their own interests by their perjured testimony, and witnesses who testified in fear of their lives. Hyrum Smith recorded: "Witnesses were called up and sworn at the point of the bayonet; and if they would not swear to the things they were told to do, they were threatened with instant death; and I do know positively that the evidence given in by those men whilst under duress was false" (HC 3:417).

Sidney Rigdon, similarly, asserted, "I do not recollect one single point about which testimony was given, with which I was acquainted, but was misrepresented, nor one solitary witness whose testimony was there written, that did not swear falsely," and went on to state: "There were things there said so utterly without foundation in truth —so much so, that the persons swearing must at the time of swearing have known it. The best construction I can ever put upon it is that they swore things to be true which they did not know to be so; and this, to me, is willful perjury" (HC 3:465).

Second, the defendants claimed that when they furnished the court with the names of the defense witnesses, these persons were arrested and imprisoned. As Hyrum Smith described Judge King's response,

"The Judge sat and laughed at the good opportunity of getting the names, that they might the more easily capture them, and so bring them down to be thrust into prison, in order to prevent us from getting the truth before the pretended court, of which he was the chief inquisitor or conspirator" (HC 3:418–19). With Judge King threatening to close the investigation unless the defense produced some witnesses, the defendants spied a Mr. Allen standing outside the courthouse and motioned for him to come inside. He did, and they tried to call him as a witness, but the prosecution objected.

> Upon this, General Doniphan arose and said, "He would be ———
> ——— if the witness should not be sworn, and that it was a damned shame that these defendants should be treated in this manner,—that they could not be permitted to get one witness before the court, whilst all their witnesses, even forty at a time, have been taken by force of arms and thrust into that damned 'bull pen,' in order to prevent them from giving their testimony."
>
> After Doniphan sat down, the Judge permitted the witness to be sworn and enter upon his testimony, but as soon as he began to speak, a man by the name of Cook, who was a brother-in-law to priest Bogart, the Methodist, and who was a lieutenant [in the state militia], and whose duty at that time was to superintend the guard, stepped in before the pretended court, and took him [the witness] by the nape of his neck and jammed his head down under the pole, or log of wood, that was around the place where the inquisition was sitting to keep the bystanders from intruding upon the majesty of the inquisitors, and jammed him along to the door, and kicked him out of doors. He instantly turned to some soldiers who were standing by him and said to them, "Go and shoot him, damn him; shoot him, damn him."
>
> He fled for his life, and with great difficulty made his escape. (HC 3:419)

Third, the court's refusal to take into consideration the events that had triggered the alleged acts of retaliation dismayed the Mormons. The attacks on the Mormons and their loss of lives, property, and rights as citizens were treated as irrelevant. Their claims that in many instances the Saints had armed themselves as an authorized militia went unheeded.

The hearing concluded on 25 November 1838, with Judge King releasing twenty-three of the fifty-three defendants for lack of evidence and binding over the others on charges including larceny, burglary, receiving stolen property, arson, treason, and murder (Document 1838, 37; HC 3:211). Although the Mormons viewed this as King's pronouncement of guilt, it was merely a preliminary hearing to determine whether sufficient evidence existed to present it before a grand jury. Surely sufficient evidence was presented to justify binding the parties over. Moreover, their incarceration had the further effect of defusing an explosive situation. On 28 November all but the Mormon leaders were released or admitted to bail. The remaining defendants—Joseph and Hyrum Smith, Sidney Rigdon, Lyman Wight, Parley P. Pratt, and six others—were committed to jail in either Liberty, Clay County, or Richmond, Ray County.

Mormons believed thereafter, whether justified or not, that they had been railroaded at the King "inquisition." During his incarceration, Joseph Smith wrote to the Saints, who had found refuge in Illinois, that his imprisonment was strictly the result of religious prejudice (HC 3:226, 229).

The imprisoned church leaders suffered long incarceration and great hardship. Repeated efforts to obtain a formal trial on the charges or to be released on writs of habeas corpus or bail proved futile. The Mormons repeatedly sought a change of venue to Marion County because of King's prejudice and the animosity pervading the northern counties of Missouri;[4] nonetheless the prisoners appeared in Daviess County for grand jury proceedings on 6 April 1839 before the newly appointed judge, Thomas C. Burch, the prosecutor at the Richmond hearing. Smith indicates that the legislature had already granted a petition changing venue to Boone County, and notice reached the court the first day of the grand jury hearing (HC 3:310). The grand jury at Daviess County nonetheless refused to defer: after hearing evidence for three days, they presented formal indictments against the defendants for "murder, treason, burglary, arson, larceny, theft, and stealing" (HC 3:309, 315).

After presenting the indictments, the court, pursuant to the legislative directive, turned the prisoners over to the Daviess County sheriff for transfer to Boone County. The Clay County prisoners—Joseph and Hyrum Smith, Lyman Wight, Alexander McRae, and Caleb Baldwin—escaped while in transit (probably with the connivance of their guards), and no trial ever took place. Parley P. Pratt, Morris Phelps, King Follett, and Luman Gibbs, still imprisoned in Richmond, were later transferred to Boone County. Pratt and Phelps escaped from the Boone County jail on 4 July 1839 (Pratt 1938, 243–54). Follett and Gibbs were the only defendants actually tried, and both were released for want of evidence (Pratt 1938, 262).

Meanwhile, the body of the church petitioned the legislature for relief. The citizens of Caldwell County organized a committee to memorialize before the Missouri legislature the depredations and atrocities suffered by the Mormons. On 10 December 1838, the lengthy indictment (HC 3:317–24) was signed by the committee, and one week later David H. Redfield delivered the petition to Representative John Corrill to present to the Missouri legislature.

Two weeks before the petition was presented Governor Boggs reported to the legislature on the "Mormon War." He provided "all the information in his possession" and included certain documents from some of the completed trials before Judge King (HC 3:217). On 18 December 1838, two days after Redfield arrived in Jefferson City with the Saints' version of the issue and one day before Corrill presented their petition to the Missouri House of Representatives, a joint committee issued a report and resolutions based entirely on the governor's information and documents. The committee concluded that it would be "unwise and injudicious" to base a final report on evidence "in a great degree, *exparte* and not of the character which should be desired for the basis of a fair and candid investigation." The documents before the committee, purportedly court records from Ray County, had "not been certified in such manner as to satisfy the committee of their authenticity" (HC 3:235–36). The report concluded that the pendency of the trials against the church leaders vitiated the need for immediate investigation into the matter.

The Missouri House discussed the Saints' petition and request for investigation of the "Mormon affair" on 19 December. Redfield reported to Joseph Smith, still in prison, that three representatives declared the petition to be false from beginning to end and urged, "The quicker they get that petition from before this body the better." However, four other representatives indicated a willingness to consider a legislative investigation since, as one reasoned, certain parties "want this petition ruled out of the House for fear their evil doings will be brought to light; this goes to prove to me and others, that the petition is true" (HC 3:238–39).

Still, a bill requiring investigation was tabled by a vote of 48 to 37. A joint committee was commissioned to investigate, and funds were appropriated for the deposition of witnesses, clerks, rooms, records, and fees. But no investigation occurred, and neither the petition nor any record of the legislative debate over it was included in the legislature's investigative report (Document 1838; HC 3:238). The matter was not taken up again until the 1840 legislative session.

According to Missouri Senator Lewis F. Linn and Representative John Jameson in Washington, D.C., Smith's pending trial was the reason the state legislature postponed any investigation of the "Mormon affair" (HC 4:83). The prior committee report in response to Governor

Bogg's report may have been precedent for the later determination not to investigate the issue. However, Redfield told Elias Higbee that the legislature's delay and subsequent lack of any investigation whatsoever came "in consequence of one of their members being in the massacre at Haun's Mill, viz., Mr. Ashley" (HC 4:84).

Since both the courts and legislature of Missouri had failed to provide a suitable, impartial investigation for church members, the Mormons were forced into exile under threat of continued mob persecution that the extermination order ostensibly legitimized.

Under these ominous circumstances and without many of their leaders, the Mormons retreated to Quincy, Illinois. During their exodus "more than $300,000 worth of property was forcibly abandoned," George A. Smith later recalled (Arrington, Fox, and May 1976, 37).

Apprehensive impatience on the part of the church leaders may have been one reason the Missouri systems failed to aid the Saints. Had Joseph Smith and the other leaders not escaped from Liberty Jail, a trial or legislative investigation almost certainly would have followed since Missouri was thoroughly embarrased on the national scene by the order of extermination. The escape of the church leaders provided a convenient end to the dilemma the Missouri officials faced.[5]

Missouri governors continued efforts in the years following to have Joseph Smith extradited from Illinois to stand trial on the "King charges" and other offenses. Only Smith's martyrdom ended the persecution he had received from Missouri mobs and civil officers. The Missouri chapter jaundiced the Mormons permanently against any further reliance on gentile civil laws or institutions for bastions of justice and security.

5

The Illinois Period

When church leaders first arrived in Illinois in the spring of 1839, they realized that efforts to secure redress from either the Missouri courts or legislature for the property and lives lost were an exercise in futility. The church leadership therefore began looking elsewhere for the desperately needed money.

Sidney Rigdon, who was released on bail in January of 1839, immediately petitioned Illinois officials for support. Governor Thomas Carlin assured Rigdon "that he would lay our case before the legislature of this state . . . and he would use all his influence to have an action which would be favorable to our people." Rigdon wrote this jubilant news to Joseph Smith on 10 April 1839 (HC 3:310). He also added the unwelcome news that the Missouri legislature had not acted on the Mormon request for an investigation:

> Our plan of operation is to impeach the state of Missouri on an item of the Constitution of the United States; that the general government shall give to each state a Republican form of government. Such a form of government does not exist in Missouri, and we can prove it. . . .
> Our plan of operation in this work is, to get all the governors, in their next messages, to have the subject brought before the legislatures; and we will have a man in the capital of each state to furnish them with the testimony on the subject; and we design to be at Washington to wait upon Congress, and have the action of that body on it also; all this going on at the same time, and have the action of the whole during one session. (HC 3:311)

The "impeachment" of a state as nonrepublican was unprecedented. However, the notion of obtaining congressional relief against state depredations, based upon the guarantee clause of the Constitution was a sound one. Article IV, section 4 of the Constitution provided that "the United States shall guarantee to every state in this Union a Republican form of government." The Supreme Court has consistently held that one must look to the political branches of government—

the Congress and the President, not the courts—to protect whatever rights might follow from this provision.[1] Unless the guarantee clause were to be rendered a nullity, therefore, congressional interpretation should follow.

Joseph Smith, Rigdon, and Elias Higbee, accompanied by Orrin Porter Rockwell, left for Washington in October 1839 with a petition authored by Lyman Wight outlining their hardships and claiming redress from the national government (HC 4:24–38). The day after their arrival they were introduced to Van Buren, who frankly stated that although their cause was just, he could do nothing for them because he would "come in contact with the whole state of Missouri" (HC 4:40, 80). Such an open admission of concern for political consequences surprised Joseph Smith. The president was legally quite limited in providing relief had he desired to do so, other than giving his personal endorsement of the church's grievances; however, Mormon reaction has rather naturally emphasized the president's political motivations and discounted the more weighty legal incapacity, which Van Buren apparently left unexplained. Van Buren's brutal self-concern angered Smith even years later as he reflected on the short interview (HC 4:40; 5:393; 6:203).

In Van Buren's defense, it should be remembered that Smith was pleading a case based, as he saw it, upon the First Amendment rights of the Mormons, particularly the free exercise of religion clause. Smith saw this as the bulwark that should have protected the Mormon people in their enjoyment of their rights. In fact, it was almost always within the context of a discussion of these First Amendment rights that Joseph Smith made reference to the Constitution or to its framers as "inspired." But from the time of *Barron v. The Mayor and City Council of Baltimore* in 1833 (US 32:243), the Supreme Court had held that the Bill of Rights, including the First Amendment, was a limitation only upon the federal government.[2] Van Buren's forbearance, therefore, was constitutionally sound.

The "Mormon" problem perplexed the congressmen whom the Saints next petitioned. Henry Clay is said to have retorted, "You had better go to Oregon," and John C. Calhoun shook his head solemnly, saying, "It's a nice question—a critical question, but it will not do to agitate it" (HC 5:393). Nonetheless, Senator Richard M. Young of Illinois, whose home state had a more accommodating attitude toward the Mormons, agreed that if supporting documents and affidavaits could be produced, he would petition the Senate for assistance.

After receiving the necessary documentation, Senator Young, on 28 January 1840, "presented the memorial of Joseph Smith, Jr., Sidney

Rigdon, and Elias Higbee, in behalf of 'The Latter-day Saints,' commonly called Mormons, praying for a redress of grievances, inflicted on them by the people of the State of Missouri" (*Congressional Globe*, 28 Jan. 1840, 149). Young moved that it be printed and referred to the Judiciary Committee. The debate on the petition focused on the extraordinary nature of the petition and the propriety of Congress stepping into a state affair. Several expressed shock at the alleged outrages against the Mormons. Others revealed their quandary about how to proceed. Senator Lewis F. Linn of Missouri felt that a sovereign state was about to be put on trial, with an inferential slur thereby placed upon all its citizens.[3] Several felt that state forums were the appropriate place to redress the grievances. On the motion of Senator John Norvell of Michigan, the petition was tabled following the debate, "with the understanding that it would be called up at an early day" (*Congressional Globe*, 28 Jan. 1840, 149).[4] Additional documents were presented to Congress supporting the petition, and on 12 February 1840 the matter was referred to the Senate Committee on the Judiciary (*Niles National Register* 57:398; *Congressional Globe*, 12 Feb. 1840, 185). Elias Higbee reported the committee investigation that followed (HC 4:81, 83, 85, 88).

For three days, 20–22 February, the Judiciary Committee considered the Mormon petition. Representatives from Missouri argued that the matter should properly come before the state legislature, which had declined to act on the matter solely because of the pending trials, but that justice could be had if the Saints petitioned the correct state institution. In defense, Higbee argued that the Mormons could find no justice in Missouri since the governor had issued an order for the extermination of all Latter-day Saints. Simply being in Missouri would endanger the lives of the petitioners. John Jameson, a representative from Missouri, admitted that the "extermination order" existed. Such an admission must certainly have piqued the curiosity of members of the Judiciary Committee; but the extraordinary nature of the petition, the question of the Senate's jurisdiction, and the political undesirability of siding with the Mormons resulted in an unfavorable disposition by the committee.

On 4 March, Senator Wall reported to the Congress on behalf of the Judiciary Committee: "*Resolved*, That the Committee on the Judiciary be discharged from the further consideration of the memorial in this case, and that the memorialists have leave to withdraw the papers which accompany their memorials" (*Congressional Globe*, 4 Mar. 1840, 233). The committee report found that the petition had "been drawn up at great length" but failed to allege any offense for which the United States was liable. In spite of the plea that justice was unobtainable among the Missourians, the committee responded that an appeal to the state courts or legislature "will never be made in vain by the injured or oppressed. It can never be presumed that a state either wants the power, or lacks the disposition to redress the wrongs of its citizens committed within her own territory, whether they proceed from the lawless acts of her officers, or any other persons" (Senate Judiciary Committee 1840).

The Mormons did not act upon the advice of the Senate committee, probably because of the remote chance of success in the Missouri courts and the outstanding warrants for the arrest of the church officials. The church, however, did not completely abandon efforts to press national representatives for justice in later years (HC 4:427; 6:84–88).

The whole experience, from the perspective of the Mormons, led them to conclude that the political branches of the federal government —as well as each branch of Missouri state government (the courts, the legislature, and the governor)—were incapable, incompetent, or at least disinclined to offer either protection or redress. If indeed the law was to be their protector and shield, it must somehow be structured to meet their peculiar needs and be interpreted and enforced by sympathetic individuals.

THE NAUVOO CHARTER

The disheartening Missouri episode created a resolve among Mormons to rely no longer on "gentile" government to protect their civil rights. Instead the Mormons turned inward, forging a society that combined democratic and theocratic elements of government that would provide for substantial autonomy, insularity, and self-sufficiency. In search of those objectives, the Saints developed Nauvoo into a sanctuary arguably untouchable by state law.

Practical considerations doubtless played a part in the displaced Mormons settling in Nauvoo. First, land developer Dr. Isaac Galland made a generous offer of the Nauvoo lands to the Mormons. Second, Illinois was a frontier area, just beginning to construct and pay for new railroad and canal systems. It needed people (Flanders, 97). Third, the lines between the political parties in the state were being sharply drawn. The possibility of gaining a political advantage from Mormon bloc-voting was probably in the minds of the Democratic party that first welcomed the Saints to Quincy. In fact, Mormon historian B. H. Roberts has blamed the political battles of the period for much of the trouble in Nauvoo:

> This effort to win the Saints to one political party or the other continued to be a factor in their affairs so long as they remained at Nauvoo. *It was owing to this rivalry for their support that doubtless made it possible for the Saints to obtain larger grants of power for their city government, and greater political privileges and influence in the State than otherwise could have been obtained by them.* It also was this rivalry for their favor . . . that made them alternately fulsomely flattered and heartily disliked; fawningly courted, and viciously betrayed. (HC 4:xxi; emphasis added)

The first recorded reference to a town charter for Nauvoo appears in the minutes of a December 1839 meeting of the Nauvoo High Council. It had been operating even before the Nauvoo Stake was organized, ever since the first lands had been purchased near Commerce, Illinois, earlier in the year (HC 4:39, 12). Smith was not involved in the meeting; he had gone to Washington, D.C., to guide the efforts to get congressional redress for the Missouri grievances. The high council appointed Hyrum Smith, George W. Harris, and Oliver Granger to a committee to petition "the legislature to define new boundary lines of the City of Nauvoo, and also of Commerce, and do all other needful acts relative to those cities" (HC 4:39). In order to "define new boundary lines" and alter existing lines for the development of the municipality, legislative recognition of the political entity would be required. Therefore, the high council gave the committee authority to pursue a city charter for Nauvoo.

Although Nauvoo was not granted her charter until December 1840 and it was not effective until February 1841 (HC 4:239, 245), the absence of a properly authorized municipal government did not create a power vacuum. The Nauvoo Stake of Zion was established in October 1839 and became the generally recognized governing authority until its authority was transferred, at least ostensibly, to the city government where ecclesiastical leaders simply donned municipal hats of authority (Kimball 1966, 1).

The Nauvoo Charter, like other charters of frontier groups seeking self-governance, was composed with the intention of obtaining as much autonomy as constitutionally could be secured (Kimball 1975, 495). Joseph Smith and a recent convert, John C. Bennett, both claimed credit for the charter but probably worked together on it prior to general church ratification at a general conference on 4 October 1840.

Smith and Bennett, along with Robert B. Thompson, Smith's personal secretary, were appointed as a committee to "draft a bill for the incorporation of the town of Nauvoo" and, barely an hour later, the congregation approved an outline of the charter (Kimball 1971, 66, 78; HC 4:206). Bennett presented the charter to the Illinois legislature in November 1840. The House and Senate approved the charter with little debate, and the governor routinely signed it (Journal of the Senate, 1840–41, 23, 45, 61, 89; Journal of the House, 1840–41, 101, 110; HC 4:239; Kimball 1966, 15–17).

Contemporary Illinois historians attribute the passage of the charter, with its extraordinary provisions, to political expediency and "the inexperience and legal incapacity of many legislators and the press of other business"—notably, the critical fiscal problems Illinois faced in 1841 (Stevens, 341; Ford, 265). The charter probably would have been passed unamended regardless of the capacity of the legislators because of the seemingly innocuous nature of most of its provisions and because it was in the state's interest to give favorable attention to the Mormons. The legislative motive in passing the Nauvoo Charter was public knowledge, as evidenced by Assemblyman William J. Gatewood's sarcastic attempt to have the title of the bill incorporating Nauvoo changed to read "A Bill for the Encouragement of the Importation of Mormons" (Journal of the Senate, 1840–41, 61).

The Charter was obviously modeled after the city charter of Springfield, which the legislature had passed earlier in 1840 (Wakole 1971; HC 4:239–48). However, there were three notable exceptions. First, Nauvoo was to raise and keep a militia, to be called the "Nauvoo Legion."[5] Second, the Nauvoo Municipal Court had power "to grant writs of habeas corpus in all cases arising under the ordinances of the City Council" (HC 4:242–43). Third, a municipal university, the "University of the City of Nauvoo," was authorized. This last provision was similar to those in the charter of the Fairfield Institute, which John C. Bennett had cosponsored in 1837 (Kimball 1971, 76).

The Nauvoo Charter was just one manifestation of a general interest of Illinois settlers in local self-governance. From 1818, when Illinois became a state, until 1837, no city charters were granted, but from 1837 until the Nauvoo Charter 1840, five were granted (Kimball 1971, 68–70). The Mormon petition was part of a new wave of requests for incorporation. That session the legislature passed forty-seven acts of incorporation, eight of which were for city charters (Flanders 1965, 96).

James L. Kimball, Jr. has compared the Nauvoo Charter with the charters of the five Illinois cities that had previously been granted charters: Chicago and Alton in 1837, Galena in 1839, and Springfield and Quincy in 1840. All six charters reveal "tendencies toward democratization" (Kimball 1971, 70). For example, short terms for elected officials were common—one year in Chicago, Alton, and Galena, and two years in Nauvoo, Quincy, and Springfield. The Nauvoo Charter did not specify qualifications for political office, but all the others required American citizenship and residency. This probably reflected the numbers of Canadian and English converts in Nauvoo and the frequent absences of men on missions. The lack of citizenship and residency requirements meant Mormons could step into civic affairs with no waiting period.

Another variation in the Nauvoo document is the provision allowing the city council to remove city officials "at pleasure," whereas the charters of the other cities only referred to the council's appointment power (Kimball 1971, 71–73). This provision may have been inserted to ensure sympathetic rule. Nauvoo also provided for both aldermen and councilors, while most other systems provided for one or the other (Kimball 1971, 73).

The Nauvoo Charter specifically gave the city council the right to pass any ordinance "not repugnant" to the Constitution of the United States or that of Illinois. This provision has been criticized, but the charters of Galena, Quincy, and Springfield had similar provisions (Kimball 1971, 73). These charters were the closest in time to the Nauvoo Charter, perhaps signifying a trend in which Nauvoo simply participated. Nauvoo, Springfield, and Quincy also granted near-identical legislative powers to the council (Kimball 1971, 73). In fact, the Nauvoo Charter incorporated by reference the provisions of the Springfield Charter defining the powers of the city council (HC 4:242). The same legislature that granted these broad powers to the Nauvoo City Council, however, repealed the corresponding section of the Quincy charter (Kimball 1971, 73–74 n. 15).

Nor are the Charter's other criticized provisions unique. The provision granting city courts the power to issue writs of habeas corpus had a precedent in the Alton Charter, as amended 1 June 1839 (Kimball 1971, 75). The Nauvoo Municipal Court was the third of its kind, with other courts in Chicago and Alton (Kimball 1971, 73). However, Nauvoo's method of selecting judges was different. In Chicago and Alton, judges were appointed by the governor and approved by the General Assembly. In Nauvoo, the mayor was automatically the chief justice of the municipal court, and the aldermen served as associate justices, an office only Nauvoo had (Kimball 1971, 73–74). Thus, the lawmaker was also the law interpreter, creating a concentration of power that was absent in the other cities.

The appeals process was also different. Chicago's and Alton's municipal courts shared concurrent jurisdiction with the county circuit courts; appeals went directly to the Illinois Supreme Court. In Nauvoo, however, appeals were first taken to the circuit court of Hancock County, a limitation rather than an expansion of judicial power.

Kimball concludes that about 80 percent of the charter sections were comparable to sections in other charters and that "the powers of the courts were well hedged and easily within the era's . . . range of acceptance" (Kimball 1971, 75).

Still, differing conclusions about the Charter remain. B. H. Roberts asserted that the charter was designed to erect a virtual city-state to protect the temporal welfare of the church (HC 4:xxiv). Anti-Mormon writers conclude that the Charter was merely a way for Mormons to codify their disregard for the law of the land and to abuse the rights of others (Ford, 265; Wallace 1902). This was probably not true at its inception, although it may have been used for both of these ends. The charter did not create abuse, but it may have created the possibility for it.

The Mormons, however, did not feel they were abusing the Charter. Rather, they viewed the Charter as granting them protection from the abuses of the democratic process they had already experienced in Missouri—perhaps more protection than the Illinois legislature ever intended.

It is easy to see how Mormons would cling to the law to protect them after they had seen it used to persecute them. According to Kimball, they considered their charter, once received, as a veritable Magna Charta, "a sacred, indestructible, inviolate instrument to be used for protection and power. In constitutionalism there was security; laws and resolutions were but water and sand. By invoking primary bases of law, Joseph attempted to avoid what he termed rapacious and evil misuses of the law" (Kimball 1975, 496). Joseph Smith himself said he "concocted" the Nauvoo Charter "for the salvation of the Church, and on principles so broad, that every honest man might dwell secure under its protective influence without distinction of sect or party" (HC 4:249). That is to say, once the Mormons had what they thought to be legal protection in the form of the Charter, which they saw as a constitution embodying complete and irrevocable powers of local governance, they were willing to give it the most liberal construction possible, a "constitution-like" interpretation, before suffering persecution again. Indeed, Joseph Smith often used the charter as justification for almost any action of Nauvoo governance and clearly felt that Nauvoo was a state within a state. On one occasion, he explained his almost sacramental interpretation of Nauvoo's charter:

> If there is not power in our charter and courts, then there is not power in the State of Illinois nor in the Congress or Constitution of the United States; for the United States gave unto Illinois her Charter or Constitution, and Illinois gave unto Nauvoo her charters, ceding unto us our vested rights which she has no power to take from us. All the power there was in Illinois she gave to Nauvoo . . . This city has all the power that the state courts have, and was given by the same authority—the legislature. (HC 5:466)

Smith found support for this interpretation in the section of the Charter that granted the city council power to enact ordinances "not repugnant to the Constitution . . ." (HC 4:242). Mormons interpreted this to suggest that the Nauvoo government was not subject to the laws of Illinois, but only to the constitutions of Illinois and the United States. Furthermore, the charter provided that the city council "shall have exclusive power within the city . . . to pass such ordinances, as may be necessary and proper for carrying into execution the powers specified in this Act." Thus, Smith believed, the council had power to enact any constitutional ordinance necessary and proper for governance. When some criticized Smith's use of the writ of habeas corpus under the charter, he justified this interpretation of the city's charter powers:

> The city council have passed an ordinance "that no citizen of this city shall be taken out of this city by any writ, without the privilege of a writ of habeas corpus." There is nothing but what we have power over, except where restricted by the constitution of the United States. . . . If these powers are dangerous, then the constitution of the United States and of this State are dangerous; but they are not dangerous to good men: they are only so to bad men who are breakers of the laws. So with the laws of the country, and so with the ordinances of Nauvoo: they are dangerous to mobs, but not to good men who wish to keep the laws. (HC 5:470)

This constitutionlike interpretation resembles the authoritative interpretation of the federal constitution's "necessary and proper" clause by Chief Justice John Marshall in *McCulloch v. Maryland* (US 17:316), upholding the constitutionality of a national bank.

Another doctrine added credibility to Smith's idea of Nauvoo as a city-state. Although the United States Supreme Court in *Charles River Bridge v. Warren Bridge* (US 36:420) had just rejected the notion that state legislatures could grant charters irrevocable by later legislatures, the 1819 case *Dartmouth College v. Woodward* (US 17:518), which had held that a later legislature could not unilaterally modify a charter granted by an earlier legislature, still influenced the thinking of many in state and local government. Public grants and charters were widely viewed as irrevocable and were interpreted broadly as conveying all the governing power that the granting body could convey (Kimball 1975, 495–96). This popular view was expressed in an editorial in the *Wasp*, a local Nauvoo newspaper, in March 1843, questioning:

> What reliance can be placed upon a legislature that will one session grant a charter to a city, with "perpetual succession," and another session take it away? . . . The house, in the dignity of its standing, passes a bill, at the request of the people, telling them that they shall have a charter granting them several privileges, and telling them that it shall be perpetual, without any repealing clause. (HC 5:306)

The editorial emphasized the natural and expected reliance upon such a grant and concluded that repeal therefore was not possible.

With Nauvoo's governmental machinery in place, Joseph Smith and the city council attempted to insulate themselves from what the Mormons saw as continuing harassment through vexatious lawsuits. To accomplish these ends, the council passed numerous ordinances, some of which would be considered unconstitutional by today's standards.

On 1 March 1841, an ordinance was passed guaranteeing freedom of religious belief and practice for "Catholics, Presbyterians, Methodists, Baptists, Latter-day Saints, Quakers, Episcopalians, Universalists, Unitarians, and all other religious sects and denominations whatever" (CCR, 13). Anyone "disturbing or interrupting" any religious meeting was subject to a fine not exceeding $500 and a jail term of up to six months.

An ordinance "concerning vagrants and disorderly persons" was both sweeping and ambiguous:

> Sec. 1. Be it ordained by the City Council of the City of Nauvoo, that all vagrants, idle or disorderly persons, persons found drunk in or about the streets, all suspicious persons, persons who have no fixed place of residence, or visible means of support, or cannot give a good account of themselves, persons guilty of using indecent, impertinent, or unbecoming language towards any City officer when in the discharge of his duty, or of menacing, threatening, or otherwise obstructing said officer, shall be convicted thereof before the Mayor, or Municipal Court, and be required to enter into security for good behaviour for a reasonable time, and indemnify the Corporation against any charge, and in case of

refusal or inability to give security they shall be confined to labor for a time not exceeding ninety days, or be fined in any sum not exceeding five hundred dollars, or be imprisoned not exceeding six months, or all, at the discretion of said Mayor or Court. This act to take effect and be in force from and after its passage. (CCR, 31)

Today the ordinance would almost certainly be unconstitutional on its face because of its overbreadth and potentially chilling effect on judicially recognized rights to travel and freely associate (*Papachristou v. City of Jacksonville*, US 405:156 [1972]; *Coates v. City of Cincinnati*, US 402:611 [1971]; *Palmer v. City of Euclid*, US 402:544 [1971]; *Bachellar v. Maryland*, US 397:564 [1970]). At the time, the ordinance would probably have been thought neither unusual nor unconstitutional. Until the late 1900s, virtually every state had statutes proscribing idle, lewd, and disorderly conduct or other forms of vagrancy (ALR 3d 25:797). Before the 1960s, when vagrancy statutes came under increasing attack, such statutes and ordinances were generally upheld against constitutional challenges. For example, in 1908, *Ex parte Mc-Cue* (Cal. App. 17:765; P. 96:110) sustained the constitutionality of a statute that punished "idle or lewd or dissolute" persons, and in 1911, *Ex parte Branch* (Mo. 234:466; SW 137:886) sustained a statute punishing those "wandering around . . . without any visible means of support." Much earlier, in 1847, *St. Louis v. Bentz* (Mo. 11:61) held that a vagrancy ordinance was a valid exercise of a municipality's police powers. Furthermore, there is no evidence that the Mormons in Nauvoo applied their vagrancy ordinance in a manner that distinguished between Mormons and non-Mormons, or that it was used to intimidate lawful conduct.

Another ordinance, probably stimulated by the Mormon leaders' experience with vexatious lawsuits, provided that if any person attempted to prosecute another in a criminal case and lost, the costs of the suit would be borne by its instigator, if the court found it to constitute "malicious prosecution" (CCR, 33).

Incorporating an identical provision from the Springfield Charter, the Nauvoo Charter granted the council power to "tax, restrain, prohibit, and suppress tippling houses, dram shops, gaming houses, bawdy and other disorderly houses" and to license and restrain every kind of gambling (HC 4:246, 242). The strictest fines were reserved for owners of brothels. One ordinance provided that owners of brothels could be fined from $500 to $50,000 and imprisoned for six months for each day of operation. Persons who frequented such establishments were to be fined $500 and imprisoned six months for each offense. Adultery and fornication were punished by fines of $500 to $50,000 plus six months in jail, with acknowledgment by the guilty party constituting sufficient proof (CCR, 77).

In 1843 and 1844, as the noose tightened around Nauvoo, the city council increased the police power of city officials. Ordinances were passed that allowed them to detain and question strangers about their purpose in the city, to enter and search hotel rooms, and to prevent "foreign" service of process (that is, service by any jurisdiction other than Nauvoo) without local approval. Other ordinances allowed for writs of habeas corpus issued by Nauvoo officials to protect church leaders against trials beyond the city and the state. By today's standards, all these ordinances were of doubtful constitutionality.

The first expansive police-power ordinance, passed 21 December 1843, concerned "strangers and contagious diseases" and was based loosely upon the provision of the charter that granted legislative power "to make regulations to secure the general health of the inhabitants, to declare what shall be a nuisance, and to prevent and remove the same," a provision that also appeared in the Springfield Charter (HC 4:246, 242). The ordinance provided that "for the peace, . . . good order, convenience, cleanliness, health and happiness" of the city, the city council, marshall, constables, and city watch were authorized to "require all strangers" who entered or were "tarrying" in the city to provide their names, former residence, and purpose for entering the city. Failure to comply with such questioning subjected the "strangers" to fine and imprisonment under the terms of the vagrancy and disorderly persons ordinance. Further, persons "strolling about the city at night" (i.e., after 9:00 P.M. and before sunrise) could be confined for trial under the same ordinance. Another section dutifully made mention of contagious diseases so as to touch on the empowering provisions of the charter. Finally, police officials were authorized to enter hotels "and such other habitations as they may judge proper" and require the occupants to give immediate "information of all persons residing in said hotel or habitation," as to occupation, residence, and purpose within the city. A few days later the police force was substantially enlarged so that it could implement these ordinances (CCR, 182–83). A system of informal, civil, "martial law" was gradually being imposed by a people increasingly under siege.

Nine days later, on 21 December 1843, an ordinance was passed to "prevent unlawful search and seizure of person or property by foreign process in the city of Nauvoo." This act required that all writs of warrants "issued out of the city" be executed in the presence of the Nauvoo marshall after receiving the "approval and signature of the Mayor." Any officer who attempted to serve foreign process without

such approval and without the presence of the marshal was subject to fine and imprisonment (CCR, 197–98). Bennett, who served
as Nauvoo's first mayor, resigned in May 1842, and the city council
immediately replaced him with Joseph Smith, who had been serving
as mayor pro tem since January 1842 (HC 5:12; 4:501). The council
also named Hyrum Smith as vice-mayor, a position not found on the
original city council. Foreign process, then, could only be served by
the marshal of Nauvoo, and only after Joseph had signed the back of
the process.

This last ordinance raised the objections of three Carthage lawyers,
who expressed their concern to Joseph Smith. They said that the
citizens of Carthage felt this ordinance was designed to "hinder the
execution of the statutes in the city [i.e., Nauvoo], consequently they,
the old citizens, felt disposed to stop the execution of processes issuing from the city in the County" (CCR, 199). Smith explained that the
statute was designed to prevent what he not unreasonably considered
to be kidnapping by process. Less convincingly, he added that thieves
might be more successfully apprehended "by throwing all foreign
processes into the hands of the Marshal, who would be most likely
to know the hiding places of fugitives from justice who might seek to
secret themselves in our midst" (CCR, 199). Still, a conciliatory section
was added to the ordinance:

> "Sec. 4. Be it ordained by the city council of the city of Nauvoo, that
> nothing in the foregoing ordinance shall be so construed so as to prevent,
> hinder, or thwart the designs of justice, or to retard the civil officers of
> the State or County in the discharge of their official duties, but to aid
> and assist them within the limits of this city." (CCR, 200)

However, the flames of fear and prejudice the council had fanned
by its actions did not die down. The final ordinances leading up to the
murders of Joseph and Hyrum Smith and the Saints' expulsion from
Nauvoo were those dealing with habeas corpus and the destruction
of the *Nauvoo Expositor*.

HABEAS CORPUS

The Nauvoo Charter provided that "the Municipal Court shall have
power to grant writs of habeas corpus in all cases arising under the
ordinances of the City Council." A writ of habeas corpus (an order
by a court or judge requiring that a person in custody be brought
before the court to determine the legality of his or her detention) had
been a mainstay of British common law and was no less significant

in American law (Oaks 1965a). This provision of the charter logically became the foremost weapon in the Mormons' protectionist arsenal. As one might expect, it proved to be an important focal point for opponents of Joseph Smith and the Mormons. Flanders has summed up the issue with only a little more bite than may be warranted:

> The court was in the future to issue such writs to free arrested persons, in particular Joseph Smith, regardless of the jurisdiction under which they were arrested. . . . The habeas corpus provision was designed to make Nauvoo an island of legal safety in which Mormons arrested by "outside" civil officers could be freed by legal process. The net result was not only to help protect the Mormons from legal persecution, real or imagined, but also to make "outside" law enforceable in Nauvoo only if the city government concurred. . . . The habeas corpus clause of the charter and the cavalier fashion in which the Mormons used it generated much popular fear and hatred, and were the points upon which legal attacks on the whole charter finally focused. Smith's riddled body at Carthage jail and the dissolution of the city corporation marked the conclusion of the issue. (Flanders, 99)

Flanders implies that the Mormon people expressly included such a power in their charter to avoid the reach of law into the city. This is probably untrue since Nauvoo was not the first Illinois city to be granted the power to issue writs of habeas corpus. It is more probable that the provision was included in the charter with little thought of its potential effectiveness in stopping foreign process or of its necessity for the Saints' protection, despite their recent experience in Missouri. The habeas corpus provision acquired its force through use, until it came to be relied on whenever a problem with outside law arose.

The past intruded into Nauvoo in the form of an attempt by Missouri officials to remove Joseph Smith so that they could try him on the charges of murder, treason, and robbery for which he had been incarcerated in Liberty Jail. In their petition to Congress for redress in early 1840, the Mormons had cited the failure of Missouri authorities to seek extradition as evidence that the charges against Smith were vexatious and intended merely to drive the Mormons from Missouri (HC 4:35–36).

The *Times and Seasons* reported to its readers on 15 September 1840:

> The governor of Missouri, after a silence of about two years, has at last made a demand on Governor Carlin of Illinois, for Joseph Smith, Jun., Sidney Rigdon, Lyman Wight, Parley P. Pratt, Caleb Baldwin, and Alanson Brown, as fugitives from justice.
> The demand it seems has been complied with by Governor Carlin, and an order issued for their apprehension; accordingly our place has

recently received a visit from the sheriff for these men; but through the tender mercies of a kind Providence, who by His power has sustained, and once delivered them from the hands of the blood-thirsty and savage race of beings in the shape of men that tread Missouri's delightful soil; they were not to be found—as the Lord would have it, they were gone from home, and the sheriff returned, of course without them. (HC 4:198)

In June 1841—after the Nauvoo Charter had been operating for over four months—another attempt was made to extradite Smith for trial in Missouri under the same writ that was returned without the prophet the previous September. Smith had been visiting Illinois Governor Thomas Carlin at his residence in Quincy on 4 June. The governor had received the requisition from the governor of Missouri for Smith's arrest but said nothing to him. Within hours of Smith's departure for Bear Creek, Illinois, Carlin sent a posse and sheriff to apprehend him. The posse arrested Smith in Bear Creek on 5 June. The party returned to Quincy, where Charles A. Warren, master in chancery, issued a writ of habeas corpus. Smith met Judge Stephen A. Douglas, who was visiting in Quincy, and made arrangements to be heard on the writ in Douglas's court in Monmouth, Illinois, on 8 June, when Douglas commenced his regular term. Douglas had helped get the Nauvoo Charter through the state legislature and had taken additional pains to ensure a friendly Mormon vote. In 1840, he had argued the alien vote case, *Spragins v. Houghton* (Ill. 3:377), before the Illinois Supreme Court and had successfully moved for a continuance until after the 1840 elections. This motion probably averted an unfavorable decision from the Whig-controlled court. When the court reconvened in December 1840, it unanimously held that aliens were entitled to vote, thus permitting early Mormon immigrants to vote. Perhaps because of his role in the alien vote case, Douglas was named to the Illinois Supreme Court the following year, when the Democrats successfully overhauled the state judiciary and increased the number of supreme court justices from four to nine (Stevens, 341, 333–35; Fiedler, 201–4).[6]

Smith returned to Nauvoo until his appearance before Douglas on 8 June. On 10 June 1841 Douglas ruled that the writ authorizing the arrest of the prophet for the Missouri charges was invalid since a similar writ had been returned unexecuted under the same indictment the prior September: "The writ being once returned to the Executive by the sheriff of Hancock county [it] was dead, and stood in the same relationship as any other writ which might issue from the Circuit Court, and consequently the defendant could not be held in custody on that writ" (HC 4:370). Joseph Smith may well have been impressed on this occasion by the power of the writ and the possibilities for its use in Nauvoo.

Under the Mormons' view of their charter, it granted Nauvoo the same power of habeas corpus held by the state of Illinois over any person the city council designated by ordinance. By passing broad ordinances respecting the power of habeas corpus, the Nauvoo City Council could acquire apparent jurisdiction for writs of habeas corpus over citizens arrested by any authority. And this is just what the council did.

On the evening of 6 May 1842, Lilburn Boggs, former governor of Missouri, was wounded at his home in Independence by an unknown assailant. The Quincy *Whig* reported rumors that the Mormons were behind the assassination attempt, primarily because Boggs had been responsible for their exodus from Missouri (HC 5:14–15). Smith denied the charge in a letter to the editor of the *Whig*. He pointed out that Boggs had other enemies, since he was running for the state senate, and expressed intense exasperation: "I am tired of the misrepresentation, calumny and detraction, heaped upon me by wicked men" (HC 5:15). Boggs accused Smith of ordering the murder and Orrin Porter Rockwell, Smith's bodyguard, of actually doing the shooting (HC 5:67, 226–27).

In July in anticipation of extradition requests from Missouri, the city council bolstered the jurisdiction of the municipal court by passing the following ordinance:

An Ordinance in Relation to Writs of Habeas Corpus

Sec. 1. Be it, and it is hereby ordained by the city council of the city of Nauvoo, that no citizen of this city shall be taken out of the city by any writs without the privilege of investigation before the municipal court, and the benefit of a writ of habeas corpus, as granted in the 17th section of the Charter of this city. Be it understood that this ordinance is enacted for the protection of the citizens of this city, that they may in all cases have the right of trial in this city, and not be subjected to illegal process by their enemies. (HC 5:57)

Governor Carlin reasonably considered the ordinance and the Mormons' interpretation of legislative power under the charter to be at odds with the legislative intent of the bill incorporating the City of Nauvoo. In a letter to Emma Smith,[7] September 1842, he said:

I have examined both the Charters and city ordinances upon the subject and must express my surprise at the extraordinary assumption of power by the board of aldermen as contained in said ordinance! From my recollection of the Charter it authorizes the Municipal Court to issue writs of habeas corpus in all cases of imprisonment or custody arising from the authority of the ordinances of said city, but that the power was granted, or intended to be granted, to release persons held in custody under the authority of writs issued by the courts or the executive of the state, is most absurd and ridiculous; and to attempt to exercise it is a gross usurpation of power that cannot be tolerated.

I have always expected and desired that Mr. Smith should avail himself of the benefits of the laws of this state, and, of course, that he would be entitled to a writ of habeas corpus issued by the Circuit Court, and entitled to a hearing before said court; but to claim the right of a hearing before the Municipal Court of the city of Nauvoo is a burlesque upon the city Charter itself. (HC 5:153–54)

In other words, under Carlin's interpretation of the city charter, the municipal court had power to issue a writ of habeas corpus only when the prisoner was held under the authority of the city of Nauvoo.

Although Carlin's position would probably prevail today, the Mormon position was not unreasonable. In fact, given the type of city government created by the charter, it may have been the most reasonable interpretation. The charter provided that the justices of the municipal court should be the mayor and aldermen of the city—the same persons normally responsible for exercising the city's authority to arrest and confine persons. As legal scholar Dallin Oaks (1965b, 881) concludes:

If imprisonments brought about by its own membership were the only kinds of official restraints that the municipal court could examine by habeas corpus, the habeas corpus power conferred in the charter would be practically meaningless. In this view, the charter must [have] contemplate[d] that the municipal court's habeas corpus power [would] be available to review some confinements other than those initiated by the membership of the municipal court itself.

Furthermore, some of the best lawyers in Illinois had repeatedly assured the Mormons that the municipal court "had full and competent power to issue writs of habeas corpus in all cases whatever" (Ford, 325).[8] All of this led Joseph Smith to exclaim:

Whatever power we have exercised in the *habeas corpus* has been done in accordance with the letter of the charter and Constitution as we confidently understood them, and that, too, with the ablest counsel; but if it be so that we have erred in this thing, let the Supreme Court correct the evil. We have never gone contrary to constitutional law, so far as we have been able to learn it. If lawyers have belied their profession to abuse us, the evil be on their heads. (HC 6:539)

Not long after the Nauvoo City Council strengthened its powers of habeas corpus, Missouri Governor Thomas Reynolds asked Illinois to extradite Joseph Smith and Orrin Porter Rockwell so that they could face charges for the attempted murder of ex-Governor Boggs. The request was based on two affidavits signed by Boggs.

Boggs's affidavit concerning Rockwell could properly have been used to extradite Rockwell if he were found in Illinois; however, the affidavit about Smith made no allegation that Smith had ever been in the state of Missouri, and thus could not logically support a request for his "return." More importantly, it did not allege that he had ever committed a crime in Missouri. B. H. Roberts noted that "in what Boggs failed, Governor Reynolds made up; and upon his own responsibility, in his demand on Illinois, charged that Joseph Smith was 'a fugitive from justice,' and had 'fled to Illinois'; a statement that was at once untrue, and wholly gratuitous" (CHC 2:150). Technically, Smith was a fugitive from justice in Illinois because the old Missouri charges of murder and treason were still outstanding. However, the Reynolds requisition was based solely on Boggs's affidavit, to which the old charges were irrelevant. Ignoring this defect, Illinois Governor Carlin issued a warrant for the arrests of both Rockwell and Smith for extradition to Missouri (HC 5:86). The two were arrested in Nauvoo and would have been taken to stand trial in Missouri except for a writ of habeas corpus from the Nauvoo Municipal Court demanding that the arresting officers deliver Smith and Rockwell to the court for an examination of the process under which they had been taken into custody.

According to Smith's account, "These officers refused to do so, and finally without complying, they left us in the care of the marshal, without the original writ by which we were arrested, and by which only we could be retained, and returned to Governor Carlin for further instructions, and myself and Rockwell went about our business" (HC 5:87). Seven months later, in March 1843, Rockwell was recognized in St. Louis and jailed by Missouri authorities. He was finally released because of insufficient evidence (HC 6:135–41). For the first time, the power of habeas corpus assumed by the Nauvoo Municipal Court over the jurisdiction of the state of Illinois had been used to secure the safety of a church official.

On 8 August, the day of Smith's arrest and release under the writ, the city council passed an extraordinary ordinance. It allowed the municipal court to look into the procedural correctness and legality of any writ of process, foreign or local, and also (if the court concluded that the writ of process was procedurally valid) to "then proceed and fully hear the merits of the case, upon which said arrest was made, upon such evidence as may be produced and sworn before said court." If upon investigation the municipal court concluded that the writ of process has been issued "through private pique, malicious intent, or religious . . . persecution, falsehood or representation," then the court could quash the writ. (It should be remembered that as mayor, Smith also served as the chief justice of the municipal court.)

Another section of the ordinance provided that upon the disqualification of the chief justice, another alderman from the city council would act as chief justice (HC 5:87–88). Three months later the city council would pass another ordinance, spelling out in more detail the procedures to be followed in obtaining a writ (HC 5:185–92). This latter ordinance, by enacting the provisions of the Illinois Habeas Corpus Act of 1827, sought to give the municipal court power to issue writs of habeas corpus for "any person or persons . . . committed or detained for any criminal or supposed criminal matter"—regardless of where they were held. To the extent the ordinance authorized the municipal court to reach outside the state by its use of habeas corpus, it "undoubtedly exceeded the charter authority" (Oaks 1965b, 888 n. 118).

These powers gave the council a virtual carte blanche. If they felt it more advantageous, they could declare the writ valid and examine the merits of the case. This had the benefit of ending the matter once and for all. Or, if they preferred, they could simply declare that the writ, even if valid on its face, was issued through private pique or discriminating intent and was therefore inoperative.

The power and propriety of going behind the writ was the subject of great debate at that time. B. H. Roberts notes that Judge Stephen A. Douglas refused to go behind the writ at the trial at Monmouth, himself doubting whether he had the power to do so. Other area judges also refused (HC 5:xxv). And by today's standards, as well as historically, their view was probably correct. At common law and under the law of most states habeas corpus was meant only to determine whether the arrest warrant had been issued correctly and perhaps whether there was probable cause for the arrest, that is, to determine whether the person in custody was being deprived of liberty without due process of law.

But Illinois law of the time apparently attached broader significance to habeas corpus. An 1849 book on habeas corpus explained that a few states at that time had added an "engraftment upon its use," namely, "hearing the whole merits and facts of the case upon habeas corpus, *deciding* upon the guilt or rather upon the *innocence* of the prisoner, and absolutely discharging him without the intervention of a jury, where the court is of opinion that the *facts* do not sustain the criminal charge" (Oaks 1965b, 883). Oaks believes that the writ of habeas corpus was used in this manner in the federal district court for Illinois when Joseph Smith finally submitted himself to federal authorities on the Missouri extradition request (Oaks 1965b, 883 n.128).

In Illinois this expanded role for habeas corpus appeared in two 1833 statutory provisions. One allowed a petitioner for habeas corpus to "allege any facts to shew, either that the imprisonment or detention is unlawful, or that he is then entitled to his discharge." The other authorized the court to "proceed in a summary way to settle the said facts, by hearing the testimony . . . and dispose of the prisoners as the case may require" (Oaks 1965b, 883). Thus, a prisoner in Illinois could use the writ of habeas corpus to obtain judicial review of his case, present evidence on the merits, and receive a judicial determination of his guilt or innocence. This determination was not conclusive, however. If new evidence surfaced, the person could be arrested again and fully tried on the merits. Still, there was legal support for the city council's actions. As Oaks (1965b, 884) concludes:

> The Nauvoo Municipal Court may have erred in its application of these principles, and some of its members seem to have misapprehended the significance of the discharge—considering it a final adjudication of innocence that would preclude any further arrest or trial—but the power that the court exercised was clearly authorized by law, not in defiance of it.

The assumption of such broad authority, and the exclusion of federal and state judicial jurisdiction, alarmed the citizens of Illinois, who saw in it evidence of Mormon attempts to create a sovereign political body under the federal system, distinct from the state of Illinois. The Mormons sincerely believed they had legislative power bounded only by the United States and Illinois constitutions, but no apprehensions would be calmed when Joseph Smith made such statements as, "Relative to our city charter, courts, right of habeas corpus, etc., I wish you to know and publish that we have all power; and if any man from this time forth says anything to the contrary, cast it into his teeth" (HC 5:466).

After the arresting officers left Smith and Rockwell to seek instruction from Governor Carlin, Smith prepared a writ of habeas corpus for the master in chancery, as a hedge against the possibility that Nauvoo's power of habeas corpus over state courts' jurisdiction would be invalidated (HC 5:89). The writ was not used, however, because Smith and Rockwell went into hiding rather than be subjected to arrest again. During their seclusion, in August 1842, Joseph's wife, Emma, wrote to Carlin, asking him to cease attempts to have her husband arrested and taken to Missouri (HC 5:115–17). Carlin responded that his actions were not a matter of his discretion: "With the constitution and laws before me, my duty is so plainly marked out that it would be impossible to err, so long as I abstain from usurping the right of adjudication" (HC 5:31). As a result, Smith remained in hiding near Nauvoo until Carlin was replaced by Thomas Ford in December 1842.

Joseph surrendered to the custody of General Wilson Law of the Nauvoo Legion on 26 December 1842 (HC 5:209), only after being convinced of the likelihood of succeeding on a writ of habeas corpus. Justin Butterfield, U.S. District Attorney for Illinois, had provided a lengthy opinion examining the legality of the Missouri extradition attempt and concluding that "the governor [had] undoubtedly been misled by the evasive affidavit which accompanied the requisition." Butterfield stated that "the supreme court [would] discharge [Smith] upon habeas corpus" (HC 5:179). Incoming Governor Ford wrote Smith on 17 December 1842:

> I submitted your case and all the papers relating thereto to the judges of the Supreme Court, or at least to six of them. . . . They were unanimous in the opinion that the requisition from Missouri was illegal and insufficient to cause your arrest, but were equally divided as to the propriety and justice of my interference with the acts of Governor Carlin. It being, therefore, a case of great doubt as to my power, and I not wishing, even in an official station, to assume the exercise of doubtful powers, and inasmuch as you have a sure and effectual remedy in the courts, I have decided to decline interfering. I can only advise that you submit to the laws and have a judicial investigation of your rights. If it should become necessary, for this purpose, to repair to Springfield, I do not believe that there will be any disposition to use illegal violence towards you; and I would feel it my duty in your case, as in the case of any other person, to protect you with any necessary amount of force from mob violence whilst asserting your rights before the courts, going to and returning. (HC 5:205–6)

Ford's statements respecting the opinion of the Illinois Supreme Court were corroborated by Butterfield's letter of 17 December 1842 and by Sangamon County Probate Judge James Adams's assurances (HC 5:206).

Smith obtained a writ of habeas corpus from Judge Nathaniel Pope of the U.S. District Court in Springfield, Illinois (HC 5:212–13). Judge Pope held that the Missouri extradition attempt based on the shooting of Boggs was improper because Boggs had not alleged that Smith had been in the state of Missouri during the time relevant to the charges, nor had he alleged that Smith had fled Missouri as a fugitive from justice (F. Cas. 22:373; also HC 5:223–31). Smith returned to Nauvoo's security once again.

The Nauvoo City Council's efforts to bolster the city's powers of habeas corpus drew the attention of the Mormons' opponents, and the powers under the Nauvoo Charter increasingly became a political issue. Efforts were made to repeal part or all of the charter in the legislature in 1842 and 1843, but a coalition of Mormon supporters blocked repeal efforts (HC 5:294–96, 298, 437).

During these troubled times, the value of the writ of habeas corpus in saving Smith and others from legal harassment seemed to escalate. From the spring of 1843 to June 1844, the Nauvoo Municipal Court issued three writs of habeas corpus on Smith's behalf, releasing him from arrest by state authorities. The first was issued in June 1843, when, on requisition from the governor of Missouri, Governor Ford issued a new writ for Smith's arrest (HC 5:433, 464–65). According to the *Illinois State Register*, John C. Bennett, who had had a falling out with Smith, was responsible for reviving the old Missouri charges (HC 5:513–15). The article concluded that Smith's arrest was a ploy by the Whigs to win the Mormons' support in the upcoming elections since Ford was a Democrat and those who came to Smith's aid were Whigs. Unlike the earlier extradition request, this requisition alleged that Smith had been charged with treason in Missouri and had fled from justice to Illinois (HC 5:464).

To make this arrest, Joseph H. Reynolds, the sheriff of Jackson County, Missouri, and Harmon T. Wilson, the constable of Carthage, Illinois, waited until Smith was far from the safe confines of Nauvoo before they acted. Representing themselves as Mormon elders, they surprised Smith outside of Dixon, Illinois, where he was visiting relatives. They arrested him without showing him any writ or serving any process, and threatened to take him to Missouri before he could obtain a writ of habeas corpus or otherwise assert his rights. They also refused his requests for legal counsel, and when two local attorneys tried to come to Smith's aid, the officers slammed the door in their faces and threatened to shoot them (HC 5:440–42). Thinking quickly, one of Smith's friends charged Reynolds and Wilson with threatening his life and with threatening and assaulting Smith, whereupon the local constable arrested them (HC 5:443). Smith also brought a civil action against Reynolds and Wilson for battery and false imprisonment, asking $10,000 in damages. The officers were arrested on a writ of *capias ad respondendum*, a writ for the arrest of the defendant in a

civil action until he furnishes security for the plaintiff's claim. Reynolds and Wilson were required to put up $10,000 bail. When they
could not post the bail, they were placed in the custody of the sheriff
of Lee County, Illinois. Smith noted with some satisfaction: "Reynolds
and Wilson felt bad when these last writs were served on them, and
began to cool in their conduct a little" (HC 5:444) (The officers borrowed a page from Smith's book and eventually obtained a writ of
habeas corpus themselves [HC 5:544].)

All this bought enough time for other friends to notify the master in
chancery, who issued two successive writs of habeas corpus for Smith.
The first writ was returned marked "Judge absent." The master in
chancery made the second writ returnable "before the nearest tribunal
in the Fifth Judicial District authorized to hear and determine writs of
habeas corpus" (HC 5:447). Smith and his lawyers[9] determined that
Nauvoo was the nearest place where writs of habeas corpus could be
heard (HC 5:456).

Reynolds and Wilson were determined not to go to Nauvoo, and
they tried repeatedly to have Smith kidnapped and taken by force to
Missouri. But by this time news of the prophet's arrest had reached
Nauvoo, and a company of 175 men from the Nauvoo Legion set off
on horseback to rescue Smith. When the first of the company reached
Smith, he exclaimed: "I am not going to Missouri this time. These
are my boys." Reynolds and Wilson were soon outnumbered, and the
party arrived in Nauvoo on 30 June 1843 without further incident (HC
5:447–49).

The procession into Nauvoo must have been a curious sight. Joseph
Smith described the relationship among the parties: "I was a prisoner
in the hands of Reynolds, the agent of Missouri, and Wilson, his
assistant. They were prisoners in the hands of Sheriff Campbell [of
Lee County], who had delivered the whole of us into the hands of
Colonel [Stephen] Markham [of the Nauvoo Legion], guarded by my
friends, so that none of us could escape" (HC 5:459). The contingent
was met on the way to town by a group of Nauvoo citizens. Mormons
lined both sides of the streets, and the group "was greeted with the
cheers of the people and firing of guns and cannons" (HC 5:459).

The Nauvoo Municipal Court convened immediately and issued a
new writ of habeas corpus, ordering Reynolds to deliver Smith, which
he did (HC 5:461–64). He then left for Carthage, threatening to raise
the militia and return (HC 5:473). Meanwhile, the municipal court
heard the testimony of witnesses for Smith and ordered the prophet
discharged "for want of substance in the warrant upon which he was
arrested, as well as upon the merits of said cause" (HC 5:474). Re-

leased from custody by the municipal court's issuance of the writ of habeas corpus, Smith spoke to the people on the nature and importance of the writ:

> The city council have passed an ordinance "that no citizen of this city shall be taken out of this city by any writ, without the privilege of a writ of habeas corpus." There is nothing but what we have power over, except where restricted by the constitution of the United States. . . . The constitution of the United States declares that the privilege of the writ of habeas corpus shall not be denied. Deny me the writ of habeas corpus, and I will fight with gun, sword, cannon, whirlwind, and thunder, until they are used up like the Kilkenny cats. We have more power than most charters confer, because we have power to go behind the writ and try the merits of the case. . . . (HC 5:470–71)

Reynolds and Wilson tried to incite the people of Carthage to mob action and petitioned Governor Ford for a posse to retake the prophet. Learning this, the Mormons sent the governor a petition of their own, asking him not to issue any more writs, together with a certified transcript of the Nauvoo Municipal Court proceedings (HC 5:478). After investigating the allegations on both sides, Ford decided not to call out the militia to retake Smith (HC 5:533–36).

Almost a year passed before Smith again made use of a writ of habeas corpus. In May 1844 apostate Mormon Francis M. Higbee, the son of Smith's good friend, Judge Elias Higbee, and a John C. Bennett sympathizer, brought a civil action against Smith in Carthage, alleging $5,000 in damages. Smith's history gives no indication of the nature of Higbee's complaint and calls it a ploy to place Smith in the hands of his Carthage enemies (HC 6:356, 358). He was arrested on a writ of *capias ad respondendum*. Smith promptly obtained a writ of habeas corpus from the Nauvoo Municipal Court. It is unclear whether the court tried the case on its merits, but "the case was argued at length." Smith was allowed to testify and to present the testimony of eight other witnesses on Higbee's character. Higbee did not appear although he had been notified of the proceedings and told to "show cause" why Smith should not be released (HC 6:360). The court found that the suit "was instituted through malice, private pique, and corruption," dismissed the suit, ordered Smith discharged, and required Higbee to pay costs (HC 6:361). As vexatious as Higbee's suit may have been, it was commenced under the authority of the state law, through Hancock County, and the best disposition of the matter would have been a return before the county court.

Smith's final use of habeas corpus occurred in June 1844 when he was arrested by a Hancock County authority on charges of causing a "riot" by ordering the destruction of the *Nauvoo Expositor* as a public nuisance. The writ of arrest was returnable before the issuing justice "or some other justice of the peace" (HC 6:453). Illinois law at the time permitted but did not require the officer to bring the prisoner before the issuing justice (Oaks 1965b, 864). The arresting officer refused to permit Smith to be heard before the justice of the peace in Nauvoo. When Smith petitioned for a writ of habeas corpus, the Nauvoo Municipal Court assumed jurisdiction and heard testimony on the merits of the case. It concluded that Smith had acted within his authority in destroying the press and that his orders were executed in an orderly manner. It ordered him "honorably discharged" and ordered Francis Higbee, the complainant, again to pay the costs (HC 6:456–58). The next morning, Smith took his seat as chief justice of the municipal court and presided over the hearings on his codefendants' petitions for habeas corpus. The court again heard testimony and ordered the defendants discharged (HC 6:461). In non-Mormon eyes, the municipality had once again preempted Illinois state authority.

The Nauvoo court went one step further during 1844. In April one Jeremiah Smith was "expecting to be arrested by the U.S. Marshal for getting money which was due him, as he says, at Washington" (HC 6:343). U.S. Circuit Judge Nathaniel Pope issued a warrant for the arrest of Smith, and on 29 May Luther Hickock, named in the writ, arrested him in Nauvoo (HC 6:416). Jeremiah petitioned for a writ of habeas corpus before the Nauvoo court over which Joseph Smith presided. Before the hearing Joseph learned that he and Jeremiah were related, but Joseph did not disqualify himself from hearing Jeremiah's case. T. B. Johnson, the complainant, denied the court's jurisdiction over the affairs of the United States government: "Your writ of *habeas corpus* [has] nothing more to do with this case than with a man in the moon" (HC 6:418). Johnson was irritated, with good reason, at the municipality's audacity in assuming jurisdiction over federal authority:

> I come here as an agent of the United States. The prisoner has been taken out of my hand, I consider illegally. I do not come here to prosecute or to defend a writ of *habeas corpus*. There is no law for these proceedings. I know my rights. If this court thinks it right to discharge the prisoner, let them do it—let them do it. I do not ask any favors of the court—I ask justice. The laws of Illinois have no power over the United States laws. Let this court discharge him, and I shall take another course—I do not say against you as a court. I came here to arrest Jeremiah Smith. (HC 6:419)

The municipal court disregarded Johnson's assertions and released Jeremiah Smith, giving, among other reasons, the fact that Smith had already been tried for the same offense before another court and acquitted (HC 6:422). Johnson threatened to bring in federal troops "for the purpose of resisting the authority and power of the Municipal Court," whereupon Joseph Smith had a warrant issued for Johnson's arrest on the grounds that he was threatening the peace of the city (HC 6:423).

Although the Nauvoo court repeatedly exercised its powers of habeas corpus in the face of state authority, this test case of its power before federal authority revealed its inadequacy. Jeremiah Smith ultimately deferred to federal authority and was tried in Springfield, armed with letters of introduction from Joseph Smith. His cause was upheld (HC 6:422–23, 501).

Although it seems obvious today that federal authority would override a municipal court, it was not so clear at the time. In the pre–Civil War era, such questions of state powers vis-a-vis the federal government were still unresolved. "Indeed, courts that had ruled on the matter prior to 1844 were practically unanimous in the opinion that state courts had the power to issue the writ of habeas corpus for persons held by federal officers," observes Oaks (1965b, 878–79; also 1965a, 275 nn. 166–67). As late as 1858, a leading treatise on habeas corpus law had declared that it was "settled that state courts may grant the writ in all cases of illegal confinement under the authority of the United States" (Oaks 1965b, 879). It was not until 1859 that the Supreme Court finally resolved the question and established the principle that state courts had no power to release persons from federal custody (*Ableman v. Booth*, US 62:506). Nevertheless, critics of the Nauvoo court's use of habeas corpus could argue that the Illinois Habeas Corpus Act of 1827 prohibited the court from exercising its powers to release federal prisoners. Section 8 of that act declared: "No person shall be discharged under the provisions of this act who is in custody under . . . [an] order, execution, or process issuing out of" a federal court (Oaks 1965b, 879). However, since the Nauvoo Municipal Court derived its habeas corpus powers from the Nauvoo Charter and not from the Habeas Corpus Act, the Nauvoo court may not have been subject to that provision, which, arguably, applied only to the state supreme court and circuit courts. It clearly was not subject to the 1827 act if the Mormons' interpretation of their charter was correct—that Nauvoo was subject only to the *constitution* of Illinois and not to its laws. The whole habeas corpus question was mooted in January 1845 when the Nauvoo Charter was repealed (CHC 2:468).

THE *NAUVOO EXPOSITOR*

If the escalating furor surrounding the Mormons' controversial use of the powers of habeas corpus had not turned uncommitted Illinois citizens against them, the *Expositor* affair did.

During the spring of 1844 a group of influential Nauvoo citizens became disaffected from the church, and particularly from its prophet. The faction was led by William Law, Wilson Law, Francis M. Higbee, Chauncey L. Higbee, Robert D. Foster, and Charles A. Foster. These men initially were alarmed at rumors spread by John C. Bennett about the personal morality of church leaders, particularly their practice of plural marriage. Alarmed that Joseph Smith had cloaked himself with both religious and temporal power, the group started to become critical of Smith, and became publicly antagonistic about the subject of polygamy. The group is even said to have formed its own religious society, with William Law as president and Austin Cowles and Wilson Law as his counselors (HC 6:347). The group continued its attacks on church leaders, and Joseph Smith in particular, until he became unusually abrasive in his public responses. Hyrum Smith felt obliged to intervene. The prophet wrote: "My brother Hyrum called in the evening, and cautioned me against speaking so freely about my enemies, &c., in such a manner as to make it actionable. I told him six months would not roll over his head before they would swear twelve as palpable lies about him as they had about me" (HC 6:403). In fact, Hyrum would be the only person besides Joseph named in the *Expositor's* scathing attack on the church's leaders.

The verbal abuse turned into a series of lawsuits and legal proceedings exchanged between the unnamed group, whom Smith called the "anties" (short for "anti-Mormons"), and church leaders. Smith was accused of perjury and polygamy (HC 6:405, 412–13). The anties were variously charged with assault, perjury, gambling, defamation, insulting city officials, and resisting arrest; court-martial proceedings were also instituted against the Law brothers, who were officers in the Nauvoo Legion (HC 6:344–51). The exchange climaxed when the anties acquired a printing press with the intention of publishing a newspaper to expose church leadership. A prospectus for the proposed paper—the *Nauvoo Expositor*—declared:

> A part of its columns will be devoted to a few primary objects, which the publishers deem of vital importance to the public welfare. Their particular locality gives them a knowledge of the many *gross abuses exercised under the "pretended" authorities of the Charter of the City of Nauvoo*, by the legislative authorities of said city and the *insupportable OPPRESSION of*

the Ministerial powers in carrying out the unjust, illegal and unconstitutional ordinances of the same. The publishers therefore deem it a sacred duty they owe to their country and their fellow-citizens, to advocate through the columns of the *Expositor*, THE UNCONDITIONAL REPEAL OF THE NAUVOO CITY CHARTER. (HC 6:443)

On 7 June 1844, the first and only issue of the *Nauvoo Expositor* was printed. It contained bristling editorials about the integrity and morality of the government under the Nauvoo Charter and the leaders of Nauvoo. Joseph Smith was focused upon, as all rumors of polygamy pointed to him—correctly, as we now know (Newell & Avery, 1985)—and all political power was vested in him.

The Nauvoo City Council met the following day, Saturday, 8 June, and discussed the problem of the *Expositor*. Most of the six-plus hours of discussion were devoted to the character and conduct of the *Expositor*'s publishers. The council suspended Sylvester Emmons, a non-Mormon member of the council and editor of the *Expositor* (HC 6:430, 434–39). The severity of the paper's charges and the social prominence of its publishers convinced the aldermen that what they perceived as a flagrantly libelous publication could not be allowed to continue. They felt the *Expositor* represented a threat not only to Smith and other leaders, but to the entire citizenry of Nauvoo. Of course, given the type of slipshod and sloppy journalism that was prevalent elsewhere in the country at the time, their concerns were probably more in the area of squelching off dissenters who acted from within the community, given that there were plenty of critics outside of Nauvoo that were not as harshly dealt with, if at all.

The city fathers believed that the Charter was a legal shield and protection for the Saints within Nauvoo's jurisdiction and that any weakening of it, such as the *Expositor* advocated, would jeopardize the personal security of the citizens.

The city council reconvened on Monday, 10 June, to continue the discussion. Smith called the *Expositor* part of a plot by his enemies to destroy the peace of Nauvoo and incite mob action against the Saints. He called the paper "a greater nuisance than a dead carcass," advocated its removal, and warned that if the council failed to take official action against the paper, the Saints might take the law into their own hands (HC 6:441–42, 581). Smith concluded that "the Constitution did not authorize the press to publish libels, and proposed that the Council make some provision for putting down the *Nauvoo Expositor*" (HC 6:443).

John Taylor declared: "We are willing they should publish the truth; but it is unlawful to publish libels. The *Expositor* is a nuisance, and stinks in the nose of every honest man." Another councilman said that "a nuisance was anything that disturbs the peace of a community," and read from Blackstone, the foremost legal authority of the day, on private wrongs. He concluded that "the whole community has to rest under the stigma of these falsehoods. . . . It is right for this community to show a proper resentment; and he would go in for suppressing all further publications of the kind." Hyrum Smith suggested that the best way to suppress the publication of such slander was to "smash the press and pi [scatter] the type" (HC 6:445).

In spite of the general feeling of outrage and resentment, Benjamin Warrington, a non-Mormon, suggested a warning and fine. After discussion, it was determined that imprisonment would not stop the libelous communication and that those responsible could not pay the damages the falsehoods produced. Accordingly, the city council passed the following resolution, Warrington casting the only negative vote:

> Resolved, by the City Council of the city of Nauvoo, that the printing-office from whence issues the *Nauvoo Expositor* is a public nuisance and also all of said *Nauvoo Expositors* which may be or exist in said establishment; and the Mayor is instructed to cause said printing establishment and papers to be removed without delay, in such manner as he shall direct. (HC 6:448)

The council also passed an ordinance governing libels, empowering the mayor (Joseph Smith) and the municipal court (of which Smith was chief justice) to convict those who published libelous statements designed to excite "the public mind against the chartered privileges, peace, and good order" of Nauvoo. Upon conviction, a person could be fined up to $500 or sentenced to six months in jail or both (HC 6:433–34). Smith, as mayor, immediately ordered the marshal to destroy the press and burn all copies of the *Expositor*. At the same time, he issued an order to Jonathan Dunham, acting major-general of the Nauvoo Legion, to assist the marshal with the Legion, if necessary (HC 6:448). That evening the press was carried into the street and smashed; the type was scattered, and the remaining copies of the paper were destroyed.

The destruction of the *Nauvoo Expositor* has been criticized as illegal. Governor Ford called the act a violation of the Constitution and "a very gross outrage upon the laws and liberties of the people" (HC 6:534). Even B. H. Roberts, the Mormon historian, admitted that "the attempt at legal justification is not convincing" (CHC 2:232), though he believed the act was justified "on the grounds of expediency or necessity" (HC 6:xxxviii).

However, in common law, conduct that injured the public health, morals, safety, or general welfare was a public nuisance. If less drastic measures could not effectively remove the danger, public officials could "abate" the nuisance, that is, remove or destroy it. Whether the city council was justified in taking the action it did therefore depends in part on the nature of the charges and their reasonably foreseeable effect on the general welfare of Nauvoo. This issue has been fully discussed by Dallin Oaks (1965b, 868–73, 877–902) and is summarized here.

The *Expositor* attacked Joseph Smith and his associates on three grounds: religious, political, and moral. The religious charges were that Smith had fallen away from the true gospel and was teaching false doctrines, most notably polygamy. Since the Illinois Constitution of 1818 (Oaks 1965b, 884) protected "the rights of conscience" and freedom of religion, the suppression of the *Expositor* cannot be justified by the differences in the religious beliefs of its publishers and those of the Nauvoo City Council. (At this time the First Amendment of the United States Constitution offered no protection to the *Expositor's* publishers, since it applied only to the federal government.)

The second major complaint was that church leaders had united the authority of the state with that of the church in Nauvoo. Specifically, the paper complained of Joseph Smith's candidacy for the presidency, Hyrum Smith's candidacy for the legislature, and the Nauvoo Municipal Court's use of its powers of habeas corpus.[10] The charge was essentially true. Church leaders dominated the political branches of Nauvoo's local government and had obliterated any lines between church and state. By criticizing what they perceived as abuses, the *Expositor's* authors were merely fulfilling an important role of a free press.

The newspaper's final charges were directed primarily at Joseph and Hyrum's personalities, describing the two men as liars, con men, and base seducers responsible for the deaths of many of their alleged female victims. Because of the Smiths' prominent place in the community and the esteem in which they were held, the council could reasonably fear that the *Expositor's* sensational attacks on their morality might incite the Mormons to attack the press, which in turn might bring anti-Mormon mobs down on Nauvoo. On the other hand, the council reasoned, if the *Expositor* was left free to circulate such rumors about the church leaders, such anti-Mormon mobs were almost certain to take action. As Oaks notes: "Subsequent events, notably the mob murder of Joseph Smith and the eventual explusion of the Mormons from Nauvoo by armed mobs, suggest that these fears were not groundless. Each of these aspects of the *Expositor's* charges was a legitimate concern of the city government, and possible basis for its suppressionary action" (1965b, 885). Joseph Smith gave a similar justification for the council's action:

> Can it be supposed that after all the indignities to which we have been subjected outside, that this people could suffer a set of worthless vaga-bonds to come into our city, and right under our own eyes and protec-tion, vilify and calumniate not only ourselves, but the charac of our wives and daughters, as was impudently and unblushingly done in that infamous and filthy sheet? There is not a city in the United States that would have suffered such an indignity for twenty-four hours. (HC 6:581)

Whether or not suppression of the *Expositor* was justified, such action may have exceeded the council's authority. Oaks notes three ob-jections that have been made to the legality of the suppression. First, it has been claimed that the council exceeded its legislative power to define a nuisance by general ordinance and infringed on the judicial prerogative to judge individual acts. Second, newspapers cannot be abated as nuisances, regardless of what they print. Finally, even the Mormons' broad interpretation of the Nauvoo charter could not sup-port an action that conflicted with the state constitutional provision ensuring the liberty of the press (Oaks 1965b, 885).

The first criticism appears to have been unfounded. Although the concept of separation of powers is at the heart of the federal constitu-tion, it has less application to local government. The Nauvoo Charter provided for a system of government that vested legislative and judi-cial powers in the same people. This combination of legislative and judicial powers was not unique. However, Joseph Smith seemed to think that the mere fact that the municipal court justices also served on the city council enabled the council to exercise judicial powers (HC 6:584–85). This argument overlooks the necessity of notice and the right to a jury trial in most judicial proceedings (Oaks 1965b, 886). The council's legislative powers, granted by the legislature, also in-cluded the power to "make regulations to secure the general health of the inhabitants, to declare what shall be a nuisance, *and to pre-vent and remove the same*" (HC 4:246; italics added). This summary power to abate nuisances without notice or judicial proceedings was recognized at common law. In 1832 New York's highest court had re-lied on the same authority as the Nauvoo City Council—Blackstone's *Commentaries*, the most authoritative statement of the common law in nineteenth-century America—to uphold a city's destruction of a structure without a judicial hearing (*Hart v. Mayor of Albany*, Wendell 9:571).[11]

The argument that the *Expositor* could not be legally removed as a nuisance because it was a newspaper, while undoubtedly the law today, had little support in the law of the time. Governor Ford insisted that the action was unprecedented in American legal history (HC 6:535–36). Joseph Smith cited as authority for the council's action an apparently unpublished Ohio case (HC 6:539; Oaks 1965b, 888 n. 154). He added, without citing authority, that "it is common for police in Boston, New York, &c., to destroy scurrilous prints: and we think the loss of character by libel and the loss of life by mobocratic prints to be a greater loss than a little property" (HC 6:539). Subsequently, in 1854 the Illinois Supreme Court said that obscene publications such as books could be categorized as public nuisances. The court added that it could find no case holding void an ordinance that provided for the abatement of a nuisance (*Goddard v. President of Jacksonville*, Ill. 15:589, 594–95). As late as the 1920s, the Minnesota Supreme Court twice upheld an injunction against a newspaper that had been found to be a nuisance (*State v. Guilford*, Minn. 174:457, NW 219:770, *aff'd* Minn. 179:40, NW 228:326 [1929], *rev'd sub nom. Near v. Minnesota ex rel. Olson*, US 283:697 [1931]). The passage from Blackstone's *Commentaries*, probably the 1832 American edition taken from the eighteenth English edition, specifically stated that "a libellous print of paper, affecting a private individual, may [probably] be destroyed" as a private nuisance (Oaks 1965b, 889). The reason Blackstone gave for summary abatement of private nuisances was that they "require an immediate remedy; and cannot wait for the slow progress of the ordinary forms of justice" (Blackstone 2:5). The Nauvoo City Council could reasonably have felt that such quick action was necessary in the case of the *Expositor*.

The council's powers to deal with a public nuisance, which the *Expositor* may have been, would have been even greater than its powers to abate a private nuisance. Because the *Expositor* threatened to provoke mob action by both sides and offended the public morals with its graphic accounts of the Smiths' alleged immorality, the city council could have found, as it did, that the newspaper had a deleterious effect on the public morals and well-being and was therefore a public nuisance. But such a finding would only have justified destroying the individual newspapers, not the press itself, since the nuisance was not in the press but in the way it was used. Thus, the destruction of the press was unwarranted, and the city councilmen were liable to its owners for its destruction.[12]

The most serious criticism of the council's action—and the one that most incited public sentiment against Nauvoo—was that it violated the constitutional guarantee of a free press. The Illinois Constitution's Declaration of Rights, section 22, stated:

> The printing presses shall be free to every person, who undertakes to examine the proceedings of the General Assembly or of any branch of government; and no law shall ever be made to restrain the right thereof. The free communication of thoughts and opinions is one of the invaluable rights of man, and every citizen may freely speak, write, and print on any subject, being responsible for the abuse of that liberty. (Oaks 1965b, 892)

However, in 1844, freedom of the press did not have the broad meaning we attach to it today. Early constitutional guarantees of a free press were meant only to prevent prior restraints on publications in the form of licensing and censorship. They provided no protection to those who abused their freedom by publishing irresponsible and defamatory statements and, in fact, the Illinois Constitution specifically provided that editors should be "responsible for the abuse of that liberty."

The legal authority the city council relied on for its action—Blackstone's *Commentaries*—supported this view. Liberty of the press, it said, consisted only "in laying no *previous* restraints upon publications, and not in freedom from censure for criminal matter when published" (Blackstone 2:113). At the time of the *Expositor* incident, the Illinois Supreme Court had not interpreted its state constitutional guarantee, but the Pennsylvania Supreme Court, in construing that state's constitutional provision (upon which the Illinois provision was based), explained the scope of the guarantee as follows: "Publish as you please in the first instance without control; but you are answerable both to the community and the individual, if you proceed to unwarrantable lengths. . . . The common weal is not interested in such a communication *except to suppress it*" (*Respublica v. Dennie*, Yeates 4:267, 269–70; italics added).

Thus, the law of the day supported the council in taking some action against the *Expositor*'s publishers. The critical question was whether the action they chose was justified. In 1948—over a century after the *Expositor* affair—the Illinois Supreme Court found that those who "abused" the liberty of the press under the Illinois Constitution could only be liable in damages or subject to criminal penalties (*Montgomery Ward & Co. v. United Retail, Wholesale & Dep't Store Employees*, Ill. 400:38, 46; NE 79:46, 50). In 1844, however, there was no direct legal authority against the use of a municipality's powers to suppress a newspaper it had found to be a nuisance. Oaks (1965b, 902) concludes:

Once the Nauvoo City Council had concluded that its nuisance-abatement powers extended to the abatement of newspapers publishing scandalous or provocative material, it would be unrealistic to have expected them to observe limitations that were not articulated clearly in any constitution, statute or court decision of their day. To charge them with a willful violation of the Illinois free-press guarantees, one must overlook the suppressionist sentiments of the age in which they lived and attribute to them a higher devotion to the ideals of a free press than was exhibited [throughout the nineteenth and much of the twentieth centuries].

Even if legally justified, the council's action was still unwise. In June 1844, the mounting political and religious pressures on the populace of Illinois, Missouri, Iowa, and Ohio were creating an explosive climate of opinion. The destruction of the *Expositor* was more than the citizens could bear. The threat of the "Mormon kingdom" under the cover of the Nauvoo Charter led to the murders of Joseph and Hyrum Smith before the month was out and ultimately to the ruin of Nauvoo. Joseph Smith's comments respecting the *Expositor*, as recorded in the proceedings of the city council, would prove prophetic. He had said that "he would rather die tomorrow and have the thing smashed, than live and have it go on, for it was exciting the spirit of mobocracy among the people, and bringing death and destruction upon us" (HC 6:442). Francis M. Higbee's rhetoric just before the posse destroyed the *Expositor* press has a similar prophetic quality: "If they lay their hands upon [the press] or break it, they may date their downfall from that very hour, and in ten days there will not be a Mormon left in Nauvoo. What they do, they may expect the same in return" (HC 6:451).

The expansive interpretation of powers under the Nauvoo Charter from the spring of 1841 to the summer of 1844 was unacceptable to most people. They shared the feelings of one early historian, who concluded: "The government of Nauvoo was not in accord with the laws of the state" (Urch 1928, 94). Smith's death in June 1844 destroyed Mormon resolve to argue for their perceived rights under the charter, and the Nauvoo Charter was repealed by an unpetitioned act of the Illinois legislature during the 1844–45 session.[13]

THE MURDERS OF JOSEPH AND HYRUM SMITH

The destruction of the *Nauvoo Expositor* was the death-knell for the legal sanctuary the Mormons had created in Nauvoo. The *Warsaw Signal* had previously expressed the prevailing sentiment: "Joe Smith is *above the law*. He *cannot be punished* for any crime" (Oaks and Hill,

13). The antagonism was so high that the *Warsaw Signal* commented two weeks later, on 29 May 1844:

> We have seen and heard enough to convince us that Joe Smith is not safe out of Nauvoo, and we would not be surprised to hear of his death by violent means in a short time. He has deadly enemies—men whose wrongs have maddened them. . . . The feeling of this country is now lashed to its utmost pitch, and will break forth in fury upon the slightest provocation. (Oaks and Hill, 14)

The *Quincy Whig* reacted to the attack on the *Expositor* by calling it an example of the Mormon attitude toward law and rights. "It is not surprising that the Missourians were raised to madness and drove them from the state" (Oaks and Hill, 15). Thomas C. Sharp, editor of the *Warsaw Signal* and one of nine men later charged with Smith's murder, wrote excitedly on 12 June: "We have no time for comment: every man will make his own. Let it be made with POWDER and BALL!!!" (Porter, 23). One week later he declared: "We hold ourselves at all times in readiness to co-operate with our fellow citizens . . . to exterminate, utterly exterminate, the wicked and abominable Mormon leaders" (Oaks and Hill, 15).

It is not surprising then that Joseph Smith was apprehensive about going to Carthage to answer complaints of riot in connection with the demolition of the *Nauvoo Expositor*. Only two weeks earlier Joseph H. Jackson, Robert D. Foster, and William Law had accused Smith of adultery and perjury before a grand jury, and Smith had traveled voluntarily to Carthage almost immediately to confront his accusers and clear his name. The case was held over until the following term of court, and he returned unharmed to the security of Nauvoo. (HC 6:405, 412–13). But now the non-Mormons were in an uproar. When Constable David Bettisworth returned to Carthage without Smith, who had been willing to stand trial in Nauvoo, it was more than the Carthage citizens could take. "Joe has tried the game too often," one protested in a letter to the *Missouri Republican* (Oaks and Hill, 16).

The anti-Mormon forces recruited men to lay siege to Nauvoo and take custody of the church leaders. At Warsaw $1,000 was voted to arm the militia against Nauvoo. Three thousand men were readied in Rushville, Illinois, and groups from Iowa and Missouri were ready, as usual, to take part in a war against the Mormons (Oaks and Hill, 16). In the face of the threatened attack, Joseph Smith declared Nauvoo under martial law and sealed the city with guarded checkpoints on all roads leading to it (HC 6:497). Later, Illinois authorities in Carthage cited this response as evidence of treason, the charge that compelled

Smith to remain in Carthage, where he was killed (HC 6:561–62, 569–70). Governor Ford later maintained that if the Nauvoo Legion were called out to resist a legal posse from Carthage this might constitute treason (Ford 1854, 337). But if—as subsequent events proved—the posse was merely a front for the attempted murder of the church leaders, the treason charge was fanciful.

With a full-scale civil war near, Smith decided to retreat to the west rather than risk death in Carthage or the destruction of Nauvoo in the state's effort to obtain his custody (HC 6:545–46).

Joseph and Hyrum hid on the Iowa side of the Mississippi River on Sunday morning, 23 June 1844, to await horses and provisions for the escape to the Great Basin in the Rocky Mountains (HC 6:548). But before nightfall they were reluctantly back in Nauvoo. A delegation from Nauvoo, bearing a letter from Emma Smith, had persuaded Joseph to return and face the charges in order to protect the city. The Nauvoo townsfolk were as fearful for their lives in the volatile situation as the prophet was.

Smith and his company left for Carthage to meet Governor Ford early on Monday morning, 24 June. Ford was fully aware of the precarious situation, and on 22 June he pledged in writing to protect the church leaders if they submitted to a legal investigation in Carthage of the destruction of the *Nauvoo Expositor*:

> I am anxious to preserve the peace. A small indiscretion may bring on a war. The whole country is now up in arms, and a vast number of people are ready to take the matter into their own hands. Such a state of things might force me to call out the militia to prevent a civil war. And such is the excitement of the country that I fear the militia, when assembled, would be beyond legal control. . . .
>
> I will . . . *guarantee the safety of all such persons as may thus be brought to this place from Nauvoo either for trial or as witnesses for the accused.* (HC 6:536–37)

Before reaching Carthage, Smith's party met Captain Dunn of the Illinois militia, who had orders from Ford to take the Nauvoo Legion's state-issued arms. Smith returned to Nauvoo to expedite the peaceable surrender of the weapons and left again for Carthage that evening (HC 6:554–58). If Ford intended to prevent bloodshed by the disarmament order, he disarmed the wrong side. The Nauvoo Legion had never expressed any intention to attack the citizens of Illinois, whereas the remainder of the state militia, controlled by bitter enemies of the Mormons, had sworn their destruction.

The group arrived at midnight and quartered in the Hamilton Hotel.

On the morning of Tuesday, 25 June, the church leaders surrendered to Constable Bettisworth on charges of riot. Later that morning, the Smiths were arrested for treason for ordering martial law in Nauvoo (HC 6:561). A hearing was held concerning the charges of riot, and bail was posted. The men might have been released at that point, had it not been for the capital charges of treason still pending. The Smiths were imprisoned on a mittimus, a written order from the court instructing an officer to convey a person to the prison and commanding the jailer to keep him safely until he is to be delivered before the court. The mittimus, issued by Robert F. Smith, a Carthage justice of the peace and captain of the Mormon-hating Carthage Greys, stated that the Smiths had been brought before him for examination, though they had not. The Smiths were given no hearing on the treason charges; instead they were scheduled to be held in Carthage Jail for four days, when it was expected that Francis M. Higbee, a material witness who had unsuccessfully served as the complainant in two previous suits, would be available (Oaks 1965b, 866–67; HC 6:567–70).

Joseph and Hyrum were secured in the two-story jail. On Thursday, 27 June, Ford left Carthage and traveled to Nauvoo to search for evidence against the church leaders (Ford, 339). Why the governor of the state was required to search for the evidence is unknown. Before leaving, he discharged most of the militiamen that had gathered in anticipation of the Mormon war although he had been warned repeatedly of the brewing conspiracy against Smith's life. The evening of the prophet's arrival, Ford had heard the Carthage Greys taunt the Mormons:

> While passing the public square many of the troops, especially the Carthage Greys, made use of the following expressions, which were re-echoed in the ears of the Governor and hundreds of others, "Where is the damned prophet?" "Stand away, you McDonough boys, and let us shoot the damned Mormons." "G—d— you, old Joe, we've got you now." "Clear the way and let us have a view of Joe Smith, the prophet of God. He has seen the last of Nauvoo. We'll use him up now, and kill all the damned Mormons." (HC 6:559)

The clamor became so boisterous that Ford finally had to disperse the group. Ford also knew of the oaths of the apostate "anties" to "shed the blood of Joseph Smith . . . whether he was cleared by the law or not" (HC 6:560). Despite the obvious danger to the prisoners, Ford left the Carthage Greys, the group that had demonstrated the most vocal hatred toward Joseph Smith, to guard the jail and protect the prisoners.

Ford probably had not reached Nauvoo before a group of men with blackened faces stormed the jail, killed Joseph and Hyrum, and wounded John Taylor. Willard Richards, the only other person in the room, was not injured (HC 6:612–18).

Understandably, in the confusion immediately following the murders, many conflicting reports circulated. Evidently many Illinois citizens expected the Mormons to take bloody revenge, but instead they regrouped and eventually abandoned Nauvoo and retreated to the west.

The first—and perhaps most important—step in bringing the Smiths' assassins to justice was the selection of the grand jury, since that body would decide who to indict for the murders and whether there was sufficient evidence to bring them to trial. The grand jury called for the October 1844 term of the circuit court in Hancock County was composed entirely of non-Mormons. This seems surprising since of the three county commissioners who were responsible for selecting the grand and petit jurors, two (Andrew H. Perkins and George Coulson) were Mormons, and the third (John T. Barnett) was sympathetic toward the church (Oaks and Hill 1975, 46). The composition of the grand jury is even more surprising given the fact that state law required that the grand jury include "as nearly as may be a proportionate number [of jurors] from each township" in the county (Oaks and Hill, 47), and Nauvoo, with over half the county's population, was nearly all Mormon.

Were it impaneled today, the grand jury would not have passed constitutional muster. Even though the Fifth Amendment right to a grand jury indictment has never been applied to the states (*Hurtado v. California*, US 110:516 [1884]), due process may require that a grand jury pool represent a fair cross-section of the community (*Hobby v. United States*, US 468:339 [1984]; LaFave and Israel 1985, 626), and the exclusion of a religious group in the community would violate the cross-sectional requirement (*Thiel v. Southern Pacific Co.*, US 328:217 [1946]). However, the due process clauses of the Fifth Amendment did not apply to Illinois in 1844 because the Fourteenth Amendment, limiting state actions, did not yet exist. Moreover, the Illinois constitution in effect at the time did not contain a due process clause. It provided that "no freeman shall be . . . deprived of his life, liberty or property, but by the judgment of his peers or the law of the land" (Braden and Cohn 1969, Ill. Constitution of 1818, art. 8, § 8), but apparently this provision was never interpreted as requiring a grand jury representative of the community.

Even where a representative grand jury is not required, however, the equal protection clause of the Fourteenth Amendment today prohibits those states that choose to proceed in criminal cases by grand jury indictment, as Illinois did (Ill. Constitution of 1818, art. 8, § 10; Braden and Cohn 1969, 34–35), from purposefully discriminating against an identifiable group in selecting grand jurors (*Castaneda v. Partida*, US 430:482 [1977]). Such purposeful discrimination could be inferred from the exclusion of a religious group as numerous as the Mormons were in Hancock County. But of course the Fourteenth Amendment's equal protection clause did not exist in 1844, and the then-existing Illinois constitution did not include an equal protection clause (Braden and Cohn, 113–14).

Thus, an Illinois citizen in 1844 had no enforceable right to be indicted by a truly representative grand jury. Illinois law at the time left grand jury composition and procedure to statute and the common law (*People ex rel. Ferrill v. Graydon*, Ill. 333:429, NE 164:832 [1928]), and the applicable statute only required that, "as nearly as may be," a proportionate number of grand jurors be selected from each township (Oaks and Hill, 47). This requirement apparently was met: at least some of the grand jurors came from Nauvoo and other Mormon communities (Oaks and Hill, 48).

Even if the Smiths' accused assassins had the right to be indicted by a representative grand jury, they had no reason to challenge the composition of the grand jury. The exclusion of Mormons was in fact favorable to them, and the Illinois Supreme Court has held that a defendant may waive any defect in the grand jury's composition by not objecting to it before entering his plea (*People v. Green*, Ill. 329:576, NE 161:83 [1928]). It is doubtful whether the Mormons could have raised any challenge, since at common law only persons under prosecution for crime and those "returned" or placed on the grand jury could challenge the composition of the grand jury pool (C.J.S. 38:1015).[14]

Oaks and Hill (1975, 47–48) suggest two explanations for the exclusion of Mormons from the grand jury. It may have been the result of the efforts of George Thatcher, the clerk of the county commissioners' court and the ranking anti-Mormon in Hancock County. Although Thatcher did not have a vote in selecting the jurors, he may have been able to influence the county commissioners by suggesting that a Mormon-dominated grand jury might touch off a civil war, especially since the grand jury was to convene just after a military encampment in Hancock County that Thatcher helped arrange. On the other hand, the exclusion of Mormons may have been a deliberate effort to maintain an appearance of impartiality so as to gain the support of the uncommitted citizens of the county and state. Whatever the reason, not only were Mormons conspicuously absent from the grand jury, but so were prominent anti-Mormons. "With but few possible exceptions, the grand jury seems to have been deliberately composed of non-Mormons who were either uncommitted or sympathetic to the Mormon cause" (Oaks and Hill, 48).

Seventeen persons testified before the grand jury, and about sixty possible defendants were named. Only nine received the twelve votes necessary to indict, and only five actually stood trial. Two had reportedly died of wounds received in the attack on the jail, and the others had reportedly left the state (Oaks and Hill, 51, 79; HC 7:103).

Oaks and Hill (1975) have reconstructed and analyzed in detail the trial of Joseph Smith's accused assassins. Only a brief summary of the proceedings will be given here. The trial began on 19 May 1845. The judge was Richard M. Young, who, some five years earlier, as a United States senator from Illinois, had presented to Congress the Mormons' petition for relief (Oaks and Hill, 76). Unlike the grand jury pool, the panel of potential petit jurors, chosen by the same county commissioners, was composed of roughly equal numbers of Mormons and non-Mormons (Oaks and Hill, 224–25). The defense immediately moved the court to discharge the panel and to disqualify the commissioners and the sheriff from their duty to select the jury panel. Affidavits signed by the defendants alleged that the elected officials were prejudiced against them and had been guided by that prejudice in their selection of potential jurors (Oaks and Hill, 97–98). Although there was no assertion that the potential jurors who had been selected were prejudiced, and although there was no legal authority or precedent for such action,[15] Judge Young granted the motion and bypassed the statutory procedure without even allowing the elected officials to be heard. He instructed the parties to select two substitutes, called elisors, who in turn would select a new group of potential jurors.

The significance of this decision did not escape the local press. The *Burlington Hawkeye* (Iowa) declared on 5 June 1845: "The decision of Judge Young will hereafter be plead [*sic*] as a precedent whenever a Mormon jury is to sit in judgment in the trials of anti-Mormons and will in great measure lessen the power the Mormons have heretofore possessed in controlling the courts of that county" (Oaks and Hill, 102). When Brigham Young and other church leaders heard of the decision, they abandoned all hope of a fair decision (Oaks and Hill, 102–3).

The substitutes were ordered to impanel a new group of prospective jurors "from the bystanders" at the trial (Oaks and Hill, 104). Since the Mormons had been told by their leaders, in the interest of peace, to stay home unless they had business with the court (Oaks and Hill, 72), this order virtually guaranteed that the Mormons, who comprised about half the population of Hancock County, would not be adequately represented on the jury.

The elisors had to select four panels of twenty-four potential jurors each—for a total of ninety-six—before the prosecution and defense could agree on the required twelve jurors. The prosecution used thirty-three of its peremptory challenges to excuse jurors. The defense used only eleven, which suggests both sides recognized that the panel of jurors favored the defense (Oaks and Hill, 107). Predictably, only about four of the ninety-six (and apparently none of the final twelve) were Mormons. The religious preferences of thirteen have not been determined (Oaks and Hill, 107, 105, 224). Most of the seventeen persons listed as witnesses before the grand jury also testified at the trial. But the list may not be completely accurate. Governor Ford and John Taylor were listed as grand jury witnesses, but contemporary accounts do not mention either testifying. Furthermore, William Daniels said at the time that he was the only Mormon to testify before the grand jury. It is likely that the grand jury only considered written statements by Ford and Taylor (Oaks and Hill, 61 n. 18). Despite the availability of church members who were eyewitnesses to the events, Mormon leaders refused to help the prosecution procure witnesses (Oaks and Hill, 103). Most of the twelve were in hiding at the time, trying to keep away from writs that might bring them to hostile Carthage either to give testimony in the murder trial or to answer on charges related to the *Expositor* affair (Oaks and Hill, 108). Church members had no expectation that justice would be done and did not publish either the proceedings of the trial or its outcome in their press (Oaks and Hill, 108).

Their fears were confirmed. After six days of trial, all of the defendants were acquitted (*People v. Levi Williams*, Hancock County Circuit Court, D:291; Oaks and Hill, 185). The case against the same defendants for the death of Hyrum Smith was dismissed when the state failed to prosecute them (Oaks and Hill, 191).

BANKRUPTCY OF THE PROPHET

Creditor suits against Joseph Smith, which antedated his murder but were continued against his estate following his death, prolonged the legal problems plaguing his family and the church. Joseph personally, and the church in general, had suffered a series of financial setbacks from the failure of the Kirtland Safety Society in the Panic of 1837, to the unredressed expulsion of the Saints from Missouri in 1839, to the substantial indebtedness incurred when the Mormons purchased lands for Nauvoo from Isaac Galland and Horace Hotchbiss. To make matters worse, Mormon businessmen on 10 September 1840 signed a promissory note for the purchase from the federal government of a steamboat and other river equipment with Joseph and Hyrum Smith as guarantors (Oaks and Bentley, 751, 754). After the steamboat ran aground and the principals failed on the note, United States Attorney Justin Butterfield in April 1842 filed a complaint and received a default judgment against the Nauvoo businessmen, including Joseph, for $5,212.49¾ (Oaks and Bentley, 743–44).

This judgment coupled with Joseph's other financial disasters had prompted him to file for bankruptcy in April 1842. The newly enacted federal bankruptcy law had only become effective on 1 February of that year. The Saints learned of its provisions from Calvin A. Warren, an attorney who advertised in Nauvoo's *Wasp*, 10 April 1842, regarding the availability of the new laws for financially strapped individuals (Oaks and Bentley, 751).

Smith was not completely convinced of the morality of declaring bankruptcy, but he felt that he had no other choice (HC 4:594–95, 600). Accordingly, he prepared a list of his obligations and inventory of his property, and on 18 April 1842, he swore his affidavit of insolvency before the clerk of the county commissioners' court. His debts totaled $73,066.38, with the U.S. government obligation of $4,866.38 listed first (Brodie, 266 n.). The inventory of property listed almost $20,000 in money and notes receivable plus specified real and personal property of unestimated value (Oaks and Bentley, 752–53).

Oaks and Bentley have reported the lenient treatment generally given those taking out bankruptcy at that time:

> The persons who filed bankruptcy applications during the spring of 1842 contemplated, and most of them received, discharges from all their debts during the fall of 1842. The national mood at that time was in favor of facilitating these discharges. In fact, a Treasury circular of May 9, 1842, officially discouraged U.S. Attorneys from opposing applications in bankruptcy, and limited their fees to a mere per diem allowance of $5 while attending bankruptcy hearings to oppose such applications. On January 3, 1843, the clerk of the United States District Court in Illinois reported that no decrees of final discharge had yet been refused in that court and that only eight of the 1,433 applications then pending in bankruptcy had been opposed by creditors. (Oaks and Bentley, 754)

In spite of this widespread routine approach to bankruptcy applications, Joseph Smith's application was singled out for special treatment. John C. Bennett had published letters in the *Sangamo Journal* in June and July of 1842 accusing Smith of attempting to defraud his creditors by conveying or "secreting property . . . for the benefit of himself and family in order to obtain the benefit of the Bankrupt Act" (Oaks and Bentley, 755). U.S. Attorney Justin Butterfield wrote to the solicitor of the Treasury, Charles B. Penrose, for permission to oppose Joseph and Hyrum Smith's applications for bankruptcy, enclosing Bennett's accusations to justify the challenge.[16] He received the necessary authorization and traveled from Chicago to Nauvoo. Butterfield found abundant evidence of what appeared to be fraudulent conveyances in contemplation of bankruptcy and the concealment of assets and omissions from inventory, which he described in a letter to Penrose on 1 October 1842 (Cannon 1945, 431).

Butterfield made four general objections to Smith's petition in bankruptcy. He claimed that Smith had wrongfully (1) conveyed property to persons who were not bona fide purchasers or creditors, (2) made invalid transfers to some creditors in preference to others, (3) made transfers after the bankruptcy act was passed, and (4) concealed assets from his inventory of property filed with the petition (Oaks and Bentley, 757–59). The conveyances would have been void, however, only if they were made "in contemplation of bankruptcy" or of passage of the bankruptcy law, and there is no evidence that Smith even knew of the bankruptcy law until four days before he filed (Oaks and Bentley, 759). Butterfield did not substantiate his allegations of fraud, and the conveyances are easily explained on other grounds.

Until the winter of 1840–41, the affairs of the church and of Joseph Smith had been inseparable. After formal organization of the Nauvoo Stake and the city government, Smith began to sort out the property held in his name. At a special conference of the church on 30 January 1841, Smith was elected "sole Trustee-in-Trust for the Church of Jesus Christ of Latter-day Saints" (HC 4:286). On 8 February 1841, Smith filed a sworn statement to that effect with the county recorder, as required by Illinois law (HC 4:287; Oaks and Bentley, 746). Later that year, the Council of the Twelve Apostles, noting that "on account of the peculiar situation of the Church hitherto, it has been expedient and necessary, that the deeds, bonds, and properties of the Church should be, and have been taken and holden by committees of the Church, and private individuals," voted to have Smith "gather up all deeds, bonds, and properties belonging to the Church, and which are now held either by committees or individuals, and take the same in his own name as trustee-in-trust for the Church" (HC 4:413). At this same meeting, the Council of the Twelve also authorized Smith "to deed and make over certain portions of Church property . . . as in his wisdom he shall judge expedient" to his and his father's families, "on account of the great losses they have sustained in property by the unparalleled persecutions . . . they have sustained since the rise of the church, which has brought them to their present destitute situation." It also ratified transfers Smith had already made to family and friends (HC 4:412–13).

From about this time on, Smith began distinguishing between his personal property and property held in trust for the church (Oaks and Bentley, 745–49). The conveyances that bothered Butterfield were probably attempts to sort out ownership of property Smith formerly held on behalf of the church and efforts to provide for his family out of those properties, as authorized by the Council of the Twelve. Furthermore, Smith filed his petition for bankruptcy in April 1842, and most of the conveyances took place in 1841. The 1841 statute expressly provided that all bona fide transactions entered into by the bankrupt more than two months before the filing of a petition "shall not be invalidated or affected by this act" (ch. 9, § 2, Stat. 5:442).

As Butterfield became more familiar with the state of affairs in Nauvoo, he changed his mind. By December 1842 he was representing Smith before Judge Nathaniel Pope on the writ of habeas corpus with which Smith countered the Missouri extradition attempt, a sign of Butterfield's new and lasting respect for Smith. For his services, Butterfield accepted $40 cash and two notes from Smith for $230 each, "hardly indicating any distrust of the Prophet's personal or financial integrity" (Oaks and Bentley, 764; HC 5:232). Joseph Smith could not attend the 15 December hearing in Springfield because the extradition order in the Boggs affair was still in force; but Hyrum Smith was granted his discharge in bankruptcy, and an "arrangement" was made for the discharge of Joseph as well. The proposal for settlement with the federal government consisted of an offer to provide a bond, secured by real estate and payable in four annual installments, for the $5,212.49¾ claimed by the government (Oaks and Bentley, 762; HC 5:205).

On 17 December 1842, Butterfield wrote to the solicitor of the treasury with the details of the proposed settlement, recommending that the government accept the offer and seeking authority to settle. The solicitor declined the offer and countered by proposing that Smith be discharged in bankruptcy on immediate payment of one-third of the debt and a confession of judgment for the balance, to be paid in three annual installments secured by a mortgage on the realty. Apparently, Butterfield never received this response since he repeated his original proposal to settle in a letter on 25 May 1843. The matter was dropped for more than a year, although Butterfield and Smith continued cordial communications on different subjects until Smith's death (Oaks and Bentley, 763–65).

Joseph was murdered before his case was resolved, and when the church emigrated to Utah the case was left in the hands of unenthusiastic representatives of his estate. In 1850 the United States filed a creditor's bill in chancery to obtain payment from the estate. On 6 January 1851, Judge Nathaniel Pope entered a decree finding the United States entitled to $7,870.23 and ordering the sale of real estate to pay the entitlement. Further decrees were entered on 14 July 1851 and 13 January and 17 July 1852, following further reports by a special master appointed to investigate Smith's properties (Oaks and Bentley, 773). Pope also ruled that Emma Smith Bidamon, Joseph's widow, was entitled to one-sixth of the proceeds of the sale, as her dower interest. Significantly, neither Pope nor the special masters made any finding of fraud on the part of Joseph Smith, despite such allegations in the complaint (Oaks and Bentley, 773–75, 778).

The real property covered by the decree included all land Smith had held in his individual capacity, to which the 1842 judgment had attached as a lien,[17] and all property he had held as trustee-in-trust for the church before his death. In including church property in the decree, Judge Pope relied on a little-known provision in an Illinois statute that allowed the trustee of a religious society "to receive by gift, devise or purchase, a quantity of land not exceeding 10 acres" (Oaks and Bentley, 776). The church had relied on an earlier version of this statute in designating Smith as trustee-in-trust. But Pope shared the traditional disfavor that courts had for lands held in trust for religious groups. He held that all property conveyed to Joseph as trustee in excess of this ten-acre limit had been held by him in his personal capacity and was therefore subject to the judgment lien (Oaks and Bentley, 777).[18] The government had former church property sold, together with the property formerly owned by Joseph personally, and took its award. Total proceeds from the sale were $11,148.35. Ninety-five percent of this amount was attributable to properties Joseph had formerly held as trustee-in-trust for the church. The government recovered its full judgment of $7,870.23; Emma Smith Bidamon received $1,809.41; and the remainder apparently went to cover costs and expenses (Oaks and Bentley, 778–79).

PART II

A Turbulent Coexistence: Church and State Relations in Utah

The martyrdom of Joseph and Hyrum Smith precipitated the evacuation of the Saints from Nauvoo. Persecution continued, and the legislature repealed the Nauvoo city charter in January 1845, leaving the city without police or judicial authority. Meanwhile, church efforts centered on completing the temple and preparing to evacuate the city. The Saints, although they had planned to begin leaving in April 1846, actually started on 4 February to avoid further persecution. By May nearly twelve thousand Saints had crossed the Mississippi, and in September the remaining 640 were besieged by a military force and compelled to leave or die. Thus commenced the largest migration of a religious people in the history of the United States. Calling themselves the Camp of Israel, the migrating Saints organized in military style in camps of fifty. At Mount Pisgah, Iowa, on 26 June 1846, Captain James Allen, of the United States Army, requisitioned the Saints to provide a force of five hundred men to serve as a battalion in the impending war with Mexico. Brigham Young surprised many by supporting the call, which demonstrated Mormon loyalty to the government. This action, however, provided cash to assist in financing the move West and ensured United States control over the territory the Mormons would soon colonize. By September 1846 the advance party of Mormons had received permission from the Pottawatomie and Omaha Indians to encamp for two years on unorganized Indian territory on the west side of the Missouri. Winter Quarters, renamed Kanesville, and later still Council Bluffs, soon became a thriving, if temporary, Mormon camp. The vanguard left Winter Quarters on 14 April 1847 and arrived in the Great Salt Lake Valley on 22 July 1847. Brigham Young entered the valley on 24 July 1847 and the colonization of the Great Basin immediately commenced.

The Mormons moved to the Great Basin desert to find the autonomy that would allow them to build Zion unimpeded by religious persecution. The choice of a largely uninhabited desert as the center place for the kingdom was primarily motivated by the Saints' desire to be left alone so they could freely establish a distinctive way of life that other communities had found so threatening and offensive. Instead, they now had to deal with the federal government, initially cautious and soon hostile and bent on eradicating Mormon distinctiveness.

Non-Mormon political control over Mormon communities was not, of course, a new problem for church leaders. They had experienced minority status in New York, Ohio, Missouri, and Illinois. Joseph Smith had often sent exploring parties to uninhabited or sparsely inhabited areas of continental America looking for a place where, in the words of historian William Alexander Linn, the Saints could have "not only an undisturbed place of residence, but a government of their own" (Linn, 428; Hansen 1967, 131). The question then was not whether the Mormons wanted to govern themselves, but the extent to which a hostile federal government would allow them to pursue their Zion.

From 1846 to the 1849 organization of the provisional state of Deseret in what is now Utah, the principal governing bodies for the church were municipal high councils supplemented by bishoprics. Church administrative leaders were aided by appointed or elected marshals who meted out corporal punishment and enforced court decisions, thereby going beyond the spiritual sanctions normally associated with church courts (Jenson, 48; Nebeker, 88). In effect, the municipal high councils exercised both civil and ecclesiastical authority during the exodus period.

While church and state merged for this brief period in Mormon history, it was out of necessity rather than theological preference. Actually, the Saints were constantly "agitating for" the replacement of the ecclesiastical regime in civil affairs by "civil jurisdiction" (Jensen, 52). But the civil jurisdiction the Mormons had in mind was governance by righteous Mormons acting in civil capacities, rather than by foreign officials hostile to Mormon institutions. They believed that Mormon control over civil government could be distinct from ecclesiastical control over the church and its institutions. Consequently, the Salt Lake High Council in 1849 "voluntarily relinquished jurisdiction in city administration" (Jenson, 54). On 4 March 1849 a committee was appointed to draft a constitution to provide for civil authority until

Congress acted. It was adopted a few days later and a provisional government called the state of Deseret was organized (Bancroft, 440; Morgan 1940, 67). Under the provisions of this constitution, the Mormons planned to institute a republican form of government, loyal to the United States but with local rule, a fairly noncontroversial political aim.

With a government established, the Mormons hoped for an association with the United States that would ensure the autonomy necessary for the existence of Zion. Their experience in Missouri and Illinois had taught them that states' rights precluded federal intervention into local affairs; consequently statehood seemed the logical choice. Although their 1849 petition for statehood technically satisfied the requirements outlined in the Northwest Ordinance of 1784, because of political controversy over the slavery issue, the petition was denied. Territorial status was granted to the Mormons on 9 September 1850.

While history had shown that states' rights could protect such reprehensible institutions as slavery and such objectionable misconduct as organized religious persecution, the domain of territorial rights was much more controversial. The subject was hotly debated in the context of the slavery issue during the antebellum period, resulting in several compromises that put off but did not avoid the resolution of the issue in a civil war. Prior to the war, Southern states advocated territorial control over local matters; the Mormons, in their newly organized territory, favored this position, believing that it would protect them in their peculiar religious practices. Northern states argued for federal control over territorial matters. They hoped to eradicate the "twin relics of barbarism": slavery and polygamy. The Civil War made the slavery issue moot, and the enactment of the "Civil War" amendments —the thirteenth, fourteenth, and fifteenth—generally strengthened federal control over the states. Nevertheless, states' rights continued to be important.

If Mormons were successful in their petitions for statehood, the constitutional prospects for eradicating peculiar, social, domestic, and adjudicatory practices associated with Mormonism would significantly diminish. Even after the church had issued its 1890 Manifesto banning further plural marriages in the United States, the federal government, testing the Mormons' good faith, delayed statehood until 1896, and then allowed it only on the condition that the state constitution forever prohibit the practice of polygamy.

During this territorial period lasting nearly half a century, the Mormons learned to swim against the tide of congressional legislation and executive appointments aimed at drowning their distinctiveness.

Increasingly harsh federal legislation outlawed polygamy, disenfranchised the Mormon faithful, kept believers off juries, and ultimately disincorporated the church. With very few exceptions, federal appointees were non-Mormons who disapproved of the community they served. The three-judge federal judiciary assigned themselves the task of stamping out Mormon recalcitrance. They attacked territorial legislation that established probate courts of general jurisdiction; they launched their own campaigns aimed at ensuring polygamy convictions; they refused to naturalize many Mormon immigrants; and they facilitated vexatious litigation aimed at discrediting, if not imprisoning, Mormon leadership. It is unclear whether the judges were after elimination or assimilation. In either case, the territorial period exacerbated intolerably an already strained and mistrustful relationship between Mormons and the state.

The Mormon predicament in the West paralleled in many respects the situation the early colonists in America faced with regard to England. Most colonists were very loyal to England but strenuously objected to what they felt were serious deprivations of their constitutional rights as Englishmen, including the right to jury trial by their peers, the right to an independent judiciary, and the right to self-rule. The degree to which the English Constitution extended these common-law rights to the colonists has been hotly debated (Black, 1157–59). The Revolutionary War settled the issue decisively in the colonists' favor, and the United States Constitution consolidated the victories into a written document.

The Mormon frontier community presented a similar constitutional dilemma. The Mormons tried to protect their rights against federal encroachments, and issues involving jury trials, an independent judiciary, and self-rule were raised again in the Utah Territory. However, the Mormons were not prepared to revolt, even though political circumstances caused them to lose on these issues and more. Ultimately the Utah controversy was resolved only when the Mormons agreed to give up much of their distinctiveness in the process of accommodation and survival. Thus, whereas the American Revolution resulted in a new experiment in government, the Mormons' experience ultimately led to the loss of a religious attempt to order society on a religious basis (Mangrum, 1985).

6

The Early Attack on Polygamy

In 1856 the Republican Party platform set as its goals the eradication of the twin relics of barbarism: slavery and polygamy (*Congressional Globe*, 1860, 1410). The first goal was controversial and was achieved only through a bloody civil war. On the other hand, everyone—except the Mormons—favored the eradication of polygamy. Despite the nation's enthusiasm, however, the campaign to force the Mormons to renounce polygamy required nearly forty years. That campaign was in a sense a war, although little blood was shed and the federal weapons were legislative, judicial, and administrative. Its casualties were not only polygamy but many other distinctive aspects of Mormon society and culture.

Polygamy provided a clear rallying point for anti-Mormon forces. It was a practice so abhorrent to most nineteenth-century Americans that sophisticated constitutional arguments were not required to justify its eradication. "The traditional family was seen as the basis of civilization, and a domestic role for women was considered essential to the stability of marriage," observe two scholars of polygamy legislation. "These were the propositions which underlay the nineteenth-century hostility to modification of women's roles" (Weisbrod and Sheingorn, 830). Typical of this attitude are the views of one representative expressed during debate on the first anti-polygamy legislation: "The existence of such an institution as prevails in Utah, under the protection of the laws of the United States, is an outrage upon the moral feelings of our whole population. It is, as I conceive, an insult to our own wives and our own daughters, and the wives and daughters of our constituents" (*Congressional Globe*, 1860, 194). But the nation's leaders were not merely troubled by the Mormons' peculiar marriage practices. Washington was also troubled by Mormon society, in particular its isolation from non-Mormon America, the church's domination of Utah politics, and Mormon economic power (Arrington 1958, 356). What began as a campaign against polygamy eventually became a war against all who professed to be Mormons, a war intended to break the secular power of the Mormon church and force it into conformity with mainstream America.

For the Mormons the cost of the war against polygamy was high. Over a thousand Mormons were convicted of practicing polygamy (Arrington 1958, 359). Mormon women were jailed for refusing to testify against their husbands. Polygamous families were left fatherless, as Mormon men either went into hiding or obeyed federal law and abandoned wives and children. Federal spies tracking down polygamists disrupted Mormon communities and invaded the privacy of Mormon homes. On a larger scale, the role of the Mormon church as a guiding force in all aspects of Mormon life was destroyed. The church that Washington permitted to survive was shorn of its secular powers, and church experimentation with novel forms of social organization such as the United Order were abandoned. For better or worse, thenceforth the civil and religious powers in Utah were clearly separated, and Mormons became by and large indistinguishable from other Americans.

America also paid a price. The image of judicial impartiality was tarnished by the active role Utah's judges assumed in the war against the Mormons. In the hysteria of anti-polygamy sentiment, the Supreme Court defined the scope of constitutionally protected religious activity in a narrow and distorted fashion. Thus, in deciding whether polygamy was protected by the Constitution, America defined in general terms the extent to which religious practices could stand against the claims of the state.

Finally, there was a moral cost. Imposing conformity on a group of sincerely dedicated dissenters almost inevitably requires a level of force that debases the oppressor. In a sorry cycle, resistance breeds repression that calls forth yet more resistance and yet more savage repression. In the case of polygamy, it may be questioned whether the prize was worth the price.

THE MORRILL ACT

The practice of polygamy was officially endorsed by church leaders in 1852, although it had been practiced privately as early as the 1830s and semi-openly in Utah since the Mormons had arrived.[1] Federal officials sent to the new territory in 1851 fled that same year following conflict with Mormon leaders, and reported to Congress that the Mormons were a rebellious lot given to the open practice of polygamy (*Congressional Globe*, 1852, 89).

By 1854, polygamy came to Congress's attention when an unsuccessful attempt was made to bar polygamists from receiving grants of federal land in Utah (*Congressional Globe*, 1854, 1092). Until the federal government surveyed the land and made it available for entry, the Mormons had no title to the lands they settled and were technically squatters. Although much of Utah was surveyed by the federal government in the 1850s, Congress refused to open a land office in Utah or allow the Mormons to gain title to their lands until 1869 (Linford 1974). Despite Congress's refusal to act, the church undertook to survey lands, grant title, and settle land disputes.

The onset of the Civil War briefly shifted the focus from Utah. Congress waited until 1862 to pass legislation directly aimed at the practice the Republicans had identified as a major social issue six years earlier. In 1856 Representative Justin Morrill of Vermont had introduced legislation outlawing polygamy; six years later the bill named in his honor became law (Stat. 12:501 [1862]). The Morrill Act contained three sections. The first section provided that no person having a husband or wife living should "marry any other person, whether married or single, in a Territory of the United States." This offense was termed "bigamy" and was made punishable by fines of up to five hundred dollars and imprisonment for as much as five years. Exceptions were provided for annullments, those who had been divorced "by the decree of a competent court," and for remarriages by those whose spouses had been absent for five years and were believed dead. The second section revoked an 1855 act of the Utah Territorial Legislature incorporating the Church of Jesus Christ of Latter-day Saints. All other acts of the territorial legislature that "establish, support, maintain, shield, or countenance polygamy" were likewise annulled. Despite these provisions, the act rather hollowly provided that the right "to worship God according to the dictates of conscience" was not to be affected. The third section of the act provided that no religious or charitable organization in any territory could "acquire or hold real estate" valued at more than $50,000. Real estate acquired in excess of that limit would escheat to the United States, but property acquired prior to the act's passage was not subject to those limits.

The Morrill Act took six years to become law, not because congressmen had any sympathy for polygamy, but because polygamy had become intertwined with the issue of slavery. In the 1850s, Southern congressmen resisted any legislation that provided a precedent for federal interference with slavery in the territories, and the Republicans explicitly stated that polygamy and slavery were linked issues. Throughout the polygamy debates runs the theme that even though

polygamy is detestable, if the federal government can outlaw polygamy, it can outlaw slavery. As Representative Lawrence D. Branch
of North Carolina put it in 1860, "If we can render polygamy criminal,
it may be claimed that we can also render criminal that other 'twin
relic of barbarism,' slavery" (*Congressional Globe*, 1860, 1410). Representative Lawrence M. Keitt of South Carolina argued in the same
session that polygamy legislation would further centralize power and
undermine the federal system: "And shall we," he demanded, "under
the impulse of an honest reprobation of an offensive and hated practice in Utah, sanction this hideous usurpation of power? I never will.
If you allow Congress to declare polygamy in the Territories to be a
crime, and to punish it, where will you stop?" (*Congressional Globe*,
1860, appendix, 197).

In 1861, the Civil War removed the issues of slavery and states'
rights to the forum of last resort. Unrestrained by confusion with the
slavery issue, the Morrill Act became law in 1862.

Still, even in this first legislation, while the most flamboyant rhetoric was aimed at polygamy, Congress's target was as much the social power of the Mormon church as Mormon practices. Two of the
Morrill Act's three sections were aimed not at polygamy, but at the
church's corporate structure and economic power. This was not surprising, given Congress's distorted perception of the Mormons. The
1860 congressional debates, the only period of intensive examination,
contained a rambling indictment of all sorts of purported Mormon
practices and beliefs. Representative John A. McClernand of Illinois,
for example, described the persecution that had driven the Mormons
from Illinois in these terms:

> And what was our experience in Illinois with regard to them? It was a
> painful one, indeed, and eventuated in the exodus of the Mormons from
> the State, because they were unwilling to submit to the laws; because,
> in an attempt to trample the authority of the State underfoot, they were
> overcome. Their maxim then was, and still is, rule or ruin.
>
> The government of these Mormons is a hierarchy concentrated in one
> man, who exerts an absolute temporal and spiritual power over his fol-
> lowers. He thinks for them; and they obey him from a dread of his tem-
> poral and spiritual power. . . . The government is an artfully-contrived
> one. It combines all the incentives which can appeal to the passions of
> bad men. It concedes to the sensual many wives; to the military adven-
> turer the distinctions of military position; and to the priest abundant
> tithes and perfect impunity to the civil authority. . . . There is not now so
> absolute a hierarch living or reigning in any other quarter of the globe.
> The civil authorities kept up there by this Government are powerless—
> a mere mockery. (*Congressional Globe*, 1860, 1514)

From their mountain fortress in Utah, McClernand continued, the "Mormon banditti" preyed on and murdered innocent immigrants. He concluded from his portrait that "these Mormons should never be admitted as a distinct political community among the States" but instead be dismembered into two parts that would be attached to existing, loyal territories.

Indeed, Congress devoted little attention to balancing the rights of the Mormons against the proposed legislation, instead using lurid press accounts to dehumanize the Mormons and portray the church as little more than a bandit gang. For example, Representative Thomas A. R. Nelson of Tennessee, on the basis of a 17 March 1860 account in the *Chattanooga Gazette*, itemized alleged Mormon atrocities against immigrants, reporting that between 1850 and 1860 the Mormons had murdered 708 immigrants and plundered $1,200,000 worth of property (*Congressional Globe* 1860, appendix, 191).

Nelson then quoted a *Nashville Daily News* (25 March 1860) account of a speech given by John Cradlebaugh, an associate justice of the territorial supreme court:

> The young people are familiarized to indecent exposures of all kinds; the Mormons call their wives their cattle; they choose them pretty much as they choose their cattle; and that great pink of delicacy, Heber C. Kimball, he next in prominence, as also the next in sin, to Young calls his women his cows.
>
> Incest is common. Sometimes the same man has a daughter and her mother for wives at once.
>
> The ill-assorted children—the offspring of one father and many mothers—run about like so many wild animals. The first thing they do, after learning vulgarity, is to wear a leather belt with a butcher-knife stuck in it; and the next, is to steal from the Gentiles; then to ride animals; and as soon as they can, "by hook or by crook," get a horse, a pair of jingling Mexican spurs, and a revolver, they are then Mormon cavaliers, and are fit to steal, rob, and murder emigrants. The women and girls are coarse, masculine, and uneducated, and are mostly drafted from the lowest stages of society. (*Congressional Globe* 1860, appendix, 194)

Polygamy was thus seen as only the most vivid example of the Mormons' moral depravity. With becoming resignation, Representative John S. Millson of Virginia observed:

> I do not know that we could have looked for a different state of things in that Territory, considering the character of the people who have taken possession of it. We certainly had no right to expect from them a very high degree of morality. The disciples of Mormonism might not be pre-

sumed to display a very exemplary conduct. Not only was it not to be
expected, but perhaps it was not even to be desired, that the result
should have been different. It was fit, and it was fortunate that so low
and degrading an imposture should reveal itself in its devilish fruits.
(*Congressional Globe* 1860, 1492)

Congressional qualms with the Morrill Act focused on whether the
mild action of banning polygamy and outlawing the Mormon church
would suffice, or whether Utah Territory should be dissolved and
either dismembered or ruled by a commission directly responsible
to Congress, as was the District of Columbia. Representative Lawrence O. Branch of North Carolina outlined the choices this way:

> There are two modes, sir, in which we can reach this practice. . . . One
> mode is by a total repeal of the territorial government of Utah. In case
> we adopt that course, two courses would still be open to us in carrying
> out that policy. We could either attach Utah to the adjacent Territories, or
> we could put the people of Utah under the general laws that have been
> passed for the government of our citizens occupying the unorganized
> territory of the Union. (*Congressional Globe*, 1410)

The claim that Congress could not act against polygamy because
it was a constitutionally protected religious practice was swiftly disposed of by two arguments. Representative Roger A. Pryor of Virginia
simply denied that polygamy had any connection to religious practices:

> It is not true that polygamy pretends to any religious sanction. It is not
> true that the Mormons practice it as a pious observance.
>   I have looked through the Mormon Bible—a disgusting farrago of
> nonsense and blasphemy, written in ribald parody of the more obvious
> characteristics of Scripture phraseology—I have examined this only dog-
> matic exposition of the Mormon faith, and nowhere do I find a word of
> recognition of the practice of polygamy. (*Congressional Globe* 1860, 1496)

Moreover, the Mormons were presented to Congress as murderous
degenerates. As Representative Nelson of Tennessee and others argued, to allow them to cloak their conduct in the Constitution would
permit a sham to shield conduct beyond the pale of civilized behavior. Similarly, Pryor argued that the Mormons' assertion of religious
freedom, "if sound in principle, will avail to cover any abomination
which affects a religious character. It will suffice for the protection of
Thugism or Suttee, as well as polygamy. Plainly, then, it is an unsound
argument and a pernicious philosophy which conduces to such absurd and mischievous consequences" (*Congressional Globe* 1860, 1496).
    Second, the free exercise argument was avoided by simply terming

the act a regulation of marital relations. The free exercise issue vanished as it was clear that regulating marriage was well within the traditional powers of government. In response to the argument that the law should not interfere with intimate domestic relations, Representative John S. Millson of Virginia replied: "The law everywhere interferes with them. Marriage has always been a subject of regulation by the State" (*Congressional Globe* 1860, 1499).

Fewer qualms were raised by the provision disincorporating the Mormon church. Representatives reasoned that such a provision did not violate the First Amendment but in actuality obeyed its mandate that Congress make no law effecting an establishment of religion. Representative Nelson advanced the truly remarkable argument that "if under the Constitution of the United States it is not competent for Congress to pass any law respecting the establishment of religion, Congress has no power to delegate such authority as that to the Territory of Utah" (*Congressional Globe* 1860, appendix, 190–91). In incorporating the Mormon church, the Utah territorial legislature acted under an 1850 grant of authority from Congress (Stat. 9:453). If the church's incorporation was a law effecting an establishment of religion, then Congress was constitutionally required to nullify that action.

Amid an apparent hysteria only a few cautions were raised. None defended polygamy; but a few representatives warned that the attempt to proscribe Mormonism would likely be a bloody failure. Representative Lawrence M. Keitt of South Carolina, perhaps subtly alluding to slavery, suggested:

It is embedded in their social and religious structure, and you can only tear it up by upheaving that structure and scattering it to the winds. Are you prepared to start the Government upon this crusade against manners and morals? Are you willing to clothe it with power to ravage the Territories, to substitute the sword for trial by jury, and to carry out, by flame and violence, an indictment against a whole community? If these people are the crazy fanatics you charge them to be; if they are the religious zealots we are told they are, then your war is against opinion, and nothing but extermination will close it. (*Congressional Globe* 1860, appendix, 198)

Utah's congressional representative, William H. Hooper, a devout Mormon, had informed the House, almost surely erroneously, that as many as one-half of Mormon families were polygamous (*Congressional Globe* 1860, 1558).[2] Thus, in adopting the Morrill Act, Congress believed itself to be striking directly at half the population of Utah territory. As Representative Lucius Q. C. Lamar of Mississippi cautioned,

polygamy had, "taken root in the life of the people there. It constitutes a part of their social polity, and this [act] is very little less than
a proposition to declare an entire community guilty of a felony" (*Con-
(gressional Globe* 1860, 1501). Others counseled that the true victims of
polygamy legislation would not be the presumptively lustful Mormon
men, but innocent Mormon women and children (*Congressional Globe*
1860, 1516). Although an advocate of the Morrill Act, Representative
Daniel W. Gooch of Massachusetts noted that the real solution to polygamy was time, time in which to allow the practice to fall from its
own weight:

> I believe that the day will come when there will begin to spring up in that
> community itself, among those who have not indulged in polygamy, and
> among those who may come in, and among those who may surround
> them, a healthy reactionary influence; and I do not believe it is going to
> require a very great amount of external power to enforce the law within
> that community. (*Congressional Globe* 1860, 1542)[3]

Most representatives were unconcerned by warnings about the possible dire consequences of attempting to exterminate plural marriage.
Remarkably, however, despite all the violent rhetoric against the Mormons and polygamy, most representatives expected the Morrill Act to
be an empty gesture, a dead letter. Mormon control over Utah's government was a repeated theme in the congressional debate. In implementing the Morrill Act, representatives were not slow to point out,
Congress was adopting an anti-polygamy law to be administered by
a territorial government presumably packed with polygamists. Representative McClernand of Illinois observed:

> This is the whole extent of the remedy proposed by the committee's
> bill—a bill which assumes and relies upon the Mormons—polygamists
> themselves, to execute its provisions. Does not everyone know that the
> Mormons will not enforce such a law against themselves? That a grand
> jury of polygamists will not indict a polygamist? and that a petty jury
> of polygamists will not convict a brother polygamist. (*Congressional Globe*
> 1860, 1514; see also 1520 and appendix, 187)

The act's proponents could only respond weakly that even if the act
were not enforced, "we shall have acquitted ourselves of our duty. We
shall have wiped away a reproach from the national reputation. We
shall have put upon the statute-book our condemnation of this crime"
(*Congressional Globe* 1860, 1494).

In fact, from its passage in 1862 until the *Reynolds* case some twelve
years later, the Morrill Act was not enforced.

EARLY PROSECUTIONS

Even before Congress passed the Morrill Act, Chief Justice Delena R. Eckles, sitting as a district court judge in 1858 at Camp Scott, near present-day Fort Bridger, Wyoming, urged a grand jury to begin returning indictments for polygamy. He reasoned that the Utah Territory had been acquired from Mexico and Mexican law remained in force unless displaced by territorial law. Under Mexican law, polygamy was a crime; therefore it continued to be a crime in Utah Territory. Even thirty years later, the Utah Supreme Court adopted this view: "Polygamy has been and is now prohibited by the law of Mexico, so that even before this territory was ceded to the United States, the practice was unlawful here, under the laws of our sister republic" (*United States v. Snow*, Utah 4:313; P. 9:697, 699). Chief Justice Eckles back in 1858 was not content to rely totally on Mexican law, however. He noted that polygamy also could be prosecuted under an existing territorial statute banning adultery (CHC 4:357–58). The judge apparently neglected to note that, under Utah law, only the offended spouse could initiate proceedings (Utah Laws 1851:122, § 32). No indictments were returned, however, and the first polygamy trial was not held until 1871.

By 1871, Utah had a tough new federal judge, James B. McKean, rabidly anti-Mormon and determined to enforce the national policy against polygamy despite all opposition. The first Mormon indicted for polygamy was one Thomas Hawkins. However, Hawkins was not convicted of polygamy. Rather, he was convicted under the 1851 Utah statute of having adulterous relations with his polygamous wife, fined $500, and sentenced to three years at hard labor (Linford 1964, 330). The charges were properly brought by Hawkins's lawful wife, who was apparently unhappy at his having taken a plural wife, and her cooperation may explain why officials proceeded against Hawkins via Utah's adultery law rather than through the Morrill Act's bigamy provisions.

Indictments immediately followed against a number of leading church officials: Brigham Young; Daniel Wells, mayor of Salt Lake City and President Young's second counselor; George Q. Cannon, editor of the *Deseret News*; and Henry W. Lawrence, a leader of the Godbeite movement. These indictments were not brought under the Morrill Act either, but under a Utah statute forbidding lewd and lascivious cohabitation.

It is not completely clear why officials chose to employ this Utah statute, obviously never intended to apply to polygamous relations, rather than the Morrill Act, which had been enacted for just such situations. B. H. Roberts speculates that the prosecution chose to proceed under Utah law to avoid the difficulty of establishing both the legal and polygamous marriages of each defendant and to take advantage of the harsher penalties available under Utah law (CHC 5:394). This assessment seems reasonable, for later cases demonstrated that proving a secret Mormon marriage could be difficult, and the extent to which a defendant's wives would be permitted or could be forced to testify against him continued to trouble courts for several years.

But if the government's choice of offenses seems curious, its choice of defendants was predictable. By indicting the church's leading figures, the government sought to set a vivid example, to cow the rank and file, and to paralyze the church's leadership. Judge McKean remarked during the proceedings against Brigham Young:

> It is . . . proper to say that while the case at bar is called *The People versus Brigham Young,* its other and real title is *Federal Authority versus Polygamic Theocracy.* . . . The one government arrests the other in the person of its chief, and arraigns it at his bar. *A system is on trial in the person of Brigham Young.* Let all concerned keep this fact steadily in view; and let that government rule without a rival which shall prove to be in the right. (*Deseret News,* 18 Oct. 1871)

Young's trial was thus a showpiece designed to crush simultaneously the practice of polygamy and the power of the church.

McKean's plan failed, however, for the juries that had indicted Hawkins, Young, and the others had been improperly empaneled. In the 1872 case of *Clinton v. Englebrecht* (US 80:434), the United States Supreme Court ruled that, in his efforts to purge juries of Mormons and secure the conviction of polygamists, Judge McKean had improperly ignored Utah's jury selection procedures. As a result of the decision in *Englebrecht,* Hawkins's conviction for adultery was overturned, and the indictments against Young and the others were dismissed (Linford 1964, 331). The prosecution of polygamy was thus halted until the first *Reynolds* case, in 1874.

Given the intense public outcry over polygamy that had begun in the mid-1850s, it is only natural to wonder why the federal government waited twelve years before it brought the first prosecutions under the federal anti-polygamy statutes. Several reasons explain why the Mormons were left in relative peace for so long a time.

Perhaps most significantly, when polygamy became an issue, the nation's energies were distracted by more pressing problems: the Civil War and Reconstruction. The fight for national survival forced the

Mormon problem to wait. Having signed the Morrill Act, Abraham Lincoln reportedly compared the Mormon church to a log he had encountered as a farmer that was "too hard to split, too wet to burn and too heavy to move, so we plowed around it. That's what I intend to do with the Mormons. You go back and tell Brigham Young that if he will let me alone, I will let him alone" (Larson 1971, 60 n. 61). Lincoln's anecdote displayed sound political sense. In 1857, when federal troops had been sent to Utah to quell an imaginary rebellion, the Mormons had displayed a grim readiness to resist by abandoning their homes, withdrawing to more isolated areas, and even fighting back (Arrington 1958, 170–88). Facing a total commitment of national resources to fight the Civil War, Lincoln could ill afford conflict with Utah's large Mormon population, a group sitting astride the East's lines of communications with California. Mormon leaders during the Civil War occasionally sent reminders to Washington that separation from the Union was a possibility for Utah, just as it was for the South, should federal policies become too oppressive. For example, Heber C. Kimball of the church's First Presidency in 1861 stated:

> We shall never secede from the Constitution of the United States. We shall not stop on the way of progress, but we shall make preparations for future events. The South will secede from the North, and the North will secede from us, and God will make this people free as fast as we are able to bear it. . . . The day is not far distant when you will see us as free as the air we breathe. (JD 9:7)

Possibly as a result, General Patrick Edward Connor, the commander of federal forces in Utah, was instructed to avoid a Mormon war: "Under the circumstances, it is the course of true patriotism for you not to embark on any hostilities. It is infinitely better that you should avoid contact with them" (Dwyer, 27).

Another important factor was the weakness of federal authority over the Mormons. The handful of federal officials in Utah during the 1860s felt powerless, lost in a hostile sea of Mormons whose way of life they were challenging. Those officials did not believe they could enforce compliance with the polygamy act. In 1862, Governor Stephen S. Harding, formerly of Indiana, chastized the Utah territorial legislature for public hostility to the new anti-polygamy legislation, noting that "it is recommended by those in high authority that no regard whatever should be paid to the same" (Dwyer, 9).

Nor were the attitudes of the federal officials pure paranoia. In 1863 the mere rumor that Brigham Young was about to be arrested for polygamy brought two thousand armed Mormons to his home to resist that arrest. Conflict was avoided by lodging a friendly complaint against Young, which was later dismissed when tempers had cooled (CHC 5:28–29). Federal officials were also troubled by the shadow government Mormon leaders maintained behind the official territorial government. Governor James Doty reported to the Secretary of State in 1865 that

> the leaders of "the church" under the Territorial laws, have the appointment, and control in fact through its members, of all the civil and militia officers not appointed by the President of the United States. In addition, the same party, in 1861 formed an independent government in the "State of Deseret" whose boundaries include Utah and portions of Idaho and Arizona. This form of government is preserved by annual elections of all the state officers; the legislature being composed of the same men who are elected to the Territorial legislature, and who, in a Resolution, re-enact the same laws for the "State" which have been enacted for the Territory of Utah. (Larson 1971, 31)

Because many officers of this "ghost-state" were also members of the territorial legislature, "the decisions they made as a 'ghost' government of Deseret became law when they met as the official legislature. It was just such unusual political activity that continued to arouse suspicions in Washington" (Allen and Leonard, 312).

Federal control over the territorial government, then, was undeniably feeble. The governor, supreme court justices, and a few other officials were appointed by the president, but the territorial legislature and the bulk of the judiciary lay in Mormon hands. In 1851, officials sent by Washington almost immediately clashed with the entrenched Mormon leadership and fled back to Washington complaining, "We found upon our arrival that almost the entire population consisted of a people called Mormons; and the Mormon Church overshadowing and controlling the opinions, the actions, the property, and even the lives of its members, usurping and exercising the functions of legislation and the judicial business of the Territory" (*Report to the President*, 1852).

To fill this void, the territorial legislature expanded the powers of the territorial judiciary. Utah's probate courts, typically empowered to hear only matters related to wills, guardianships, and divorces, were granted general jurisdiction over all civil and criminal cases (Utah Laws 1851:43, § 30); a territorial marshal and attorney were established with powers paralleling those of their federal counterparts (Utah Laws 1851:56, §§ 1–3); and the drawing of jury lists was placed in the hands of the probate judges. In short, the Mormon-controlled legislature had created a rival, Mormon-controlled judicial system, with powers concurrent with the federal judiciary. Naturally, it was viewed as an effective instrument for frustrating the enforcement of the federal polygamy laws. Indeed, a vital step in the federal campaign against polygamy was the 1874 Poland Act's dismembering of the territorial judicial system.

In 1870 tough new federal officials were sent to Utah to try to bring the Mormons in line with federal authority. President Ulysses S. Grant expressed hope in his 1871 address to Congress: "In Utah there still remains a remnant of barbarism, repugnant to civilization, to decency, and to the laws of the United States. Territorial officers, however, have been found who are willing to perform their duty in a spirit of equity and with a due sense of the necessity of sustaining the majesty of the law" (Richardson, 7:151). But Grant's optimism was unwarranted, and the congressional prophecies that the Morrill Act would not be enforced so long as the Mormons retained power over Utah's judiciary remained correct. In fact, within a month of his arrival in the territory in 1870, the new governor, J. Wilson Shaffer, wrote to Congressman Shelby M. Cullom, pleading with Congress for additional powers:

> As affairs now stand the oath which I have taken to execute the laws is nothing more than a useless form, a mockery, a farce, for without the enactment by Congress of a statute containing the main features of the bill which you have introduced on the subject of Utah, I am rendered almost powerless, and the laws for ought that I or other officers of the government can do to prevent it may continue to be violated with impunity, and the federal authority openly defied and ridiculed. It is hard to be nominally governor of Utah. (Larson 1971, 73)

The new chief justice was James B. McKean, a New York lawyer long associated with Republican opposition to polygamy. For McKean, appointment to Utah's judiciary was a summons to a divinely appointed mission: "The mission which God has called upon me to perform in Utah, is as much above the duties of other courts and judges as the heavens are above the earth, and whenever or wherever I may find the Local or Federal laws obstructing or interfering therewith, by God's blessing I shall trample them under my feet" (Tullidge, 420–21). McKean and his associates acted vigorously against the Mormons, refusing to honor acts of the territorial judicial officers. Indeed, by the early 1870s conflict between the federal and territorial judicial systems was close to an impasse.

The 1850 Organic Act, making Utah a territory, had provided "that the legislative power of said Territory shall extend to all rightful sub-

jects of legislation, consistent with the Constitution of the United
States and the provisions of this act" (Stat. 9:454 [1850]). The Organic Act also made skeletal provision for Utah's judiciary but left
it to the legislature to furnish the details. The act provided for four
classes of courts. The justices of the Utah Supreme Court, all federal
appointees, also sat as territorial district court judges (Stat. 9:455).
Territorial district courts had the same jurisdiction as federal district
courts. Justices of the peace had jurisdiction limited to disputes under
$100, and finally the act provided for the creation of probate courts.
Because of these provisions, when the Mormon-controlled territorial
legislature moved to create a court system that was not dominated by
the federal government, only the probate courts were available. The
Organic Act restricted the jurisdiction of justices of the peace to minor
disputes, and the district and supreme courts were in federal hands.[4]
Thus, in 1852 the territorial legislature had granted probate courts
jurisdiction over most civil and criminal cases (Utah Laws 1851:43,
§ 30).

The problem was that probate courts were traditionally courts of
limited jurisdiction, restricted to the disposition of guardianships,
wardships, estates, and trusts. It was this deviation from the traditional role that provided a point of attack for the Utah Supreme Court
in *Cast v. Cast* (Utah 1:112 [1873]).

Cast was a divorce case, instituted in the territorial probate court
and taken to the Utah Supreme Court on appeal on the ground that
the probate court lacked jurisdiction to enter divorce decrees. Because
Congress provided in Utah's Organic Act for four types of courts,
the supreme court reasoned, Congress must have assumed that jurisdiction among these courts would "be distributed in a manner usual
to like courts in the States. If a jumbling of jurisdictions was to be
allowed, the division of the judicial power was wholly unnecessary"
(Utah 1:117). While the territorial legislature possessed broad powers
to adopt laws consistent with the Organic Act, the supreme court
held that the term "probate court" referred only to a court of limited jurisdiction, and any attempt to broaden the powers of probate
courts would be therefore inconsistent with the Organic Act. Thus,
probate courts were denied their general jurisdiction, leaving the federally controlled district courts the only remaining ones of general
jurisdiction in the territory.

The Utah Supreme Court's construction of Utah's Organic Act in
Cast was upheld by the United States Supreme Court in the 1874
case of *Ferris v. Higley* (US 87:375). The case arose when Higley sued
Ferris in Utah's probate court on a promissory note for $1,000 and

obtained a judgment. Higley took the case to the district court, which reversed on the ground that the probate court had no jurisdiction over such matters, a ruling affirmed by the territorial supreme court. Ferris appealed to the United States Supreme Court, which noted that Utah's Organic Act granted the territorial legislature the power to define the jurisdiction of probate courts only as provided by law. The Court reasoned that the "law" that restrained the actions of the territorial legislature was not merely the Constitution or the acts of Congress, but also the "general history of our jurisprudence" (US 87:383–84). Of course, the court found that the "general history of our jurisprudence" demonstrated that probate courts had generally been courts of limited jurisdiction. The Court conceded that "there may be cases when the legislature conferring new rights, or new remedies, or establishing anomalous rules of proceedings within their legislative power, may direct in what court they shall be had" (US 87:383). But the wholesale transfer of general jurisdiction to Utah's probate courts did not fall within this exception. Probate courts, by tradition, did not possess the procedural devices recognized as central to general judicial tasks: "Such courts are not in their mode of proceeding governed by the rules of the common law. They are without juries and have no special system of pleading" (US 87:382). Also, there was no appeal from the probate courts to a higher court.

The Supreme Court's analysis in *Ferris v. Higley* makes sense. It was a reasonable exercise in judicial construction for the Court to conclude that in providing for probate courts, as well as district courts of more general jurisdiction, Congress meant the usual sort of probate courts. The reasons of judicial efficiency advanced by the Court as a basis for not permitting Utah's legislature to upset Congress's intent, similarly make sense. The Supreme Court, however, was not oblivious to events in Utah and knew very well what stakes were involved in the case before it. The Court strongly intimated that it was aware that a decision restricting the jurisdiction of Utah's probate courts would also inhibit the ability of the Mormons to resist enforcement of the polygamy laws:

> The fact that the judges of . . . [Utah's district courts] are appointed by the Federal power, paid by that power—that other officers of these courts are appointed and paid in like manner—strongly repels the idea that Congress, in conferring on these courts all the powers of courts of general jurisdiction, both civil and criminal, intended to leave to the Territorial legislature the power to practically evade or obstruct the exercise of those powers by conferring precisely the same jurisdiction on courts created and appointed by the Territory. (US 87:384)

The second major battlefield in this war between federal judges and territorial officials was control of jury selection procedures. The federal judges struck at what they perceived as an important source of the church's power—pro-Mormon juries—by attacking a territorial statute that empowered the territorial marshal to summon jurors. The judges tried to deny authority to the marshal and attorney by holding that those roles were completely preempted by federally appointed officials. In a case not involving jury selection, *Snow v. United States* (US 85:317 [1873]), the Supreme Court nullified those attempts.

The *Snow* case was initiated by Charles Hempstead, the United States attorney for Utah, to receive a judicial determination whether he or Zerubbabel Snow—the territory's attorney general, elected by the legislature—was entitled to prosecute offenders of territorial law. In concluding that Snow had properly been empowered by the territorial legislature to prosecute those accused of offenses against territorial laws, the Court offered a fascinating theory of the nature of Utah's judiciary. The Court concluded that Utah's Organic Act provided for the territorial supreme and district courts to act as circuit and district courts of the United States when handling cases arising under the Constitution and laws of the United States. At all other times, they were ordinary territorial courts. The two roles were distinct; and because they were distinct, it appeared reasonable that territorially appointed officers should serve the courts when they sat as territorial courts.

The court's novel account of Utah's judiciary is inconsistent. It conflicts with the Court's own account of Utah's judiciary two years earlier in *Clinton v. Englebrecht* (US 80:434), where the Court had clearly rejected the proposition that Utah's district courts sat as United States district courts under the Organic Act. While United States courts derived their powers from Article III of the Constitution, the territorial courts exercised power pursuant to Congress's power to regulate the territories. Furthermore, as the Court recognized in *Snow*,

> strictly speaking, there is no sovereignty in a Territory of the United States but that of the United States itself. Crimes committed therein are committed against the government and dignity of the United States. It would seem that indictments and writs should regularly be in the name of the United States, and that the attorney of the United States was the proper officer to prosecute all offenses. (US 85:321)

Despite this anomaly, the fact that other territories had regularly appointed territorial attorneys persuaded the Court that Congress had either intended or acquiesced in this theoretically unsatisfactory but practical arrangement.

Snow was a victory for the Mormons, but its usefulness was limited. Because it dealt only with the powers of the territorial attorney general, it left intact an earlier, unreported Utah decision, *Orr v. McAllister*, which had ruled that territorial marshals were powerless to summon jurors (Linford 1964, 331 and n. 108; CHC 5:386 and n. 7). Judge McKean explained the consequences of this decision in a letter to President U. S. Grant on 13 February 1871:

> For near twenty years the Mormon leaders packed the Grand and Petit juries of the United States Courts with their tools and instruments. But within a few months past we have decided against this system . . . to recognize only the U.S. Attorney and the U.S. Marshal as the proper officers of our courts. One of the consequences is that we have already indicted *for capital offenses* ten or twelve Mormons—some of them bishops and other influential men in the Mormon establishment. (Dwyer, 76)

However, the practice of relying on the United States marshal to summon jurors came to grief in the 1872 case of *Clinton v. Englebrecht* (US 80:434).

In *Englebrecht*, Judge McKean, sitting as a territorial district judge, "wholly and purposely disregarded" a territorial statute directing the territorial marshal to summon jurors and instead used the United States marshal for that task. On appeal, the United States Supreme Court unanimously held that McKean's use of federal jury selection procedures was improper. As territorial courts, the district courts were bound by territorial statutes on such matters, and under Utah's Organic Act jury selection procedures were a subject properly delegated to the territorial legislature. The Court defined the powers granted to Utah in generous terms: "The theory upon which the various governments for portions of the territory of the United States have been organized, has ever been that of leaving to the inhabitants all the powers of self-government consistent with the supremacy and supervision of national authority, and with certain fundamental principles established by Congress" (US 80:441). Because the Constitution and Organic Act were silent on the issue of jury selection, the subject was left to the territorial legislature. The Court noted that Congress must have been aware of the territorial act, could have disapproved it, and yet failed to do so. Because of Congress's inaction, Utah's jury law thus "received the implied sanction of Congress" (US 80:446).[5]

The fallout from the *Englebrecht* decision was dramatic. In Utah about 130 persons who had been indicted by improperly selected juries were released and the indictments quashed (Linford 1964, 331–416). Among the cases upset were the prosecution of Brigham Young and other church leaders for "lascivious cohabitation" (CHC 5:415–

16). An elated editorial in the Mormon-owned *Deseret News*, 24 April 1872, called the decision "a very important one, . . . a virtual declaration by the highest authority in the land that no portion of the people of the United States—however abhorrent their religious faith—can be deprived of their liberties except by due process of law." George L. Woods, Utah's anti-Mormon governor, by contrast, provided President Grant with a bleak picture of affairs in Utah as a result of the decision:

> The news of the decision of the U.S. Supreme Court in the Englebrecht case strikes consternation into the ranks of the Gentiles in Utah. Under the law as laid down by the Supreme Court, a Mormon Marshall [*sic*] will summon a Mormon jury to try Mormon criminals, each, and all, of whom regard their duty to the Church as above all law. The Marshall and Attorney General are both polygamists, and the former is a criminal. . . . Henceforth, . . . law will be a farce and the officers of the government mere ninnies. . . . Their triumph in the Supreme Court makes the Mormons very jubilant, arrogant, insolent, and they feel, now, that all power is in their hands. . . . There are more than twenty murderers in Salt Lake City alone, who committed some as dark and diabolical crimes as darken the annals of human depravity, who are to be turned loose upon the community. (Dwyer, 86)

After the Supreme Court ruled that United States marshals could not summon jurors and the Utah courts had ruled that territorial marshals could not summon them, no juries were summoned. Utah's judicial system was effectively paralyzed. By the end of 1873, President Grant's optimism regarding a swift resolution of the Mormon problem appears to have vanished. In his annual message to Congress, he reported that "all proceedings at law are practically abolished by these decisions, and there have been but few or no jury trials in the district courts of that Territory since the last session of Congress. . . . To prevent anarchy there it is absolutely necessary that Congress provide the courts with some mode of obtaining jurors" (Richardson, 7:250).

Moreover, when the federal district courts tried cases arising under territorial laws, their expenses were to be paid by the territorial legislature, and almost all criminal cases arose under territorial law. When the federal judges refused to acknowledge the powers of territorial officers, the territorial legislature responded by refusing to appropriate funds for the operation of the federal courts. Washington left the federal courts destitute by refusing to pick up those expenses. Judge McKean complained to President Grant that "the Mormon Territorial Legislature will not appropriate any more funds to pay the expenses of our Courts, nor will the Territorial officials pay for Court expenses such funds as are now on hand. Even our jurors are remaining unpaid; though the Marshal has advanced from his own funds considerable sums for other unavoidable expenses" (Dwyer, 76).

McKean and others had forecast precisely the steps Congress would have to take when it became serious about curbing the power of the Mormon church and eliminating polygamy. Because a judicial system controlled by Mormons would not enforce the polygamy law, Mormon control of the judicial process in Utah would have to cease.

Representative Shelby M. Cullom had proposed a legislative solution to the problem in 1870. The Cullom Bill would have allowed the governor to appoint all local judges, notaries, and sheriffs; made federal appointees responsible for jury selection; denied the probate courts' jurisdiction in criminal cases; set fines and penalties for both polygamy and cohabitation; abolished statutes of limitation for those offenses; excluded from jury service in polygamy and cohabitation trials those who even believed in plural marriage and allowed wives to testify against their husbands in such cases; barred polygamists from voting, holding public office, and becoming naturalized citizens; and authorized the president to use military force if necessary to enforce the provisions of the act. The bill passed the House of Representatives on 23 March 1870 but was never voted on in the Senate, where the prevailing view was that the newly completed transcontinental railroad would bring "civilizing elements" to Utah that would eventually cause the Mormons to abandon polygamy (Larson 1978a, 250–51).

Such patience, however, was short-lived. In his message to Congress in 1873, President Grant called on that body to curb the powers of the Mormon-controlled judiciary. He asked Congress to nullify, in effect, the territorial statutes that had led to the conflict, concluding that such drastic measures were necessary

in order to prevent the miscarriage of justice and to maintain the supremacy of the laws of the United States and of the Federal Government, to provide that the selection of grand and petit jurors for the district courts, if not put under the control of Federal officers, shall be placed in the hands of persons entirely independent of those who are determined not to enforce any act of Congress obnoxious to them, and also to pass some act which shall deprive the probate courts, or any court created by the Territorial legislature, of any power to interfere with or impede the action of the courts held by the United States judges.

I am convinced that so long as Congress leaves the selection of jurors to the local authorities it will be futile to make any effort to enforce laws not acceptable to a majority of the people of the Territory, or which interfere with local prejudices or provide for the punishment of polygamy or any of its affiliated vices or crimes.

> I am advised that United States courts in Utah have been greatly em-
> barrassed by the action of the Territorial legislature in conferring criminal
> jurisdiction and the power to issue writs of *habeas corpus* on the probate
> courts in the Territory, and by their consequent interference with the
> administration of justice. Manifestly the legislature of the Territory can
> not give to any court whatever the power to discharge by *habeas corpus*
> persons held by or under process from the courts created by Congress,
> but complaint is made that persons so held have been discharged in that
> way by the probate courts. (Richardson, 7:209–10)[6]

Congress wasted little time in acting on Grant's recommendations.
The result was the Poland Act of 1874.

The Poland Act

The 1874 Poland Act (Stat. 18:253) resolved the rivalry between territorial and federal judicial officers by placing the judiciary firmly in federal hands. It validated previous probate court decrees but restricted
probate courts to "jurisdiction in the settlement of the estates of decedents, and in matters of guardianship and other like matters; but
otherwise they shall have no civil, chancery, or criminal jurisdiction
whatever." By contrast, district courts were given exclusive original
jurisdiction of all suits over $300. The United States marshal was em-
powered to serve all process for the district and supreme courts, and
the United States attorney was empowered as prosecuting attorney
for all criminal offenses in all courts. Counties, however, were authorized to select county attorneys to initiate prosecutions in lower courts
and to assist the United States attorney in district court prosecutions.

New procedures for the selection of jurors were adopted. Each year
the clerk of the district court and the probate court judge in each
county were to meet and prepare a jury list of 200 names, the officers
drawing alternate names. Jurors were to be drawn from that list and
summoned by the United States marshal, and the territorial act creating territorial marshals and attorneys was disapproved. Finally, the
act provided that cases of polygamy or bigamy could be appealed to
the United States Supreme Court from the Utah Supreme Court by
writ of error. Formerly, such cases could be reviewed by the Supreme
Court only where the lower court had held invalid a federal law or upheld the validity of a local law in the face of a constitutional challenge
(Stat. 1:73, 85 [1789]). By granting a writ of error, the Supreme Court
could review *any* error of law asserted to have been made by the trial
court, regardless of whether the decision had upheld or struck down
the statute in question.

The Poland Act nullified earlier Supreme Court decisions favorable to the Mormons. It nullified *Englebrecht* by creating a new jury selection process aimed at limiting Mormon control, and it nullified *Snow* by divesting the territorial attorney and marshal of most of their powers. It also reinforced the holding in *Ferris v. Higley* by restricting probate court jurisdiction to traditional probate matters such as estates, wills, and guardianships.

Enforcement of the Morrill Act

Although the Poland Act struck at the heart of Mormon resistance to the Morrill Act, it did not result in a spate of polygamy prosecutions. This delay in enforcement of the Morrill Act was due in part to defects in the act itself. It required proof of multiple marriages, and the problems posed in proving that a marriage had in fact taken place were almost insuperable.

Until 1887, marriage records were not kept in Utah or in many other western territories. Congress did not require marriage registration until the Edmunds-Tucker Act of 1887 (Stat. 24:636, § 9). Mormon weddings were often performed in temples or the Endowment House, which were open only to faithful Mormons[7]; so witnesses were scarce, and what witnesses there were often preferred to face contempt charges rather than reveal information related to temple ordinances (Davis 1962, 10). As the United States Supreme Court noted: "Polygamous marriages are so celebrated in Utah as to make the proof of polygamy very difficult. They are conducted in secret, and the persons by whom they are solemnized are under such obligations of secrecy that it is almost impossible to extract the facts from them when placed on the witness stand" (*United States v. Miles*, US 103:304 [1880]). Moreover, under Utah law, a wife could not testify against her husband.

These evidentiary problems are perhaps best illustrated by the case of *United States v. Miles*, the only Morrill Act case besides *Reynolds* to ever reach the United States Supreme Court. John Miles had apparently married three women, Emily, Caroline (also known as Carrie), and Julia, on the same day, 24 October 1874. He was charged with bigamy under the Morrill Act. It was thus necessary to prove the fact of his marriage to the three women, and therein lay the difficulty. As the Supreme Court noted: "Marriages of persons belonging to the Mormon Church usually take place at what is called the Endowment House; . . . the ceremony is performed in secret, and the person who officiates is under a sacred obligation not to disclose the names of the parties to it" (US 103:307). Miles's wife Caroline, however, was willing to testify against him. Apparently Caroline had consented to enter plural marriage only if Miles married her first. Church authorities, however, directed Miles to marry Emily, the eldest woman, first. When Caroline discovered, after the wedding, that Miles had already married one of the women, she angrily went to a United States marshal with her story (Linford 1964, 342).

Miles conceded his marriage to Caroline but denied his marriage to Emily. Because Daniel H. Wells, the presiding official, refused to testify, Caroline's testimony was essential to the state's case. At this point, the federal judges faced a conundrum. If Caroline was Miles's lawful wife, under the common law rule, her testimony was inadmissible. But her testimony helped establish that at the time Miles married her, he already had a lawful wife. And if Miles had a wife when he married Caroline, his marriage to her was invalid, she was not his wife, and therefore she was a competent witness.

The trial court resolved this perplexing question by throwing the whole matter to the jury. Caroline was allowed to testify that she had seen Miles's alleged first wife, Emily, at the Endowment House on her wedding day in wedding attire, that Emily had been at her wedding supper that night, and that Miles had referred to her as his wife (US 103:307–8). At the end of the trial, the jury was instructed that if they found that Miles was already married at the time he married Caroline, they could then consider Caroline's testimony in determining whether Miles was guilty of bigamy.

The instruction was, of course, useless because it was tautological. In effect, the jury was told that they could use Caroline's testimony to determine whether Miles was guilty of bigamy. In determining whether Caroline's testimony was admissible, the jury necessarily had to determine the issue of his guilt.

The trial court's ingenious labor-saving device was not, however, acceptable to the United States Supreme Court. On appeal, the Court ruled that "As long as the fact of the first marriage is contested, the second wife cannot be admitted to prove it" (US 103:315). The principle behind this ruling was the old rule that a witness that is "*prima facie* incompetent" cannot at the same time give evidence "to establish his competency, and prove the issue" (US 103:314).

Two escapes from this predicament were, however, recommended by the Court. First, eyewitnesses to a marriage were not necessary, for polygamous marriages could be proven like any other fact, by admissions of the defendant or by circumstantial evidence. Second, if existing laws made it too difficult to prove polygamy, "the remedy is with Congress, by enacting such a change in the law of evidence in the Territory of Utah as to make both wives witnesses on indictments for bigamy" (US 103:311, 315–16).

The final obstacle to effective enforcement of the Morrill Act was its three-year statute of limitations. Polygamists who eluded prosecution for the requisite three years were thereafter free from peril. The Mormons quickly discovered how to use this limitations period to their advantage. They allegedly began sending polygamists out of the country on three-year missions immediately after their polygamous marriages (Dwyer, 240 n. 71).

In short, even after the *Reynolds* decision upheld the Morrill Act, the first anti-polygamy statute remained, as one scholar of polygamy litigation concluded, "constitutionally pure, but practically worthless" (Davis 1962, 9–10). A combination of national events, stubborn Mormon resistance, and unwieldy federal laws allowed the Mormons to resist enforcement of the Morrill Act for over twenty years. In the mid-1870s, the *Reynolds* case signaled the end of the respite.

REYNOLDS v. UNITED STATES: A JUDICIAL TEST OF POLYGAMY LEGISLATION

George Reynolds was an English immigrant, private secretary to Brigham Young, and a polygamist (Davis 1973, 288). In October 1874, he was indicted for bigamy under the Morrill Act (CHC 5:469).

Church historians maintain that *Reynolds* began as a test case in which both the federal judiciary and the church presidency hoped to determine the constitutionality of the anti-polygamy statute. At the request of George Q. Cannon, Reynolds agreed to test the statute and cooperate in his prosecution in return for the government's agreement not to seek a harsh punishment (Whitney, 3:46–47; CHC 5:469). Non-Mormon historians assert that no deal was ever struck (Dwyer, 112–13). There is some support for the agreement hypothesis: Mormon witnesses, including Reynolds's second wife, Amelia Jane Schofield, who testified at the first trial refused to appear for the second. If there was an agreement, Mormons apparently believed the government had broken it by the time of the second trial.

Reynolds was convicted on the testimony of his polygamous wife, but the case swiftly became caught in the procedural snarls commonplace in Utah's judicial system. On appeal to the Utah Supreme Court (*United States v. Reynolds*, Utah 1:226 [1875]), Reynolds argued that the grand jury that had indicted him had been improperly constituted. The jury list had been drawn up and the jurors chosen in accordance with the newly enacted Poland Act. A Utah statute provided that a grand jury must be composed of fifteen jurors. The trial court, however, empaneled twenty-three grand jurors in accordance with federal jury practice. Reynolds argued that using federal rather than territorial law in fixing the size of the grand jury constituted error.

The Utah Supreme Court accepted Reynolds's argument and reversed his conviction, reasoning that the Poland Act nullified territorial jury provisions only insofar as it did so explicitly and not by implication. By its terms, the Poland Act dealt only with how a jury should be selected and not with its size. On more substantive issues, however, the court's opinion was less favorable to the Mormons. Reynolds argued that a grand juror had been improperly excluded for voicing religious objections to indicting individuals for polygamy. The court denied this objection: "He, upon oath, admits that his conscience forbids his aiding in the enforcement of a specific law. . . . Such a party would be wholly incompetent to sit upon a petit jury" (Utah 1:231). The court's refusal even to acknowledge the claims of religious conscience did not bode well for the Mormons.

Although Reynolds' conviction was reversed, the trial had put him in a highly vulnerable position. Reynolds' polygamous marriage was now a matter of public record. To federal officials struggling with the secrecy surrounding Mormon marriage practices, this made him a highly attractive target. Thus in October 1875, Reynolds was again indicted for violating the Morrill Act. This time, the indictment was handed down by a fifteen-member grand jury, in accordance with Utah law. The grand jury was composed of seven Mormons and eight non-Mormons (Linford 1964, 333), but was selected according to the Poland Act's procedural requirements. During this case, however, Reynolds declined to cooperate with his own prosecution. His polygamous wife did not appear; and when a marshal with a subpoena for her asked Reynolds in his home where she was, Reynolds responded only, "You will have to find out" (Kurland and Casper, 8:8). This resistance did him little good, however, for the trial court admitted her earlier testimony into evidence (Kurland and Casper, 8:9). Reynolds was again convicted and sentenced to two years' hard labor and a $500 fine. Again he appealed. This time, the Utah Supreme Court sustained his conviction (Utah 1:319, 1876).

As in the first *Reynolds* case, the court held that individuals who believed in or practiced polygamy could not be impartial jurors and thus could properly be excluded. Potential jurors had been asked if they themselves practiced polygamy and cautioned that they need not answer if doing so would incriminate them. Those who refused to answer were excluded from the jury. Because the court read invocations of the Fifth Amendment privilege against self-incrimination as equivalent to an admission of guilt for purposes of jury selection, "it was not necessary that the disqualification of the jurors should be shown by extrinsic evidence, when they, in effect, admitted it themselves."

The court also struck down Reynolds's argument that admitting his wife's testimony from his first trial was improper. Although Reynolds "was not required by law to aid the prosecution in supplying witnesses against himself," he had no right to conceal witnesses in an effort to thwart his trial (Utah 1:322). This ruling is consistent with the modern *Federal Rules of Evidence*, which states that the admission of prior testimony when the witness is no longer available is proper when that testimony was given under oath and was subject to cross-examination, as it was in Reynolds's first trial.

With but one avenue of appeal remaining, Reynolds turned to the United States Supreme Court (*Reynolds v. United States*, US 98:145 [1878]).

In his brief to the Supreme Court, Reynolds's attorneys spent little time discussing First Amendment protection of polygamy. Instead, they challenged the size of the grand jury that had indicted him, the improper admission and exclusion of jurors, the admission of his polygamous wife's testimony from his first trial, and the bench's instructions to the jury to consider the larger consequences of polygamy. All were rejected.

At trial Reynolds had challenged the seating of a juror who professed to having formed an opinion in the case. The Supreme Court held the juror's seating to be proper on the ground that his opinion in the case was merely "hypothetical" rather than deeply seated and thus did not "raise the presumption of partiality" (US 98:156). The findings of a trial court on that issue would be set aside only for "manifest" error.

Reynolds also claimed that the trial court had given the jury a prejudicial instruction. The trial judge had told the jurors:

> I think it not improper, in the discharge of your duties in this case, that you should consider what are to be the consequences to the innocent victims of this delusion. As this contest goes on, they multiply, and there are pure-minded women and there are innocent children—innocent in a sense even beyond the degree of the innocence of childhood itself. These are to be the sufferers; and as jurors fail to do their duty, and as these cases come up in the Territory of Utah, just so do these victims multiply and spread themselves over the land. (US 98:167–68)

The Utah Supreme Court had quoted only the relatively mild first sentence of this instruction, thus misleadingly characterizing its prejudicial potential (Utah 1:323 [1876]). The Supreme Court, however, concluded that there was "no just cause for complaint," for "the effort of the court seems to have been not to withdraw the minds of the jury from the issue to be tried, but to bring them to it; not to make them partial, but to keep them impartial" (US 98:167–68).

The question of prejudice is, of course, somewhat subjective, but the Court's effort to construe this instruction as an attempt to instill impartiality is a tortured reading. The challenged instruction equates Reynolds's individual case with a moral crusade, gives a lurid image of the social devastation caused by Reynolds's delusion, and suggests that a failure to convict Reynolds would be a violation of the jury's duty and the cause of future misery. By any standard, such a charge must be considered prejudicial.

The bulk of the Court's opinion was devoted to Reynolds's claim that the trial court failed to instruct the jury properly on a crucial point involving the First Amendment: that if Reynolds had engaged in polygamy as a result of a sincere religious conviction, he could be acquitted. *Reynolds* became a landmark case because of Chief Justice Morrison R. Waite's analysis of whether the First Amendment's guarantee of the freedom of religious exercise would excuse otherwise criminal conduct. First, Waite attempted to define *religion* as used in the constitutional provision that "Congress shall make no law respecting an establishment of religion, or prohibiting the free exercise thereof."

Finding no definition within the Constitution itself, Waite quoted Thomas Jefferson, a source contemporary with the First Amendment, to the effect that "religion is a matter which lies solely between man and his God; that he owes account to none other for his faith or his worship; that the legislative powers of the government reach actions only, and not opinions" (US 98:164).

Adopting this demarcation, Waite reasoned that "Congress was deprived of all legislative power over mere opinion, but was left free to reach actions which were in violation of social duties or subversive of good order" (US 98:164). The Court concluded: "Laws are made for the government of actions, and while they cannot interfere with mere religious belief and opinions, they may with practices" (US 98:166).

Waite thus grasped one-half of a profound dilemma posed by the First Amendment's protection of religion. He recognized that the First Amendment could not be read so broadly that any conduct asserted to be an exercise of religion would be immune from state regulation. "To permit this," Waite reasoned, "would be to make the professed doctrines of religious belief superior to the law of the land, and in effect to permit every citizen to become a law unto himself. Government could exist only in name under such circumstances" (US 98:167). To illustrate his point, Waite considered examples of religiously motivated conduct that no civilized society could abide:

> Suppose one believed that human sacrifices were a necessary part of religious worship, would it be seriously contended that the civil government under which he lived could not interfere to prevent a sacrifice? Or if a wife religiously believed it was her duty to burn herself upon the funeral pile of her dead husband, would it be beyond the power of the civil government to prevent her carrying her belief into practice? (US 98:166)

Because not all religious conduct could reasonably be exempted from civil control, Waite concluded that the First Amendment protected only religious belief, not conduct.

This conclusion ignored the other side of the dilemma. Religion exists as much through the conduct of an individual as through belief, and conflict over freedom of religion will arise when the majority of any community is offended by specific practices of a minority. The speech clause of the First Amendment fully protects freedom of belief or conscience. Thus, unless at least some practices offensive to the majority are protected by the First Amendment, the free exercise clause is redundant, and devoid of practical content.

After determining that the First Amendment did not bar the criminalization of religiously inspired conduct, the Court then considered whether polygamy should be deemed "subversive of good order" and, hence, properly made a crime. The Court conceded that marriage was "from its very nature a sacred obligation" and that "an exceptional colony of polygamists under an exceptional leadership may sometimes exist for a time without appearing to disturb the social condition of the people who surround it" (US 98:165, 166). However, "polygamy has always been odious among the northern and western nations of Europe" and was an offense at common law (US 98:164–65). While marriage might be a sacred obligation, it was also a civil contract regulated by law. Indeed, it was an obligation in which the state had an intense interest since "out of its fruits spring social relations and social obligations and duties, with which government is necessarily required to deal" (US 98:165). The Court cited Professor Francis Lieber, a prominent intellectual and founder of American political science who had written extensively on marriage, for the principle that polygamy fosters a patriarchal form of society "which, when applied to large communities, fetters the people in stationary despotism" (US 98:166). Lieber had "described Mormonism as characterized by 'vulgarity,' 'cheating,' 'jugglery,' 'knavery,' 'foulness,' and as bearing 'poisonous fruits' " (Weisbrod and Sheingorn 1978, 851 n. 126).

Thus, polygamy was defined as both conduct and as a social evil and therefore beyond the protection of the First Amendment. Reynolds's conviction was unanimously affirmed by the Supreme Court on 6 January 1879, over four years after he was first indicted. A petition for rehearing pointed out that Reynolds's sentence to hard labor had been improper because the statute provided only for imprisonment. The Court therefore reversed the district court's judgment in this respect and remanded the case for proper sentencing (US 98:168–69). Reynolds was resentenced to two years in prison. After being released five months early for good behavior, Reynolds was received among the Mormons as a "living martyr," and in 1890 became one of the General Authorities of the church (Davis 1973, 291 and n. 24; Jenson 1901–36, 1:206).

The Legal Contributions of Reynolds

A century later, *Reynolds* remains a basic guide to understanding the free exercise clause, but it has been significantly qualified over time. As one scholar summarizes these changes:

> No longer are courts as concerned with defining the scope of religion or determining whether governmental activity inhibits belief or action. Instead, courts consider whether religious acts can be inhibited because of some compelling state interest, and the compelling quality of society's interest is considered in light of alternative means of protecting the public. (Davis 1973, 287)

The critical element in the Court's analysis in *Reynolds*—the distinction between action and belief as a test for First Amendment protection— has apparently been largely abandoned in practice. For example, in 1972, in the case of *Wisconsin v. Yoder* (US 406:205), the Court noted that "to agree that religiously grounded conduct must often be subject to the broad police power of the State is not to deny that there are areas of conduct . . . beyond the power of the State to control. . . . In this context belief and action cannot be neatly confined in logic-tight compartments" (US 406:220).

The *Reynolds* Court quite sensibly recognized that not all conduct could be immunized from governmental scrutiny simply because it was asserted to be a religious practice. What the Court failed to consider was that religious belief and conduct could not be disentangled. As one scholar put it:

> Every great religion is not merely a matter of belief; it is a way of life; it is action. The preferred definition of "religion" given by Webster's *New*

International Dictionary is *"The outward act* or form by which men indicate their recognition of the existence of a God or gods having power over their destiny, to whom obedience, service and honor are due. . . ." One of the most scathing rebukes in religion is reserved for hypocrites who believe but fail to so act—and the Court has itself defined religion as action. (Freeman, 826)

The Court's attempt to define religion as belief alone was, moreover, undercut by the express terms of the Constitution, for what the Constitution protects is the "free exercise" of religion. In the face of this language, Tribe (1978, 838 n. 13) calls the Court's attempt to define constitutionally protected religion as belief "peculiar."

Of course, it was not enough to call the practice of polygamy unprotected conduct. The Court also had to find that practice a proper object of legislation. The *Reynolds* Court concluded that this was so because polygamy was "subversive of good order." The Court's conclusion that polygamy represented an evil sufficiently serious to override the First Amendment has been much criticized by modern commentators. One scholar suggests that the Court's opinion displays "the same undercurrent of hysteria" that ran through the national campaign against polygamy and points out that "the Court never quite explained *why* plural marriage was a threat to the public well-being" (Linford 1964, 340–41). Tribe (1978, 838 n. 15) suggests that *Reynolds* was wrongly decided because the Court overrode core personal rights of privacy and religious expression for the sake of diffuse social goals. No victims of Reynolds's conduct were produced; it was conceded that polygamous sects might be well ordered; and the Court never examined whether polygamy actually degraded women. Instead, the Court found subversion of the social order on the basis of a syllogism that polygamy meant patriarchy, which meant despotism. To avoid this amorphous social evil, the Court infringed the right to religious freedom and limited the right to marry. Davis, however, cogently points out that the state interest in prohibiting polygamy was at the time viewed as compelling, and no less restrictive alternative was available (1973, 305–306).

Even though *Reynolds* continues to be cited as binding precedent, the attitudes of courts toward religious expression are markedly different today. The *Reynolds* concept "that religiously grounded conduct is always outside the protection of the Free Exercise clause," has been expressly rejected (*Wisconsin v. Yoder*, US 406:205, 220 [1972]). Courts now require the existence of a "compelling state interest" that overrides the interest claiming protection under the free exercise clause (US 406:215).

In the 1972 case of *Wisconsin v. Yoder* (US 406:205), the Supreme

Court abandoned the action/belief distinction, implementing instead a test that balanced the competing interests surrounding the free exercise clause. In *Yoder*, Amish parents objected to the compulsory high-school education of their children on the ground that exposure to modern values and advanced education would destroy the insular society and simple life-style essential to their religion.

In *Yoder* the Court expressly rejected the belief/action distinction and adopted a balancing test which would weigh the competing interests at stake. In order for a law restricting religious conduct to stand, there must be an interest of "sufficient magnitude to override the interest claiming protection under the Free Exercise clause" (US 406:214). The Court conceded that the state interest in universal education was compelling. It concluded, however, that even such a vital interest as education could not be "totally free from a balancing process when it impinges on [other] fundamental rights and interests" (US 406:214). The Court emphasized that it was dealing with a belief that was "intimately related to the daily living" of the Amish. Balancing the state's legitimate interest against the strong interest of Amish parents, the Court concluded that compulsory education beyond the eighth grade infringed the free exercise of the parents' religious beliefs. Consequently, the Court held the Amish parents immune to criminal prosecution.

The vitality of *Yoder* was questioned ten years later in *United States v. Lee* (US 455:252 [1982]), where another Amish objected on religious grounds to paying the social security tax imposed on employers. The Court purported to apply the *Yoder* balancing test but rejected Lee's claim to an exemption from the law. Justice John Paul Stevens, concurring in the judgment, suggested a different constitutional standard for the Court's decisions in *Yoder* and *Lee*—namely, that a person who objects to a valid, neutral law of general applicability on religious grounds should have "an almost insurmountable burden" of demonstrating "that there is a unique reason for allowing him a special exemption." He found *Yoder* the "principal exception" to this rule. The majority's conclusion in *Lee*, he argued, suggested that the Court in fact placed a heavier burden on the party challenging the law than *Yoder* would warrant (US 455:262–63).

Whether the present constitutional standard is the *Yoder* balancing test or a more restrictive standard, as Justice Stevens suggested in *Lee*, the Court has clearly abandoned the rationale of *Reynolds*. Could Reynolds have been convicted today?[8] Perhaps, but had the government been required to show a compelling interest, it arguably would have had to produce evidence of the social injury caused by polygamy. The evidence available today suggests that "Mormon polygamy neither caused or could cause the degradation of women and children or the subversion of democracy" (Davis 1973, 301).

The *Reynolds* decision was, of course, not well received in Utah in 1879. It is an article of Mormon belief that the Constitution is divinely inspired (D&C 101:79–80), and the Mormons had steadfastly believed that the First Amendment would ultimately shield them from polygamy prosecutions. Brigham Young had confidently stated in 1852 that "there is not a single constitution of any single state, much less the constitution of the Federal Government, that hinders a man from having two wives, and I defy all the lawyers of the United States to prove the contrary" (JD 1:365). John Taylor, who had become president of the church on Brigham Young's death, reacted, like many Mormons, with shock at what was seen as a betrayal by the Supreme Court: "I do not believe that the Supreme Court of the United States . . . has any right to interfere with my religious views, and in doing it they are violating their most sacred obligations" (Allen and Leonard, 392).

Although the decision was a blow to the Mormons, its immediate impact was limited. *Reynolds* established that Congress had the power to punish polygamy, but, because of evidentiary obstacles and its short limitations period, the Morrill Act was a cumbersome weapon with which to act.

For all that, the period in which the Mormons could effectively resist Washington's mandate was rapidly ending. True the *Reynolds* cases had taken over four years to work their way through the judicial system, but when the Supreme Court issued its opinion, no doubt remained that the federal government had the power to outlaw polygamy. By 1880, the tone of congressional debate indicated that the government also had the will to act. Mining, commerce, migration, and the transcontinental railroad had ended Mormon isolation. To a nation that was rapidly spanning the continent and was now largely undistracted by more serious problems, polygamy loomed ever larger as a divisive issue. In a sorry cycle Congress began considering a series of increasingly severe anti-Mormon bills, not so much because of polygamy as because of prior Mormon resistance. Since polygamy was supported by the church, and because that institution was able to resist laws that simply outlawed the practice, attempts to stamp out polygamy almost inexorably became attacks on the institution of the Mormon church and Mormons in general.

7

The Decisive Attack on Polygamy

The Poland Act of 1874 removed the procedural obstacles to enforcement of the polygamy law, and prosecution slowly began with the *Reynolds* test case. It quickly became apparent, however, that the Morrill Act was ill suited for the swift and efficient prosecution of large numbers of polygamists.

In the years following passage of the Poland Act, presidents regularly, and with increasing irritation, called on Congress to pass tougher anti-polygamy laws. In 1875, President Grant brought the "anomalous, not to say scandalous, condition of affairs" in Utah to Congress's attention, although he offered no specific legislation to remedy the situation (Richardson, 7:355). In 1879, President Rutherford B. Hayes promised that Utah would not become a state so long as polygamy existed and urged that, "if necessary to secure obedience to the law, the enjoyment and exercise of the rights and privileges of citizenship in the Territories of the United States may be withheld or withdrawn from those who violate or oppose the enforcement of the law on this subject" (Richardson, 7:559–60). The next year, following a visit to Utah, Hayes complained to Congress that the Mormon church still controlled Utah and frustrated the efforts of federal officers. Concluding that polygamy "can only be suppressed by taking away the political power of the sect which encourages and sustains it," he therefore recommended that "the right to vote, hold office, and sit on juries in the Territory of Utah be confined to those who neither practice nor uphold polygamy" (Richardson, 7:606).

In 1881 President Chester A. Arthur noted the series of past executive pleas for stringent legislation to suppress polygamy. The polygamy law was, he suggested, "practically a dead letter" because of "the difficulty of procuring legal evidence sufficient to warrant a conviction even in the case of the most notorious offenders" (Richardson, 8:57). To remedy this, the president suggested that Congress require marriages to be registered with the Utah Supreme Court and that wives be qualified as witnesses against their husbands in polygamy cases.

THE EDMUNDS ACT

Finally heeding presidential exhortations, Congress acted. The 1881–82 session saw a parade of proposals to deal with the Mormon problem. Democrats generally favored stricter enforcement of existing polygamy laws, while Republicans sought to wrest political control from the Mormons (Larson 1978b, 259). The bill finally passed was sponsored by a Vermont Republican, Senator George F. Edmunds. The Edmunds Act (Stat. 22:30 [1882]) imposed civil disabilities on polygamists and dramatically simplified the prosecution of polygamy. The first section of the act provided a cosmetic change. The offense termed "bigamy" by the Morrill Act was renamed "polygamy." The section also closed a potential loophole in the Morrill Act. The offense defined in that act covered a man, having one wife, who married another wife. The Edmunds Act also provided for the conviction of men who simultaneously married two or more women. The evidentiary problem of proving polygamous marriages that had hampered enforcement of the Morrill Act was neatly solved by the creation of a new offense, unlawful cohabitation, for which no proof of marriage was required. The act of "cohabiting" with more than one woman was deemed a misdemeanor punishable by a maximum fine of $300 or six months' imprisonment or both. Nor did prosecutors have to decide which charge they could prove at trial, since the act allowed both polygamy and cohabitation to be charged in the same indictment.

Section 5 of the Edmunds Act restricted the Mormons' ability to influence prosecutions by providing that potential jurors who were or had been polygamists could be questioned on that subject and excluded for cause. A juror's responses could not be used as evidence against him in criminal proceedings, but a juror who declined to answer questions regarding his polygamous activities could be rejected as incompetent. Finally, potential jurors who believed "it right for a man to have more than one living and undivorced wife" could be rejected for jury duty. Thus, not only practicing polygamists but also all faithful church members could be excluded from jury duty under the Edmunds Act.

The act struck at the general political power of the church by denying the vote and the right to hold any elective or appointive public office to polygamists and those unlawfully cohabiting. To ensure that the Mormons' electoral power was broken, Congress declared Utah's registration and election offices to be vacant and provided for their replacement. A five-man commission was created to oversee future elections and issue certificates to those lawfully elected. It had instructions that voters were not to be denied the vote simply because they believed in, but did not practice, polygamy. This commission, known as the Utah Commission, came to exercise vast power over Utah's politics over the next decade.

In this harsh legislation only a few moderating gestures were offered to the Mormons: the president was empowered to grant amnesties to past and future offenders, and children of polygamous marriages born before 1 January 1883 were declared legitimate.

The Edmunds Act circumvented the frustrating process of curbing polygamy through judicial punishments by imposing massive civil punishments on the entire Mormon community. As conceived by its sponsor, the effect of the act would be to strip political power in Utah from Mormon hands:

> But we try the mildest of measures first. We take out by this bill from the present government of Utah all of its essential powers, because the statistics and the information that we have demonstrate that the government of the Territory of Utah from top to bottom now is and has been for a long time . . . in the hands of the polygamists. . . .
> Now this act, if it has no other effect, will have the effect of displacing from political supremacy all the persons whom the laws of the United States for twenty years have said were people who ought not to be allowed to carry on a government. (*Congressional Record* 13 [1882]:1212)

The obligatory outrage at polygamy appears predictably in the congressional debates, but overshadowing it is the threatening social power of the church, which is repeatedly described as "theocratic" in nature. For example, Senator Thomas Francis Bayard of Delaware asked:

> What are the real forces? Is it the Constitution of the United States and its laws, or is it the laws and the constitution of the Mormon Church? Does any man hesitate to answer that question? Does any man in the Senate not know that the government of Utah is the government of the Mormon Church; that it is a theocracy as perfect as ever existed on the globe? Does any man say that that is republican in theory, in doctrine, or in practice? (*Congressional Record* 13 [1882]:1157)

Picking up this theme, Senator Edmunds suggested, "Here we have a Territory, anomalous as it may appear, directly at war and directly antagonistic to all the theories of our Government and at war with the principles of our Government. It is a Territory subject to our own control, under the needful rules and regulations we may think proper to make" (*Congressional Record*, 13 [1882]:1159)

The use of polygamy as a justification for federal action against the Mormons was downplayed because it had become too feeble an excuse for such severe action. In 1862, when the Morrill Act was adopted, Congress had been led to believe that half the families in Utah were polygamous. Twenty years later, as Congress considered much harsher legislation, Senator John Sherman of Ohio stated that there were no more than 2,500 polygamists in Utah: about 7 percent of the married Mormon men (*Congressional Record* 13 [1882]:1211). These figures, which placed the issue of polygamy in a more accurate and realistic perspective, lent credibility to the position of those congressmen who urged patience and restraint in dealing with polygamy. Thus, action against the Mormon church had to be justified not merely in terms of the morally outrageous issue of polygamy but also on the basis of the church's allegedly "unrepublican" power in Utah's politics.

In 1862 scarcely anyone in Congress had spoken in favor of polygamy. Twenty years later a naked attack on the organization of a church met more resistance. Both the act's specific provisions and its underlying assumption—that Mormonism should be eradicated—were severely challenged. Senator Wilkinson Call of Florida ironically counseled:

> I think you can find better means of stamping out polygamy than one which stamps out the institutions of the country, the rights contained in the Constitution, the distinction between judicial, legislative, and executive powers, and which by a plain enactment here gives to five persons nominated by the President and confirmed by the Senate, all of whom except one may be of one political party, absolute power not only of deciding who shall be voters, but also of deciding what votes are cast and who shall be eligible to office. (*Congressional Record* 13 [1882]:1156)

An open attack on Mormonism lent new legitimacy to the spirit of religious persecution, a spirit that had been stamped out only with great difficulty. As Senator Joseph E. Brown of Georgia noted, in 1882 religious toleration was only a new and fragile achievement. Before persecuting Mormons became popular, Americans had persecuted Catholics, Baptists, and Quakers among others. He queried:

> If religious intolerance in this most enlightened and intelligent State was so great forty-eight years ago as to incite men to burn and desecrate the covenants of the Catholic Church, and the riot was permitted with impunity, how can we trust ourselves forty-eight years later to make

indiscriminate warfare upon the people of any Territory of these United States on account of any opinion of theirs, religious or otherwise? (*Congressional Record* 13 [1882]:1205)

Refraining from persecution of the Mormons need not be based on any sympathy for Mormons or for polygamy. Restraining the baser forms of mob sentiment, he argued, was ultimately a matter of self-interest:

> You are treading on dangerous ground when you open this flood-gate anew. We have passed the period where there is for the present any clamor against any particular sect except as against the Mormons; but it seems there must be some periodical outcry against some denomination. Popular vengeance is now turned against the Mormons. When we are done with them I know not who will next be considered the proper subject of it. (*Congressional Record* 13 [1882]:1205)

The most controversial section of the Edmunds Act in the congressional debate was the one creating an election commission for Utah. Senator Brown had seen similar commissions in operation during the Reconstruction in Georgia. He knew firsthand how vast the power to control elections could be: "It is virtually a returning board, and I have always found in the South that the returning board is the government of the State. They always decide elections there one way, and I think it will be so here" (*Congressional Record* 13 [1882]:1156).

Not only were the commission's powers broad, they were also unrestrained by procedural protections. In essence, the Edmunds Act imposed penalties on polygamists without benefit of trial by depriving them of the right to hold office, vote, or serve as jurors. Power to impose this penalty would lie solely in the hands of the commission. Senator Graham Vest of Missouri protested: "It is the very essence of good government and of freedom and of constitutional right that every man should be tried and convicted before punishment. The seventh section of this bill takes away from a citizen of the United States the right to vote or hold office before conviction by his peers of any crime" (*Congressional Record* 13 [1882]:1157).

The act's proponents hedged on a technicality. Congress was empowered to fix the qualifications of voters: "There may be a disqualification fixed by law for a perfectly praiseworthy act" (*Congressional Record* 13 [1882]:1201). By definition, then, they claimed, the act imposed no punishment but was merely an exercise of Congress's power to fix the qualifications requisite for participation in the political process. Senator Edmunds cavalierly acknowledged that the act's provisions "were intended to be severe. They have been said to be rough provisions. They were intended to be rough. Desperate cases need desperate remedies" (*Congressional Record* 13 [1882]:1158). Senator Bayard of Delaware, a doubt-ridden supporter of the act, conceded that its provisions were "an unrepublican theory of proceeding in regard to elections" but concluded that they were necessary to break the equally unrepublican theocracy that ruled Utah (*Congressional Record* 13 [1882]:1156).

This defense of the act fails in two respects. First, although the form of the act dealt with the qualifications of voters and office-holders, in substance and intent the provisions were punishments. Senator George H. Pendleton of Ohio conceded Congress's power to establish voter qualifications in the territories, but noted:

> I cannot resist the conclusion that the foundation of this bill, the idea that lies at its groundwork, is that these are crimes now to be defined, and to be punished not only by imprisonment and fine, but by deprivation of the right of voting and the right of holding office. I say when that is to be done it is an essential principle of our justice that this punishment shall be inflicted only after conviction. (*Congressional Record* 13 [1882]:1211)

Thus, the Edmunds Act was offered to Congress as a means of punishing Mormons. As such it was a bill of attainder and violated an express constitutional provision prohibiting bills of attainder. Second, the provisions were largely unrelated to their purported end. Whatever the faults of polygamy, no clear arguments were presented to explain why polygamists were incompetent to serve as voters or even elected officials.

While the provision creating an election commission received the closest congressional scrutiny, the act's other provisions were also criticized. Two objections were directed at the provision excluding polygamists or those who believed in polygamy from jury duty. First, Call pointed out, the provision would almost certainly result in packed, biased juries in polygamy cases:

> It imposes a religious test upon the jurors which is in violation of that cardinal provision of the Constitution of the United States, that when a man is charged with a crime he shall have a fair and impartial trial. . . . If there be anything sacred in the history of American jurisprudence and American liberty it is that a person charged with crime shall have a fair and an impartial trial by a jury of his peers, and not by a packed jury selected of men known to be opposed to him and prejudiced against him, and a religious test imposed upon them for their qualification as jurors. (*Congressional Record* 13 [1882]:1207)

Pendleton added that the broad language of the statute provided not only that practicing polygamists would be disqualified as jurors, but also those who had been polygamists.

Did you ever know a jury law which went back to the whole course of a man's life and disqualified him for sitting upon a jury unless he would swear that he is not now, and never has been guilty of any of the acts defined as crimes in the laws? . . . according to this bill he is forever deprived of the right of sitting upon a jury in these cases. . . . you deprive him of the inducement to abandon that which you define as a crime. (*Congressional Record* 13 [1882]:1210)

Also, it was urged that even if the act's cohabitation provision did not operate in a strict sense to punish past conduct, in practical effect it was too harsh. To remain within the law, polygamous Mormons would be required to immediately cease cohabiting with their plural wives. Senator Eli Saulsbury of Delaware, a supporter of the act, noted that the failure to allow Mormon men some period to provide for their illegal families would force Mormons to choose between violating the law and leaving their loved ones destitute (*Congressional Record* 13 [1882]:1207).

Finally, Senator John Sherman of Ohio fatalistically warned that the harsh provisions of the Edmunds Act, like those of the Morrill Act, would be inadequate to break the power of the Mormon church. If the estimated 2,500 polygamous leaders of the church were disenfranchised and convicted of polygamy, they would only become living martyrs; their real power would remain intact. So long as Mormons constituted the majority of the electorate, Mormons would be elected to the territorial government, and those elected would faithfully obey the disenfranchised leadership. Only when the federal government acted directly to remove political power entirely from Mormon hands would the power of the church be broken. "I believe myself," he summarized, "that the only remedy for this evil which the people of the United States will grapple with and will end some of these days, is to place in power there a government that is not controlled by Mormon votes" (*Congressional Record* 13 [1882]:1212).

Notwithstanding the debate, the Edmunds Act was passed in the Senate and passed the House by a 199–42 majority, with 51 representatives not voting. President Chester A. Arthur promptly signed it into law on 22 March 1882, and it immediately produced chaos in Utah's government. The Utah Commission was not organized in time to conduct the 1882 territorial election, but without its oversight no elections could be held. Thus, elective territorial offices fell vacant, and government in the territory ceased to function (CHC 6:61–65). Congress was forced to repair the damage by adopting the Hoar Amendment on 7 August 1882 (Stat. 22:313), allowing Utah's governor to appoint successors to the vacant offices until elections were held.

Once in operation, the Utah Commission functioned even more efficiently than its sponsors had had reason to expect. Over 12,000 Mormons in Utah were disenfranchised in the first year of its operation. If Senator Sherman's estimate was correct, this was nearly five times the number of practicing polygamists in Utah at the time.

THE PROSECUTION OF COHABITATION

In the hands of imaginative anti-Mormon jurists, the provisions of the Edmunds Act were construed broadly. Almost any contact between a Mormon man and his reputed polygamous wives constituted cohabitation. Evidentiary standards were relaxed, allowing evidence of prior conduct or reputation to be introduced to establish cohabitation. Plural wives were compelled to testify against their husbands, and jailed for contempt if they refused. Perhaps most cruelly, cohabitation was construed as a discrete offense, so that each year, month, or day of cohabitation gave rise to a new offense, subject to additional penalties.

In the latter half of the 1880s, resistance tactics the Mormons had previously employed to delay enforcement of the polygamy law no longer availed. Indeed, even Mormon efforts to comply with the law were often no protection. In late 1884, three polygamists were convicted and given prison sentences. By the end of the next year, of eighty-three indicted polygamists, twenty-three had been convicted and sent to prison while forty-six more awaited trial. Seventeen of those indicted escaped punishment by promising to obey the law in the future (Larson 1971, 110). By September 1888, the attorney general could report to Congress that, although the president had granted fourteen pardons,

> the records of the Department show that under the provisions of the anti-polygamy law of 1882 and the act of 1882 amendatory thereof, and the act of March 3, 1887 [the Edmunds-Tucker Act], there have been in the Territory of Utah 470 convictions for polygamy, adultery, and unlawful cohabitation with fines imposed, and 30 convictions where the sentence was imprisonment without fine, making a total for that Territory of 500. There have been in the Territory of Idaho 48 convictions for polygamy, adultery and unlawful cohabitation with fines imposed, and 41 convictions where the sentence was imprisonment without fine, making a total for that Territory of 89.
>
> There was 1 conviction in Utah in March, 1875, and 1 in April, 1881; in October and November, 1884, 1 in Idaho and 3 in Utah; in 1885, beginning with the March term, 39 in Utah and 16 in Idaho; in 1886, 112 in Utah and 20 in Idaho; in 1887, 214 in Utah and 6 in Idaho, and

in 1888, 100 in Utah and 5 in Idaho—in all 589 convictions. There have been collected in Utah fines and costs in the above cases to the amount of $45,956.90, and in Idaho to the amount of $2,251.10—in all $48,208 of fines and costs, and in Utah in April, 1886, a forfeiture of $25,000. (*Congressional Record* 19:9231)

By 1893, after the Mormons had renounced polygamy and prosecutions had largely ceased, there had been 1004 convictions for unlawful cohabitation and 31 for polygamy (Arrington 1958, 359).

These figures demonstrate several interesting patterns. Polygamy prosecution apparently peaked in Idaho in 1886, and thereafter the resistance of Idaho Mormons to the law was broken. Their political persecution, however, continued well after that prosecution ended. The data also indicate that the cohabitation offense was a much more effective instrument for the government than the original polygamy provision. All but thirty-one of over a thousand convictions were for unlawful cohabitation.

The mere number of polygamy and cohabitation convictions, however, understates the impact of "the raid" on Mormon society. Not just any Mormon male was allowed to practice polygamy. As a general rule, only men who were morally worthy and financially able were permitted to take plural wives. Thus, by and large, the polygamists were also the Mormons' leaders. "From the president down through the apostles and the Presiding Bishopric during the period, no general authority was a monogamist," note Arrington and Bitton (1979, 204). "The same was true of most bishops and stake presidents, as well as, for all practical purposes, their counselors." Polygamy unified the church leadership by committing them in common to a practice reviled by the outside world and by interlocking the leadership through marital ties (Arrington and Bitton, 204–5; Davis 1962, 4–5). Thus, the conviction and imprisonment of polygamists paralyzed Mormon society by removing its leadership.

Moreover, many polygamists who were not convicted were forced into hiding or to flee the United States. President John Taylor spent nearly two and a half years moving among secret sanctuaries in Utah (Allen and Leonard, 402). In a public sermon, delivered on 1 February 1885, before he went into hiding, President Taylor counseled, "When such a condition of affairs exists, it is no longer a land of liberty, and it is certainly no longer a land of equal rights, and we must take care of ourselves as best we may, and avoid being caught in any of their snares" (JD 26:156). Taylor died while in hiding on 25 July 1887. Apostle Lorenzo Snow was arrested in a secret apartment under his home in Salt Lake City (*United States v. Snow*, P. 9:503 [Utah 1886]).

Entire villages were disrupted and terrorized by federal officials and spies seeking polygamists; and by 1886 "nearly every settlement in Utah had been raided by federal marshals" (Allen and Leonard, 400).

To simplify polygamy prosecution, the Edmunds Act provided that men who "cohabit with more than one woman" were guilty of a misdemeanor (Stat. 22:31, § 3). Congress's intent, of course, was to allow the conviction of polygamists without requiring prosecutors to prove the fact of the often secret Mormon weddings and to allow for the prosecution of polygamists without regard to the statute of limitations. The Edmunds Act, however, contains no definition of what conduct constituted cohabitation, and the *Congressional Record* does not offer any evidence that Congress considered the question.

Once the act became law, the issue assumed immediate importance. Mormons who wanted to comply with the law were forced to guess what relations with their plural wives and families were permitted by the law (Linford 1964, 348). Judges were likewise called on to decide if Mormon efforts to "put their plural wives behind them" fell outside the ambit of "cohabitation."

The Mormons argued that the benchmark of cohabitation should be sexual intercourse. But the courts balked, for two reasons. First, proving sexual intercourse would be difficult. If enforcement of the Morrill Act had been paralyzed because of the difficulties entailed in proving the fact of marriage, a rather public event, the Edmunds Act would be even more useless if proof of cohabitation required proof of intercourse. Second, requiring Mormons to divulge the most intimate details of their family life before the courts would be an unendurable invasion of privacy. But to accept less intimate evidence as establishing "cohabitation" could too easily remove all standards for the determination of guilt.

The definition could not be debated with academic coolness forever. In February 1885, nearly three years after the passage of the Edmunds Act, Angus Cannon, president of the Salt Lake Stake, was indicted for unlawfully cohabiting with two of his plural wives, Clara and Amanda, both of whom lived in separate quarters in his house. A third wife lived in a house nearby. The behavior of the federal marshals when Cannon was arrested clearly indicated what was in store for the Mormons:

He [Cannon] was arrested on the street in Salt Lake City on January 19, 1885. Immediately thereafter his home was visited by a deputy marshal with a handful of subpoenas to serve on members of the family as witnesses. In a crude manner, foreshadowing the uglier features of the rising crusade, he forced entrance to the house and to the bedroom of Amanda M. Cannon, who was ill in bed. After informing her of her husband's arrest, he proceeded to read a summons demanding her appearance in court as a witness against him. Immediately after leaving the house by the front door, he appeared at the rear entrance and again thrust himself into the room to subpoena two more women witnesses. (Larson 1971, 115–16)

At trial, Cannon attempted to prove that

after the Edmunds law had passed both Houses of Congress, and before its approval by the President, the defendant announced to witness [Clara], Amanda, and their families, that he did not intend to violate that law, but should live within it so long as it should remain a law, and at the same time assign his reasons for so doing; and thereafter and during the times alleged in the indictment, he did not occupy the rooms or bed of or have any sexual intercourse with the witness, and to this extent, by mutual agreement, separated from the witness. . . . and, also, that the defendant was financially unable to provide a separate house for witness and her family. (US 116:65)

The court, however, ruled this evidence inadmissible, as irrelevant. Cannon was duly convicted and sentenced to six months in the penitentiary and a fine of $300. In May 1885, bishops and stake presidents received instructions from the underground headquarters of the church: "We do not think it advisable for brethren to go into court and plead guilty. Every case must be defended with all the zeal and energy possible" (Larson 1971, 133–34). Adhering to these directions, Cannon appealed to the Utah Supreme Court (*United States v. Cannon*, P. 7:369 [1885]).

Cannon's main objection was directed at the trial court's definition of "cohabitation." At trial and on appeal, Cannon contended that, "all cohabitation which the law deals with is sexual cohabitation; that the word as used means a dwelling together by male and female adult persons in the intimacy of husband and wife, and that sexual intercourse is necessarily implied" (P. 7:381). Under that theory of the law Cannon sought to show his agreement to leave off sexual relations with his plural wives.

The Utah Supreme Court, however, rejected Cannon's interpretation of the Edmunds Act, noting as a rule of statutory construction that, "that sense of the words should be adopted which best harmonizes with the context, and promotes in the fullest manner the policy and objects of the legislature" (P. 7:374). Congress's intent, the court concluded, was largely evidentiary, to eliminate problems attending proof of polygamous marriages. Thus, the Edmunds Act provided that unlawful cohabitation might be shown whether or not preceded by an unlawful marriage. Polygamy was made, as the court put it, "a continuous offense," and, "whether marriage took place or not, the pretense of marriage—the living, to all intents and purposes, so far as the public could see, as husband and wife—a holding out of that relationship to the world, were the evils sought to be eradicated" (P. 7:374).

Proof of sexual intercourse was not necessary to make out such an offense, because, as Justice Orlando W. Powers noted in a concurring opinion,[1] the aim of the act was not "to punish mere sexual crimes" (P. 7:381). Indeed, the court reasoned that to construe the statute as Cannon urged would render the cohabitation offense superfluous since other statutes already covered sexual offenses: "The prosecution would have to prove adultery, when adultery was not charged; would have to prove fornication, and lewd and lascivious cohabitation, when none of these charges had been made, and all such offenses had been purposely left out of the act by the law-making power" (P. 7:378). Finally, the court appealed to prior case law and general definitions of the term *cohabit* to demonstrate that *cohabitation* referred to the act of dwelling together and not sexual intercourse (P. 7:375).

The United States Supreme Court affirmed the *Cannon* decision (US 116:55 [1885]). Adopting much of the reasoning of the Utah court, the Supreme Court concluded that cohabitation was established "if he [Cannon] lived in the same house with the two women, and ate at their respective tables . . . and held them out to the world, by his language or conduct, or both, as his wives" (US 116:71). This interpretation of the Edmunds Act, the Court concluded, was deducible from "the language of the statute throughout," which dealt with marital relations, and from the existence of other statutory provisions dealing with sexual offenses. Cannon's agreement to abstain from sexual relations with his plural wives was dismissed: "Compacts for sexual non-intercourse, easily made and as easily broken, when the prior marriage relations continue to exist, . . . is not a lawful substitute for the monogamous family which alone the statute tolerates" (US 116:72). Justices Stephen J. Field and Samuel F. Miller dissented, arguing that the prohibition of cohabitation should be interpreted to mean "unlawful habitual sexual intercourse" and calling the majority's holding "a strained construction of a highly penal statute" (US 116:79–80).

A second polygamy case, decided at about the same time as the *Cannon* case, emphasized the severe consequences that would flow from the courts' broad construction of the term *cohabitation*. In *United States v. Musser* (P. 7:389 [Utah 1885]), A. Milton Musser was charged with cohabiting with his three plural wives. In an apparent effort to comply with the Edmunds Act, Musser had established each woman in a separate house and given her a deed to the property. The evidence against Musser consisted mostly of such facts as that the women and their children bore his name, that he had been seen in their company, and that he had eaten with them.

The Utah Supreme Court sustained Musser's conviction, affirming that evidence of sexual conduct was irrelevant to the charge of cohabitation. With brutal candor, the court stated that Congress had adopted the Edmunds Act because it

> knew the time had elapsed within which a very large portion of those living in polygamy could be punished for that offense, and that many of these were among the most influential men in society, being the heads of the church, and that the example of their continuing to live with their plural wives under a claim of divine right would be a scandal to society and a menace to the lawful marriage; that such examples would be a continuing invitation and apparent justification for their followers to either secretly or openly violate the law. (P. 7:391)

On the whole, the judicial refusal to make sexual intercourse the test for cohabitation was sensible. Through at least this century it has been an axiomatic standard for the irreducible minimum of personal privacy that government has no power to place spies in the bedroom (see *Griswold v. Connecticut*, US 381:479 [1965]). By construing the Edmunds Act to avoid that nightmare, the judiciary at least spared the Mormons an intolerable indignity and assault on their rights. A nation gripped by anti-Mormon hysteria, as America was in the 1880s, might willingly have accepted so odious an expansion of governmental prerogatives—with consequences that may have reached far beyond the Mormons. As it was, Mormons had to endure more than a few incidents of bedroom raids and window peeping.

In 1886, over two thousand Mormon women assembled in Salt Lake City and addressed a petition to Congress detailing the outrages they had endured during the polygamy raids: "Women are arrested and forcibly taken before sixteen men and plied with questions that no decent woman can hear without a blush. Little children are examined upon the secret relations of their parents, and wives in regard to their own condition and the doings of their husbands" (*Congressional Record* 17:3137).

The petition recounted a number of incidents in which Mormon men and women had been literally taken from their beds by federal marshals:

On January 11, 1886, early in the morning, five deputy marshals appeared at the residence of William Grant, American Fork, forced the front door open, and while the inmates were still in bed made their way upstairs to their sleeping apartments. There they were met by one of the daughters of William Grant, who was aroused at the intrusion, and despite her protestations, without giving time for the object of their search to get up and dress himself, made their way into his bed-room, finding him still in bed, and his wife *en deshabille* in the act of dressing herself.

Early on the morning of January 13, 1886, a company of deputies invaded the peaceful village of West Jordan, and, under pretense of searching for polygamists, committed a number of depredations. Among other acts of violence they intruded into the house of F. A. Cooper, arrested him, and subpoenaed his legal wife as a witness against him. This so shocked her that a premature birth occurred next day, and her system was so deranged by the disturbance that in a few days she was in her grave.

February 23, 1886, at about 11 o'clock at night, two deputy marshals visited the house of Solomon Edwards, about 7 miles from Eagle Rock, Idaho, and arrested Mrs. Edwards, his legal wife, after she had retired to bed, and required her to accompany them immediately to Eagle Rock. Knowing something of the character of one of the deputies, from his having visited the house before, when he indulged in a great deal of drinking, profanity, and abuse, she feared to accompany them without some protection, and requested a neighbor to go along on horseback while she rode in the buggy with the two deputies. On the way the buggy broke down, and she, with an infant in her arms, was compelled to walk the rest of the distance between 2 and 3 miles.

They could have no reason for subpoenaing her in the night and compelling her to accompany them at such an untimely hour, except a fiendish malice and a determination to heap all the indignities possible upon her because she was a "Mormon" woman, for she never attempted to evade the serving of the warrant and was perfectly willing to report herself at Eagle Rock the next day. She was taken to Salt Lake City to testify against her husband.

On February 23, 1886, Deputy Marshals Gleason and Thompson went to Greenville, near Beaver, Utah. The story of their conduct is thus related by the ladies who were the subjects of their violence:

Mrs. Easton's statement:

About 7 A.M. deputies came to our house and demanded admittance. I asked them to wait until we got dressed and we would let them in. Deputy Gleason said he would not wait, and raised the window and got partly through by the time we opened the door, when he drew himself back and came in through the door. He then went into the bed-room; one of the young ladies had got under the bed, from which Gleason pulled the bedding and ordered the young lady to come out. This she did, and ran into the other room, where she was met by Thompson. I asked Gleason why he pulled the bedding from the bed, and he answered: "By G-d, I found Watson in the same kind of a place." He then said he thought Easton was concealed in a small compass, and that he expected to find him in a similar place, and was going to get him before he left.

Miss Morris's statement:

Deputy Gleason came to my bed and pulled the clothing off me, asking if there was any one in bed with me. He then went to the fire-place and pulled a sack of straw from there and looked up the chimney. One of them next pulled up a piece of carpet, when Gleason asked Thompson if he thought there was any one under there. Thompson said "No," and Gleason exclaimed, "G—d d—n it, we will look anyway!" They also looked in cupboards, boxes, trunks, etc., and a small tea-chest, but threw nothing out.

William Thomas's statement:

The deputies called at our place about day break, and came to my window and rapped. I asked who was there, but received no answer. They then tried to raise the window, when I called again, and they said they were officers. I asked them to wait until I was dressed, but they said: "No, we will break in the door." I told them they had better let that alone, and they went around to mother's door, which was opened, and father was summoned. The deputies next went to the bed of Mrs. Elliotts and subpoenaed her. Gleason said, with a frightful oath, that he knew there was another woman in the house, and searched in boxes, trunks, etc. (*Congressional Record* 17:3138)

The price to the Mormons of the judicial refusal to make sexual intercourse a necessary element of cohabitation was that proving the offense became ridiculously easy for federal prosecutors. As one scholar of the polygamy trials has concluded, "There were few acquittals for Edmunds Act violations during [Chief Justice Charles S.] Zane's tenure; to be tried was, in effect, to be convicted" (Linford 1964, 348). Construing the polygamy statutes to allow offense by the mere appearance of polygamous union also entailed a shift in the tone of judicial rhetoric and imposed severe penalties on Mormon families that attempted to live within the law.

However, there was something pyrrhic in the federal victory. Prior to the *Cannon* and *Musser* cases, polygamy had presented an easy target for the moralistic rhetoric of congressmen and jurists. Orators easily justified the most repressive government measures by calling forth lurid images of licentious Mormon patriarchs. Heretofore polygamy had been depicted as a sexual offense that shocked a puritan society. Suddenly, with the *Cannon* decision the sexual activities of alleged polygamists were declared legally irrelevant and polygamy became an offense against marital relations, an offense that somehow menaced the monogamous family. As the Supreme Court construed the law, it sought

> not only to punish bigamy and polygamy when direct proof of the existence of those relations can be made, but to prevent a man from flaunting in the face of the world the ostentation and opportunities of a bigamous household, with all the outward appearances of the continuance of the same relations which existed before the Act was passed. (*United States v. Cannon*, US 116:72)

Once reformers determined to ignore the carnal aspects of polygamy, the moral foundation of the crusade against polygamy became suspect. No one could or would define in what way polygamy was a menace to American society and monogamous marriage. Indeed, the Utah Supreme Court suggested that, in adopting the Edmunds Act, Congress had the less than noble goal of enacting legislation to punish senior church leaders who had otherwise brought their conduct into compliance with the law (*United States v. Musser*, P. 7:391).

The law's directive to all Mormon men to cease cohabitation meant that wives who had been married decades before and who were now aged and infirm were to be abandoned. Frequently a polygamous wife would be "a homeless immigrant, a spinster, or the wife of a deceased relative with a family to support" (Arrington 1958, 239). Because of the Edmunds Act prosecutions, "the psychological and legal pressures led, in some instances, to abandonment of wives, who having sacrificed much, suddenly found themselves without even the tenuous security of status as a plural wife" (Arrington and Bitton, 202). Whatever polygamy's faults, in destroying it the federal government destroyed what had been an effective social welfare system (Arrington and Bitton, 200–201). Younger wives were often to be left to support and raise large families alone. Angus Cannon, for example, supported eleven children—at least two the orphaned children of a wife's niece—along with his wives. Musser had a dozen children. Thus, the moral posture of courts enforcing the Edmunds Act was dramatically altered, for no longer did courts command Mormons to abandon a life of presumed debauchery. Instead, in the name of amorphous social policies, the Mormons were called on to ignore the moral obligations of supporting aging wives and raising innocent children.

The judicial interpretation of the Edmunds Act meant the Mormons could not honor their obligations toward plural wives and children without violating the Act. To be sure, Justice Powers did offer some general guidelines in the *Musser* case:

> In my opinion a man who has heretofore contracted a polygamous mar-
> riage, and has had children by two or more women, is required, as I
> have stated, to treat those women precisely as he would be required to
> treat them if he had been divorced from them. . . . He may visit his
> children, he may make directions with regard to their welfare, he may
> meet his former wife on terms of social equality; but it is not expected,
> after the decree of divorce, that he will associate with his former wife as
> a husband associates with his wife; that he will live under the same roof,
> and, to outward appearances, live with her as a husband lives with his
> wife. (P. 7:394)

But Powers's advice was not authoritative, coming as it did in a dissenting opinion, and more authoritative sources were less helpful in
suggesting how Mormons might comply with the law. The Supreme
Court in *Cannon* stated:

> A strong appeal was made in argument to this court, not to uphold the
> rulings of the trial court, because that would require a polygamous hus-
> band not only to cease living with his plural wives, but also to abandon
> the women themselves; and this court was asked to indicate what the
> conduct of the husband towards them must be in order to conform to the
> requirements of the law. It is sufficient to say, that, while what was done
> by the defendant in this case, after the passage of the act of Congress,
> was not lawful, no court can say, in advance, what particular state of
> things will be lawful, further than this: that he must not cohabit with
> more than one woman, in the sense of the word "cohabit," as herein-
> before defined. (US 116:79)

Similarly, the Court unhelpfully advised that "he can only cease to be
such when he has finally and fully dissolved in some effective manner, which we are not called on here to point out, the very relation of
husband to several wives, which constitutes the forbidden status he
has previously assumed" (US 116:73). Utah courts continued to find
the polygamists' efforts to terminate their unlawful relationships inadequate, and continued to refuse, at times almost gleefully, to specify
what conduct would be lawful. For example, the Utah Supreme Court
responded to a defendant's plea that he knew of no way to comply
with the law, that "if the defendant has been unable to find out any
way to cease living with his polygamous women, it is not the fault of
the law that he suffers for his imperfect knowledge" (*United States v.
Peay*, P. 14:346–47 [Utah 1887]).

Polygamous Mormons were thus presented with a difficult decision:
morally, they were obligated to associate with their polygamous families to the extent necessary to provide for their welfare, but because
the boundaries of legally permissible conduct had been left unde-

fined, any contact potentially left polygamists open to prosecution. The standard adopted by the courts appears to be a classic example of a law invalid by virtue of its vagueness. It is a constitutional maxim that the terms of the law must be sufficiently clear that citizens may order their conduct in conformity with it.[2] As construed by the courts, the Edmunds Act failed to do this. The facts of *Cannon* and *Musser* indicate that both men had genuinely attempted to arrange their polygamous families in a manner that complied with the law. Yet even after the court issued its opinions in the case, it remained unclear what they might have done differently to avoid violating the law.

Indeed, more than one passage in the courts' opinions suggests that there was no way the two men could have kept from violating the Edmunds Act. As construed by the courts, cohabitation involved the appearance of plural marriage. The offense was not so much one of conduct as of appearance. What Mormon men did, therefore, did not count so much as whether they appeared to be or were reputed to be polygamists. The United States Supreme Court in the *Cannon* case stated that cohabitation was directed at the "outward appearances" of a relationship "without reference to what may occur in the privacy of those relations" (US 116:72). The Utah court stated, "Congress therefore forbade plural marriage in appearance only, as well as in form, and by the example of punishment it doubtless intended to eradicate the example of apparent plural marriages, as well as the plural marriage in form" (*United States v. Musser*, P. 7:391).

Of course, the Mormons could not comply with a statute that made their conduct largely irrelevant and considered only what they appeared to be or were reputed to be doing. After resisting enforcement of the polygamy laws for over twenty years, Mormons suddenly found themselves unable to comply with a new law that was to be vigorously enforced. Moreover, the vagueness of the offense of cohabitation infected all aspects of the judicial proceedings against the Mormons. Where the offense was so poorly defined, the range of evidence admissible to prove that offense was inevitably also poorly defined. In the *Cannon* and *Musser* cases, relatively little evidence was given as to the actual conduct of the defendants. Instead, the state offered and the court accepted testimony as to what the defendants appeared to do, what they were reputed to do, or how others regarded them.

The interpretation of the offense of cohabitation announced in *Cannon* and *Musser*, an interpretation that left the Mormons little room for compliance, was made even harsher by subsequent decisions. Although cohabitation had been termed offensive because of the appearance of impropriety—by the public flaunting of polygamy—the Mormons could not avoid prosecution by keeping the connections with their plural families discrete. In *United States v. Peay*, the court had asserted that a polygamist "must lay aside all *indicia* of the crime. He must act in good faith, and separate himself entirely from his polygamous women" (P. 14:344 [Utah 1887]). Thus, confusingly, Mormons could not even treat their plural wives as if they had been divorced or meet with them, as Justice Powers had suggested, "on terms of social equality" (*United States v. Musser*, P. 7:399). Any contact, covert or open, could apparently qualify as cohabitation.

Indeed, a polygamist might have contact with only one wife and still be convicted of cohabitation, if that one wife was not his legally recognized wife. Lorenzo Snow, for example, had married nine women over a thirty-year period, the last ten years before he was indicted for cohabitation. Two had died. In compliance, so he thought, with the law, the seventy-two-year-old Snow had established his six older wives in six separate households and refrained from almost all contact with them. He lived solely with his youngest wife, who still had infant children to raise. Nevertheless, he was convicted of cohabitation. The Mormons could not win whatever they did, for Snow's efforts to comply with the law by separating himself from his wives scandalized the Utah Supreme Court, which upheld his convictions (*United States v. Snow* P. 9:501 [Utah 1886]): "As his passion for one wife became satiated and dulled by indulgence and gratification, and his lust was again kindled by the appearance of a younger and fresher, or possibly more attractive, woman, he would marry again, until his marriages have been repeated nine times" (P. 9:503). The court purported to find Snow's case to be "one of the most aggravated cases and worst examples of polygamy" (P. 9:505). But the court's holding was based not on the fact that Snow was cohabiting or associating with more than one wife; it was based on the fact that he was with the wrong wife. Snow lived exclusively with his last wife, but she was not his legally recognized wife, and so the court deemed that Snow was also cohabiting with his lawful wife. (Determining which of a polygamist's wives was his lawful one could be trickier than it might seem. In Snow's case, for example, his legal wife was not his first one. Snow had married his first two wives simultaneously, forty years prior to his conviction. Because the simultaneous marriage was void, Snow's legal wife was his third.)

As the pace of polygamy prosecutions accelerated, the thought occurred to some eager prosecutor that the cohabitation statute would be more fearsome, the threat of punishment direr, if every defendant faced not one cohabitation charge and punishment, but many. Such a change could be simply made by considering each year, or month, or day that a man cohabited illegally the basis of a separate and distinct offense. Periods of cohabitation could thus be divided into units as small or as large as the prosecutor wished, allowing him to tailor the potential punishment to be meted out to individual defendants solely at his discretion.

A judicial test of this theory was attempted on a modest scale in the case of Apostle Lorenzo Snow. On 12 December 1885 Snow was charged by a grand jury with cohabitation in three separate indictments. Each indictment charged the same offense with the same women; the indictments differed only in that the first charged Snow with cohabitation in 1883, the second with cohabitation in 1884, and the third covered 1885. In effect, Snow was charged with a separate offense for each year since adoption of the Edmunds Act.

Snow was tried and convicted first for cohabitation during 1885. At his second and third trials, for offenses committed in 1884 and 1883 respectively, Snow raised his first conviction as a defense, claiming that it barred further prosecution for the same offense. A demurrer to this defense was sustained, and Snow was convicted on each indictment and given the maximum sentence of six months' imprisonment and a $300 fine for each conviction. Thus, through the device of segregating the charges against Snow into three charges, each for a one-year period, Snow's punishment was tripled.

Each conviction was appealed to the Utah Supreme Court (*United States v. Snow*, P. 9:501, 686 & 697 [Utah 1886]), but the court discussed the issue of the propriety of subdividing cohabitation offenses only with regard to the conviction for 1884. That discussion proved unhelpful. Snow argued that a single continuous offense could not be divided into a series of discrete offenses for the purpose of multiplying punishment. The court rejected this argument, citing *Commonwealth v. Connors* (Mass. 116:35 [1874]), which had held that maintaining a tenement for the sale of illegal liquor could be the basis of separate convictions based on different periods of time. The Utah court called it "the only case we have seen which squarely meets the issue, and it sustains the ruling of the court below in the case at bar. Coming as it does from the very able and highest court in one of the oldest commonwealths of our Union, it commands respect and consideration, and we have no hesitancy in following it" (P. 7:696). Its distinguished lineage was, however, the Utah Supreme Court's only justification for the rule that an offense could be segregated into separate offenses of different temporal duration.

Needless to say, the Utah Supreme Court's decision in *Snow* was a great shock to the Mormons. It made the penalty for cohabitation convictions far more severe and raised the specter of unlimited segregation. No stronger reason existed, in principle, for dividing cohabitation offenses into one-year units than into one-day units, since the basis of the segregation was arbitrary anyway. With sufficient application of the segregation principle, cohabitation could become punishable by lifetime imprisonment. Bad as this was, the *Snow* case had still further unpleasant surprises in store for the Mormons.

Snow's appeal to the United States Supreme Court was dismissed on the ground that the Court did not possess jurisdiction to hear it (US 118:346 [1886]). The Court's power to hear Snow's appeal on a writ of error was derived from statute and extended only so far as the terms of that statutory grant. In general, the United States Supreme Court was empowered to hear and decide cases involving money above a certain sum, issues of statutory validity, and constitutional issues. Additionally, the Poland Act provided that polygamy or bigamy convictions could be appealed to the Supreme Court through writs of error.[3] But when cohabitation was defined as an offense by the Edmunds Act, no similar provision for appeal of cohabitation convictions was adopted.

Snow's appeal, the Supreme Court concluded, came within none of those jurisdictional categories. He did not raise a constitutional issue nor challenge the validity of the act. The question of segregation of offenses was, instead, merely a question of "whether there is or is not error in the administration of the statute" (US 118:353). Such a question of the interpretation or application of a statute might be raised in any criminal prosecution and did not imply that "the validity of 'an authority exercised under the United States' is drawn in question" (US 118:353).

Similarly, jurisdiction over Snow's appeal could not be based on the Court's power to review polygamy or bigamy convictions. Polygamy and cohabitation were distinct offenses, and jurisdiction granted over one class of offenses did not imply a power to review offenses that were similar but based on a different statute (US 118:351). Disingenuously, the Court suggested that Congress's failure to provide a method of appealing cohabitation convictions was intentional, since cohabitation was defined as a relatively minor offense, carrying much lesser penalties than did bigamy or polygamy. This rationale was very feeble. The ground of Snow's appeal was precisely that the cohabitation statute had been construed in a way that allowed the imposition of penalties as great as, or potentially much greater than, those imposed for bigamy or polygamy.

In denying Snow's appeal for want of jurisdiction, the Court realized that it had already improperly heard and decided one other cohabitation case, *Cannon v. United States* (US 116:55 [1885]). The Court therefore vacated its decision in that prior case as having been issued without jurisdiction over the subject matter (US 118:355).

With the principle of segregation approved by the Utah Supreme Court and the possibility of further review seemingly removed by the United States Supreme Court's holding in *Snow*, federal prosecutors swiftly began expanding their use of the segregation of offenses, testing how far the principle could be pushed. The first expansion was in the 1886 case of *United States v. Groesbeck* (Utah 4:487). Nicholas H. Groesbeck was indicted on two identical counts of cohabitation with his three wives. As in *Snow*, the only difference between the charges was the time covered by each; but unlike *Snow*, the period of each offense had been halved from one year to six months. Also unlike Snow, Groesbeck was not granted a separate trial on each charge.

On appeal, the Utah Supreme Court sustained both these innovations. The fact that the single trial had allowed the jury to improperly consider Groesbeck's first conviction in determining his guilt on the second charge was disregarded. The court concluded that, in considering the question of Groesbeck's guilt as to the second charge, the jury was entitled to consider his prior relations with his wives, evidence presented in connection with the first charge. Moreover, consolidation of offenses into a single trial saved the state the burden and expense, and the defendant the harassment, of multiple litigation.

The Utah Supreme Court also advanced some sort of reasoned justification for the segregation of offenses principle. To allow Groesbeck to be charged and convicted for only one count of cohabitation for his period of continuous cohabitation with his wives would be unfair, the court reasoned. Such a rule might allow more serious offenders to be treated more leniently than lesser offenders. For example, the court reasoned, a polygamist who ceased cohabiting with his wives one year after the Edmunds Act was adopted but then began cohabiting with them a year later would be liable to two charges of cohabitation for his two years of cohabitation. By contrast, Snow would face only one charge for three years of cohabitation. Thus, without the segregation of offenses, "the greater the cohabitation the less the punishment; the less the cohabitation the greater the punishment" (Utah 4:493). Similarly, a rule that allowed only one charge of cohabitation to be raised, however long the period of cohabitation had been, gave polygamists no incentive to conform to the law, for an individual's liability was not increased if he continued to cohabit nor limited if he ceased.

The court's reasoning in this respect is flawed. First, under the segregation rule, in principle and in practice, there was no necessary relation between the length of an offender's offense and the number of charges raised against him. Because the basis of segregation was inherently arbitrary, any offense—no matter how long or short its duration—could be divided into as many separate offenses as was desired. Snow, for example, had engaged in polygamy for a period of forty years and was charged with three offenses spanning the three years since adoption of the Edmunds Act. Groesbeck, on the other hand, was assigned two-thirds the punishment given Snow, for a period of cohabitation of one year. Conversely, if cohabitation were treated as a continuous offense, under the principles governing the treatment of continuous offenses even lapses in cohabitation would not necessarily segregate the offense into separate offenses.

Snow, meanwhile, with no avenue of further appeal available, began serving his sentences for the three convictions. After serving the first six-month sentence, Snow again appealed to the United States Supreme Court, this time on an application for a writ of habeas corpus. He claimed that his further detention in the Utah prison was unlawful since the two remaining sentences were the result of an unlawful segregation of a single offense. The Supreme Court heard this case on 21 January 1887 (*In re Snow*, US 120:274). As before, the government contended that the Court lacked jurisdiction because Snow had already raised and received a ruling on the issue of segregation at trial and in his prior appeal, an issue reviewable only if a writ of error were allowed in cohabitation cases. The Court, however, held that it did have jurisdiction because "not only had the court which tried them no jurisdiction to inflict a punishment in respect of more than one of the convictions, but, as the want of jurisdiction appears on the face of the judgment, the objection may be taken on *habeas corpus*, when the sentence on more than one of the convictions is sought to be enforced" (US 120:285).

The Court's opinion constituted a mild but clear rebuke to Utah's judicial officers for attempting to impose so patently objectionable a device as the segregation of offenses. Cohabitation was, the Court stated, "inherently, a continuous offense, having duration; and not an offense consisting of an isolated act" (US 120:281). Because cohabitation was an offense of reputation and appearance, any division of the offense into separate charges must be "wholly arbitrary," leaving open the door to as many or as few divisions as the prosecution chose to make:

On the same principle there might have been an indictment covering each of the thirty-five months, with imprisonment for seventeen years and a half and fines amounting to $10,500, or even an indictment covering every week, with imprisonment for seventy-four years and fines amounting to $44,000; and so on, *ad infinitum* for smaller periods of time. . . . (US 120:282)

To prevent such arbitrary judicial conduct the law provides that inherently continuous offenses "can be committed but once . . . prior to the time the prosecution is instituted" (US 120:282).

In conclusion, the Court demolished the legal precedent of *Commonwealth v. Connors* by pointing out that in a subsequent case, *Commonwealth v. Robinson* (Mass. 126:259 [1879]), the Massachusetts court, on the same facts as in *Connors*, had rejected the segregation principle and treated the offense as continuous (US 120:286). The Utah Supreme Court's holding in *Snow* was, thus, left bereft of both reason and legal authority.

The Utah Supreme Court grudgingly bowed to the United States Supreme Court, but it suggested in an 1887 case that the bar against the segregation of offenses would be narrowly construed, warning that an offense would be treated as continuous only where "the cohabitation is by the same man, with the same woman, continuously and uninterruptedly" (*United States v. Eldredge*, P. 13:680; P. 14:42).[4] By implication, thus, the court left open the possibility that cohabitation offenses might still be divided where there had been some breaks in the periods of cohabitation—a common occurrence since Mormon men frequently went on missions. Where an accused had more than two wives, the court's dicta suggested that cohabitation with each would be made the basis of a separate offense.

Despite the decision in *In re Snow*, courts could still impose multiple punishments for what was in reality one offense. The Edmunds Act itself specifically allowed polygamy and cohabitation charges to be combined (Stat. 22:31, § 4 [1882]). However, because the offenses were statutorily distinguished, a man could be convicted of marrying a polygamous wife and then convicted for subsequently living with her. For example, in *Clawson v. United States* (Utah 4:34 [1885], affirmed, US 114:477 [1885]). Rudger Clawson, later an apostle, was convicted of polygamy for marrying a second wife and sentenced to three and one-half years' imprisonment and a $500 fine. He was also convicted of cohabiting with that wife and sentenced to six months and a $300 fine. But cohabitation was much easier to establish than polygamy; and fewer than fifty polygamy convictions were ever handed down.

In 1889 the United States Supreme Court, in *Hans Nielsen* (US 131:176), limited the combination of different offenses. In September 1888 Nielsen had been indicted for two offenses, adultery and cohabitation. Both charges were directed at Nielsen's conduct with his polygamous wife Caroline. The cohabitation charge covered from 1885 to 13 May 1888; adultery was charged for 14 May 1888. Nielsen pleaded guilty to the charge of cohabitation and was sentenced to three months' imprisonment and fined $100. When arraigned on the adultery charge, however, Nielsen claimed his conviction for cohabitation barred his further prosecution. After serving his sentence for cohabitation, Nielsen was tried and convicted of adultery and sentenced to an additional 125 days' imprisonment. Nielsen's appeal from this sentence was taken to the United States Supreme Court by way of a petition for writ of habeas corpus.

The Court swiftly disposed of two issues. As it had in the *Snow* case, the United States argued that Nielsen could not raise a collateral attack on the trial court's judgment through a habeas corpus proceeding. The Court noted that Nielsen's petition, however, raised a constitutional issue:

> In the present case, it is true, the ground for the *habeas corpus* was, not the invalidity of an act of Congress under which the defendant was indicted, but a second prosecution and trial for the same offense, contrary to an express provision of the Constitution. In other words, a constitutional immunity of the defendant was violated by the second trial and judgment. It is difficult to see why a conviction and punishment under an unconstitutional law is more violative of a person's constitutional rights, than an unconstitutional conviction and punishment under a valid law. (US 131:183)

Secondly, the argument that the offenses could be distinguished because they dealt with different periods of time—adultery having been charged for the day after the alleged period of cohabitation—was quickly dismissed on the authority of *In re Snow* (US 131:185–86).

Thereafter, the Court's analysis becomes more difficult because of the gap between legal rules and reality in the area of polygamy laws. In real terms, Nielsen's convictions for cohabitation and adultery were manifestly improper, for he was being punished for but one offense: having a polygamous wife. Legally, though, the answer was not so clear. Adultery was an offense based on unlawful sexual conduct. Cohabitation, by contrast, was not based on an accused's sexual conduct, but rather on his appearance of having a polygamous wife. Legally, the elements of the offenses differed, and thus a conviction for both offenses on the basis of the same activity appeared permissible. "A single act may be an offence against two statutes," observed the Court, quoting *Morey v. Commonwealth* (Mass. 108:433 [1871]). "And if each statute requires proof of an additional fact which the other does not, an acquittal or conviction under either statute does not exempt the defendant from prosecution and punishment under the other" (US 131:188).

Within the framework of unrealistic legal rules, however, the Court managed to arrive at a sensible result. In Nielsen's case, the charge of cohabitation amounted to dual punishment for the same offense. While it was true that sexual intercourse need not be proved in an unlawful cohabitation case, "this was only because proof of sexual intercourse would have been merely cumulative evidence of the fact" (US 131:187). Since Nielsen and Caroline had lived together as husband and wife, sexual intercourse (the essential element of the adultery charge) could be assumed. Thus, when Nielsen was convicted of cohabitation, he was convicted of all the elements of adultery and could not be separately punished for that offense. However, the court left open the question whether Nielsen's acquittal on the cohabitation charge would have barred his prosecution for adultery, perhaps envisioning the more frequent situation in which the couple committing adultery do not cohabit as husband and wife.

With *Hans Nielsen*, draconian attempts to make the polygamy laws even more severe by piling offenses together or fractioning a single act into many separate offenses ceased. Until the conclusion of the polygamy prosecutions in the early 1890s, prosecutors contented themselves with simply enforcing the laws vigorously, a process that was itself painful and disruptive enough for the Mormon community.

In addition to segregating offenses, federal prosecutors and judges tried to facilitate convictions by making it easier to prove cohabitation.

It is well known that the guilt of one accused of a crime must be established "beyond a reasonable doubt." This heavy burden of proof minimizes the risk that an innocent party will be punished. Less well known, however, is that burdens of proof can be effectively shifted through the use of presumptions. A presumption of fact directs the finder to accept a given fact as true unless or until contrary evidence is produced. A conclusive presumption directs the fact-finder to accept a fact as true despite any contrary evidence introduced to rebut it. Properly used, presumptions can effectively help juries assess evidence or force reluctant parties to produce evidence to which they alone have access. Misused, presumptions can deprive an accused person of the right to be presumed innocent until the state has proven guilt.

The offense of cohabitation, as interpreted by the Utah courts, consisted of appearing to consort with two or more women. Thus, it was not necessary to prove that a marriage had taken place, and polygamy was not a necessary element of the offense. Such a definition of cohabitation created the theoretical possibility that a polygamist might abandon his first or legally recognized wife, live exclusively with a later plural wife, and not be guilty of cohabitation. So long as a man cohabited with only one woman, the statutory terms seemed to be satisfied, regardless of whether that woman was the man's lawful wife.

A construction of the Edmunds Act that allowed a polygamist to retain whichever one of his wives he wished, so long as he retained only one of them was, of course, not well received by the courts. Their solution was a presumption that a man cohabited with his legal wife. When first announced in the case of *United States v. Snow* (P. 9:501 [Utah 1886]), it was offered as a rebuttable presumption of fact. The court noted that "a lawful marriage of itself affords a strong presumption of matrimonial cohabitation, because such cohabitation is in accordance with duty, and usually attends such a marriage" (P. 9:504). A presumption of cohabitation was justified by two reasons. First, society's policy of encouraging marital fidelity supported the creation of a presumption that encouraged spouses to honor their marital duties. Secondly, the presumption was justified as a factual generalization. Because, as a matter of fact, most legally married couples did cohabit, it was convenient for courts to assume so in polygamy cases until contrary evidence was presented. At first, however, this presumption was somewhat tentative since a presumption of cohabitation appeared to require at least some independent evidence of actual cohabitation.

Given the judicial purpose, however, a factual basis for a presumption of cohabitation with a lawful wife would not do. The fact that most lawfully married couples cohabited could not deter some polygamists from demonstrating that the assumption was incorrect when applied to them. Thus, the courts very quickly deemphasized the factual rationale for the presumption and instead emphasized its legal and social policy rationale. As they did so, the strength of the presumption of cohabitation increased, and the extent to which it could be refuted by contrary evidence diminished. For example, on Snow's appeal of his second conviction, the court stated: "If a man has a wife—a lawful wife—the strong presumption is that he lives and cohabits with her. This presumption is so strong that in some instances he is not permitted to deny access, and we do not know but that such should be the rule in this class of cases" (P. 9:688). Chief Justice Charles S. Zane dissented, arguing that since cohabitation with more than one woman was essential to the offense, that fact should have to be proved by the state (P. 9:696–97).

A year later, in 1887, the court again emphasized the strength of the presumption of cohabitation with a lawful wife (*United States v. Clark*, P. 14:288). Presumptions of cohabitation were deemed not to be "slight presumptions of fact" but strong presumptions based on social policy: "that holy union without it is a sham—a mere semblance. Without matrimonial association the institution of marriage, upon which the happiness and welfare of society so largely depends, is shorn of its power to promote chastity and to exalt virtue" (P. 14:291). A lawful marriage, thus, gave rise to a *prima facie* presumption of cohabitation. Probably, the court meant that the presumption would be accepted without any independent evidence of actual cohabitation, although if contrary evidence were introduced, the presumption could be rebutted.

Finally, in 1888 the Utah Supreme Court so diluted the amount of evidence required to render the presumption of cohabitation with a legal wife conclusive, that, in effect, the presumption became conclusive in law. In *United States v. Harris* (P. 17:75), the court approved jury instructions to the effect that "if in this case, or any other, the legal wife of the defendant lives in the same vicinity with him, bearing his name, in a household maintained in part by him; that is cohabitation with his legal wife. It is absolutely and conclusively cohabitation with his legal wife; because, whatever he does with her is done as a husband" (P. 17:76).

Under this standard even the remotest contact between a man and his legal wife constituted cohabitation. In *Harris*, for example, the defendant, John Harris had agreed to separate from his legal wife, who lived in a house nearby. He had been seen, however, in her yard watering his horses at her well, and "he sends her provisions; and, whenever she has wanted a sack of flour, he would take it to her and put it in her flour-bin" (P. 17:78). These "contacts" justified a conclusive presumption that Harris cohabited with his lawful wife. Indeed, the court suggested that Harris's very act of agreeing to separate from his wife, accompanied by a conveyance of property to her, constituted cohabitation.

In *United States v. Smith* (P. 14:291 [Utah 1887]), James Smith was convicted despite the absence of any evidence that he had been in his lawful wife's home "more than once during the last two years (and that was on a funeral occasion)." However, there was abundant evidence "that he has been seen during the time in the house-yard, at the well, and at the door of the house in which she lived" (P. 14:294). The defendant's explanation that his blacksmith shop was located thirty to fifty feet from the house was ignored.

Under such a standard, it seemed unlikely that any polygamist could insulate himself sufficiently to avoid a finding of cohabitation with his lawful wife. Certainly, this presumption of cohabitation created a strong disincentive for polygamists who wished to support and care for the women they had married.

Conversely, *Harris* provided some measure of relief to polygamists. If cohabitation with one's lawful wife was strongly presumed, the court announced, "When you come to cohabitation with the illegal wife, then the presumptions are all against it" (P. 17:76). Under this standard then, Mormons were strongly pressured not only to adopt monogamous marital relations, but to adopt them only with wives recognized as lawful.

Even this standard was not reliable, however, for on other occasions the court suggested that a man might be presumed to cohabit with his unlawful wives, as well as with his lawful one. For example, Lorenzo Snow's support of his plural wives served to raise a presumption of cohabitation (P. 9:686). The Utah Supreme Court reasoned:

> Would not a man so living be cohabiting with all the women he was thus maintaining and supporting and holding out as wives? We think the conclusion is inevitable that he would. He could be the head of each and all of these diverse establishments, and they would be all one "Snow family." (P. 9:690)

A year later, in *United States v. Smith* (P. 14:291 [Utah 1887]), the court rather ambiguously suggested that both legal and illegal marriages raised a presumption of cohabitation. Although the presumption of cohabitation with an unlawful wife was weaker than the presumption with regard to a lawful wife, the court failed to define just how much or what sort of evidence would be required to rebut the presumption of cohabitation with regard to a polygamous wife. Together, the two presumptions effectively shifted the burden of proof in cohabitation trials. Because a polygamist was presumed to cohabit with both his lawful and unlawful wives, he was presumptively guilty of cohabitation unless he could effectively rebut those presumptions. In essence he was presumed guilty unless he could prove his innocence.

The prosecutor's ease in proving cohabitation was further enhanced by judicial rulings on the type of evidence that could be admitted to establish cohabitation. To a great extent, these rulings were simply a product of the amorphous definition of cohabitation adopted by the

court. Because cohabitation was held to be an offense of appearance
and repute, evidence of appearance and repute could, of course, be
admitted to establish the offense. Beyond that, however, lax evidentiary standards in cohabitation trials were a matter of judicial policy.
In *United States v. Snow*, the court, noting the strong legislative policy
of stamping out all vestiges and appearances of polygamy, concluded
that to achieve Congress's goal, loose evidentiary standards were required:

> In these polygamic relations there never is and cannot be that intimate
> association, and habitual attention given by the man to the various
> women, as exist between a husband and his wife in the monogamic state.
> Consequently, in the very nature of things, the proof of cohabitation
> cannot be made as clear as in the case of a monogamic marriage, simply
> because the facts of which proof is to be made do not as abundantly
> exist. (P. 9:687)

Moreover, the Mormons and the judges apparently differed in their
perceptions of affairs in Utah. Many Mormons apparently attempted
to live within the cohabitation law, as they understood it, while still
honoring their legal and moral obligations to support their wives and
raise their children. But in these Mormon efforts, the judges saw only
attempts to evade the law:

> If a living, staying, dwelling, eating, sleeping, and lodging in each house
> must be shown by direct proof, and the law fails in its object, and it
> will be a vain and a fruitless effort to destroy the outward semblance of
> polygamy—the ostentatious display of the polygamic relation—without
> additional legislation. The shrewd and cunning polygamist can easily
> evade the law as it stands without an interpretation. (*United States v.
> Snow*, P. 9:692)

The courts therefore admitted circumstantial evidence: "language,
and conduct, and appearances, and expressions," could serve as evidence of cohabitation (*United States v. Musser*, P. 7:394 [Utah 1885]).
As already noted, the fact that a man was seen watering his horses
at a plural wife's well or taking her provisions suggested an unlawful
cohabitation. A birthday party given for an aging polygamist and
attended by his plural families similarly indicated a continued cohabitation (*United States v. Snow*, P. 9:689).

If these examples indicate a loose standard of evidence, admitting
reputations as proof of cohabitation had almost no limitations. To
convict a man of cohabitation, it was sufficient to show that he and
his plural wives "were living in the habit and repute of marriage, and
to all outward appearance they were living and associating together

as man and wife[;] it was not necessary to show that they occupied the same bed, slept in the same room, dwelt under the same roof, or that they were guilty of sexual intercourse" (*United States v. Snow*, P. 9:506). Of course, to allow convictions on the basis of reputation transformed courtrooms into courts of public opinion.

At these outer reaches of the limits of judicial propriety, however, a few cautionary voices were raised. The Arizona Supreme Court acknowledged evidence of reputation "standing alone, would amount to nothing in such a case," but in conjunction with "all the other proof and circumstances," reputation could be considered by a jury (*United States v. Tenney*, P. 8:296–97 [1885]). The supreme court of Idaho, a state not given to charity toward Mormons, excluded evidence of reputation altogether in cohabitation trials, ruling in 1889 that "the defendant's guilt may be established by his own acts, but certainly to assume the guilt without proof of the acts would be manifestly improper" (*United States v. Langford*, P. 21:409).

Evidence that the defendant had fled to avoid arrest was deemed admissible as circumstantial evidence of guilt. For example, in *Snow*, it was held that "the jury, in ascertaining whether the appellant was guilty or not, had the right to take into consideration his concealment at the time of arrest, and also the manner of concealment" (P. 9:691). In *United States v. Kuntze* (P. 21:407 [1889]), the Idaho Supreme Court also held that a defendant's flight could be considered by the jury, although by itself it could not warrant a conviction.

If a defendant's guilt could be established by a presumption that he cohabited with his wives, lawful and polygamous, prosecutors still had to prove that the defendant had married those women before raising that presumption. Until the Edmunds-Tucker Act in 1887, most western territories had no laws governing the performance of a marriage or its public recordation, and the agreement of a couple to live together as man and wife could constitute a marriage. No witnesses were required. Because the task of establishing Mormon weddings had rendered the Morrill Act nearly useless, courts lowered evidentiary standards, allowing marriages also to be proven by scraps of circumstantial evidence. Because a marriage might have been entered into informally, equally informal proof was admissible: "Proof that two parties have treated each other as husband and wife, have lived together as such, and have held each other out to the world as such, is sufficient to enable a court or jury to find that at some previous time the parties did, as a fact, consent to be married" (*United States v. Simpson*, Utah 4:229 [1885]). Polygamy and cohabitation, then, could each be proven by evidence that a couple had the appearance of being married.

Thus, statements by a defendant that a woman was his wife, made out of court and before any charges had been made against him, could be introduced at trial to prove his marriage. Similarly, a defendant's out-of-court statements could, by themselves, be sufficient to prove cohabitation. In *United States v. Schow* (Utah 6:381 [1890]), the defendant "was convicted alone on the proof of his admissions made out of court." Indeed, a hot-headed Mormon could pay dearly for intemperate public remarks. For example, in *United States v. Smith* (P. 14:288 [Utah 1887]), James Smith was convicted on testimony that the "defendant said 'we' or 'they' (not positive which) 'would never give it up; that the law against it was unconstitutional; and that he had just as good a right to decide on it as the Supreme Court'" (P. 14:292). Thus, a rash criticism of Supreme Court decisions was transformed into an admission of guilt of cohabitation.

Cohabitation trials also raised the issue of what time periods of cohabitation could establish the offense. Because cohabitation became an offense only on enactment of the Edmunds Act in 1882, prior conduct should have been irrelevant in cohabitation cases. In fact, however, courts admitted evidence of a defendant's conduct with his wives prior to passage of the Edmunds Act on two alternative theories. The harsher theory again depended on a presumption: If an individual entered into an evil relationship at any point in time, a presumption existed that the relationship continued unless evidence of its cessation were brought forward. Thus, in *United States v. Cannon*, the court quoted with approval the rule that "a meretricious intercourse in the beginning is presumed to continue, unless there be evidence of a change" (P. 7:379 [Utah 1885]). In *United States v. Musser*, the court explained its position more carefully. If a lawful relationship was formed, then made unlawful, the law would presume that the innocently intentioned parties had terminated the relationship unless the contrary was proven. "But if the relationship was unlawful in its inception, and the intention was unlawful, then it would be necessary to presume a change of both intention and relationship" (P. 7:396 [Utah 1885]), and such a presumption would be too much. Polygamy had been unlawful, the court pointed out, since the Morrill Act in 1862 and for more than a generation under common law in the territory. At this point, the court's analysis becomes confused, for while this line of reasoning suggests that a defendant's prior conduct could be admitted as evidence of his present guilt, the court also recognized that a defendant must be presumed innocent until proven guilty. Instead of resolving this dilemma, the court simply concluded that a defendant's cohabitation prior to passage of the Edmunds Act was evidence of his propensity to violate the law and of his evil intentions. As such, the evidence could be thrown in, along with all the other circumstantial evidence, for the jury's consideration: "A disposition and intention to violate the law in entering into the relationship with these women being shown, it affords an inference of some effect upon the man, when considered with the other evidence, at the time of the offense charged" (P. 7:395–96).

The reasoning of the court is almost directly antithetical to modern rules of evidence. For example, Rule 404(a) of the *Federal Rules of Evidence* provides that, with few exceptions, "evidence of a person's character or a trait of his character is not admissible for the purpose of proving that he acted in conformity therewith on a particular occasion. . . ." Similarly, under 404(b) of the federal rules, evidence regarding prior "crimes, wrongs, or acts" of a defendant is inadmissible. Under Rule 609 evidence of certain crimes may be admitted but only to impeach the credibility of the defendant's testimony.

The other rationale for allowing evidence of a defendant's conduct prior to passage of the Edmunds Act was less ambitious. Marital relations, the court in *Musser* reasoned, are likely to be enduring relationships: "That relation is usually preceded and attended by affections and feelings peculiar to it, and more permanent in their character, and they give rise to conduct indicating their existence, and thereby indicating marriage" (P. 7:396). In other words, just as a murder trial might admit evidence of the defendant's behavior and feelings regarding the victim prior to the murder, evidence of how the defendant regarded his plural wives prior to 1882 could be admitted to show how he regarded them at the time of the offense (P. 7:395–96). Similarly, in *United States v. Peay* (P. 14:342 [Utah 1887]), the court deemed it permissible to admit evidence of prior conduct on the grounds that "it was not introduced to show acts or conduct for which the party was liable, or to show a cohabitation for which the defendant would be liable under this indictment. It was merely to illustrate and explain the evidence as to what took place during the time laid in the indictment" (P. 14:344). In *United States v. Smith* (P. 14:288 [Utah 1887]), a similar guideline was explained: "We are of the opinion that it was proper for the jury to consider appellant's conduct towards the women during the time covered by the indictment in the light of his previous relations to and conduct towards them" (P. 14:293).

This rationalization, too, is unsatisfactory. While, as the court in

Musser reasoned, evidence of prior conduct may be admitted to establish the defendant's motive or knowledge, evidence of prior conduct admitted in the polygamy trials was not evidence of some different conduct at a prior time. Instead, it was evidence of cohabitation, precisely the offense charged. Such evidence could only have prejudiced or confused a jury, making it likely that a defendant would be improperly convicted on the basis of his prior conduct or that the jury would improperly conclude that because the defendant had previously cohabited, he must have been guilty of cohabitation as charged.

In summary, early in the prosecution of cohabitation, the courts announced that the nature of the offense required liberal standards of evidence. But in loosening the rules of evidence to serve Congress's policy of ensuring the punishment of polygamy, the courts undermined the elemental bases of judicial procedure and due process of law. The most basic assumptions—that an accused is presumed innocent and must be found guilty beyond a reasonable doubt by competent evidence—were sapped of all strength by evidentiary rulings. Because evidence of an accused's prior conduct could be admitted to build an inference of guilt, polygamists could not avoid prosecution even by avoiding their wives altogether. Innocent statements against the polygamy laws could be construed as admissions of guilt, and even the most innocent or distant of contacts between a man and his plural wives could trigger a presumption of cohabitation under the standard that anything a man does with a lawful or unlawful wife is presumed to be marital conduct.

The court opinions of this era are replete with circular reasoning. It is assumed that the women with whom a man is charged with cohabiting are his plural wives. And if it is not assumed, then proving that they are his wives is simple enough, because the fact of marriage was demonstrated by the fact that a couple appeared to be married. Then, if those women were presumed to be wives, any contact at all between the accused and those women was held to constitute cohabitation. Even if no contact were shown, cohabitation might be presumed on the basis that a marriage not proved to have been effectively terminated or a prior cohabitation could be presumed to continue into the present. The courts were indeed accurate when they identified cohabitation as being an offense of appearance or reputation, for under such evidentiary standards an accused's actual conduct seemed largely irrelevant. Mormons widely reputed to be polygamists could, by using strings of presumptions and the testimony of what people thought their marital relations were, be quickly convicted whatever they tried to do.

Most important, these interpretations of evidentiary law allowed the state to deny association and responsible care, on the part of former marriage partners, and parents and children. Surely the interest of the state should have been to see that children and dependent former wives were cared for, even as plural marriage ended. But this interpretation of rules of evidence forbade such sensible and compassionate treatment. Instead, the interpretation and evidentiary rulings of cohabitation cases produced heart-rending suffering. Men were forbidden to associate with their own children or to provide for their former wives. Women were denied care from and association with former husbands. The law, not limited to prohibiting future polygamous marriages, fell with all its severity upon people whose relationships had most often been established when the law did not unambiguously forbid them.

Wives as Witnesses

To convict Mormon men of polygamy offenses, certainly no more effective and knowledgeable witnesses could be found than those men's wives. Two obstacles, however, appeared to bar the use of this pool of witnesses. First, many if not most Mormon wives were unwilling to testify against their husbands. Second, even if they were willing to testify, common law rules of evidence and territorial statutes appeared to bar spouses from testifying against their husbands or wives. The polygamy prosecutions partially overcame both obstacles.

At common law, a spouse was not competent—was not permitted—to testify against his or her spouse. Polygamy prosecutions, however, raised perplexing variants that made application of this rule problematic. For example, did this spousal disability rule apply to illegal, polygamous wives as well as to legal wives? If polygamous wives were competent witnesses, what was to be done when it could not be determined which was the lawful and which were the plural wives?

These issues were first confronted in the case of *United States v. Miles* (US 103:304 [1880]), which held that a wife who agreed to testify against her husband to prove an earlier marriage must be treated as his lawful wife. The *Miles* Court, however, noted that eyewitness testimony was not necessary to prove a polygamous marriage.

Such spousal immunity issues generated by the peculiarities of polygamy baffled the courts for several years. In 1886 the Utah Supreme Court heard an appeal from a case in which the defendant, Barnard White, had been convicted of cohabiting with his lawful wife and his polygamous wife (*United States v. White*, P. 11:570). White was indicted on 9 January 1886. His lawful wife, Diana, died shortly thereafter, and he then legally married his polygamous wife, Jane Fyfe White, on 12 April 1886, two months before his trial. According to the court, "It transpired from the testimony that the sole object in having the marriage ceremony performed was to close the mouth of the witness, and to prevent the government from obtaining her testimony" (P. 11:570). The Utah Supreme Court reversed the trial court by holding that the wife's testimony had been improperly admitted. Because she had not been the defendant's lawful wife at the time of the alleged offense, the offense could not be used against her and, thus, no exception to the rule excluding a wife's testimony was available. The defendant's motives in legally marrying the woman who had been his polygamous wife were legally irrelevant (P. 11:571).

United States v. Kershaw (P. 19:194 [Utah 1888]) presented yet another variation of the evidentiary puzzle posed by a polygamous wife's testimony. Andrew J. Kershaw was charged and convicted not of polygamy, but of adultery. In fact, however, the basis of the charge was Kershaw's polygamous marriages. The evidence against him consisted of the testimony of one Mary E. Ramsden, his polygamous wife and accomplice in the offense. On appeal, Kershaw contended that this evidence was insufficient to sustain his conviction, for a Utah statute (Utah Laws 1878, 118, § 273) provided that an accused could not be convicted on the testimony of an accomplice unless that testimony were corroborated by other evidence that independently tended "to connect the defendant with the commission of the offense." In sustaining Kershaw's conviction, the Utah Supreme Court concluded that Mary's testimony was, in fact, corroborated by her reputation as Kershaw's polygamous wife (P. 19:195).

Finally, the United States Supreme Court considered the question of polygamous wives' testimony in United States v. Bassett (P. 13:237 [Utah 1887], reversed, US 137:496 [1890]). William E. Bassett had been convicted of polygamy and sentenced to a term of five years and a fine of $500 on the strength of the testimony of his first wife. Bassett's conviction was upheld and his objection to the testimony of his first wife overruled by the Utah Supreme Court.

The Utah court recognized the general rule that a wife was not a competent witness against her husband but also noted that that rule was subject, under common law and Utah statute, to several exceptions. A Utah statute, for example, provided that a wife could testify against her husband in a civil action by one spouse against the other or in a criminal action for a crime committed by one against the other (P. 13:240). The general rule rendering a spouse incompetent as a witness is logical. Ensuring private and open communications between marital partners is worth the loss of some potential evidence. Similarly, the exceptions to that rule in the case of an action or crime by one spouse against the other ensure that a spouse is not deprived of all access to the judicial system in cases of conflicts where the lines of marital communication are likely to have been already disrupted.

In *Bassett*, the Utah Supreme Court concluded that polygamy was, in fact, an offense by the husband against his lawful wife:

> The husband is bound by that contract [marriage] not to marry another woman, while the marriage is in force. . . . The law recognizes the marital rights of a woman or man, . . . and the breach thereof by a second marriage, or by cohabitation with another woman as a wife, is often more injurious to the feelings of the lawful wife, as well as in other respects, as would be a deprivation of personal security or of personal liberty—more injurious than the shake of a fist, coupled with a threat or an attempt to commit a bodily injury. (P. 13:240)

Because polygamy was an offense against a man's lawful wife, then, the general rule of spousal disability did not apply, and the wife was a competent witness. The Utah Supreme Court's position on this issue was reaffirmed in *United States v. Cutler* (P. 19:145 [Utah 1888]). Chief Justice Zane in dissent argued, however, that even though he agreed with the majority's reasoning that polygamy was a crime against a man's lawful wife, the Utah evidentiary rules permitting a lawful wife to testify should not be applied to polygamy cases. Inasmuch as polygamy was an offense defined by federal statute, Zane reasoned, federal rules of evidence excluding a wife's testimony, should have been employed (P. 19:146–47).

However, the United States Supreme Court continued to disregard territorial efforts to allow disaffected spouses to testify against their polygamous husbands. The Court rejected the territorial court's analysis in *Bassett* on two grounds. First, it concluded that the Utah courts had applied the wrong territorial evidentiary statute. The statute applied by the territorial court, allowing a spouse to testify in criminal actions for offenses committed by one spouse against the other, was found in Utah's civil code. A second, older statute, contained in Utah's criminal code, provided that a spouse might testify only in cases of "criminal violence" upon one spouse by the other. The Court concluded that although the section of the civil code was more recently adopted and would thus otherwise take priority over older inconsistent acts, in fact, the criminal code provision should have been applied in *Bassett*, a criminal case (US 137:503). Under Utah's criminal code, a wife might only testify against her husband if he had committed some act of criminal violence against her. Polygamy could not rationally be construed as an act of criminal violence.

Less technically, the Court concluded that even under the standard employed by the Utah courts, a wife would not be a competent witness against her husband in a polygamy trial. That is, polygamy could not be properly viewed as an offense against the wife: "Polygamy and adultery may be crimes which involve disloyalty to the marital relation, but they are rather crimes against such relation than against the wife; and, as the statute speaks of crimes against her, it is simply an affirmation of the old familiar and just common law rule" (US 137:506). Certainly, a lawful wife's feelings might be outraged at being made a party to a polygamous union, but that outrage could not, even by strained judicial interpretation, be construed as a crime sufficient to outweigh the powerful social interest in preserving the rule of marital silence (US 137:505–6).

Nearly seven years after the United States Supreme Court first excluded the testimony of a polygamous wife, in *Miles*, and suggested that the remedy to such evidentiary problems lay with Congress, Congress finally made it easier to prove polygamy by passing the Edmunds-Tucker Act.

THE EDMUNDS-TUCKER ACT

The mining boom and the completion of a transcontinental railroad in 1869 increased the non-Mormon presence in Utah. There were an estimated 14,000 non-Mormons in Utah in the late 1870s, but "they were still no numerical threat to Mormon supremacy," with the Mormon population in Utah and the surrounding states estimated at 150,000 in 1880 (Arrington 1958, 353; Dwyer 1971, 167). Thus even after the Utah Commission's mass disenfranchisement of Mormons, Mormon voters still controlled Utah's electoral machinery. Three years after passage of the Edmunds Act, President Grover Cleveland reported to Congress that although the Utah Commission had excluded all practicing polygamists from voter rolls and removed them from all offices,

> yet at the last election in the Territory all the officers elected, except in one county, were men who, though not actually living in the practice of polygamy, subscribe to the doctrine of polygamous marriages. . . . Thus is the strange spectacle presented of a community protected by a republican form of government, to which they owe allegiance, sustaining by their suffrages a principle and a belief which set at naught that obligation of absolute obedience to the law of the land which lies at the foundation of republican institutions. (Richardson 1896–99, 8:361)

Cleveland, however, called on Congress only to prevent the further importation of Mormons into the country. The year before, Cleveland's predecessor had urged sterner measures. In 1884 President Chester A. Arthur called on Congress to finally resolve the Mormon question by assuming "absolute political control of the Territory of Utah" and ruling the territory through federally appointed commissioners (Richardson 1896–99, 8:250).

Dissolution of Utah Territory was an ultimate political weapon that Congress had repeatedly threatened to use since 1860, and no doubt such a move would have effectively ended Mormon resistance. But even depriving Utah of its territorial status would have been an indirect means of achieving Congress's objective: destroying the Mormon church. When Congress adopted its strongest anti-Mormon legislation in 1887, it attacked the perceived problem directly. Instead of dismantling Utah's government, Congress dismantled the church.

Since 1882 Senator Edmunds had continually introduced legislation to strengthen the provisions of the Edmunds Act. Finally, in 1887, Congress acted on one of his proposals. The Edmunds-Tucker Act (Stat. 24:635 [1887]) was a collection of provisions aimed at diverse goals. Some provisions further tightened the polygamy laws. Others further restricted the civil freedoms of Mormons. A few were aimed directly at the church.

Sections 1, 2, and 6 of the act eliminated several evidentiary obstacles to polygamy prosecution. The Edmunds-Tucker Act overrode the common-law rule that a wife could not testify against her husband by declaring the wife to be a competent witness "in any prosecution for bigamy, polygamy, or unlawful cohabitation." The severity of this change was moderated by two provisions: a wife could not be compelled to testify, and her testimony could exclude any communication between spouses made "during the existence of the marriage relation, deemed confidential at common law."

To prevent witnesses from hiding, the act provided that a witness who might disobey a subpoena could be immediately compelled to appear by "an attachment . . . issued by the court, judge, or commissioner, without a previous subpoena." Such a witness might be released, however, by posting a bond. Finally, a Utah statute that permitted adultery prosecutions to be initiated only by the offender's spouse was annulled, allowing adultery prosecutions to be "instituted in the same way that prosecutions for other crimes are."

Sections 9 and 10 of the act solved the problem of evidence that had rendered the Morrill Act useless: proving Mormon marriages. Section

9 required that "every ceremony of marriage, or in the nature of a marriage ceremony" be certified by a certificate identifying the date, participants, and officiating officer. This certificate was to be filed with the probate court and would constitute "prima facie evidence of the facts required by this act to be stated." Violation of this provision was categorized as a misdemeanor but carried severe penalties: fines of up to $1,000 and/or up to two years' imprisonment. Section 10 carefully provided that in addition to the new marriage registration provisions of section 9, marriages could also be proved "by any evidence now legally admissible for that purpose."

The jurisdictional restrictions imposed on Utah's probate courts by the Poland Act were reiterated. Under sections 12 and 19 territorial provisions for the election of probate judges were nullified, and probate judges became presidential appointees to ensure that no obstruction of the polygamy laws would arise from that quarter.

Further collateral punishments were imposed on the members of polygamous households by the act's nullification of several Utah intestate succession statutes. An 1851 territorial statute provided that "illegitimate children and their mothers inherit in like manner from the father, whether acknowledged by him or not, provided it shall be made to appear to the satisfaction of the court, that he was the father of such illegitimate child or children" (Utah Laws 1851, 71, § 25). The Edmunds-Tucker Act nullified this provision and instead provided that illegitimate children born one year after the act's passage could not inherit from their fathers. Section 18 of the act negated an 1872 territorial act abolishing dower, a widow's right to one-third of her husband's real property (Utah Laws 1872, 27, § 3). By reestablishing dower, Congress reasserted the primacy of the first wife over plural wives' claims to their husband's estates.

A number of civil penalties were directed more or less indiscriminately against Utah's Mormon population. Several measures attempted to break the electoral and political dominance of the Mormons in Utah. Women had been granted the vote in 1870 (Utah Laws 1870, 8). Several scholars suggest that women were enfranchised to demonstrate to the world that women were not debased and subservient in Mormon society (Weisbrod and Sheingorn 1978, 852 n. 130). Now, apparently on the theory that Mormon women submissively voted according to their husbands' dictates, section 20 of the act disenfranchised Utah's women. Section 21 provided for the use of secret ballots in Utah's elections, tardily echoing a provision already adopted by the territorial legislature (Utah Laws 1878, 32, § 11). The secret

ballot issue provides a grimly humorous look at the Mormon predicament. Prior to passage of the territorial act, Utah's non-Mormons had
complained that the use of marked ballots allowed Mormon leaders to
watch over voters and control elections. After the legislature adopted
the secret ballot, they complained that unmarked ballots allowed the
Mormons to flood the polls with ineligible voters, including aliens
(Dwyer, 131–33).

The act further removed control of the electoral machinery from
the hands of Utah's Mormon-controlled legislature by abolishing territorial laws that had established election districts and apportioned
representatives. Redistricting was placed in the hands of the territorial governor, secretary, and the Utah Commission. The powers of the
Utah Commission were reaffirmed, and voters were required to take
a preregistration oath affirming that the applicant would obey the polygamy laws and "will not, directly or indirectly, aid or abet, counsel
or advise, any other person to commit any of said crimes." A similar
oath was required of territorial officers and jurors, and all those convicted of polygamy or who "cohabit polygamously" were denied the
right to vote, serve as jurors, or hold office.

Additional governmental powers believed to be sources of Mormon
influence were removed from territorial control. Section 22 abolished
the territorial superintendant of district schools and replaced him with
an officer appointed by the territorial supreme court. This new official
was directed to collect a variety of demographic data, including the
percentage of Mormon teachers and students in the school system.
As Utah's non-Mormon population had grown, the gentiles chaffed
ever more vocally at Mormon control of the public school system and
sent many of their children to parochial schools, thus furthering the
gulf between Utah's Mormon and gentile populations. In 1885, Utah's
governor had reported to the Secretary of the Interior:

> The public school system is very generally established over the Terri-
> tory, but it is a source of great complaint by a large number of the people
> who are taxed for the support of schools into which their children never
> enter. . . . The sum of it is, that the public schools receive as a body the
> Mormon children, and the schools established by the . . . denominations
> receive . . . the non-Mormons. (Dwyer, 170)

The governor's report reflected the conclusions of Utah's non-
Mormons:

> The American residents in Utah are taxed to support purely Mormon
> schools which they never patronize. The Government should at once take
> charge of the public school system in Utah by appointing an American as

superintendant of public instruction and taking the school system out of the hands of the Mormon priesthood, who are training up the children and youth of the Territory to hate country and all American institutions. (Dwyer, 168)

The Edmunds-Tucker Act allayed these concerns by placing control of public education in the hands of federal officials. Jacob S. Boreman, a retired territorial judge, was appointed superintendent of schools. The Mormons' ability and will to resist were fading, and they submitted peacefully to this change. In 1889 Boreman reported:

In a few localities where the influx of new people and the infusion of new life have caused a change, the control of the schools is passing out of the hands of those who heretofore controlled them.

The Mormon people do not show that independence of action that is so characteristic of the American people, but are obedient, even against their better judgment, to the will of their Church leader. (Dwyer, 173)

Section 27 of the Edmunds-Tucker Act abolished the territorial militia, the Nauvoo Legion, and provided for a new militia, organized according to United States law, with all general officers to be appointed by the governor. The militia had long provided a psychological defense against federal persecution and had actually tested its mettle in the 1857–58 campaign against Johnston's Army. The threat of armed resistance may well have forced Washington to moderate its treatment of the Mormons. Thus, abolishing the territorial militia, like the new school policy, furthered Congress's aim of systematically rooting out sources of Mormon resistance, organization, and strength.

Of course, the ultimate source of Mormon organization was the church itself. The Morrill Act of 1862 had voided the territorial statute incorporating the Mormon church and declared property acquired by the church exceeding $50,000 in value escheated to the United States. That provision had remained unenforced, but the Edmunds-Tucker Act (sections 13–17) remedied this neglect by reaffirming the church's disincorporation, directing the attorney general to institute proceedings "to wind up the affairs of said corporation conformably to law," and granting courts "power in a summary way to compel the production of all books, records, papers, and documents of or belonging to any trustee or person" managing church property, and to transfer church property, to be "applied to the use and benefit of the common schools in the Territory." The Perpetual Emigrating Fund Company, an organization created by the church to aid the immigration of Mormons to Utah, was similarly dissolved and its assets declared escheated to the United States. The territorial legislature was specifically forbidden to organize or recognize any similar company in the future, or to "pass any law for the purpose of or operating to accomplish the bringing of persons into said Territory for any purpose whatsoever."

Under even the most generous standards of legislative latitude, the Edmunds-Tucker Act skirted the boundaries of constitutionality. It was legislation that nakedly attacked a religious institution and imposed civil punishments on an entire group of people solely for their religious beliefs. Indeed, it is questionable whether the act can be defended even as a necessary means to break polygamy, assuming that this would be a legitimate governmental end. By the time it was adopted, it was clear that the Edmunds Act was working and that the drastic measures of the Edmunds-Tucker Act were excessive. By 1887, Congress was aware that polygamists were relatively few, perhaps only 2,500 in number. Liberalized procedures and broader definitions of the offenses that polygamists could be charged with had broken the prosecutorial logjam. By 1887, the relatively few polygamists in Utah were being vigorously tracked down and swiftly prosecuted.

All this, however, played little part in Congress's consideration of the Edmunds-Tucker Act. By 1887, polygamy was clearly a peripheral concern. Congress was concerned mainly with the church's power, the way the church intertwined with Utah's territorial government, and with the loyal obedience of the Mormons to church leaders' directives. The Mormons' dogged resistance to the prior series of harsh federal measures enraged Congress. Even in 1882, when the Edmunds Act was adopted, Congress was caught up in a national hysteria that saw obliteration of the Mormon faith as the ultimate and only acceptable goal. The Edmunds-Tucker Act was the fruit of that hysteria.

Shortly after passage of the Edmunds Act, the agitation for even harsher measures had begun. In 1884, President Arthur urged Congress to take control of the territory:

> I still believe that if that abominable practice [polygamy] can be suppressed by law it can only be by the most radical legislation consistent with the restraints of the Constitution.
>
> I again recommend, therefore, that Congress assume absolute political control of the Territory of Utah and provide for the appointment of commissioners with such governmental powers as in its judgment may justly and wisely be put into their hands. (Richardson, 8:250)

The next year, President Cleveland urged that no further Mormons be allowed to enter the country (Richardson, 8:362).

In Congress, supporters of the act expressed few qualms at mandating the dissolution of a religious organization. Senator John T. Morgan of Alabama observed: "I believe that if ten or twenty years ago we had exercised the unquestioned power residing in Congress of repealing that church charter out and out, disbanding its organization, and scattering its property into the hands of whoever it might belong to, we should by this time have arrested entirely the evil of polygamy in Utah" (*Congressional Record* 17 [1886]:504). By narrowly construing the First Amendment's reach, some congressmen concluded that the Mormon church did not merit constitutional protection. To them, the constitutional guarantee of freedom of religion meant primarily a freedom to practice one of the Christian faiths established at the time of the Revolution. More recent churches did not qualify. As Senator Morgan concluded:

> In dealing with this corporation or with its associated ecclesiastical organization I do not feel that I am dealing with a religious establishment. I feel that I am dealing with something that is entirely irreligious, that has no just pretension at all to be called a religion in a Christian country. It would be a very fair religion in China or in any Mohammedan country; it would do very well for the Congo Free State perhaps; but in Christian America this can hardly be rated as an establishment of religion. (*Congressional Record* 17 [1886]:509)

This line of reasoning justified destroying the Perpetual Emigrating Fund Company because of wild accusations from the press that the Mormons imported innocent women from Europe to impress into polygamous marriages. It was charged in Congress that the church was "devoted to gathering the most ignorant and degraded of all classes of community in all the States and in all other countries [to Utah] for the purpose of imposing upon them the doctrines and the practice of polygamy" (*Congressional Record* 17 [1886]:509).

Yet even as Congress debated its most repressive measures against Mormons, the tone of congressional debate had changed. Over twenty years earlier, when Congress debated passage of the Morrill Act, the debate was laden with references to Mormon atrocities against wagon trains passing through Utah, the barbaric customs and manners of the Mormons, and the near-universal practice of polygamy. Utah's increasing contact with the rest of the nation had intensified the scrutiny —a mixed boon—but it appears to have abated the most outrageous misperceptions of the Mormons. By 1887 it was the power of the Mormon church as an institution that troubled Congress most, and the strengths of Mormon culture even won a grudging recognition from such foes as Senator Morgan (*Congressional Record* 17 [1886]:504). Needless to say, opponents failed to see the organization of the Mormon church as the cause of those virtues.

Opponents of the Edmunds-Tucker Act argued that the act's provisions amounted to an exercise in religious persecution. Senator Wilkinson Call of Florida, for example, argued:

> It is the second step towards the establishment of religious persecution and intolerance. It is but a thin disguise for the acute lawyers who have prepared this bill to assert that it is no violation of the Constitution of the United States or of the principles of civil liberty or religious tolerance upon which this Government is founded. (*Congressional Record* 18 [1887]:1900)

Seizing church property violated not only the First Amendment, but also the constitutional directive that government not take private property without just compensation. As Senator George Graham Vest of Missouri argued, "It is naked, simple, bold confiscation, and nothing else. It is taking the money subscribed, I care not for what purpose, by individuals, and applying it in the discretion of Congress to an object which was not contemplated by the corporators" (*Congressional Record* 18 [1887]:1897).

Similar objections were raised to a number of the act's specific provisions. The provision requiring a test oath of voters, jurors, and officials, pointed out Senator Vest, was futile and unworthy of American republicanism. It was futile because "if these Mormons are the fanatics that they are proclaimed to be . . . there is not one of them that will not commit perjury in order to vote and in order to carry out his treasonable purpose against the Government. If they are what they are denounced to be, these test oaths will do no good; they will merely add perjury to their other crimes" (*Congressional Record* 18 [1887]:1898). The measure was unrepublican because citizens could not be expected to defend a government's institutions simply because an oath to do so was exacted from them. Citizens of a free society freely defended their institutions because they accepted and believed in those institutions. If that support crumbled, no oaths could restore it (*Congressional Record* 18 [1887]:1898). The provision declaring the children of polygamous marriages illegitimate was similarly misguided. Senator Call warned that "the child born of innocent purposes and under a form of religious belief [would] be an outcast from human sympathy" (*Congressional Record* 18 [1887]:1901). By its severity, the act would make martyrs of the Mormon leaders and victims of their innocent offspring (*Congressional Record* 17 [1886]:507).

Notwithstanding these objections, the Edmunds-Tucker Act was passed by Congress and became law on 3 March 1887, without the president's signature, because he failed to act on it.

This final act of Congress presented the church's leaders with a hard decision: they could abandon polygamy and the practices that made the church a unique community and, by that capitulation, hope to save some portion of the church as an organization, or they could cling to their beliefs, continue to resist, and risk being utterly destroyed. As a result of the ongoing polygamy prosecutions, many of the church's leaders had fled to Mexico or Canada, were in hiding, or were in prison. Without effective leadership, experiments in social organization like the United Order had already crumbled. The seizure of church property—property inseparably tied to the Church's social programs and the territory's economy—brought terrible pressures to bear. Finally, the church capitulated. On 24 September 1890, President Wilford Woodruff issued the Manifesto, in which he declared "my intention to submit to those laws, and to use my influence with the members of the Church over which I preside to have them do likewise" (D&C Official Declaration 1). The Manifesto was read in general conference on 6 October 1890, and Lorenzo Snow, president of the Quorum of the Twelve, moved that "we accept his declaration concerning plural marriages as authoritative and binding" (D&C Official Declaration 1). "Although official accounts of this meeting state that the congregation voted unanimously to sustain the Manifesto," notes historian D. Michael Quinn (1985, 48), "that was not the case. William Gibson, later a representative in the Utah legislature, voted against it. . . . The majority of the congregation refused to vote at all when the Manifesto was presented . . ."

With the reluctant concession of the Manifesto, federal pressure against the Mormons abated. Ultimately, what remained of the church's property was returned, Utah was finally admitted to statehood in 1896, and the polygamy laws faded into history. No remnant of the polygamy laws remains in force today. However, the polygamy laws have left an enduring mark on the Constitution and on standards of judicial interpretation and an ineradicable mark on the Mormon church. The novel social organization the Mormons created in Utah largely vanished as a result of federal pressure, and the scope of Church's involvement in the lives of its members—for good or ill —was irrevocably limited by the federal government's demand for secular dominance in Utah.

Judicial Consequences of Edmunds-Tucker

The Edmunds-Tucker Act made proving polygamy easier because it provided that a wife was a competent witness in polygamy, bigamy, and cohabitation trials and required that records be kept of weddings in the territories (Stat. 24:635–36, §§ 1, 9). Even these provisions contained one restraint on spousal testimony, however; only a wife willing to testify would be heard.

Notwithstanding the clear command of the Act, a number of Mormon women were required to testify against their husbands or be held in contempt of court. Probably the most egregious instance of judicial misconduct in this regard is the case of Belle Harris (*Ex parte Harris*, P. 5:129 [Utah 1884]). In 1883 Mrs. Harris was summoned before a Utah grand jury during the course of its investigation of polygamy charges. Evidence before the jury indicated that Mrs. Harris was the second wife in a polygamous household. Mrs. Harris, however, refused to answer any grand jury questions regarding her marital relations on the ground that "her marriage is a matter of which this grand jury has no concern, and that such question is improper" (P. 5:130). On her refusal, Belle Harris was taken before a district judge and, on 10 May 1883, was fined $25 and ordered to be imprisoned "until she shall appear before the said grand jury and answer said question" (P. 5:130). On 15 May the grand jury was about to be discharged. Belle Harris was again brought before it for questioning. Again she refused and was returned to prison, and the grand jury was discharged.

Mrs. Harris's petition for habeas corpus was denied by the Utah Supreme Court, which found the lower court's procedure proper. Citing the *Miles* decision, the court concluded that the grand jury had determined that Mrs. Harris was a polygamous wife and therefore not entitled to spousal testimonial immunity. Her reasons for refusing to testify were dismissed as "puerile" and contemptuous of the dignity of the court (P. 5:131).

Relying on an established principle governing civil contempt proceedings, Mrs. Harris argued that her imprisonment after dismissal of the grand jury was improper, because she could not comply with the court's order after 15 May. The intent of civil contempt proceedings is coercive; sanctions are imposed to compel an individual to obey the court's order. Where, for any reason, that order can no longer be obeyed, sanctions should be removed since they no longer serve any useful purpose (Dobbs, 97–98). The Utah Supreme Court, however, argued that she had been given a chance to comply and informed that that would be her last chance until 29 August, when the grand jury would be reconvened. Belle Harris and her baby ultimately spent three and a half months in prison (*Congressional Record* 17 [1886]:3137).

As the *Harris* case illustrates, the power of contempt could be a fearful weapon. On the basis of the most sketchy or nonexistent of hearings, Mormon wives who refused to testify against their husbands could be sent to prison for indefinite periods. The 1886 petition

Mormon women sent to Congress called the legislature's attention to the plight of Mormon wives and itemized their victimization by Utah's judiciary:

In the third district court, November 14, 1882, Annie Gallifant, having been asked by the grand jury a number of questions which she declined to answer, one of them being as to the name of the man to whom she was married, she was brought into court, and still declining, was sent to the penitentiary, where although daily expecting to become a mother, she was kept until the grand jury was discharged. On the trial of John Connelly she was again brought into court and asked, "When did you first cohabit with your husband?" "How long after you commenced cohabiting with your husband was it that your child was born?"

On May 22, 1884, in the same court, Nellie White, for refusing to answer personal questions in regard to her relations with Jared Roundy, was sent to the pentitentiary, under the same roof with murderers, burglars, and other convicts, and confined there until July 7, the grand jury being kept over and not discharged for the purpose of protracting her imprisonment until the beginning of a new term.

In the court of United States Commissioner McKay, June 20, 1885, Elizabeth Ann Starkey was brought in as a witness against Charles S. White. On refusing to answer the question, "Have you ever in this country, within the last two years, occupied the same bed with defendant?" she was sentenced to one day's imprisonment and a fine of $50, and placed in the custody of the United States marshal until payment.

On June 22 she again declined to answer, and was fined $100 and committed until payment.

On June 24 she refused to answer similar personal questions to the grand jury, and was committed to the penitentiary until August 21, but was again imprisoned and kept till October 6. While in prison she was approached and grossly insulted by an employe of the marshal.

On the 15th of September, 1885, Eliza Shafer was sent to the penitentiary for refusing to answer the question, "Have you within three years last past, lived and cohabited with J. W. Snell as his wife?" The court ordered her imprisonment until the question was answered.

On February 15, 1886, Mrs. Martha J. Cannon was brought into the third district court, and the grand jury complained that she would not answer certain questions, among them the following: "Are you not now a pregnant woman?" "Are you not now with child by your husband, George Q. Cannon?" On still declining to answer the court adjudged her guilty of contempt, and pending sentence she was placed under bonds of $2,500, which were subsequently raised to $5,000.

On March 2, 1886, Miss Huldah Winters was arrested by Deputy Marshal Vandercook at her home in Pleasant Grove, 40 miles distant, no charge being preferred against her, but it was suspected that she was a plural wife of George Q. Cannon. She was brought to Salt Lake City and conducted to the court-house, where she was required to furnish bonds for $5,000 for her appearance from time to time as she might be wanted.

Under the suspicion that any woman or young lady is some man's plural wife she is liable at any time to be arrested, not merely subpoenaed, but taken by force by deputy marshals and brought before a grand jury, and examined and browbeaten and insulted by the prosecuting attorney or his minions. But this is not all. In defiance of law and the usages of courts for ages, the legal wife is now compelled to submit to the same indignities.

On February 20, 1886, in the third district court, in the second trial of Isaac Langton, upon whom the prosecution had failed to fasten the slightest evidence of guilt, Prosecuting Attorney Dickson exclaimed, "If the court will allow me, I would like to call Mrs. Langton" (defendant's legal wife). After a strong protest from the attorneys for the defendant the court permitted the outrage, and against her and her husband's consent she was compelled to testify for the prosecution, the evidence, however, completely exonerating the husband, who was discharged.

But this has now been set up as a precedent, and within the past few days a legal wife has been taken before the grand jury, as many have been before, who refused to give evidence, but this time was compelled to answer the questions propounded by the public prosecutor against the lawful husband. (*Congressional Record* 17:3137–38)

Again in 1888 Congress's attention was called to the unlawful detention of Mormon wives who refused to testify against their husbands by Representative James N. Burnes of Missouri, who read to the House a report by a visitor to Utah's prison:

I found in one cell (meaning a cell of the penitentiary in Utah) 10 by 13½ feet, without a floor, six women, three of whom had babies under six months of age, who were incarcerated for contempt of court in refusing to acknowledge the paternity of their children. When I plead [*sic*] with them to answer the court and be released, they said: "If we do, there are many wives and children to suffer the loss of a father." (*Congressional Record* 19 [1888]:9231)

The icy response by Representative Charles Dougherty of Florida seemed to summarize the feeling of the House: "Sir, in this matter I have no sympathy except for the children. The women, when they went into this polygamous relation, knew that they were violating the laws of the land of which they could not but be cognizant" (*Congressional Record* 19 [1888]:9232).

In 1887, Congress had appropriated funds for an industrial home in Utah to provide a haven for "indigent women and children whom the rigors of Federal laws against polygamy had made homeless and husbandless and fatherless" (*Congressional Record* 19:9225). The home was a resounding failure, housing at its maximum only ten individuals connected with polygamy (*Congressional Record* 19: appendix, 562; CHC 6:184–86).

Judicial use of the contempt power in the polygamy cases thus presented many Mormon families with a cruel dilemma. If the wife called as a witness submitted and testified, her husband would almost surely be convicted and imprisoned. If she refused, her husband might escape conviction, but the wife would be imprisoned. Thus, at least one Mormon husband, Rudger Clawson, directed his wife to testify at his trial after she had spent a night in the penitentiary for refusing to do so (Larson 1971, 108).

In retrospect, it is difficult to offer any explanation for this judicial conduct toward Mormon wives besides a spirit of vindictiveness. The polygamy laws, which were being vigorously enforced in the latter part of the 1880s, imposed ample punishment on polygamous males, but provided no equivalent punishment for the women who stubbornly clung to polygamy. The imposition of contempt sentences on wives who refused to testify introduced a sort of random sexual equality in the federal punishment of polygamy. However, it seems implausible that Utah's courts believed that they needed to compel Mormon women to testify to convict their polygamous husbands. Courts had reduced the quantum of evidence required to establish polygamy or cohabitation to such a low level that in almost any case ample alternative sources of proof must have been available. These prosecutions, which step over the line to become persecution, signal clearly that it was Mormonism itself, not just polygamy, that the federal government wished to eradicate.

8

The War against Mormon Society

In Utah, where they had been driven by their persecutors, the Mormons founded a novel society. In it, secular and religious authority were intermingled; social, economic, religious, family, and political life were bound together under the doctrines of the church into a cohesive way of life. It was a society radically different from mainstream America.

Public debate on the "Mormon issue" and the legal conflict between the Mormons and the federal government largely centered on the issue of polygamy. But there were other points of conflict between the Mormons and the rest of the nation. Most aspects of Mormon life that made the Mormons distinctive came under attack by the federal government. For the more farsighted critics, the church's economic, social, and political power were more significant than the issue of polygamy, and the curtailment of the church's social and political activities by the federal government may have had a more enduring impact on Mormonism than the prohibition of polygamy.

Historians have begun to recognize that the conflict over polygamy masked a more important attack by the federal government on some of the most unique features of Mormon life. Leonard J. Arrington (1958, 356), has noted:

> That the issue of polygamy played a major role in this campaign can hardly be denied, but it seems to have been neglected that Mormon collectivism, in economics and politics, was also under attack. The crusade which stamped out polygamy also succeeded largely in putting an end to most of the unique and noncapitalistic economic institutions for which the Mormons had been noted.

Other historians note that as early as the 1850s, national concern with the Mormons focused not only on polygamy, but also on the church's involvement with and control over Utah's politics and government (Allen and Leonard, 296).

A few records of the era even suggest a somewhat cynical view that polygamy provided no more than a convenient excuse for the nation to crush Mormon society. A Massachusetts paper, for example, editorialized:

> Popular judgment is today repeating the same blunder in the matter of Mormonism. Attention is fastened upon a single aspect of Mormonism, the revolting immorality of polygamy, and this conspicuous offensive part is mistaken for the whole just as the conspicuous barbarism of slavery was mistaken for the whole of Southern policy. . . . If they persist in this mistake the country will one day have another rude and terrible awakening. It will one day be discovered all at once that the essential principle of Mormonism is not polygamy at all but the ambition of an ecclesiastical hierarchy to wield sovereignty; to rule the souls and lives of its subjects with absolute authority, unrestrained by any civil power. (Larson 1971, 207)

In much the same spirit, Utah's governor wrote the Secretary of the Interior in 1885 that he regarded Utah's monogamous Mormons as more despicable and deserving of punishment than the polygamists because, "where two men claim to believe that polygamy is divinely appointed, the one who follows that belief into a conscientious practice is the honester of the two. If you punish the honester one, you at least should disfranchise the other" (Dwyer, 145).

Of course, some of the charges leveled against the Mormons were a product of religious bigotry and lurid imagination. In the early years of Utah's settlement, congressmen alleged that Utah was a bandit empire peopled by a barbarous tribe who lived by preying on innocent settler caravans. As late as 1893, Congress's debate on the admission of Utah as a state was enlivened by a reiteration of the charges that Utah's citizens were murderers, polygamists, and thieves (Harrow, 66–67). These charges can be looked at, though, in light of the 1851 proclamation of polygamy by Brigham Young, the Mountain Meadows Massacre (which by then had become a matter of intense speculation in California), and extreme prices that the Mormons charged the emigrees traveling through Utah for goods and supplies. While the charges are obviously emotion-charged and argumentative, they do have a subjective basis in fact.

As communication between Utah and the East improved, the wildest sorts of charges died out, to be replaced by better-founded accusations. Indeed, as time passed, the continuing controversy between Utah and Washington became itself an independent charge against the Mormons. Thus, the Supreme Court in commenting in 1890 on the justification for the government's seizure of church property noted: "Whatever persecutions they may have suffered in the early part of their history, in Missouri and Illinois, they have no excuse for their persistent defiance of law under the government of the United States" (*The Late Corporation of the Church of Jesus Christ of Latter-day Saints v. United States*, US 136:49).

Not unexpectedly, the more vigorously Washington enforced policies the Mormons perceived as hostile, including the polygamy laws, the stiffer Mormon resistance became. Equally expectedly, the more Mormons resisted, the more they were seen as a rebellious, lawbreaking people. To the church's enemies, Mormon resistance provided a powerful argument for new, more sweeping legislation that undercut any aspect of Mormon society enabling the Mormons to resist national policy. The Mormons reacted defensively to threats to the life they had so painfully built in Utah. Mormon words and acts at times played into the hands of their enemies, and the Mormons were too suspicious of non-Mormons who settled in Utah. On the other side, Congress and the Mormons' enemies preyed on ignorance and bigotry to destroy a society that they never even bothered to try to understand.

SOURCES OF GRIEVANCE

By choice as well as by necessity, Mormon society in Utah was tightly organized around the church. Church doctrine supplied guidance in most aspects of life, and the church's organization supplied direction, leadership, and resources throughout Mormon society. In this truly religious community, only the fuzziest of barriers, if any, separated Mormon secular activities from the clearly religious ones. Such an organization was, of course, a source of controversy in a nation devoted to the separation of church and state.

For the Mormons, the cohesiveness of their institutions meant that a challenge to any one Mormon practice would almost inevitably call all of Mormon society into question. To hostile observers of the Mormons, the cohesiveness of those institutions presented only the sinister impression of power-hungry church leaders. Thus, at the same time that the nation sought to eliminate polygamy, the federal government also sought to limit the church's political, social, economic, and religious power and the institutions through which that power was expressed.

Political Power in Utah

Having been driven to Utah by persecution and having repeatedly observed the failure of government officials to protect them from their persecutors, Mormons may well have harbored mixed feelings toward the United States. At the time they moved to Utah, the land was Mexican territory, and there is some evidence that they contemplated establishing an independent state there. Arrington (1958, 41–42) finds evidence that the Mormons fully intended to settle and petition for admission as a state; however, the ambiguities in their attitude toward the Union were apparently sufficient to raise concerns in Washington. Before and during the Civil War, periodic veiled references by Mormon leaders to the possibility that Utah might withdraw from the Union furthered such rumors. Indeed, rumors of armed revolt in Utah prompted the infamous invasion of the territory by federal troops in 1857–58. Although Mormon leaders defused Washington's immediate fear that insurrection was underway in Utah, the Mormons showed they were ready and able to resist outside aggression.

Of course, in the 1850s and 1860s, Utah was a dim and distant threat to the seat of government in Washington. But it was strategically located along the major paths of western migration and the routes to already-settled California. For a nation recently traumatized by secession, the perceived political aspirations of the Mormon church seemed to threaten national unity and expansion. The Civil War represented a national resolve to defend national unity at all cost, to eliminate obstacles to the nation's destined expansion across the continent, and to eliminate any social systems that threatened that unity and expansion. Having paid the price of allowing an incompatible society to become too powerful and entrenched, the nation reacted vigorously to the Mormon threat.

The self-reliance and colonizing energies of the Mormons, admirable traits in themselves, could not help but foster a fear of secession on the part of the nation's leaders. When the Mormons moved west they laid claim to, and actively began settling, an area far larger than present-day Utah. Their original state of Deseret encompassed nearly one-sixth of the present area of the United States (Arrington 1958, 84–85). Missionaries recruited shiploads of convert immigrants to Utah to settle this immense desert empire. To political observers in Washington, the Mormons' ambitious growth might have suggested future peril.

Of course, the end of the Civil War and a continuing wave of non-Mormon, westward migration made the possibility of Mormon secession less and less likely. The Mormon challenge to federal political power, however, simply changed its form. Political institutions originally initiated by the Mormons remained firmly in Mormon hands. Almost all those who possessed leadership abilities in the territory were leaders of the Mormon church as well as political leaders. In

1863, for example, eleven of the twelve Mormon apostles sat in the territorial legislature, and on 16 January 1878 the *Salt Lake Tribune* reported that the legislature that year included "six Apostles, twenty-three bishops and other inferior priests" (Larson 1971, 53 n. 43). Finally, the great mass of Utah's population was Mormon, more devoted to the church and its direction than to the federal government.

The Mormons' quest for political control and autonomy in the Great Basin was exemplified by their efforts to obtain statehood in the face of difficulties experienced by no other state (Flynn, 314). These difficulties were compounded by the outside animosity toward polygamy. Between 1849 and 1894, Utah constitutional conventions adopted six constitutions in attempts to obtain congressional sanction for statehood.

Finally in 1894, Congress passed an Enabling Act officially authorizing Utah to convene a constitutional convention and containing various sections relevant to statehood. In 1895 the Utah constitutional convention, borrowing from the earlier Utah and other state constitutions, drafted what eventually became Utah's constitution. It was approved by the voters in 1895, and President Grover Cleveland proclaimed Utah a state on 4 January 1896 (Flynn, 322–24).

Judicial Power in Utah

Even as they were fighting the forty-year political war over statehood, the Mormons battled on another front over control of the judiciary. On 9 January 1850, the legislature for the proposed state of Deseret established a court and the offices of prosecuting attorney, court clerk, sheriff, justice of the peace, and constable in each county (Morgan 1940, 171–73). The Mormons never intended to abandon their ecclesiastical courts even with the establishment of their own civil courts; each had different purposes and jurisdiction. The civil courts handled criminal matters and actions involving nonmembers, while the ecclesiastical courts continued to hear charges involving the violation of church standards as well as private disputes between members.

Under Deseret's laws the county court, which consisted of a chief justice and two associate justices, played an important role in local governance. In judicial affairs the county courts held general jurisdiction and could hear appeals from justice of the peace courts. Influenced by the informality of their church-court counterparts, these civil courts administered justice without regard to the technical forms of pleadings used in other jurisdictions. In addition to these courts, probate courts were established in January 1851 with "power to probate wills and grant administration of estates of deceased persons whose property lay in this court" (Allen 1956, 14).

The Organic Act creating the Territory of Utah on 9 September 1850 substantially shifted control of the judiciary in Utah. Under the provisions of the act, the judiciary for the territory consisted of a supreme court, comprised of the justices of three judicial districts, district courts, and such probate courts and justices of the peace as established by territorial legislation (Stat. 9:453).

On 20 September 1850 President Millard Fillmore appointed the first federal judges in the territory of Utah: Joseph Buffington of Pennsylvania as chief justice, with Perry E. Brocchus of Alabama and Zerubbabel Snow of Ohio as associate justices. Snow was the only Mormon. Buffington declined the appointment and was replaced by Lemuel G. Brandebury of Pennsylvania. Historian Howard Lamar described Brandebury and Brocchus as "political hacks" and concluded, "Had Fillmore searched the length and breadth of the land he scarcely could have found men less suited to deal with the Saints than the two non-Mormon judges" (Larson 1971, 8 n. 18). Brocchus, the last of the officials to arrive in Utah, arrived on 17 August 1851. In early September he was invited to speak at a general conference of the church. He showed a severe lack of tact by chastising the congregation for their religious beliefs and practices for nearly two hours, until in reaction the congregation became disorderly. Later that month, on 28 September 1851, the non-Mormon federal appointees, including Brandebury, Brocchus, and Secretary of State B. D. Harris, abandoned their offices and returned to Washington after having been in Utah for little more than a month (Kilts, 41–43; Bancroft, 456–61). Mormons thereafter referred to these officers of the court as the "run-away officials."

The explanation given for their precipitous departure varies with the persons giving the account. The report filed by the officials with the President provided the following excuses:

> We have been driven to this course by the lawless acts, and the hostile and seditious feelings and sentiments of Brigham Young, the Executive of the Territory, and the great body of the residents there, manifested toward the Government and the officers of the United States in aspersions and denunciation so violent and so offensive as to set at defiance, not only a just administration of laws, but the rights and feelings of citizens and officers of the United States residing there. (*Congressional Globe*, 1851, 86)

The allegation that hostile attitudes made it impossible to achieve a "just administration of laws" is anomalous, points out one scholar, since "there is no apparent record of any of them ever holding court in their respective district" (Kilts, 45). The *Deseret News* (3 Apr. 1852) attributed their departure, at least in part, to the unwillingness of the

Mormons to sue in gentile courts: "It is certain however that Judge Brocchus found an empty docket on his arrival there and no disposition amongst the people to give him employment. They would not go to the law 'any how he might fix it,' so he resolved to throw up his sinecure and return eastward."

This initial experience with unfriendly federal judges soon became the pattern. Mormons viewed these "foreign" judges as serious threats to their rights of self-governance and religious distinctiveness. The federal judges interpreted Mormon recalcitrance as evidence of their un-American tendencies that would have to be rooted out by the force of the law. The term "mission jurist" (Whitney, 2:542) characterized those federal judges who announced they felt they had a mission to reform Mormons. For example, James B. McKean, a minister's son and former congressman appointed territorial chief justice by President Grant, indicated that his mission to break up Mormonism was as "high above his mere duty as judge as heaven is above earth" (Bancroft, 440). Orson F. Whitney, author of an early Utah history and later an apostle, felt that these judges "resolved that the liberties and even the lives of the leaders of the devoted community should not stand in the way" (2:546). The condemnation visited upon them by "gentile" appointees to the federal judiciary irritated the Mormons, who questioned the moral integrity of the judges. A federal appointment to Utah during its early territorial years, with its accompanying inconveniences, was usually not sought by men of distinction who had other alternatives. As a result, the appointees were often men who did not command the respect of those whom they judged. Bancroft (1890, 429), in reviewing the federal appointments between 1852 and 1856, reflects the Mormons' view that they had good reason to feel disgusted with the quality of the appointees: "If it was true that the magistrates appointed by the United States were held in contempt, there was sufficient provocation. Two of them . . . deserted their posts, a third was probably an opium-eater, a fourth a drunkard, a fifth a gambler and a lecher." With the federal judges posing a threat to Mormon control over the civil court system in Utah, as well as to the survival of religious institutions such as polygamy and ecclesiastical courts, and with judges of dubious credentials and morality personally insulting the people they were judging, Mormon hostility to gentile law, lawyers, and courts increased. Frustrated by the federal government's appointments to the territorial judiciary, the Mormons turned to the territorial legislature in an effort to circumscribe the influence of a hostile federal judiciary.

Contrary to popular belief, the common law of England was never entirely adopted in America, except to the extent it fit the needs and circumstances of the adopting jurisdiction. Mormons believed their needs and circumstances differed from other jurisdictions in many important respects and that the common law of Utah—the decisional law of the Utah judges—ought to reflect those differences (Linford 1979, 224–28).

An instructive example is one of the first murder trials in the territory. Howard Egan had been a guard to Joseph Smith and as a frontiersman had assisted several wagon companies across the plains. While Egan was away assisting some Forty-Niners to California, one James Monroe seduced one of Egan's polygamist wives. She later gave birth to Monroe's child. In 1851 Egan caught up with the fleeing Monroe near the territorial border and killed him for his misconduct. Egan was exonerated in a church investigation. Justice Zerubbabel Snow, sitting for the recently absent Justice Brandebury, arraigned Egan on 17 October 1851. W. W. Phelps and George A. Smith, a Mormon apostle who was arguing his first case, defended Egan. Seth M. Blair, another prominent Mormon, was the prosecutor. In his closing remarks to the jury, Smith argued not only that it was within the jury's power to nullify the law and absolve Egan from guilt even if they found that he had shot Monroe, but also that such an act was not contrary to the common law of the frontier. He argued that the common law of England had no binding force on plain mountain men, who were instead subject to the plain "mountain common law" that provided that "the man who seduces his neighbor's wife must die" (Kilts, 50–55 and Appendix 9; also Cannon 1983, 310–14). Judge Snow did not subscribe to Smith's view that different common-law rules applied in Utah than applied elsewhere, but he instructed the jury that if it found that the murder had been committed in unorganized territory of the United States, it was to convict, but if within the Territory of Utah, to acquit, since it was sitting as a federal court and had no jurisdiction over crimes committed within the territory. The jury acquitted Egan, but it is not clear whether its decision turned on the court's lack of jurisdiction or whether it found that the court had jurisdiction and chose to apply Smith's "mountain common law."

This practice of fashioning the common law to local circumstances did not last. The president removed Snow. For the duration of the territorial period the Mormons fought against the adoption of the English common law into the territory by the only avenue they had left —territorial legislation. Following the informal pleading practice used in the church courts, the territorial legislature in 1851 established that "all technical forms of actions and pleadings are hereby abolished"

(Utah Laws 1851:29, § 7). In their stead the Mormon-dominated legislature adopted an early form of notice pleading for the purpose of minimizing both delays and the subversion of substantive justice by legal technicalities inherent in more technical pleading forms (Utah Laws 1851, § 8). In a further effort to pattern the civil practice after the church courts, the territorial legislature in 1854 prohibited the use of legal precedent as a ground for a decision in any case:

> All questions of law, the meaning of writings other than laws, and the admissibility of testimony, shall be decided by the Court; and no laws or parts of laws shall be read, argued, cited, or adopted in any courts, during any trial, except those enacted by the Governor and Legislative Assembly of this Territory, and those passed by the Congress of the United States when applicable; and no report, decision, or doings of any Court shall be read, argued, cited, or adopted as precedent in any other trial. (Utah Laws 1854:32, § 1)

Finally, the territorial legislature attempted to modify the common-law system of adversarial justice. While legislation permitted (but did not require) the employment of counsel, it added that "no person or persons employing counsel, in any of the courts of this territory, shall be compelled by any process of law to pay the counsel, before or after, or during the process of trial in the case" (Utah Laws 1852:37, § 2). The statute also required counsel to present all the facts, even if adverse to his party's interest (Sec. 5, repealed by Utah Laws 1874:7, § 2)—again, a practice followed in the ecclesiastical courts but not the civil courts at common law.

Because payment was optional with the client, it was hoped that a professional bar would be avoided. Legal services were to be seen as a community service. But in practice a professional bar nonetheless gradually developed. Lawyers obtained their fees in advance of the service to be performed. Apparently, conduct becoming those who would inhabit Zion was not as easily obtained as the passage of legislation.

These legislative efforts to align the practice in the federal courts with that in church courts did not sit well with gentile judges and attorneys, who had been trained under common-law, adversarial systems of justice. As a result the issue arose as to whether the common law was binding in Utah by virtue of either the Organic Act or common practice. In an effort to forestall the reinstatement of the common law as the rule of decision in Utah courts, the territorial legislature in 1882 enacted a statute giving priority to rules of equity, which Mormons believed served justice better than common-law rules (Utah Laws 1882:73, § 1). The 1884 legislature likewise directed the courts to construe liberally the code of civil procedure applicable in the territory despite the fact that it was in derogation of the common law and by common-law rules should have been strictly construed (Utah Laws 1884: 154, § 3).

Mormons also relied on the legislative appointment of territorial marshals and attorneys to limit the obtrusive interference of the federal judiciary. Unfortunately for the Mormons, federal judges simply deferred, even with regard to territorial matters, to federal marshals and attorneys (who were decidedly anti-Mormon). Judge John Cradlebaugh, for example, ruled in 1859 that the United States marshal—not the territorial marshal—was the proper official to serve process for territorial prosecution, and that the United States attorney—not the territorial attorney—was the proper official to prosecute cases under territorial laws. This legal controversy over whether the territorial official or federal appointees should handle the prosecution of territorial crimes continued until the United States Supreme Court finally resolved it in 1873 in favor of the territorial officials (*Snow v. United States*, US 85:317; see Alexander, 30–34). Unabashed by this legal pronouncement, Congress abolished the offices of territorial marshal and attorney in the Poland Act of 1874. It effectively elevated the federal judiciary and federal officers over their Mormon counterparts. In 1874 the Supreme Court sustained this subjection of the Mormons to federal authority in *Ferris v. Higley* (US 87:375).

The Poland Act also curbed the power of the Mormon-controlled probate courts. Mormons had made every effort to expand the jurisdiction of probate courts as an alternative to the federal courts. Prior to the Poland Act's restriction of probate jurisdiction, these courts handled a great deal of litigation (Allen 1968, 138–39). To the extent a choice was possible, Mormons would litigate in the probate courts issues that could not be handled in the church courts; they generally avoided the federal courts. Critics of the probate court system argued that Mormons enjoyed an unfair advantage over gentiles in these courts, imposing their own form of persecution on nonmembers. Mormon judges and juries would allow religious bias to control their decisions, they argued. (The issue of jury nullification, implicit in this criticism, would apply to federal courts as well since the probate courts empanelled jurors for both.) Mormons countered that they respected the constitutional rights of all persons and were only desirous of ensuring fair legal proceedings.

Critics used this claim of Mormon prejudice to support passage of the Poland Act even though congressional delegate George Q. Cannon presented in rebuttal a statistical analysis of these courts in operation demonstrating consistency of treatment between Mormons and non-Mormons: Of eighty-four civil cases tried in the probate court of Salt Lake County between Mormons and non-Mormons, only twenty-five were decided in favor of Mormons (*Congressional Record*, 1874, 4471).

Several later studies also have demonstrated that the probate courts treated Mormons and non-Mormons consistently throughout the history of the probate courts. One study, by Jay E. Powell (1970), expanded and refined Cannon's statistical approach. In one selected probate court Powell studied, that of Elias Smith, probate judge for Salt Lake County between 1852 and 1882, the decisions were consistent for all civil litigants. Powell's study for the years 1852 to mid-1855 shows that in fact the probate courts were harder on Mormons than on non-Mormons when considering crimes such as theft or murder. Powell found that the conviction rate for Mormons in probate courts on such charges was double that for non-Mormons (p. 259). Such harshness is understandable given the Mormons' desire to build Zion and their strict moral code.

Interestingly, church leaders "rarely appeared before the court" in this first decade despite their extensive property holdings. Brigham Young, for example, filed only two suits, both of which "were withdrawn before trial upon payment of the demanded sums" (Powell, 276 and n. 6). Ten other suits brought on behalf of the Perpetual Emigration Fund "were occasioned by debtors intending to leave the territory without settling up" (Powell, 260). These suits by leaders or on behalf of church interests probably went to the probate courts because the defendants would not have responded to the limited ecclesiastical sanctions available to the church courts.

An analysis of the fairness of probate courts for Utah County for random periods between 1855 and 1872 is consistent with Powell's study, concluding that the "probate judges and jurors fairly administered all the law to both Mormons and non-Mormons" (Gee, 146). The author speculates:

> The true basis for the accusations cast at the probate courts and the Mormons necessarily rests upon extradocumentary evidence, not upon the records reflecting the actual quality of justice delivered by Utah probate judges and jurors. One source of conflict may have been the district judges' distress at having their powers assumed by inferior courts or their aggravation at being deprived actual business and fees. Perhaps the conflict erupted as it did because of the attachment of the issue of the courts' controversy surrounding the practice of polygamy. (Gee, 146–47)

This assessment appears to be closer to the truth than the anti-Mormon criticisms that were brought against the probate courts during the conflict over the range and limit of federal authority in the Utah territory.

If Mormons had to bring suit they generally looked to the probate courts, but the injunction against suing brethren applied to Mormon-dominated probate courts as well as federal courts. Thus Powell's study indicates "that a clear majority of civil suits were between outsiders—usually emigrants on their way to the coast" (Powell, 259). The Saints, however, preferred the probate courts for criminal actions against members, as well as actions against "gentiles" or apostates who were not amenable to the jurisdiction of the church courts. In addition, the church encouraged use of the probate courts for the limited purpose of obtaining formal decrees, usually after the church courts had resolved the matter, in divorce or probate cases where a legally binding decree was necessary in dealing with the outside world.

Mormons were anxious to preserve their influence over civil affairs through the probate courts, even while enforcing the "exclusive jurisdiction" rule of church courts for religious disputes. As a result the probate courts played an important role in civil litigation in the Utah Territory until the Poland Act limited their jurisdiction.

Economic Power in Utah

Utah was a harsh country, and the Mormons survived their first years in that desert environment only through "central planning and collective labor" (Arrington 1958, 45). If dealing with gentiles had brought them betrayal and misery, the Mormons could become self-reliant. By living far from the rest of the nation and by relying only on themselves, Mormons excluded the temptations and dangers of the outside world and increased the value of each individual member to the whole. The ideal of a religious community built on cooperation and centralized direction thus meshed with the requirements of their harsh new home and with their sensible desire to avoid more contact with the gentiles.

The church's program for economic self-sufficiency was established almost immediately. On 28 July 1847, only four days after his arrival in the valley, Brigham Young asserted that "The Kingdom of God cannot rise independent of the gentile nations until we produce, manufacture, and make every article of use, convenience, or necessity among our own people" (Arrington 1958, 47). As a practical matter, only the church could focus the resources and provide the direction for the creation of the Mormon-owned industries that would make the Mormons independent. Thus, with steady persistence but varying degrees of success, the church capitalized, directed, and promoted such basic industries as iron works, textile factories, sugar refineries, paper mills, pottery works, and railroads.[1]

On the one hand the church encouraged the establishment of Mormon-owned industries, and on the other it actively discouraged church members from trading with gentile merchants and forcefully encouraged Mormon merchants to join church-controlled cooperatives. Early on, trade with gentile merchants became a substantial drain on the territory's limited currency and resources. Church leaders further suspected that the gentile traders had encouraged the federal invasion of Utah in 1857 (Arrington 1958, 294). Eventually, in 1868 the church initiated an all-out boycott against gentile merchants.

As a commercial alternative, the church authorized the formation of a cooperative association of Mormon merchants, Zion's Co-operative Mercantile Institution. The board of directors of ZCMI was empowered to pay tithing on profits to the church, set uniform policies and standard retail prices, and distribute profits among shareholders. Brigham Young threatened to boycott Mormon merchants who were reluctant to join the new association along with the gentiles (Arrington 1958, 249, 298–300).

The boycott made ZCMI a financial success. The boycott's impact on gentile merchants, however, is less clear. Walker Brothers complained bitterly that sales fell from $60,000 to $5,000 per month as a result of the boycott. The firm had been founded by English converts who were excommunicated after their arrival in Utah, ostensibly over tithing disagreements with Brigham Young, although their disagreements with the prophet also extended to price-setting policies. Tax lists of the period belie their claimed losses, however, and show no perceptible decline in the firm's business (Arrington 1958, 306–7). Arrington concludes that Walker Brothers survived by absorbing the trade of non-Mormon merchants who left Utah, but that the boycott prevented the firm from expanding as rapidly as it might have otherwise. Twenty-three other non-Mormon Salt Lake merchants offered to leave Utah if the church would purchase their inventories and property, an offer Brigham Young declined (Arrington, Fox, and May, 86–87). The major gentile firms in Utah survived through their growing trade with non-Mormons and mining centers.

Because of the shortage of currency in Utah, ZCMI paid its employees in its own scrip, redeemable in goods at ZCMI. The Internal Revenue Service imposed a 10 percent tax on this scrip on the ground that it was being used as money. In 1878 the collector of internal revenue for Utah, O. J. Hollister, presented ZCMI with a $17,000 tax bill (Arrington, Fox, and May, 100). Seven years after the Mormons paid this tax under protest, and after substantial litigation, the money was returned (Arrington 1958, 312–13). A number of other church enterprises using scrip in this manner were also subjected to the 10 percent tax (Arrington, Fox, and May, 129–30).

Much of this economic and industrial activity came under the direct control of Brigham Young as trustee-in-trust for the church. As Arrington (1958, 431) notes, the term *trustee-in-trust* "is probably a corruption of the common legal term 'trust in trust for. . . .'" As trustee-in-trust, the president had power to receive, acquire, manage, or convey property for the use and benefit of the church (Arrington 1958, 30, 431). Direction for economic enterprises was also provided by Zion's Central Board of Trade, an advisory group established in 1878, the year after Brigham Young's death. Composed of fifty men representing each valley or stake, the board "was an attempt on the part of the church to get together a group of her best business and professional people to help work out solutions to the various economic problems which would arise from time to time" (Arrington 1958, 344).

Although the Board of Trade might have given centralized direction to Utah's economy, focused Mormon energies and resources, and brought the best thought to bear on Mormon economic problems, it really had no chance to do so. Antipolygamy persecution was in full force, and by 1884 legal prosecutions had removed almost all the leading citizens from Mormon society. As the church's central authority crumbled, the board ceased to function (Arrington 1958, 349).

These Mormon economic institutions and planning all worked toward the same practical ends: to make Mormons independent and to exclude outside influences. Beyond this, however, was the spiritual goal of sanctification through the communal ownership of property.

Joseph Smith had announced a revelation on the law of consecration in 1831:

> Behold, thou shalt consecrate all thy properties, that which thou hast unto me, with a covenant and a deed which cannot be broken; and they shall be laid before the bishop of my church, and two of the elders, such as he shall appoint and set apart for that purpose. . . . The bishop of my church, after that he has received the properties of my church, that it cannot be taken from the church, he shall appoint every man a steward over his own property, or that which he has received, inasmuch as shall be sufficient for himself and family. (Arrington, Fox, and May, 15; see also D&C 42:30–32)

Initial attempts to implement this ambitious program in Kirtland and Missouri collapsed under the weight of persecution. In Nauvoo in

1841 the church retreated from the law of consecration to the law of tithing (Arrington, Fox, and May 1976, 15–38). In Utah, however, attempts were made to implement the ideals of the law of consecration again but on a more limited scale.

In the 1850s, Brigham Young vigorously urged renewed adherence to the law of consecration, and thousands of Mormon settlers heeded him. Arrington, Fox, and May (1976, 62, 66) have located 2,682 deeds of consecration recorded in Utah counties between 1855 and 1858. After 1858 the consecration of property ceased, perhaps because of obstructions created by the federal government. In the 1850s, because Congress had not extended the federal land system to Utah, the Mormons were technically squatters on the public domain. By transferring their insecure land claims to the church, which was highly unpopular in Washington, they risked losing their land completely (Arrington, Fox, and May, 77).

In 1874, Brigham Young again attempted to create a communal spirit and life-style among the Mormons through the United Order movement. The movement called for church members to contribute their property to a cooperative in return for capital stock in the order, and to contribute their labors to the order and subsist on its produce. Over 150 of the orders were organized from entire settlements (Arrington 1958, 328–29). The orders were incorporated under the laws of the Territory of Utah, apparently to create a mechanism for conveying property "that lawyers cannot pick to pieces and destroy" and so "apostates cannot afflict us" (Arrington, Fox, and May, 140–41). This concern seems drawn from the history of the law of consecration in Illinois and Missouri, where gentile judges had not recognized the validity of conveyances to the church, where apostates had successfully sued to recover consecrated property, and where apparently some impoverished opportunists converted to Mormonism, received an inheritance, and then left with their newly acquired property (Arrington, Fox, and May, 21, 23, 25–26).

Economic historian Leonard Arrington (1958, 330) has characterized the United Order movement as "a deliberate flight from the gradually developing exchange economy into the less advanced, but more autonomous, self-sufficing household and village economy of the frontier."

Although orders varied from Orderville, where even meals were communal, to much looser forms (Arrington 1958, 330–37), all of them experienced problems that have historically beset experiments in communal living: restraining the acquisitiveness of some, shaking the sloth of others, balancing the order's total produce and consumption, and allocating its produce among members. Perhaps these problems would have been sufficient to doom the Mormon experiment, but external pressures applied by the federal government hastened the demise of the movement.

The moderately successful Brigham City order, for example, was crippled when a federal official placed an embargo on the withdrawal of timber from the area where the order's sawmill was operating and another official attempted to levy a tax on the order's scrip (Arrington 1958, 332). The specter of gentile judges levying judgments against an order's property, leaving entire settlements destitute, was a constant fear, especially after one member obtained a $10,000 judgment against the Beaver order (Arrington, Fox, and May, 240). Church leaders were faced with a difficult problem. They

> wanted to break with traditional economic and social usages, inaugurating a new, more just order, but were hindered by the knowledge that hostile judges were scrutinizing their every act, prepared to bring the full weight of the law to combat any activities contrary to accepted American practice. Wanting to break out of the world, they knew that they were yet in the world and must accordingly scale their designs to the limits worldly authorities could impose. . . . One needed only look to the southern states, then being reconstructed in the wake of the Civil War, to see how willingly federal officials trampled on local autonomy if they sensed among the populace a disloyalty to traditional American values. (Arrington, Fox, and May, 162)

The effects of indirect federal oppression were even more devastating. The polygamy prosecutions that resulted in the imprisonment or exile of most of the Mormons' leaders removed from Mormon society those individuals who could make the communal experiments work. With no one left to organize activities and adjudicate the inevitable frictions, the order movement swiftly collapsed. For example, when Lorenzo Snow, superintendent of the Brigham City order, was imprisoned for polygamy in 1885, the order was dissolved (Arrington 1958, 332). The Orderville order was similarly decimated by polygamy prosecutions and dissolved in 1885, whereupon many of its members moved to Mexico and started a similar settlement (Arrington 1958, 337). Arrington concludes:

> It is a testimony to the effectiveness of the cooperative and United Order movements that Mormon cooperative ventures and collective institutions had to be destroyed, as most of them were during the "Raid" of the 1880's, before the "peculiar" theocratic economy of Zion could be accommodated and absorbed into the general economy of the nation. (Arrington 1958, 338).

The final blow to Mormon efforts to insulate their economy and to translate their religious values into economic institutions came with enforcement of the Edmunds-Tucker Act in 1887. That act dissolved the Corporation of the Church of Jesus Christ of Latter-day Saints and provided for the seizure and redistribution of church property. The seizure of property broke the church as the dominant figure in Utah's economy. Although much of the property was later returned, the government had decisively ended church efforts to organize and lead the economic lives of its members.

CIVIL RIGHTS VIOLATIONS: THE ASSAULT ON MORMON POLITICAL POWER

America is deeply committed to the proposition that an individual's religious convictions should not operate as a political disability. America's persecution of the Mormons in the nineteenth century eroded that commitment, but even here there were limits. During the period of conflict between the Mormons and the federal government, Congress never directly passed a law depriving Mormons of their civil rights simply because they were Mormons, even though, as applied by hostile federal judges and officials, some laws came close to that result.

From the inside, Utah's Mormon society was a coherent whole in which members' lives centered on their church. The political aspect of those lives was a natural and normal extension of their religious convictions. From the outside, Utah was a political machine, where Mormon voters blindly obeyed the dictates of church leaders and where the church dominated and manipulated the political process. These two viewpoints remained irreconcilable.

Washington had any number of politically sensible reasons for wanting to destroy this theocratic control over Utah's politics. The fact that church control over Utah's political system helped to sustain polygamy gave Washington an excuse for attacking Mormon political power. Thus attacks on the political rights of Mormons were deemed acceptable if done in the guise of stamping out polygamy, whereas such acts might have been found constitutionally unacceptable had they been framed simply as attacks on Mormons.

During the polygamy prosecutions, the Mormons' civil rights were abridged in five significant and specific respects: Mormons were denied the right to serve as jurors; Mormons were denied the right to hold elective and public offices; Mormons were denied their franchise; children of polygamous marriages were denied inheritance rights; and the immigration of Mormons into the United States was obstructed and foreign-born Mormons denied citizenship. The Mormons also experienced vexatious litigation unrelated to polygamy and cohabitation prosecutions. On a general level, their most basic freedoms were massively invaded. The totality of federal actions against the Mormons directly restricted their freedom of religion and the pervasive federal pressure indirectly chilled their religious expression. Throughout the polygamy prosecutions, federal attempts to simplify and expedite the conviction of polygamists routinely denied Mormons due process of law. In violation of the Fourth Amendment's restrictions on unreasonable searches and seizures, Mormon homes were raided and Mormon families terrorized. Finally, long after more sparsely settled territories with weaker social structures were granted statehood, Utah remained a territory governed by officials appointed by a hostile federal government. In denying Utah's repeated petitions for admission into the Union as a state, Congress denied Utah's citizens the republican form of government to which they were entitled.

The Exclusion of Mormons as Jurors

On 1 December 1879, President Rutherford B. Hayes called on Congress to withdraw the privileges of citizenship from Utah to break the territory's resistance to enforcement of the polygamy law (Richardson, 7:559). Again, in 1880, Hayes urged Congress to enact legislation so that "the right to vote, hold office, and sit on juries in the Territory of Utah [would] be confined to those who neither practice nor uphold polygamy" (Richardson, 7:606). Congress responded to these pleas with the Edmunds Act in 1882. That act broadly provided that past or present polygamists and those who believed in it could be excluded from jury duty. Potential jurors could further be questioned under oath regarding their polygamous activities or beliefs and could be rejected for failing to answer such questions (Stat. 22:31, § 5).

Supporters claimed this measure was necessary to ensure the effective prosecution of polygamists (Richardson, 7:606; Dwyer, 42–43). Federal officials had for some time vigorously argued that Mormon jurors would refuse to convict their coreligionist believers in polygamy, even though the first polygamy indictment in the *Reynolds* case, handed down in October 1874, was by a grand jury composed of seven Mormons and eight gentiles (Linford 1964, 333 and n. 108). Moreover, Congress ignored pleas that the Edmunds Act imposed "a religious test upon the jurors which is in violation of that cardinal provision of the Constitution of the United States, that when a man is charged with a crime he shall have a fair and impartial trial" because it ensured that Mormons would face "packed" juries, composed almost solely of their enemies (*Congressional Record* 22:1207). The law disabling Mormons as jurors was, nonetheless, enacted by Congress and upheld by the courts. Indeed, the Edmunds Act only ratified a position adopted by the courts two years earlier, in *Miles v. United States* (US 103:304 [1880]).

Convicted of polygamy under the Morrill Act, Miles argued on appeal that a large number of potential jurors had been improperly excluded because they had testified that they believed in polygamy. Miles argued that the examination of the proposed jurors and the rulings of the court showed that the court had in effect administered an unlawful religious test to exclude all Mormons from the jury (US 103:309). The rationale for excluding Mormon jurors was the assumption that the Mormons would be biased in favor of Miles. In upholding the Utah court, the Supreme Court relied on an 1878 territorial statute that provided that a juror could be disqualified "for the existence of a state of mind . . . which leads to a just inference, in reference to the case, that he will not act with entire impartiality" (US 103:305). The Supreme Court upheld the standards established by this Utah statute and noted that it would have reached the same result even without the statute, since under common law a juror could be excluded for actual bias: "It needs no argument to show that a jury composed of men entertaining such a belief could not have been free from bias or prejudice on the trial for bigamy, of a person who entertained the same belief, and whose offense consisted in the act of living in polygamy" (US 103:310).

The Court thus brushed aside the rather subtle psychological questions raised by the issue of bias. Clearly, potential jurors' disagreement with the legal standards they are charged to enforce raises potential problems of bias. Equally clearly, it is a relatively common problem. Jurors who dislike the tax laws serve on tax cases; jurors who find the taking of human life offensive are called on to decide on the death penalty in murder cases. In either instance a juror's competence to serve is determined as a factual matter on the basis of whether that belief is so intense as to prevent the potential juror from setting aside his personal values and enforcing society's norms. *Miles* announces no such factual, balancing standard. The Court ignored the testimony of one of the excluded jurors that, although he believed in polygamy, he would find the defendant guilty of violating the law if the evidence so warranted (US 103:307). Rather, the Court held that a belief in polygamy, of whatever intensity, was sufficient to disable a Mormon from jury duty.

Miles's constitutional claims were similarly dispatched. The claim that the procedure of testing potential jurors' attitudes toward polygamy constituted an unlawful religious test was held irrelevant: "Whether or not that bias was founded on the religious belief of the juror, is entirely immaterial, if the bias existed" (US 103:310). Likewise, the Court simply asserted that the exclusion of Mormons from juries deprived the potential jurors of no rights, and, "if the jurors themselves had no ground of complaint, it is clear the defendant had none" (US 103:311).

Since the Supreme Court had upheld the exclusion of Mormon jurors on the basis of Utah statute and common-law principles, the provision of the Edmunds Act excluding Mormon jurors was predictably sustained, in *Clawson v. United States* (US 114:477 [1885]). Clawson was indicted for cohabitation and polygamy by a grand jury from which Mormons had been systematically excluded. Although the Edmunds Act effectively excluded Mormons as "jurors" in polygamy cases, Clawson argued that this exclusion did not extend to *grand* juries (US 114:483–84). Clawson's argument possessed a certain logic. Grand jurors could be called on to issue indictments for a variety of offenses during their term of service. To the extent that grand juries functioned as watchdogs of the community, excluding Mormons from them excluded the large majority of Utah's citizens from that important function. By thus extending the Edmunds Act disability to grand juries, the Court excluded Mormons from ruling on *any* indictments, simply to avoid possible Mormon bias with respect to a single class of offenses. The Supreme Court, however, without considering this consequence, held that the term *juror* encompassed both grand and petit jurors and that the Edmunds Act must therefore be read broadly to disable Mormons from service on any juries (US 114:483–84).

The procedure for selecting jurors under the Poland Act effectively filtered out Mormons from jury duty, even before the Supreme Court condoned their total exclusion. The lists from which potential jurors were taken, were drawn up by probate judges and the clerk of the court, each official drawing alternate names for the list. The probate judges, being Mormons, selected mostly Mormons for the list, while the non-Mormon court clerks selected non-Mormon jurors. From the start, then, Mormons, who constituted the majority of Utah's population, were systematically underrepresented in the jury selection process. Mormons who made it onto the jury list, however, could now be challenged and removed for bias. *Clawson* illustrates the problems engendered by this procedure. If Mormons were eliminated, the pool of eligible jurors was drastically reduced. Indeed, when it came time to select the petit jury for Clawson's trial, the pool of jurors on the list —some two hundred prospective jurors—had been exhausted, and eleven of the twelve finally chosen were individuals assembled by the U.S. marshal on orders from the court (US 114:484).

The exclusion of Mormons from juries was not absolute, even in polygamy trials, but the exceptions only serve to demonstrate how effectively Utah's jury system was tilted against the Mormons. In *United States v. Bassett* (P. 13:237–39 [Utah 1887]), for example, one of the jurors called was Andrew Larsen, formerly a practicing polygamist who had been granted a presidential pardon when he renounced the practice of polygamy. Despite objection, Larsen was accepted as a juror on the rationale that the terms of his pardon had legally obliterated his prior conduct. Excluding Larsen from jury duty would have thus imposed a civil disability on him, contrary to the terms of his pardon. In this instance, however, it was not the prosecution that objected to the inclusion of a reputed polygamist on the jury, but the defendant.

Perhaps such narrow legalisms encouraged the Mormons to attempt their own hair-splitting tactics. *United States v. Brown* (P. 21:461–62 [Utah 1889]) was a criminal perjury case brought against a potential juror in a polygamy case. Brown testified, while being questioned as a potential juror, that he did not believe polygamy to be right. The United States prosecutor knew that Brown was a loyal Mormon, and challenged his testimony. At his perjury trial, Brown explained that his testimony was not false because his adherence to polygamy was not a matter of "belief"; rather, he "knew it was right, for he had a testimony which gave him a knowledge that it was right" (P. 21:462). Brown's rather precise analysis did not convince the court, and he was convicted of perjury.

In theory at least, Mormons were prohibited from serving as jurors only in polygamy trials. Idaho, a hotbed of anti-Mormon sentiment, carried Congress's efforts a step further. An Idaho statute provided that only qualified electors could serve as jurors. Because Idaho law excluded Mormons from the vote, they were automatically barred from jury service as well. Even this draconian, blanket disability was upheld by the courts. In *Territory v. Evans* (P. 23:232 [1890]), the Idaho Supreme Court conceded that the law would, in some counties, exclude so many citizens that juries could not be selected but still upheld the exclusion of Mormons. The court reasoned, "We are justified in supposing the law-maker took notice of the generally admitted fact that the members of that church are more obedient to its teachings, which are antagonistic to the laws of the land, than to the latter" (P. 23:233).

The Exclusion of Mormons as Voters

While the Edmunds Act excluding Mormons from polygamy trial juries was rationally related to the federal government's goal of eliminating polygamy, other "anti-polygamy" measures of that act were directly aimed at Mormon political power. One provision denied polygamists the right to vote (Stat. 22:31, § 8). To enforce this provision, Utah's registration and election offices were declared vacant, and a five-man commission was appointed to oversee Utah elections (Stat. 22:32, § 9). During its first year the Utah Commission barred over 12,000 Mormons from voting in Utah. This was nearly one-fourth of eligible Mormon voters, and far exceeded the number of polygamists in Utah (Allen and Leonard 1976, 395). To "purify" Utah's political system, the Utah Commission, on its own initiative, came up with a test oath that all qualified voters were required to take. This oath specified that the affiant was neither a polygamist nor a cohabitant (US 114:19 [1884]). Mormons objected to this oath, among other reasons, because it operated as an ex post facto law by imposing a civil disability on Mormons who had entered polygamous unions prior to passage of the Edmunds Act. Furthermore, the Utah Commission apparently rejected the affidavits of those who had abandoned their polygamous marriages and excluded all Mormons who were reputed polygamists. Variant affidavits from Mormons who claimed to have entered no polygamous unions since passage of the Edmunds Act were likewise rejected.

The Utah commission's exclusion of Mormon voters met an immediate judicial challenge. Mormon voters sued the commission members, who had refused to place them on the voters' rolls. In *Murphy v. Ramsey* (US 114:15), the United States Supreme Court rebuked the commission, but its decision had mixed results for the Mormons. The Court did hold that the powers of the Utah Commission were restricted to ensuring that elections in Utah were fairly and properly conducted, and that the commission had no further power to establish voter qualifications or to administer a voter's oath. On the other hand, the Court held that since the commission was legally powerless to exclude voters, it was not legally liable for the acts of voting officials who wrongfully obeyed the commission in excluding the Mormons (US 114:36–37).

On the substantive question of the scope of the Edmunds Act's disfranchisement of polygamists, the *Murphy* Court again ruled against the Mormons. Because the act's provisions extended to cohabitants and polygamists without exclusion, it barred those who became polygamists before the act's passage as well as those who did so after 1882 (US 114:42). Nor was the statute an ex post facto law. The act applied only to those who continued to practice polygamy and not to those who had abandoned that practice. Therefore it was not retrospective (US 114:43). The Court alluded, however, to the problem faced by the Mormons: Because polygamy had been judicially defined as a state of being rather than an unlawful act, the Court could point to no conduct sufficient to terminate that unlawful status. A polygamist "might in fact abstain from actual cohabitation with all, and be still as much as ever a bigamist or a polygamist. He can only cease to be such when he has finally and fully dissolved in some effective manner, which we are not called on here to point out, the very relation of husband to several wives, which constitutes the forbidden status he has previously assumed" (US 114:42).

Moreover, fair or not, Congress held the sole power to determine the qualifications of voters in the territories and could legally set any eligibility requirements it pleased (US 114:44–45). The Court did not question whether other constitutional provisions, such as the First Amendment, might impose some rational restrictions on Congress's power to set voter qualifications. It was clear, however, that the Court considered the exclusion of polygamist voters to be a wholesome and rational measure:

> For certainly no legislation can be supposed more wholesome and necessary in the founding of a free, self-governing commonwealth, fit to take rank as one of the co-ordinate States of the Union, than that which seeks to establish it on the basis of the idea of the family, as consisting in and springing from the union for life of one man and one woman in the holy estate of matrimony; the sure foundation of all that is stable and noble in our civilization; the best guaranty of that reverent morality which is the source of all beneficent progress in social and political improvement. And to this end, no means are more directly and immediately suitable than those provided by this act, which endeavors to withdraw all political influence from those who are practically hostile to its attainment. (US 114:45)

Any measure of victory the Mormons won in this case must be rated as slight indeed. The Utah Commission remained charged with the duty of excluding polygamists from the franchise. Although the stricken voter oath had been administered unfairly, it had given the Mormons one protection: it established, in a manner at least conceivably open to challenge and rebuttal, whether individual Mormons were polygamists. Without the oath, the Utah Commission could exclude polygamists from the voter rolls without challenge, solely on the basis of reputation and rumor.

Although it abused its powers, the Utah Commission could legally exclude only practicing polygamists from voting. The legislatures of Utah's neighboring states attempted to carry this premise a step further. In 1887, Nevada adopted a statute excluding all Mormons from voting, holding elective office, and serving on juries. This law was challenged in *State v. Findley* (P. 19:241 [1888]) and stricken by the Nevada Supreme Court. Because the Nevada Constitution defined the qualifications of voters and included no religious test, the state legislature could not constitutionally adopt a religious test for voters (P. 19:242–43).

In Idaho, the Mormons faced even tougher sanctions. A large and violent anti-Mormon group in that state actively oppressed the Mormons. In 1885 the territorial legislature had adopted a statute similar to Nevada's, excluding all Mormons from voting. In 1888 Idaho's statute was sustained by the Idaho Supreme Court in *Innis v. Bolton* (P. 17:264). The Idaho court concluded that Congress had properly delegated the power to establish electoral qualifications to the territory and that the Idaho statute was consistent with and complemented the Edmunds Act's exclusion of polygamists. Congress's act excluding polygamists did not preempt the territories from imposing further restrictions, including the exclusion of all Mormons, who were deemed to be supporters of polygamy (P. 17:266–67).

To deal with the argument that the Idaho exclusion was an unconstitutional religious test, the court adopted the proposition set forth in *Reynolds v. United States* (US 98:145 [1878]) that freedom of religion encompassed only belief and not conduct. Even monogamous Mormons were deemed to have aided and abetted the unlawful conduct of polygamists, and therefore the exclusion of all Mormons from the vote was a reasonable means of curbing unlawful conduct (P. 17:267–68). Moreover, as the Supreme Court in *Murphy v. Ramsey* noted, the vote was a privilege that Congress could limit at will.

The Idaho court in *Innis v. Bolton* treated disfranchisement as a political question, left to legislative discretion regardless of the propriety or legality of polygamy. Thus the court scarcely dealt with the purported evils of polygamy. By contrast, the United States Supreme Court used the Idaho situation as the soapbox for a remarkable diatribe on polygamy (*Davis v. Beason*, US 133:333 [1890]).

Following the Idaho court's decision in *Innis v. Bolton*, a number of

Idaho Mormons, believing either that the church no longer advocated polygamy or that the Idaho statute would no longer prevent non-polygamous Mormons from voting, tried unsuccessfully to register to vote in the 1888 election (Wells 1978, 112–19). Some members then decided to take the only way left to them. They resigned their church membership and sought to register as voters (Wells 1978, 119–22; *Shepherd v. Grimmett*, P. 31:793 [Idaho 1892]). In some cities, Idaho election officials simply ignored the affidavits of the supposedly former Mormons and refused to allow them to vote. One seceder, Samuel D. Davis, managed to get his case heard by the United States Supreme Court (*Davis v. Beason*, US 133:333 [1890]). The Supreme Court similarly ignored the claim of Davis and his co-defendants that they were no longer Mormons and were thus improperly excluded from the vote. If the Mormon seceders had been acting in good faith, then Idaho's law was truly harsh. Under such a standard, an individual who was once identified as a Mormon could not escape the law's punishments even by abandoning his religion. To punish an individual for his faith was wrong; to punish him for his former faith was worse.

However, the Supreme Court did not deal with the issue of membership. Instead, the Court confined itself to the question of whether the Malad district court, in which Davis had been convicted of criminal conspiracy, had jurisdiction. The resolution of this issue in turn depended on whether Idaho's territorial legislature had power to require prospective voters to take an oath denying membership in any organization teaching polygamy. The Court assumed that Davis and others had "unlawfully procure[d] themselves to be admitted to registration as electors" (US 133:334). Their conspiracy consisted of offering affidavits that they were not Mormons "when, in truth, each of the defendants was a member of an order, organization and association, namely, the Church of Jesus Christ of Latter-Day Saints" whose members could not vote under the Idaho statute (US 133:334–35).

The initial portion of the Supreme Court's opinion in this case is an extensive account of those social policies supporting its conclusion that polygamy was abhorrent, in language that reached new heights of invective. The reasoning, of course, was familiar: polygamy destroyed family, freedom, and civilization and degraded women. The logic of the Court's decision in *Reynolds* was emphatically spelled out. Religion was reduced to purely a matter of belief and sentiment with conduct (including "form of worship") completely separate and outside the protection of the First Amendment (US 133:342).

However, even with such a restricted definition of the First Amendment's protection, the Court's judgment was too much. The Idaho statute disabled as voters those individuals who adhered to or believed in organizations promoting polygamy. No further action was necessary to invoke the act's sanctions. Thus, the act imposed penalties simply on the basis of belief. The only clearer instance of statutory invasion of the First Amendment would be a statute directly forbidding belief in the rightness of polygamy. Even if the First Amendment was deemed to protect only matters of belief, belief was exactly what Idaho's voter statute punished individuals for.

With the issue of freedom of religion dispatched, the Supreme Court swiftly denied Davis's remaining arguments. Idaho's statute was within the territory's power to set voter qualifications. It conflicted with no act of Congress. Moreover, Idaho's statute, according to the Court, rather sensibly prevented Mormons from overturning the criminal laws against polygamy with their votes (US 133:348).

The substance of Idaho's test oath statute was even more firmly embedded in Idaho's constitution when Idaho was admitted to statehood in 1890. Section 3, Article 6, of the Idaho constitution provided:

> No person is permitted to vote, serve as a juror, or hold any civil office who . . . is a bigamist or polygamist, or is living in what is known as patriarchal, plural, or celestial marriage . . . or who in any manner teaches, advises, counsels, aids, or encourages any person to enter into bigamy, polygamy, or such patriarchal, plural, or celestial marriage . . . or who is a member of, or contributes to the support, aid, or encouragement of, any order . . . which teaches, advises, counsels, encourages, or aids any person to enter into bigamy . . . or which teaches or advises that the laws of this state prescribing rules of civil conduct are not the supreme law of the state.

The Idaho Supreme Court upheld this provision in *Shepherd v. Grimmet* (P. 31:793–94 [1892]).

Finally, Congress passed the Edmunds-Tucker Act in 1887, disfranchising Mormon women and ending one of Utah's most significant advances in civil rights. In 1870, Utah's territorial legislature had granted women the right to vote, following Wyoming Territory in granting women full political equality, excepting the right to hold public office (Weisbrod and Sheingorn 1978, 828 n. 3). Initially, Utah's action won support even among the Mormons' enemies, who believed Mormon women would swiftly use their new political power to end polygamy. The Mormons, conversely, may have granted women the vote to demonstrate that polygamy and Mormon society in general did not oppress Mormon women (Weisbrod and Sheingorn 1978, 853–54 n. 134, 852–53 n. 130).

Mormon women, of course, did not use their votes to end polygamy, so Mormonism's critics reversed their position. Enfranchised Mormon women came to be seen as an impediment to the elimination of polygamy and the destruction of the Mormons' political power. Observers concluded that Mormon women were utterly dominated by the church leaders; women's votes thus only enlarged Mormon political power. The Edmunds-Tucker Act provided "that it shall not be lawful for any female to vote at any election hereafter held in the Territory of Utah for any public purpose whatever, and no such vote shall be received or counted or given effect in any manner whatever" (Stat. 24:639, § 20).

Given the judicial conclusion that the franchise in territories was a privilege that Congress could arbitrarily restrict, Congress's disfranchisement of Utah's women was legal. Its efficacy in hastening the end of polygamy, however, may be doubted. Congress's all-out assault on Mormon political rights destroyed healthy and progressive social experiments as well as those tainted by polygamy. One rationale for a federal system of government is that separate local governments provide laboratories for new experiments in social organization and government. Ideas proven in one area may then be adopted in other states. In the nineteenth century, territorial Utah was one of the most innovative areas of the country, both socially and politically. In its opposition to all things Mormon, the federal government crushed much that was valuable and much that otherwise might have been sooner adopted in other states.

The Exclusion of Mormons from Public Office

To the extent that Mormons were excluded from the vote, they were also and quite locally excluded from all elective and other public offices. Thus, the 1882 Edmunds Act excluded polygamists from public office, and Idaho's statute excluded all Mormons from public office.

The Edmunds Act, in creating the Utah Commission to oversee Utah's elections, mandated that no election could take place without the commission's supervision (Stat. 22:31, § 8). Because the commission was unable to arrive in Utah in time, no election was possible in 1882 (*Wenner v. Smith*, P. 9:293 [Utah 1886]). So that elective offices would not stay vacant pending the next election, Congress hastily passed the Hoar Amendment allowing Utah's governor to appoint officials to fill vacant elective offices until the next election (Stat. 22:313 [1882]).

Some disagreement arose regarding the effect of the Hoar Amendment. The Mormons maintained that under Utah law, where an election was not held, incumbent officials simply retained their office.

Thus, the governor had no appointments to make, for no offices were vacant. Utah's governor, Eli H. Murray, a gentile who was hostile to the Mormons and frustrated by their political obstructionism, decided that in spite of contrary Utah law, the offices were vacant. In September and October of 1882, he appointed a total of 174 replacements to public office, almost all gentiles (CHC 6:65–66).

Mormons reacted angrily to this attempted ouster, and many refused to surrender their offices. Others instituted action to validate their claim that no offices had been vacated through the failure to hold elections when scheduled. In an unreported case, *Kimball v. Richards* (discussed in *Wenner v. Smith*, P. 9:297–98 [Utah 1886]), the Utah Supreme Court held that the Hoar Amendment had, in fact, vacated Utah's elective offices, despite the amendment's failure to specifically state this.

Despite this judicial setback, some Mormon officials still refused to relinquish their offices. The 1886 case of *Wenner v. Smith* (P. 9:293) illustrates this continuing resistance. Defendant Smith had been elected probate judge of Salt Lake County in 1880. By virtue of the Hoar Amendment, the governor considered Smith's office to be vacant and appointed Uriah J. Wenner as his successor in September 1882 to serve for eight months, the maximum allowed by the Hoar Amendment. Smith, however, refused to turn over the office, books, papers, and duties to Wenner and continued to receive the fees and salary of the judgeship. Wenner sued to recover those sums.

On appeal, the Utah Supreme Court concluded that Wenner's appointment was lawful. Moreover, the court concluded, because the Edmunds Act declared polygamists unfit to hold public office and because Smith was a polygamist, his judgeship had been vacated by the Edmunds Act without reference to the Hoar Amendment. Thus, Wenner had been wrongfully denied the office and was entitled to recover the fees.

THE ASSAULT ON MORMON SOCIETY

Like a vise, federal pressure affected every part of Mormon society. Prying spies seeking to discover polygamists and midnight raiders invading homes posed constant concerns. Polygamists who voluntarily obeyed the government's dictates faced different strains, for obedience to the government meant abandoning wives and children. The polygamist who tried to care for and support his plural wives walked a tightrope. If he was too visible in his support, he was likely to be condemned for continuing to cohabit with his plural wives.

The cumulative pressure brought to bear by the federal government on Mormons changed the Utah society. This sort of pervasive pressure is exemplified by federal intervention into inheritance rights and immigration. In one sense, these two issues span a society's most individualistic and most collective concerns. The laws of inheritance profoundly concern individuals, for they govern how and to what extent one generation may pass on its accumulated labor and wealth to the next and in a tangible sense stretch the individual's own impact and existence beyond the span of his or her life. Immigration laws touch a society as a whole in somewhat the same fashion, regulating the flow of human wealth and talent into a society.

The Laws of Inheritance

Under common law, illegitimate children, if recognized by the law at all, could inherit property only from their mothers (Ritchie, Alford, and Effland 1977, 71–72). Utah's territorial legislature reversed this common law-rule, and provided in 1852 that "illegitimate children and their mothers inherit in like manner from the father" (Comp. Laws 1876, 268, § 677).[2] It is, of course, a rather fine question whether the children of polygamous Mormon marriages were illegitimate. Under common law and federal law after passage of the Morrill Act, polygamous marriages were unlawful, and the offspring of such unions were presumably illegitimate. In Utah, where such marriages were recognized, the children were not illegitimate, but territorial law rendered the question moot. Whether or not they were illegitimate, plural wives and their children were entitled to inherit equally with a decedent's first wife and children.

This state of affairs presented Congress with a problem. Clearly, it was the nation's policy to forbid polygamy and crush institutions that supported and furthered the practice. Utah's law allowing polygamous wives and children to inherit in the same manner as monogamous heirs arguably furthered the practice of polygamy. On the other hand, to overturn Utah's laws and prohibit the children of polygamous marriages from inheriting property was equally clearly a cruel punishment that would be levied primarily against innocent children. Perhaps in some attenuated sense it might be said that denying a polygamous parent the right to leave property to his children would punish the parent by denying him the right to provide for his unlawful families after his death. Compared to the punishment inflicted on the children, however, such a deprivation is simply too indirect to be significant.

Sensibly, Congress simply left the issue alone until 1887. Indeed, in

the Edmunds Act Congress specifically provided that children of polygamous marriages born prior to 1883 were to be deemed legitimate
(Stat. 22:31, § 7). The continued Mormon resistance to enforcement of
the polygamy laws, however, finally eroded Congress's moderate attitude toward the children of polygamy. In the Edmunds-Tucker Act,
Congress annulled the Utah statute by providing that "no illegitimate
child shall hereafter be entitled to inherit from his or her father or to
receive any distributive share in the estate of his or her father: *Provided,* That this section shall not apply to any illegitimate child born
within twelve months after the passage of this act" (Stat. 24:637, § 11
[1887]). As might be expected, Congress's ambivalent attitude and
legislation spawned litigation.

The question of the status of polygamous children first came before
the Utah Supreme Court in the case of *Chapman v. Handley* (P. 24:673)
in 1890. George Handley died intestate in 1874, leaving an estate of
$25,000, a surviving widow, and eight children, four of them the off-
spring of a then-deceased plural wife. These polygamous children
claimed an interest in Handley's estate under the Utah statute allowing illegitimate children to inherit from their parents. Handley's other
children invoked the Morrill Act to block their claim. Their argument
was that the Utah law violated public policy in general by supporting
polygamy. More specifically, because Utah's statute supported polygamy, the Morrill Act had expressly annulled it. The issue, then, was
whether a law allowing illegitimate children to inherit supported polygamy. The court expressed no doubt that the statute "was intended
to, and did tend to, support, maintain, and countenance polygamy"
(P. 24:675).

Although the court recognized that its conclusion punished the innocent children of polygamy, it noted that "Congress has recognized
the potency of denying to illegitimate children the rights of legitimacy
and inheritance as a means of breaking up and discouraging polygamy
in the acts of 1882 and 1887" (P. 24:675). The denial of inheritance,
by this rather twisted reasoning, ultimately benefited illegitimate children because it helped destroy the polygamous marital system that
produced them.

The problem in *Chapman v. Handley* arose because George Handley
had died intestate. Presumably, then, even if the law did not allow
his polygamous children to share in his estate under the laws of in-
testacy, Handley could have provided for the children in a will. The
Utah Supreme Court, however, cast doubt upon even this alternative. Noting the provision of the Edmunds-Tucker Act that prohibited
illegitimate children from inheriting, the court commented that, "so

emphatic is the language of the latter act that it may well be doubted whether testamentary provision can be made for them" (P. 24:675).

In 1891, the year after the decision in *Chapman v. Handley*, another case involving the same issues and similar facts was brought before the United States Supreme Court. In *Cope v. Cope* (US 137:682), however, the Supreme Court arrived at a different conclusion: "Legislation for the protection of children born in polygamy is not necessarily legislation favorable to polygamy. There is no inconsistency in shielding the one and in denouncing the other as a crime" (US 137:687). Utah's act, rather than promoting polygamy, simply protected the children of polygamy: "It may be said in defence of this act that the children embraced by it are not responsible for this state of things, and that it is unjust to visit upon them the consequences of their parents' sins" (US 137:685). Further, Utah's statute was not implicitly annulled by the Morrill Act in 1862. Rather, all of Congress's acts relating to illegitimate children should be read together, and "the later acts should also be regarded as legislative interpretations of the prior ones" (US 137:688). In 1882 Congress had explicitly legitimated the children of polygamous marriages, and not until 1887 did it specifically bar their inheritance rights. These later actions demonstrated that in 1862 Congress had not meant to annul the Utah statute allowing illegitimate children to inherit. In fact, the Court continued, "Not only does Congress refrain from adding to the odium which popular opinion visits upon this innocent but unfortunate class of children, but it makes them the special object of its solicitude, and at the same time offers to the parents an inducement, in the nature of a locus penitentiae (an opportunity to change one's mind), to discontinue their unlawful cohabitation" (US 137:689).

After 1890, when the church formally renounced plural marriage, Utah again adopted a statute entitling the children of polygamous marriages to inherit property. The legislature further provided that any heir who had been previously denied an inheritance on the basis of his polygamous lineage could petition the courts for a redistribution of the estate (Utah Laws 1896, ch. 41, 128–29).

On the strength of this provision and in the wake of *Cope*, George Handley's polygamous children petitioned Utah's courts to award them their rightful share of their father's estate. If the purpose in denying illegitimate children a share in their parents' estate was to strike a blow at polygamy, then that purpose was served when the Mormons abandoned that practice. With that excuse removed, all that remained to justify the inheritance bar was a senseless vengeance against innocent children. By retroactively removing that bar, Utah's statute simply removed a penalty that no longer had even a pretext of justification.

Apparently in a vengeful mood, Utah's Supreme Court declined to accept this reasoning. Instead, the court struck down the statute. The court reasoned that the Utah act reopened cases that had been resolved by the judiciary, thus second-guessing judicial judgment. Under the separation of powers, this interference with the judicial process was unconstitutional:

> In effect the courts are required to disregard as final all judgments and decisions rendered in such cases. We must hold the act of 1896 invalid, because in its passage the legislature assumed to exercise judicial powers, and also because they assumed the right to require the courts to regard judments as impeachable that were unimpeachable under the laws in force at the time they were rendered, and by which vested rights were established and evidenced. (*In re Handley's Estate*, P. 49:832 [1897])

Curiously, the court did not mention the United States Supreme Court's decision in *Cope v. Cope* as a basis for its reconsideration of this case, even though that decision in effect overruled the territorial court's decision in *Handley*.

The court's action was a bitter but somewhat empty gesture. Since the Edmunds Act in 1882 legitimated polygamous children, the court's ruling affected only the estates of those polygamists who had died prior to passage of the Edmunds Act. If the court's action had any justification, it was the dubious virtue of refusing to disturb old and settled accounts even at the price of failing to right past wrongs.

Immigration Laws

For the Mormons, Utah became the point from which they would carry the word of their gospel throughout the world and to which Mormon converts from around the world would gather. Spiritually, immigration was the gathering of the Saints into the Mormon community. Economically, the immigrants brought the skills and hands needed to settle the wilderness.

With typical initiative, the Mormons organized the immigration of large numbers of converts through the Perpetual Emigrating Fund Company (Arrington 1958, 97–108). This church-sponsored company provided agents to arrange the converts' passage from Europe to America and from there to Utah. It also paid the passage for those too poor to pay their own way. The fund was theoretically perpetual because immigrants were supposed to repay the company for the money advanced for their passage, after they arrived in Utah. In actuality the fund received little in the way of repayments from the immigrants and was instead supported by contributions from church members (Arrington 1958, 101). By 1870, the year after the transcontinental railroad was completed, the Perpetual Emigrating Fund had helped over 51,000 Mormon immigrants reach Utah (Arrington 1958, 99).

This large-scale flow of new, foreign Mormons into Utah naturally alarmed the church's enemies, who feared that the faith of the converts would revitalize the church's doctrines. An 1881 essay in *Harper's Magazine* stated, Mormonism "is an institution so absolutely un-American in all its requirements that it would die of its own infamies within twenty years, except for the yearly infusion of fresh serf blood from abroad" (Mulder 1956, 417). The point was made more luridly by fictionalized reports that the Mormons imported young, innocent girls to become polygamous wives in a sort of religious white slavery (Mulder, 428). President Ulysses S. Grant reflected this view when he recommended to Congress in his annual message on 7 December 1875 that it "drive out licensed immorality, such as polygamy and the importation of women for illegitimate purposes" (Richardson, 7:356).

A decade later, in 1885, President Grover Cleveland recommended to Congress that it prevent the importation of Mormons into the country (Richardson 8:362). Congress acted, in part, on this advice when it adopted the Edmunds-Tucker Act in 1887. Section 15 of that act dissolved the Perpetual Emigrating Fund Company and forbade the territorial legislature from acting in any fashion to encourage immigration into Utah (Stat. 24:637). In 1891 Congress again acted, adding polygamists to the list of classes excluded from the country (Stat. 26:1084, ch. 551, § 1; Mulder, 427).

In dissolving the Perpetual Emigrating Fund and seizing its assets, the federal government made a rather poor haul. Besides a little office furniture, books, records, and $2.25 in silver, federal officials found only $417,968.50 in uncollectable promissory notes (Mulder, 426–27). Moreover, the Perpetual Emigrating Fund was a withering organization by the time Congress dissolved it. By the 1880s, immigration to Utah had slowed to a trickle, and those immigrants that came mostly paid their own passage. The company, however, had served its purpose, assisting over 100,000 Mormon converts to migrate to Utah by 1887 (Arrington 1958, 381–82).

Congressional action to halt Mormon migration was simply the last step in federal efforts to obstruct immigration. Through diplomatic channels, the executive branch of the federal government attempted to persuade European governments to block the departure of European Mormons. In 1879 Secretary of State William M. Evarts sent a message to diplomatic offices in Europe calling on Europe's governments for assistance:

> Under whatever specious guise the subject [of polygamy] may be presented by those engaged in instigating the European movement to swell the numbers of the law-defying Mormons of Utah, the bands of organizations which are got together in foreign lands as recruits cannot be regarded as otherwise than a deliberate and systematic attempt to bring persons to the United States with the intent of violating their laws and committing crimes expressly punishable under the statute as penitentiary offenses. (Mulder, 423)

This diplomatic effort met with some ridicule from the British press, which noted that converting to Mormonism was not necessarily equivalent to adopting polygamy (Mulder 1956, 423–24). However, many European governments offered their support. Norway and Sweden agreed to discourage Mormon missionary activity, and Germany banished all Mormon missionaries (Mulder, 424).

In America, immigration officers instituted a program of harassing and excluding Mormon immigrants. Because the passage of many poorer immigrants was assisted by the church federal officials attempted to bar those immigrants as paupers. From 1886 on, many Mormon immigrants were detained as paupers, and a few were even returned to Europe (Mulder, 427–28).

In Utah, the Mormon-controlled probate courts freely granted naturalization to immigrants. In 1866, Thomas J. Drake, an associate justice of the Utah Supreme Court sitting as a district court judge in Provo, barred this procedure, holding that the probate courts were without power to grant naturalization. He further ruled that all prior naturalizations granted by the probate courts were null and void (Mulder, 429).

In 1870 Chief Justice James B. McKean, presiding over the district court in Salt Lake City, ruled that a mere belief in polygamy was sufficient grounds for refusing to naturalize an alien regardless of whether the applicant was involved in its practice (*In re Sandberg and Horsley*, reported in *Deseret News*, 19 Oct. 1870, 436; CHC 5:386–87). McKean failed to cite any precedent for his arbitrary holding, basing his decision on his interpretation of the naturalization statute. But McKean's ruling required more of applicants than was required of natural-born citizens, an open denial of belief in polygamy.

Finally, in 1889 Justice Thomas J. Anderson denied citizenship to foreign-born Mormons because the religious covenants administered in the Endowment House required them to pledge allegiance to the church's laws above and against those of the United States (Mulder, 431). After the church renounced polygamy in 1890, Chief Justice Charles S. Zane ruled that foreign-born Mormons could be naturalized (Mulder, 432).

VEXATIOUS AND ANTI-MORMON LITIGATION

Polygamy was not the only front in the legal battle against the Mormons. Their opponents repeatedly used lawsuits as harassment, focusing particularly on Mormon leaders. Some of the claims were legitimate,[3] but the Mormons nevertheless perceived the assault as motivated by religious discrimination.

The earliest criminal charges against Brigham Young and other church leaders arose out of the Utah War of 1857–58. Acting on reports that the civil government of the Utah Territory was in a state of "substantial rebellion" against the federal government, President James Buchanan sent an army of 2,500 men to Utah in 1857 to restore order, reaffirm federal supremacy, and to install the newly appointed gentile governor of Utah, Alfred Cumming of Georgia, to replace Brigham Young. Encamped for the winter at Camp Scott, near Fort Bridger, on 21 November 1857, Cumming issued a proclamation to the people of the Utah Territory announcing his appointment, declaring the territory in a state of rebellion, and asserting that treason had been committed by "lawless individuals" in an effort to restrain the federal troops (CHC 4:314–15). In the proclamation and in a personal note to Brigham Young, Cumming blamed Young for authorizing "violent and treasonable acts" that had resulted in the destruction and theft of United States property. As governor, Young had issued a proclamation forbidding the United States armed forces from entering the territory and encouraging the people to prepare to repel any United States aggression.

Patrols of the Nauvoo Legion had burned government supply trains en route to Utah (CHC 4:273–74, 283–86), and their scouts put a scorched-earth policy into effect, destroying both Fort Bridger and Fort Supply in the process (Brooks 1962, 144–45). But these acts did little to hinder the progress of the army, and had the Utah winter not descended when it did, there could have been a very different ending to the story.

> Had the weather permitted them [Johnston's army] to proceed, war would have been inevitable, for the Mormon army of twenty-five hun-

dred men was stationed at strategic points, and reserves were all alerted for action at an hour's notice. (Brooks 1962, 146)

Shortly after Cumming's proclamation, Delena R. Eckles, the new chief justice of the territory, organized a district court at Camp Scott. A grand jury impaneled for the court investigated the alleged rebellion and indicted Brigham Young and sixty of his associates for treason (CHC 4:317–18). This action raised a serious jurisdictional question because the court was ostensibly called only "to insure security of life and property in Camp Scott and its vicinity" (CHC 4:318).

Young's proclamation and the Utah militia's destruction of United States property certainly left the Mormons open to charges of treason. From their perspective, however, the federal troops were a continuation of the persecution and mob action they had earnestly attempted to escape. Brigham Young saw the intrusion as an unconstitutional infringement of religious and political freedom and therefore felt justified in his proclamation (CHC 4:310–11, 411–13). Perhaps because of the jurisdictional concern and the generally "unsettled state of things" in the territory, no proceedings were ever conducted on the indictments (CHC 4:359).

Two years later, Young again became the subject of criminal investigation. A group of men at Camp Floyd, later Fort Crittendon, a federal facility some forty miles south of Salt Lake City, employed a young Mormon engraver to join their conspiracy to counterfeit United States quartermaster orders (CHC 4:505–10). He duplicated the plate at Camp Floyd. After the crime was discovered, one of the principals turned state's evidence and blamed the young Mormon. The engraver had worked for Brigham Young, and one of Young's employees was also implicated for supplying the paper for the counterfeit notes. On the strength of these connections, the officers at Camp Floyd hoped to implicate Young and made plans to arrest him, but Governor Cumming refused to assent to Young's arrest on such a groundless charge. The federal troops thought of acting without Cumming's cooperation but decided not to when the governor ordered the Mormon militia to prepare to repel any attempts to arrest President Young (CHC 4:509–10).

In 1866, non-Mormons again attempted to link the Mormon leader to criminal activity. Dr. J. King Robinson, an anti-Mormon from Maine, was murdered. Robinson had already been involved with Salt Lake City officials in disputes over his "bowling saloon" that the city attorney, Hosea Stout, called a "gambling house, and a liquor hell-hole besides, diametrically opposed to city ordinances" (*Deseret News* 14 Nov. 1866). The police had destroyed it because of ordinance violations, and Robinson's suit to recover damages was pending at the time of his death. Furthermore, Robinson had seized eighty acres of city property, claiming that the city corporation had no legal existence because the city charter had not been subjected to the requirements of the territorial organic act. The district court had rejected this argument a month earlier (*Deseret News*, 24 Oct. 1866).

Special prosecutor John B. Weller, speaking for the coroner's court, laid suspicion for the murder on church leaders (Stenhouse 1873, 735–41). In a vehement denial, Brigham Young challenged the accusers to trace the murder to him or refrain from the damaging insinuation (JD 11:280–82). The coroner's inquest was unable to produce "one particle of proof" connecting any church leader to the murder (CHC 5:204). The verdict of the coroner's jury was that "the deceased had died by the hands of some persons unknown to the jury" (*Deseret News*, 14 Nov. 1866).

With President Grant's appointment of Chief Justice James B. McKean in July 1870, efforts to harass the Mormons through the judicial system increased. The Mormon church generally and Brigham Young in particular became the objects of blatant religious discrimination.

In 1871 Salt Lake City Mayor Daniel H. Wells, Hosea Stout, and W. H. Kimball were charged with the murder of a man named Yates and arrested (Jenson 1899, 86). President Young was also indicted, based on the questionable confession of the notorious Bill Hickman, who had confessed to some twenty murders (CHC 5:405). Hickman consented to testify before the grand jury to implicate Young and the others. R. N. Baskin, acting United States district attorney, encouraged the indictment and claimed that the Hickman confession was corroborated by "statements of other persons," which he never produced (CHC 5:406).

Judge McKean's disposition of the charge was typical of his anti-Mormon sentiment. He set Wells's bail at $50,000 and denied bail for the seventy-one-year-old Young, after the United States district attorney had requested that it be set, if at all, at $500,000 (*Deseret News*, 10 Jan. 1872). Before the case could come to trial, however, the United States Supreme Court handed down the decision in *Clinton v. Englebrecht* (US 80:434 [1871]), overturning the criminal proceedings in Utah for the previous eighteen months on the grounds that the juries had been improperly impaneled (CHC 5:412–14). All indictments during the period were declared void, forcing the release of about 120 persons, including the defendants in the Yates murder case. President Young hoped to be released in time for the church's conference on 6

April 1872, but the United States marshal delayed. Young was forced to obtain a writ of habeas corpus from the probate judge of Salt Lake County before the marshal would release him (CHC 5:415), and the conference was adjourned to 28 April to allow President Young to attend.

Three years later, Brigham Young's enemies tried to implicate him in the infamous Mountain Meadows massacre, which had occurred almost twenty years before. To fully understand that event, one must understand the mind-set of the Mormons in 1857. On July 24, 1857, during the celebration of the tenth anniversary of the settlement of the Great Basin, Brigham Young informed his people that an army was marching on Utah. This provoked anti-American sentiment, and the people were prepared to fight for Zion. A part of this war hysteria was a mistrust of all outsiders, and an order from Brigham Young to stop all trading with emigrees (Brooks 1962, 15–30). It was in this climate of hostility that an emigrant group entered the territory.

According to the Mormons, the emigrants boasted of having mobbed the Mormons in Missouri and participated in the assassination of Joseph and Hyrum Smith. The newcomers threatened to return from California to destroy the Mormon settlements and poisoned a spring and an ox carcass, which resulted in the deaths of several Indians, a settler, and several cattle (CHC 4:142–43). When the group reached the Mountain Meadows, about 300 miles southwest of Salt Lake, Indians and nearby Mormon settlers attacked them, killing between 115 and 120 men, women, and children (Brooks 1962, 69–96). Seventeen young children were saved (CHC 4:157–58). Responsibility for the massacre remains unclear, but attempts were made to place blame on the Mormon leadership.

John D. Lee, an Indian agent near Mountain Meadows at the time of the massacre, confessed to his involvement in the crime and was first tried in July 1875. "The scarcely veiled object of the prosecution was to extract from Lee a confession that would afford grounds for an indictment of Brigham Young himself" (Dywer, 100). Leonard Arrington observes:

> It seems quite obvious [from the minutes of the first trial] that federal prosecutors were using John D. Lee as a symbol rather than trying him individually. R. N. Baskin, for example, in his statement to the first trial jury stated that in reality "the Mormon theocracy" was "responsible" for the "heinous crime"—perpetrated at Mountain Meadows. "It seems to me," he said, "that a part of the Mormon Religion is to kill—and a part and parcel of it—and a great part of it is to shed human blood for another. . . . There is no use to disguise it when counsel said that the

Mormon Church was on trial—I am willing to accept the gentleman's statement. . . ." Baskin went on to compare the Lee case to the Dred Scott case in which, he said, Dred Scott was a symbol, but "the whole system of negro slavery was involved." So it was with the Mountain Meadows affair: "In as much as this crime was concocted by the leaders of the Mormon Church . . . , and the further fact shows it was the result of a secret and misterious [sic] organization which strikes misteriously and secretly and seals the lips of those who participated in it. . . . I am willing to accept the gentleman's proposition, that it is the Mormon Church that is now on trial." Baskin then went on to involve Brigham Young: "I do hold Brigham Young responsible; I do hold the system which has carried out which distinctly teaches and carries out in its preaching and practices the shedding of human blood to atone for real and imaginary offenses. I hold, I arraign this iniquitous system, and the leaders of the church." (1960, 43 n. 60)

To the prosecution's disappointment, Lee implicated no one higher in authority than local church leaders in Iron County. Baskin refused to accept his confession, claiming it had not been made in good faith.

The jury for Lee's first trial, composed of both Mormons and non-Mormons, could not agree on a verdict, and the case was remanded for a new trial. The assistant prosecutor claimed that the jury split down religious lines—the non-Mormons voting for conviction and the Mormons favoring acquittal (CHC 4:606 n. 23). "It seems clear," writes Arrington, ". . . that through Lee the prosecution was attempting to fasten the crime upon the Mormon Church and its leaders. In such a contest it is not surprising that the Mormon jurors acquitted Lee. To convict him would have been tantamount to convicting themselves" (1960, 43 n. 60). When the case was retried, the prosecution changed its approach, explaining to the jury that its intention was "to try John D. Lee, and not Brigham Young and the Mormon Church, who are not indicted" (*Deseret News*, 16 Sept. 1876). Under the circumstances the all-Mormon jury had no difficulty finding Lee guilty of first-degree murder. "Nearly all works which mention the second Lee trial point to a 'conspiracy' on the part of the Mormon Church to 'sacrifice' Lee in return for the prosecution's promise not to involve the church," Arrington notes (1960, 43 n. 60). However, another possible explanation for the prosecution's change of approach might be that it merely repudiated its claim against the church for convenience and success rather than as a result of a conspiracy because of the difficulty of obtaining a conviction in the first trial. In any case, after the Utah Supreme Court affirmed the lower court's judgment, Lee was executed by gunshot at the site of the Mountain Meadows massacre.

Criminal law was not the only means used to harass church leaders. The church's enemies also filed vexatious civil suits. The case of *Godbe v. Young* (Utah 1:55 [1870] reversed, US 83:564 [1872]) illustrates how the church's opponents sought slender opportunities to embroil the church in litigation and exemplifies Judge McKean's willingness to affirm dubious procedural rulings to the disadvantage of Mormon leaders. William S. Godbe, excommunicated in 1869 over political and economic differences with church leaders, filed suit against Brigham Young as trustee-in-trust of the church for money Godbe had allegedly advanced him. At the trial Godbe produced evidence tending to show that he had advanced money to Brigham Young in some capacity. The critical question was the nature of that capacity. Brigham Young contended that he had received the money as agent for the Deseret Irrigation and Canal Company, and not as trustee-in-trust for the church. After the parties had rested, Godbe called a local bookkeeper to testify. His testimony consisted of statements made by a third party suggesting that the irrigation company was so mixed up with the church as to make the distinction meaningless. Young's counsel objected on the grounds that the evidence was not in rebuttal and therefore could not be introduced once the parties had rested their case. The testimony was clearly inadmissible, being hearsay, yet it was admitted over the defendant's objection, and the trial judge told the jury it could consider the testimony "for what it was worth" (in US 82:564). The Utah Supreme Court affirmed, Judge McKean writing the opinion. He admitted that the trial court had erred in admitting the evidence but ruled that the defense had made the wrong objection, thereby waiving any other (Utah 1:57). The United States Supreme Court reversed the Utah court for allowing into evidence testimony that was clearly hearsay (US 82:565).

Another example of McKean's bias was his willingness to adopt inconsistent legal positions to the detriment of the Mormons. In *Young v. Young*, Ann Eliza Webb Young sued Brigham Young for divorce in 1873, claiming neglect, cruel treatment, and desertion (CHC 5:442–43). The suit was filed on 28 July, 1873. Claiming that Young was worth $8 million and had a monthly income of $40,000, she asked for $1,000 per month pending the trial, a total of $20,000 for counsel fees, and $200,000 for her maintenance. Brigham Young denied her charges and claimed to have a worth of only $600,000 and a monthly income of $6,000. More fundamentally, he pointed out the inconsistency of granting a divorce and alimony for a marriage that was not legally recognized. Since he had married Mary Ann Angell at Kirtland, Ohio, in 1834 and was still lawfully married to her, he argued that the court should not grant the divorce and award alimony unless it was willing to recognize the validity of "plural or celestial marriages." He acknowledged that his 1868 marriage to Ann Eliza had been in violation of the law and was illegal from the beginning but also claimed the marriage was invalid because Ann Eliza was the legal wife of James L. Dee when he married her, a fact unknown to him at the time (CHC 5:443–44; *Deseret News*, 2 Sept. 1874). Since Ann Eliza's complaint and prayer for damages consisted of an attempt to extort, according to B. H. Roberts, Brigham Young felt justified in taking advantage of "every technicality that the law permits" (CHC 5:444).

The proceedings were protracted. Ann Eliza took advantage of the drawnout proceedings to capitalize on her celebrity: "She toured the eastern states, lecturing on the horrors of polygamy" (Dwyer, 90–91). Finally, on 25 February 1875, McKean, as judge of the third district court, rendered a decision on the issue of alimony pending the trial. He ordered the defendant to pay $3,000 attorneys' fees within ten days and, within twenty days, alimony of $500 per month pending trial, "to commence from the date of filing of the complaint herein," that is, beginning a year and a half previously, a decision Roberts describes as "doubtless in legal annals a curiosity" (CHC 5:443 and n. 16). On advice of counsel, Young did not pay counsel fees and was brought before McKean on contempt charges. Young stated that he had appealed the decision to the territorial supreme court and had filed a motion to stay execution of the order pending the appeal, as he understood it was his right to do (*Deseret News*, 17 Mar. 1875). McKean adjudged Young guilty of contempt and sentenced him to a $25 fine and twenty-four-hour imprisonment. The $3,000 attorneys' charges were immediately paid; and Young, who then was in poor health, was driven through a snowstorm to the penitentiary, where he spent the night (CHC 5:445–46).

A week later President Grant removed the unpopular McKean from office. A press dispatch reported that he was removed for "several acts . . . which are considered ill advised and tyrannical, and in excess of his powers as a judge" (*Deseret News*, 16 Mar. 1875). George R. Maxwell, the registrar of the territorial land office and the instigator of the suit by Ann Eliza Young, was also replaced, "for fanatical and extreme conduct" (CHC 5:443, 446, 450–52). Justice McKean continued to reside in Utah until his death in 1879. Brigham Young was brought before McKean's successor, David B. Lowe of Kansas, in April 1875 to show cause why he had not paid the $9,500 accumulated alimony to Ann Eliza Webb Young according to McKean's order. The court reasoned that alimony could not be awarded unless a valid marriage existed. Since Young had alleged that the marriage was illegal and the allegation was not denied, it had to be considered true, and the order was set aside (*Deseret News*, 12 May 1875).

Judge Lowe resigned shortly thereafter and was succeeded by Alexander White. Before White's arrival, the case was taken before the interim judge for the third district, Jacob S. Boreman, formerly judge of the second judicial district, who shared McKean's anti-Mormon sentiments. Boreman readjudicated the matter and ordered Young imprisoned until he paid the $9,500. When Justice White arrived, he held that Boreman's action was "unauthorized and void" and ordered Young released (CHC 5:453). However, White's appointment was never confirmed by the Senate. After three months his name was withdrawn, and he was replaced by Chief Justice Michael Schaeffer. Schaeffer reduced the alimony to $100 per month, making the accumulated sum $3,600. In April 1877, nearly four years after the original charges were filed, the divorce action finally came to trial; the marriage was adjudged void from the beginning, and all orders to pay alimony that had not been complied with were revoked (CHC 5:453–54; *Deseret News*, 2 April 1884). Brigham Young was nevertheless required to pay the costs of the action. Roberts waxed indignant: "This case of 'Young v. Young' was malicious and vindictive and instituted purely for extortion, and for the vexation and annoyance of Brigham Young. It was brought into court against the plainest principles of law, and its record is a disgrace to those who instituted it" (CHC 5:454). Schaeffer's decision so upset Young's enemies, however, that they successfully lobbied for Schaeffer's removal.

DISESTABLISHMENT OF THE CHURCH

In its early years, the church's leaders harbored a deep distrust of lawyers and the formalities of the law. In Utah, church leaders attempted to neutralize legal harassment through a counter-use of the law. In 1851, the assembly of the state of Deseret passed an ordinance incorporating the Church of Jesus Christ of Latter-day Saints. When Utah became a territory in 1855, this charter was readopted by the territorial legislature. By the terms of this charter, the church was granted vast powers. It could acquire and sell property, regulate marriages, register births and deaths, and make all laws, rules, and adjudications it deemed necessary. It was also not subject to legal review (*United States v. Church of Jesus Christ of Latter-day Saints*, P. 15:474–75 [Utah 1887]).

Having been legally endowed with all necessary powers, the church was presumably freed from petty legal challenges. Armed with these powers, it became deeply involved in members' economic lives. It established itself as a major business interest in Utah, and consistent with the church's communal doctrines, held a major portion of the Mormons' collective wealth. These policies made the church quite vulnerable to federal pressure. The seizure of church property would be a devastating blow to the entire Mormon community. The federal government did not hesitate long before it used this ultimate weapon. The Morrill Act of 1862 revoked the charter incorporating the Mormon church, at least insofar as that charter supported or aided polygamy (Stat. 12:501, § 2).

No attempt was made to enforce the forfeiture of church property, but the church took this warning seriously even though the act was generally believed unconstitutional. To bring themselves into what they believed to be a technical compliance with the act, the Mormons initiated a policy of placing property in the hands of the trustee-in-trust (Arrington 1958, 356). Thus, title to church property was legally held by individual church leaders in trust.

With the 1887 Edmunds-Tucker Act, Congress told the church to abandon the practice of plural marriage or face destruction. The mechanism of destruction was to be confiscation of church property. Section 13 of the act directed the attorney general of the United States to institute proceedings pursuant to the Morrill Act of 1862 to confiscate all church real estate in excess of $50,000 in value (Stat. 24:637). Proceeds from this confiscation and the assets of the Perpetual Emigrating Fund Company were to further schools in the territory. Property used exclusively for purposes of worship, parsonages, and burial grounds were exempted from this provision.

Congressional legislation specified that only the church's real property was subject to seizure; but because the Morrill Act arguably revoked the church's charter in its entirety, the church no longer existed in the eyes of the law as a body capable of holding property. Thus, such personal property as stocks, livestock, and furniture were left ownerless and forfeited to the state.

Anticipating passage of the Edmunds-Tucker Act, Mormon leaders increased their efforts to place the church's property beyond the reach of the federal government. First, they continued placing property in secret trusts held by loyal church members. These properties included:

> the tithing office and grounds in central Salt Lake City; three lots adjoining the tithing grounds; the Church Historian's Office and lot; the office and residence of President Taylor; the lots on which Zion's Savings Bank,

Z.C.M.I., and other church enterprises were erected; the granite quarry in Little Cottonwood Canyon containing the stone used in building the Salt Lake Temple; some coal mines near Coalville; all of the capital stock of the Deseret News Company; half of the capital stock of the Zion's Savings Bank & Trust Company; and two-thirds of the stock of the Bullion, Beck, and Champion Mining Company. Other properties whose exact ownership status was not established by subsequent judicial investigation may have been similarly held. These included some lots fronting Temple Block in Salt Lake City; the Salt Lake City Social Hall; the iron and coal claims of the church near Cedar City; Lee's Ferry, Arizona; the sugar plantation and works in Laie, Hawaii; shares of stock in the First National Bank of Ogden and the First National Bank of Provo; and real estate along the Mormon Trail in Iowa and Nebraska. (Arrington 1958, 362)

Second, the church organized a number of nonprofit associations to hold church real and personal property:

The St. George, Logan, and Manti temple associations were organized in 1886 for the purpose of placing legal custody of the three temples in the hands of local ecclesiastical authorities. Similarly, the Salt Lake Literary and Scientific Association was given title in 1885 to some church properties facing the Salt Lake Temple Block, including the Council House and the Deseret Museum. Finally, the numerous ward and stake ecclesiastical associations were given title between 1884 and 1887 to local meetinghouses, tithing houses, granaries, and to capital stock in community stock herds, general stores, irrigation projects, and other local enterprises in which the local or general church had a financial interest. These properties had been held variously in the name of general and local church leaders. Not transferred to the stake and ward ecclesiastical associations at this time were the tithing receipts, the value of which on hand throughout the territory at any moment of time probably varied between $200,000 and $300,000, which was approximately one-half the value of a year's tithing receipts. Although physically located in the wards and stakes, tithing properties remained in the name and at the disposition of the trustee-in-trust. (Arrington 1958, 362–63)

Third, shortly before the effective date of the Edmunds-Tucker Act, a number of church properties—including the Salt Lake Temple Block and the controlling shares of stock in ZCMI, the Deseret Telegraph Company, and the Salt Lake City Railroad Company—were simply sold or assigned to friendly individuals (Arrington 1958, 363). By this means, the property at least remained within the Mormon community.

All these efforts to avoid the Edmunds-Tucker Act sanctions were of limited use. On 30 July 1887, the United States attorney for Utah initiated proceedings before the territorial supreme court to dissolve the church corporation and to recover all property held by the church except for any real property acquired prior to 1862 and under $50,000 in value. At that time, the church's trustee-in-trust remained in possession only of the Salt Lake Temple block, the Office of the President of the Church, the Church farm in Salt Lake City, Indian farms, and $240,000 cash. It was hoped that the temple and president's office would be exempt as a place of worship and a parsonage under the terms of the act. Because the cash was being expended for charitable purposes, church leaders hoped it would not be seized. The Indian farms were liabilities. Thus, by the express terms of the act, few assets seemed subject to seizure by the federal government (Arrington 1958, 364–65).

As in the *Reynolds* polygamy trial, the Mormons overestimated the readiness of the courts to accept their legal arguments. But unlike the consequences of *Reynolds*, the property confiscations were a death blow.

In the first challenge to the Edmunds-Tucker Act's seizure provisions, *United States v. Church of Jesus Christ of Latter-day Saints* (P. 15:473 [Utah 1887]), the Mormons argued that the territorial charter given to the church constituted a right that Congress could not constitutionally nullify. Relying on the landmark case of *Dartmouth College v. Woodward* (US 17:518 [1819]) for the proposition that the charter of a private corporation was a contract between the state and the corporation, the Mormons argued that their right to acquire and hold property was a vested, contractual right that could not be impaired. This argument was rejected. The court rather vaguely suggested that a legislature could not properly delegate so broad a range of powers as the Mormon church was granted in its charter.

More convincingly, *Dartmouth College* had concerned the inviolability of contracts made by states as sovereign authorities. Utah was not a state. Under its enabling act, Utah's territorial legislature acted subject to Congress's acquiescence. Congress could nullify any act of the territorial legislature. Thus, the court concluded, the charter gave the church no vested rights but merely allowed it to exercise the enumerated powers "during the pleasure of Congress" (P. 15:478).

Against this, the Mormons raised an ingenious argument. In the Morrill Act in 1862, of course, Congress annulled the church's charter but, the Mormons argued, only insofar as it furthered or supported polygamy. By implication, therefore, Congress approved of all portions of the church's charter that did not support polygamy (P. 15:478–79). The court rejected this analysis: "We do not think that the act of congress of 1862 affords the inference that so much of the charter as remained in force was in effect a law of the United States" (P. 15:479).

Thus, whatever corporate powers of the church were not negated by the Morrill Act were nullified by section 17 of the Edmunds-Tucker Act (P. 15:479–81).

The court noted that under common-law rules a corporation's officers and agents cease to have any right to the use or benefit of corporate property when the corporation is dissolved. The court therefore appointed Frank H. Dyer, United States marshal in Utah, as receiver to take control of and manage the church's assets (P. 15:482–83; Arrington 1958, 368). Not surprisingly, Dyer's tenure was stormy. Dyer vigorously pursued hidden Mormon assets, and the Mormons resisted. Many of the receiver's claims were compromised; and in lieu of surrendering property, the church agreed to pay the receiver nearly a quarter of a million dollars (Arrington 1958, 371). What Dyer recovered represented only about one-third of the Church's total assets (Arrington 1958, 371).

Courts were willing to set aside conveyances where the church attempted to hide its property, but the property was simply too widely scattered for a cumbersome judicial recovery to be effective. Complex transactions sometimes had to be unraveled to identify church property. In February 1887, John Taylor, president of the church and trustee-in-trust for church property, held various donations for use in building the Salt Lake Temple. Anticipating passage of the Edmunds-Tucker Act, Taylor assigned this property to another corporation, the Church Association of the Salt Lake Stake of Zion. In turn, on 12 March 1887, this group assigned the property to William B. Preston, presiding bishop of the Church (*United States v. Late Corporation of Church of Jesus Christ of Latter-day Saints,* P. 18:35 [Utah 1888]).

In opposing the receiver's attempt to recover this property, the Mormons apparently did not challenge the claim that "the purpose for which the property was to be used was not changed by any of the transfers. It was used by each holder or possessor for aiding in the construction of the temple" (P. 18:37). Instead, the Mormons argued that the receiver stood in the stead of the dissolved church corporation and could only challenge any conveyances if the church might also have challenged them. The Court rejected this claim. Because the church corporation had been dissolved by statute, the receiver acted not for the dissolved corporation, but as the Court's agent. From this premise, the Court had little problem in setting aside this series of conveyances as a fraudulent attempt to conceal church assets. As the Court concluded:

> On their faces, and by the evidence, they seem to have been aimless transactions, made with suddenness, and in a hurried and confused manner, for some purpose not avowed. . . . It is not unreasonable to

conclude, from all the circumstances, that the object of the transfer by Taylor, trustee, to the church association, was to save that property from the impending forfeiture.

[The transfers] were not made in good faith, but for the evident purpose of defrauding the government of the benefits to be acquired under the statute. (P. 18:39)

Obviously, the Mormons were not pleased with the receiver's efforts. Discontent also surfaced from a rather unexpected source. Under the Edmunds-Tucker Act, assets seized from the church were to be applied to the territory's common schools. Thus, a group of trustees of Utah's school districts petitioned the Supreme Court to investigate charges that the receiver had settled claims against Mormon property for inadequate amounts, rented church sheep herds for an inadequate fee, failed to pursue and recover church property, and tried to charge an exorbitant fee for his services (*United States v. Late Corporation of Church of Jesus Christ of Latter-day Saints*, P. 21:503 [Utah 1889]). The Court refused the school trustees' petition to be made parties to this investigation on the ground that the petitioners' interests were too remote from the controversy. However, the Court felt the charges were serious enough to proceed with an investigation of the receiver's conduct. After collecting 1,151 pages of testimony on the charges, a special examiner found the charges to be unwarranted. Although the Court concurred in exonerating Dyer, it cut his compensation from the $25,000 he claimed to $10,000 (P. 18:507–8, 518).

Dyer resigned in 1889, commenting:

> The hostility of the Mormon people to this law and the proceedings to enforce it are well known. It was believed that in anticipation of its passage large amounts of property really owned by the Church, but held in the names of private parties in trust in its favor, had been conveyed to evade the enforcement of the law. It seemed to the Supreme Court, that the means and powers which as Marshal I had at command, would greatly facilitate my acquisition of this property as Receiver. . . . I accepted this post with hesitation, though had I then known of its magnitude I would have declined it altogether. I gave a bond for the faithful performance of my trust in the sum of a quarter of a million dollars, and although there was voluntarily delivered to me by the Church authorities property to the amount of One Hundred and Forty-Five thousand dollars in value, in less than eight months I had with the aid of persons . . . in my employment unearthed of property held in secret trusts and reduced into my possession . . . a further amount . . . aggregating nearly Six Hundred thousand dollars. (Dyer to Pres. Benjamin Harrison, 9 Mar. 1889, in Dwyer, 242)

Arrington concludes that the receivership system was probably more at fault than was Dyer but documents several rather clear instances of misconduct. For example, Dyer invested $250,000 in church funds in gentile banks without interest, and purchased lucrative Salt Lake Gas Company stock, which he held as trustee of church assets (Arrington 1958, 376–77). Whether through Dyer's mismanagement or not, the seizure of property had a dreadful effect on Church finances. By the time church assets were finally returned, many had been liquidated in an effort to get the church out of business, though there is no evidence that the receivers sold the properties for less than market value (Arrington 1958, 378). To compromise the receiver's claims against church property, church authorities had been forced to borrow nearly $250,000 from gentile banks. Saddled with extensive charitable commitments to needy Mormons, commitments caused in part by the dislocations brought about by federal persecution of the Mormons, the church was unable to rapidly pay off those debts. Thus, the compounding of interest on these loans created a mountainous debt (Arrington 1958, 371–72).

In 1889, an appeal on the validity of the Edmunds-Tucker Act's provisions for dissolving the church and seizing its property reached the United States Supreme Court (*The Late Corporation of the Church of Jesus Christ of Latter-day Saints v. United States*, US 136:1 [1890]). The arguments of the church's attorneys displayed a clear political realism. They made no arguments based on the free exercise of religion. The sanctity of religious expression had failed to persuade the Court in the past. Instead the Mormons argued for the sanctity of contract: the church's charter was a contract that Congress could not lawfully break by revoking the charter. In the Morrill Act and before, Congress implicitly recognized that charter. Even if Congress were allowed to wrongfully break that contract, no precedent or rationale existed for seizing church property. Instead, if the corporation were to be dissolved, its property rightfully reverted to the church's membership.

The Court rejected each piece of the argument in turn. Congress's power to legislate for the territories was reaffirmed. Although the grant of powers to the church was lawful when made by the Utah legislature, it remained so only as long as Congress acquiesced. The property held by the church was, or should have been, donated for public and charitable purposes. Instead, the church employed it to promote polygamy. By depriving the church of its property, then, Congress directed that property to its proper end, and furthered Congress's policy of blocking the spread of polygamy (US 136:43–50). As legal precedent, the Court elaborately outlined the ancient doctrine of cy pres. Under this legal principle, if a charitable trust could not be fulfilled according to its terms, the state would apply the trust property to those charitable uses that most nearly approximated the original purpose of the grant. By analogy, the Mormons' continued unlawful adherence to polygamy made a return of church property to the members improper. Because the original purpose of church donations could not lawfully be accomplished, the property should then be applied to other charitable goals.

Although rejected, the Mormons' arguments were not without effect. The Court's decision was a close one, with four justices dissenting. Accepting that Congress had the power to legislate for the territories, the dissenters argued that Congress "is not authorized under the cover of that power to seize and confiscate the property of persons, individuals, or corporations, without office found, because they may have been guilty of criminal practices" (US 136:67).

Recognizing that the original decree might need to be modified slightly, the Supreme Court remanded the case to the territorial court for further consideration. Utah's supreme court undertook to determine specifically how to dispose of the property, but before this issue could be resolved, the church officially renounced polygamy in October 1890. That action created a powerful claim for the courts to abandon a meaningless effort to seize church property. However, despite a vigorous dissenting opinion, Utah's supreme court refused to abandon the forfeiture proceedings and created a trustee to apply church property "to the support and aid of the poor of the church, and to the building and repairing of its houses of worship" (P. 31:436).

A small amount of real property was, however, returned to the church by Utah's courts. The Morrill Act allowed the church to retain real property to which it had a vested right prior to 1862. In 1862, however, because there was no land office in Utah, the federal government retained legal title to all Utah's lands. Technically, then, the church could not have held a vested right to any land. For once, however, the courts behaved relatively generously toward the Mormons. Waving aside technical objections, the court held that, from settlement, the Mormons acquired a real interest in the lands they settled even though the federal government retained legal title. Thus, property such as the tithing yard, which was owned by the church in 1863, remained in the church's possession (*United States v. Tithing Yard and Offices*, P. 34:55 [Utah 1893]). Property such as the Gardo House, historian's office, church coal lands, and church farms, which the church acquired after 1862, were forfeited (*United States v. Gardo House and Historian Office*, P. 34:59 [Utah 1893]). As with much other property, the church had in fact retained control over the Gardo House through much of the period of federal seizure. After seizure, the church continued to rent the house for four years. The skyrocketing rental imposed by the receiver, which increased from $900 to $5,400 per year during this period, finally forced the church to abandon the property (Lyman 1973, 135 n. 20).

With the judiciary unable and unwilling to return most church property, Congress finally closed the book on federal efforts to destroy the Mormon religion. In 1893, Utah's congressional delegate, Joseph L. Rawlins, introduced a resolution directing the return of the church's personal property. With minor amendments the resolution passed Congress, and on 10 January 1894 what was left of the church's personal property was returned: "Furniture in the Office of the President of the Church, in the Church Historian's Office, and the Office of the Receiver; 4,732 shares of stock in the Deseret Telegraph Company; and $438,174.39 in cash" (Arrington 1958, 378). On 8 June 1896, the church's real estate, consisting of Tithing Office property, the Historian's Office, the Gardo House, the Church farm, and coal lands, was returned (Arrington 1958, 378).

In the battle of wills between the church and the federal government, the government was victorious. It suppressed polygamy and crippled the church's political, social, and economic power in the territory. Faced with a choice between a principled commitment to polygamy and survival as an organization, the church chose to survive. In Utah's early days, the church was the focal point of life in the territory. After the 1890s, the church remained a dominant force, but it became more nearly like one among many churches in a rapidly pluralizing society.

Some of the measures imposed by the Edmunds-Tucker Act bore a hypocritical tinge. Restricting the Mormons' civil rights was clearly a blow to the Mormons' political power. Defending these actions as anti-polygamy measures was simply a smokescreen. The confiscation of church property was, at least, refreshingly candid. No effort was made to defend the measure as an anti-polygamy move. For the most part, the courts analyzed the provisions for dissolution of the Mormon Church in terms of a power struggle: the church was a political threat that Congress was empowered to and chose to eliminate.

By the standards of political morality, it is perhaps sensible that civil and religious rights give way to national unity and political integrity in an ultimate confrontation. It may even be argued, though not very realistically, that continued conflict between the Mormons and the government had provoked such an ultimate confrontation by the

1890s. The clear failure of law that emerges from the three decades of conflict between Mormons and the government, from 1862 to 1892, is the failure of intermediate bulwarks of civil rights, those mechanisms that supposedly mediate conflicts between individual rights and political and national interests at levels less than ultimate conflict. In nearly each instance along this path, the rights of Mormons were thrust aside with little of the serious reflection that should have been accorded each interest. Even those unsympathetic to the Mormons might note, as a few reflective observers of the time did, that the practice of neglecting individual rights can become a habit that affects everyone's rights.

PART III

The Ecclesiastical Court System
in the Great Basin

———

Mormon theology characterized Zion as a temporal as well as spiritual community of Saints. The group solidarity accompanying early efforts to establish Zion was a major cause of the persecution Mormons received in Missouri and Illinois. After they migrated to the deserts of the Great Basin, the Saints pursued their radical theory of Zion as an alternative to the social experiment of pluralistic America. A critical part of this effort was the establishment and maintenance of their own court system. Through their ecclesiastical courts Mormons were able to offer an alternative to the divisive influence of the adversarial legal system with its technical pleadings, rules of evidence, and pettifogging lawyers. More importantly Mormons were able to introject their own notions of community and temporal affairs into the resolution of social conflict. The ecclesiastical court system facilitated a radical change in the laws governing the distribution of land, water, and other natural resources. Church courts also permitted religious perspectives to be determinative in conflicts arising out of contractual or tortious disputes. Finally, the courts provided forums for the mediation of conflict in polygamous families. In each of these substantive law areas the existence of the church courts enhanced the independence of the church from the state, thereby lending credibility to the theological concept of Zion.

No attempt has been made to trace the impact of court proceedings on the lives of the litigants. Surely the results were not acceptable to all involved, and church leaders undoubtedly decided unfairly in certain cases. Since infallibility never became part of Mormon teachings, members faced the dilemma of steering their continued church membership between Scylla and Charybdis: mandatory church directives versus perceived unjust outcomes. The existence of an alternative secular court system that often handed down decisions at odds with priesthood decisions exacerbated this difficult dilemma. Day-to-day working relations with governing priesthood leaders also emphasized the foibles of those who wielded so much authority in Mormon communities, and perhaps created predispositions that influenced the outcome of particular cases. Deciding issues of conflict on a case-by-case basis always asks for more Solomonic wisdom than is readily available; abiding by such outcomes tests even the most faithful and obedient at times.

What can be said, based on the records examined, is that priesthood leaders seemed to exert remarkable, at times heroic, efforts in mediating community conflicts, and members of the church complied with directives at a level that is difficult to understand apart from their consistent efforts to achieve a Zion society. As the impetus to establish a separate socioeconomic community waned toward the end of the nineteenth century, the necessity of maintaining a separate court system eroded. For the second half of the nineteenth century, however, church courts played an important role in furthering the cause of Zion.

9

Mormon Law, Gentile Law

Mormon general authorities publicly condemned members for suing other Saints "before the ungodly" and frequently extolled the comparative advantages of resolving disputes within the church court system. This counsel was not purely advisory. The processes and substantive results adopted in the church courts effectively controlled personal and property relations between members of the religious community during the Utah period. If these church standards, which often involved qualifications of legal entitlements (rights under the civil law), were to have any chance of enduring within the larger American community, then the Mormons had to defer virtually completely to religious norms rather than secular ones. The "exclusive jurisdiction" rule ensured that members would not vacillate between church and civil courts, depending on the advantages of each given different circumstances. If they valued church membership, they had to order their personal and financial affairs with other members in accordance with religious norms and precepts, rather than secular alternatives. By living the higher law of Zion, members thus retained their right to fellowship. The potential for unfairness certainly was a real threat during this period. Undoubtedly some Saints begrudgingly deferred to the church courts, and it is likely that many disapproved of the outcome or processes in individual cases. Since much of this study is dependent upon the church court records, it is difficult to assess long-term effects of reconciliation efforts. Nonetheless, the evidence available suggests both an attempt by priesthood leaders to achieve results acceptable to all involved and little recidivism amongst the litigants.

The few historians who have written on the subject have assumed that Mormons looked to their own courts only when civil alternatives were unavailable or only so long as the Mormons maintained an independent and self-sufficient economy. Both of these assumptions are historically inaccurate and misinterpret the purposes and effects of the church courts' jurisdiction over civil disputes between members. Church leaders persisted throughout most of the nineteenth century in their efforts to maintain an exclusive jurisdiction rule in civil matters because Mormon legal processes and results accorded better with their vision of Zion. Although exceptions were occasionally recognized, the real force of the rule abated only when, under federal government pressure, the church renounced plural marriage and political direction of its members in the 1890s, both key elements in the cause of Zion.

EXCLUSIVE JURISDICTION

Church members who violated the exclusive jurisdiction rule by suing their brethren in civil courts were guilty of "unChristianlike conduct" and subject to being disfellowshipped. This caused some members to leave the church for the privilege of suing in the civil courts, but the strict penalty was justified as inherent in the vision of Zion as a unified people. By choosing Zion one necessarily relinquished some individual rights. Insisting on these rights, therefore, implied a decision to give up membership in Zion.

Records of church court intervention in a court dispute between Judge Zerubbabel Snow and a local constable filed in the early 1880s provide an informative overview of the exclusive jurisdiction rule. Judge Snow was a highly influential Mormon attorney and was appointed as one of the first associate justices of the federal court in Utah on 2 September 1850. After the runaway gentile judges—Brandebury and Brocchus—left Utah in September 1951, the legislature established broad probate jurisdiction and authorized Snow to serve in all the federal judicial districts until the president should supply again a full bench for the supreme court of Utah. Judge Snow held the first United States District Court at Salt Lake City and presided over the first murder trial in Utah in October of 1851, wherein Howard Egan was acquitted for the killing of James Monroe, the seducer of Egan's wife. Judge Snow later served as Utah's attorney general (elected by the territorial legislature) where he ultimately won an important Mormon victory establishing the rights of the territorial marshal and attorney general to prosecute territorial cases in *Snow v. United States* (U.S. 85:317 [1873]). Snow had also been counsel, along with Aurelius Miner and Enos D. Hodge, in the successful (*Clinton v. Englebrecht*, U.S. 80:434 [1871]) case where Judge McKean's assault on Brigham Young and others through illegal jury selection had been overturned. In the Poland Act of 1874, Congress abolished the territorial offices and sent Snow into private practice. As a private practitioner Snow often defended Mormons on polygamy charges, including Brigham Young in *People v. Brigham Young*.

Unintimidated by Judge Snow's legal credentials, a Mormon constable, CC, on 19 January 1880 filed an action against Judge Snow, for his unChristianlike conduct in suing the constable before the United States Third District Court for the Territory of Utah. There was no particular LDS issue that would have made church court jurisdiction absolutely necessary. (Ecclesiastical Court Cases, 1839–1965, LDS Church Archives are hereinafter cited by date and folder [Fd.] number.) Snow had sued CC in federal district court for misfeasance in his capacity as constable. He successfully argued that CC, in an action distributing a debtor's assets, had improperly preferred an attorney's claim for legal fees over Snow's creditor claim. Snow had offered at the outset to provide the constable with an indemnity bond in support of Snow's claim of priority. CC, however, to whom the attorney creditor had assigned his interest, went ahead and essentially preferred his own assigned interest, leaving a balance insufficient to satisfy Snow's claim.

Snow received a judgment for $182.60—$132.60 of which was for court costs and attorney fees assessed against the constable as the losing party. CC consulted with the ward teachers and then filed a complaint against Snow in a bishop's court, charging unChristianlike conduct. After hearing the evidence the bishop censured both parties: the constable for purchasing the attorney's claim and then paying himself ahead of Snow, and Judge Snow for his unChristianlike conduct in suing the constable before the district court. Since both had acted improperly he ordered Snow to repay $100 of the $182.60 that he had recovered from the constable.

Four years later Snow appealed from the bishop's court to the Salt Lake High Council. Snow argued two points that he believed justified a reversal of the judgment. The first was a technical point—that the real party in interest to the suit was not himself, but his non-Mormon son—to whom he had apparently assigned his creditor's interest.

His assigned high council speaker responded that the church courts did not look to form but to substance. "We only want to look at Brother Snow, not at his son. He [Snow] only turned the case over because he did not want to sue his brother before a Gentile court, which his son would do, because he was not in the church. He advised him to do it and was glad he did it." Judge Snow, according to church teachings, should have possessed an attitude of brotherly love, but instead had been glad that his son was not a member and could freely sue in civil courts. The high council obviously believed that Snow was trying to take advantage of his son's nonmember status when he should have been seeking ways to resolve the controversy in a brotherly manner.

The second point Snow argued in favor of reversal went to the heart of the charge against him in challenging the exclusive jurisdiction rule:

> I [Snow] have heard that we were not permitted to go to law with each other except before the Church. I have been a member fifty-two years last May; up to this time I have never preferred a charge against a brother except this time, and if I am in error now, I ought to pay Brother[CC], everything that he has lost, but if I am not, then I ought not to pay him one dime.
>
> I have been an officer in this territory many years, part of the time as prosecuting attorney . . . also as a judge. . . . I think I may be in a position before long to have to bring a number of suits against men, and shall never ask this council if I dare start these suits. I insist that I have as good right to my money as the president of the Church has to his. I claim I have a right to seek justice, and that when I seek that I am not seeking revenge; and that when I am restrained from getting my rights till I have to go and ask if I can get them my liberty is hampered.

The high council disagreed and sustained the Bishop's decision "that Brother Snow acted unchristian-like in suing Bro. [CC] before the district court." The high council required him to pay the constable $132.60, "that being the amount of expenses of the Court, interest, etc. incurred on going to law." The judgment thus affirmed Judge Snow's original $50 claim while reaffirming the prohibition against suing in gentile courts.

Snow then appealed to the First Presidency for a reversal of the policy. He expressed his willingness to continue complying with the exclusive jurisdiction rule if the First Presidency found merit in its continuation:

> I have known for some time the views of the church on these points, but I have differed with them in judgment and still do offer. For this reason I want President Taylor and others to know it. But still as before, if the final decision be against me on the principle [of suing brothers before gentile courts] I shall comply with it.

Although there is no decision from the First Presidency in the file, Snow must have lost his appeal because the church clearly continued its policy of demanding that members not sue other members in the civil courts.

By 1884 the exclusive jurisdiction rule had been church policy for more than forty years. Though it became increasingly anachronistic, the church delayed laying it aside for a longer period than has earlier been supposed. Church court records indicate few conflicts over the jurisdiction issue in hearings held after statehood was granted. However, at least some priesthood courts sanctioned members for suing other members in the civil courts as late as 1900 (1900, Fd. 7). The only recorded authoritative pronouncement is a 1908 recommendation by a committee of apostles that the church courts no longer be used for the collection of ordinary debts.

EXCEPTIONS, WAIVER, AND JUSTIFICATION

Exceptions, waiver arguments, and special circumstances justifying the filing of civil actions in certain instances gradually modified the strictures of the exclusive jurisdiction rule even while it was the norm. For example, the church courts did not entertain criminal cases, reaffirming the probation against suing in the gentile courts.

Although criminal behavior (excepting polygamy offenses) was manifestly inconsistent with good standing in the church, the limited sanctions of excommunication and disfellowshipping available in the church courts required that the state handle cases that could require incarceration or fines.

Even in criminal law, however, the Saints' vision of Zion led them to deny the state complete autonomy. For example, it was considered unChristian to assist in any way with the prosecution of polygamy. Also, the availability of criminal prosecutions did not preclude a church court from also hearing the case to decide whether to impose ecclesiastical penalties. And if the church courts exonerated a member of all criminal culpability, a priesthood court might hold that a member's attempt to bring charges in a secular court would constitute unChristianlike conduct.

While church courts generally heard only cases between faithful members, occasionally gentiles or apostates would voluntarily appear. Since nonmembers could not be sanctioned by a church court, priesthood leaders would hear a claim involving a nonmember only if he ensured his compliance by posting a bond. If a member was allowed to sue an "unrepentant" member (a member who would not abide a church court disposition) in the secular courts, the convention was to rely wherever possible on Mormon-controlled probate courts so long as their jurisdiction continued.

Initially, church courts took jurisdiction of cases even when a final decision had been rendered in the civil courts. In an 1862 case the losing defendant in a civil case brought the plaintiff before the Salt

Lake State High Council, charging unChristianlike conduct. Although one councillor argued against it (saying that the "case does not belong here—here are two brethren who have gone to law, and because one is worsted, he don't like it, when they go to law they should abide the law, and not make a hack of the priesthood"), the high council decided to take the case anyway. The council held for the plaintiff, but for a lower amount, and required him to pay the expenses incurred by the defendant in the civil court proceeding (1862, Fd. 7).

Twenty-five years later, waiver was addressed differently in a case heard by the Salt Lake High Council on 31 October 1887 (1887, Fd. 9). In that case the civil plaintiff was a widow with six children. The civil defendant had provoked her into suing him over a property dispute. After losing in the trial court and the appellate court, the civil defendant went to the bishop and asked that the widow's membership be tried for unChristianlike conduct.

MS explained that she had been coerced into seeking legal assistance: "I've had no wish to go to law with [AE]. I only acted in self defense. I did not do this till I was forced by threatening letters and language by [AE]." She also asked the bishop to remember that she was a widow and the AE had attempted to take advantage of her defenseless plight:

> You must remember I have six children but no husband to counsel with, I don't want to do wrong. I don't want to be forced out of the church for this land at the same time I don't want my brethren to be deceived and think they are doing right when wrong and fraud were the underlying motives in this land dispute. [AE] did not value his church standing when he threatened me with the law. He has only applied to the Church when he found the law would not sustain him.

The bishop considered the special circumstances of the case and decided that the defendant had waived his right to have the matter adjudicated by the church courts when he provoked the widow into seeking legal assistance.

Waiver became an accepted defense in the last decade of the nineteenth century, as the Mormons slowly gave up the distinctive practices that justified the exclusive jurisdiction rule. Thus when a land case that had been litigated in the United States District Court in Provo was appealed in 1898 to the First Presidency (consisting of Wilford Woodruff, George Q. Cannon, and Joseph F. Smith) the First Presidency advised the high council: "If the plaintiff in the present case was sued by the defendant before the courts of law and said nothing about it until after the decision was rendered, it might be held that he had submitted his controversy to the courts of law and ought to abide its decision" (1890–98, Fd. 1).

Church officials also justified filing civil actions where the defendant, though a member, was unlikely to obey a church court resolution. Bishop Kesler of the Salt Lake 16th Ward, for example, refused to condemn EM for filing simultaneous actions in his bishop's court and the Third District Court because EM argued persuasively that the defendant TB would only abide a church determination if a civil action were pending:

> I entered a suit against him in the District Court to protect myself. But told my lawyers to hold the case until we could get a hearing before church courts. I told [TB] if it could be settled here I would withdraw the suit and pay the costs. I believed he was defrauding me and this is the reason I filed the case in the District Court.

Bishop Kesler accepted EM's explanation, found TB liable to EM, and disfellowshipped TB "until such time as he makes full satisfaction to Bro [EM]" (1889, Fd. 4). Threatening disfellowshipping for failure to abide a church court's disposition of a conflict between members cleared the way for civil litigation as a last resort. Thus in an 1891 case where CP refused to pay the judgment to AR, the bishop disfellowshipped CP and gave AR permission to employ Zerubbabel Snow to collect the debt in the courts (1891, Fd. 10).

OPPOSITION TO CHURCH JURISDICTION

The ecclesiastical sanctions imposed upon members who went to civil rather than church courts usually discouraged civil filings. Some members, however, resented ecclesiastical intervention in secular affairs and publicly sought to attack the exclusive jurisdiction rule in an effort to discredit the church before an already-hostile federal government and gentile neighbors. These attacks posed a real conundrum for church leaders. Advocating an exclusive jurisdiction rule risked increasing the animosity of the anti-Mormon community, but abandoning the rule meant turning away from the effort to achieve a Zion community.

A case filed in the bishop's court in the Paris Second Ward in Idaho on 23 February 1889 illustrates the dilemma. In the church action, HW preferred charges against Mrs. RR for successfully suing him for breach of trust in the administration of a probate estate in the civil probate courts (1885–89, Fd. 1). Upon receiving the summons to appear before the bishop's court, Mrs. RR had her attorney, H. W.

Smith, send HW's attorney, J. C. Rich, a letter threatening public exposure if the church courts intervened:

> If any Bishop's Court tries to modify the judgment of the District Court or compel a satisfaction of it without payment by threat of excommunication or otherwise, we will have another lawsuit. . . . I have forbourne to do so. But I will not be much longer delayed in this matter. I would as soon have their methods exposed as not, and am perfectly willing to assist at the exposition. We would then see whether they would make good their oft repeated declarations as to non-interference in temporal affairs.

Bishop West exonerated Mrs. RR because the probate was "a legal matter that must necessarily be conducted under legal form."

Bishop West's decision, however, must be read in light of the circumstances. The church court actually found that HW had been an honest but careless administrator. Nevertheless church intervention was impractical because HW had stipulated to a compromise judgment in the civil action and the award had become the separate property of each heir. Thus church intervention would have required each heir to agree to any recovery the church deemed appropriate. Expediency, therefore, required that the church not seek to set aside the civil disposition of this probate matter. HW, in effect, had waived his opportunity to invoke the exclusive jurisdiction rule.

Two letters in the file add further background. In the first letter, dated 11 February 1888, the First Presidency wrote to Bear Lake Stake President William Budge, to recommend that the matter be settled peacefully. Although Mrs. RR had been in error "for not having submitted her grievances to the Councils of the church before going to law," allowing H. W. Smith to drag "the doings of the High Council before the courts as he threatens to do, would be a great injury to our cause." In the second letter dated 26 June 1888, President Budge made it clear to Mrs. RR that he disapproved of her suing at law:

> I have been informed by the brethren that you are under the impression that I advised you to keep the action in court which you commenced against [HW]. A little explanation will show you that you misunderstood my meaning. Everyone in this country knows, that during the time of my labors I have constantly counselled the Saints to avoid going to the law with each other where it could be avoided, and I have advised the withdrawal of actions where it could legally be done.
>
> [HW] has made a complaint against you for taking him to law when he is willing to have all business difficulties adjusted by the help of the brethren and that without cost, and in the spirit of friendship. The Bishop's Court is willing to investigate truly and faithfully, and it is their duty to see that your interests legal, as well as in the church, are not

endangered, and it is your duty as a Latter-Day Saint to be subject to the regulations of the Church and its decisions. (1885, 89, Fd. 1)

These letters antedating Bishop West's decision establish that the stake leaders and the First Presidency condemned Mrs. RR's filing a civil suit against HW even though she was not disfellowshipped for doing so.

The conflict between the exclusive jurisdiction rule and the need to allay non-Mormon disapproval became increasingly focused in the 1890s. When social and political pressures forced the Mormons to abandon polygamy and bloc voting thereafter the justification for church courts hearing secular matters wore thin. Thus by 1900 the exclusive jurisdiction rule was no longer emphasized.

MORMON OPPOSITION TO LAWYERS

Lawyers were in a precarious position in the early decades of Mormon history. Priesthood leaders consistently condemned them for urging vexatious lawsuits, for charging exorbitant fees in a cash-poor frontier economy, for the subordination of "truth" to the adversary ethic, and for their use of legal technicalities. The church therefore banned lawyers from church courts, although lawyers involved in previous civil litigation of a case occasionally appeared as witnesses. Presumably, Mormon lawyers earned their fees representing Mormons in criminal actions and suits against either apostates or non-Mormons, and by representing nonmembers.

The propriety of lawyers representing members in civil suits against other Mormons was a matter of concern for faithful Mormon attorneys. If it was unChristian for a member to sue another member in the civil courts, what about the Mormon lawyer who represented a civil complainant? Also, did a Mormon lawyer have any church-approved way of recovering fees once he had represented a member in a suit in the gentile courts? These and related issues became matters of discussion in church court proceedings. Thus in an 1882 case heard by the Box Elder High Council, Mormon attorney George Marsh found his own membership in question for "wrongful [sic] counselling, aiding and abetting" a Mormon plaintiff in a civil suit.

In defense of his action, Marsh explained that "he was a counsellor at law; had taken the oath to that effect [he had been admitted to the Utah bar in 1877 after studying law at home]—had no business to ask parties whether they were Mormon or gentiles." The speaker for CR stated that he believed Brother Marsh "has not acted wisely in laboring to aid a wicked man in evading rights and justice." The speaker for Marsh agreed! Marsh had been unwise "in accepting the engagement of a wicked man to defeat justice." The stake president, "after listening attentively to all decided that Brother Marsh had acted unwisely in this matter. Thought that none was prejudiced against Brother Marsh, deemed it right and proper to adhere to the rules of the church and settle all our difficulties by arbitration." Accordingly, "as a partial reimbursement for the losses and damage sustained through prosecution of this case," Marsh was ordered to pay the civil defendant fifty dollars.

The high council unanimously sustained the stake president's decision. Marsh then appealed to the First Presidency. Marsh claimed he had "done his sworn duty" and pointed out that two Mormon attorneys, Franklin S. Richards and Judge R. W. Williams, had represented the civil defendant. President John Taylor and George Q. Cannon, his first counselor, read the minutes of the high council proceeding and sustained its decision 13 May 1885.

Church officials also condemned Mormon lawyers for their exorbitant fees. A number of plaintiffs sought relief in the church courts from what they considered unreasonable attorneys fees. In one case, for example, RB preferred charges before the Salt Lake High Council against Zerubbabel Snow on 13 June 1871, for "suing him before Judge Clinton, for counsel services [which he considered extortionate] when he was willing it should be brought before the priesthood" (1871, Fd. 10).

In another case, brought in September 1871 before the Salt Lake High Council, Aurelius Miner, Ogden city attorney, preferred charges against the Ogden City Council for failure to pay him for services rendered (1870, Fd. 15). The Ogden City Council had refused to pay Miner a retainer, preferring to pay only for services actually rendered. Since the Mormons avoided the courts, the city council had not called upon Miner's legal services very often; as a result Miner was unable to make an adequate living. Miner presented the written testimony of Mormon attorney Zerubbabel Snow, who argued the equities of a retainer fee:

> A city attorney ought to be able to aid and actually advise the City Council and the City Officers in their official business which he cannot do without pay. In my judgment the simple engagement as attorney for a city is worth from three to five hundred dollars per year though no important legal proceedings may be had or needed. I do not know what business if any had been done by Brother Miner for Ogden but if he had been the city attorney he ought to be paid for it even though through his prudent management no legal proceedings have been had. (1870, Fd. 15)

The court denied the claim.

An 1879 case clearly evidences the jaundiced view of lawyers held by many Mormons. Dr. John M. Bernhisel filed a complaint against his friend and associate Judge Snow, alleging that Snow had overcharged him for attorney's fees. On appeal before the Salt Lake High Council, Bernhisel testified that he had engaged Snow to collect a mortgage debt of $7,300 from a non-Mormon "for 5% which is the usual rate for collecting large amounts." After losing Bernhisel's case in the territorial courts, Snow appealed to the United States Supreme Court. In February 1874 the Supreme Court ruled in Bernhisel's favor. The trustee of the money, however, had misapplied most of the funds, and since Snow had failed to see that the trustee had sufficient security, the monies were lost. Nevertheless, Snow had had the trustee deed some property to him as partial payment for legal fees, and had sent Bernhisel "an enormous bill." Bernhisel refused to pay on the grounds that the bill was higher than agreed upon, that Snow was responsible for Bernhisel's loss as a result of his mishandling of the case, and because "I had put $8,000 in his way, by having him appointed associate justice of the Supreme Court of the territory, and it cost me about as much trouble to obtain his appointment as my suit cost him." Bernhisel further alleged that Snow had overcharged him on some smaller collections. According to Bernhisel, Snow "now has property which cost between $7,000 and $8,000 for collecting about $1,430 and attending to two or three petty suits." Snow's non-Mormon partner, Judge Enos Hoge, testified that their fees were reasonable and that the "cheapest we ever got a suit attended to in Washington was for $500, and I consider that $1,000 which we charged the Doctor for attending to that case was very cheap."

After hearing testimony for two days, high councillors on both sides spoke. The speaker representing Bernhisel's interest argued for compromise:

> There is a difference in regard to the agreement as to what the fees were to be. . . . It would seem to me more in accordance with the Golden Rule and the feelings that should exist between brethren for Brother Snow, inasmuch as the Doctor had lost so heavily to make some allowance for his losses and to make charges as light as possible. . . . I consider the circumstances taken as whole entitle the Doctor to some remuneration.

Snow's speaker evidenced total distrust for attorneys:

> Brother Bernhisel brought a difficult case to the judge and he should have understood lawyers well enough to know that they always look after their own fees before they pay anything over to their clients. The Doctor was unlucky. . . . Brother Bernhisel knows that lawyers don't engage in business in a brotherly way, they have to be acquainted with

all sorts of tricks and games that we don't know anything about, and the Judge did well, and looked after himself first. . . . I am surprised that a man of Doctor Bernhisel's experience should complain of a lawyer for making exorbitant charges. I never knew them to make any other kind.

In closing remarks, Snow justified the $1,000 fee and the difficulties of a Mormon attorney: "A Lawyer is at great expense in keeping up a library and an office in a central place, costing in the aggregate near $100 per month. It has been shown Mr. Hoge received $500 for his services, but there has been no complaint of his being exorbitant, simply because he don't happen to belong to the church." Stake President Angus M. Cannon rendered the decision: although Bernhisel had received only $825 out of a debt of possibly $8,000 while the attorney had received $1,000, Bernhisel should have reduced any fee arrangement to writing. Since he had not, the church courts would not intervene. He also counseled Bernhisel:

The more experience I have with lawyers the less I want to have to do with them, and the more I see the necessity of having a thorough understanding with them to commence with, for they will generally try to get what they can out of you, and if there is any quarrelling to do it is better to do it on the start, and this is well not only with lawyers but with all that you employ.

It was hardly a reassuring message for Mormon lawyers.

LEGAL TECHNICALITIES

Mormon judges, whether sitting as bishoprics, on high councils, or on courts of appeal deemed gentile law largely irrelevant; they fashioned decisions to fit the needs and circumstances of citizens of Zion. Because court files were confidential, specific cases generally had no precedential value, though official policies, such as the preference for local boundaries over federally approved boundaries, were regularly dispositive of applicable cases. The discussion in some cases indicates an awareness of past cases, but few decisions relied on the binding force of an earlier decision.

The distinctiveness of church courts was deliberate and self-conscious. In 1852, five years after the Mormons arrived in the Great Basin, the Salt Lake High Council heard a dispute over the ownership of a cow. One party objected to the evidence proffered by the other party as inadmissible in a court of law, but a speaker for the other party responded:

This is a court got up by Divine Revelation to adjust difficulties among members of the Church, and we occupy the position of servants also to those passing through here, who put themselves under our protection. We wish it understood that technicalities that are taken advantage of elsewhere are laid aside here and all we wish is to get all the truth and justice of the case agreeable to the Revelations. (1852, Fd. 9)

The evidence in this case did not establish clear ownership by either party. In a court of law, the plaintiff would have lost because he had not met the burden of persuasion, but the church courts applied different rules. After acknowledging the failure to arrive at a clear resolution, the high council asked the stake president for a decision, feeling that it "would be full of light according to the office upon him."

Procedural rules in the church courts typically were less important than procedure in the civil courts. Similarly, church courts repudiated substantive civil rules that did not serve the cause of Zion. For example, in an 1848 case (1849, Fd. 18), DG had lent JN an ox in Winter Quarters to assist him in his travels to the Salt Lake Valley. Once he arrived, JN sold the ox to PN, who butchered it, even though DG had told him that he, rather than JN, owned the ox.

DG brought PN before the bishop's court, but the bishop decided that DG should have brought the action against JN and dismissed the action. On appeal the Salt Lake Stake High Council acknowledged that the bishop was correct "according to Gentile law," but decided that "Gentile laws on customs" should not apply, and reversed the decision. PN was ordered to pay DG $40, the ox's value as estimated by a butcher.

Although the church courts felt unhampered by civil rules they occasionally considered them if they served the best interest of the community. In one interesting 1873 case involving the computation of interest on a contract, the Salt Lake High Council permitted the parties to be represented by counsel, who were to argue the "law" because the high council thought Zion would be better served by following the relevant civil rule (1873, Fd. 10). The high council undoubtedly hoped to establish consistency in commercial business practices, a necessary virtue even in Zion. The case represents an exception to the usual practice, not a move toward "economic assimilation." In other areas of law, church courts routinely excluded attorneys, disregarded legal precedent, and fashioned decisions as required by the equities of the particular case.

Nor was the area of commercial law always in conformity with civil rules. Other business cases were treated according to "Zion" rules rather than the civil law. For example, in 1869 the Salt Lake High Council heard the case of DT, a mill owner who had become indebted to so many creditors that he decided to turn over his entire affairs to Charles C. Rich. Rich was to act as trustee for the benefit of DT's creditors (1869, Fd. 9). Before the accounts could be settled equitably, TT commenced a suit against DT before the Third District Court for the outstanding amount DT owed him. DT asked the high council to make TT stop the civil action so that all the creditors could benefit equitable.

All DT's creditors appeared, recommending various compromises so that each creditor would be allowed some proportion of his claim. After hearing the evidence and the proposed compromises, the high council proposed reorganizing DT's debts and ordered TT to dismiss all proceedings in the Third District Court. Rich was appointed trustee of DT's property for the benefit of the creditors, and DT continued to run the mill under Rich's supervision. Rich also saw that DT had enough of the proceeds to sustain his family. All of the creditors, including TT, apparently found the solution satisfactory.

INFLUENCE ON CIVIL AFFAIRS

Church courts provided legitimacy for priesthood control over temporal as well as spiritual affairs. Through church court proceedings, priesthood leaders told Mormon civil officials how to exercise their civil authority and asked them to sustain ecclesiastical resolutions of conflict even when church intervention conflicted with their official responsibilities. Civil officials in turn asked church courts to make recalcitrant citizens do their civic duty.

While the federal government, by appointing non-Mormons, controlled the most significant political offices in Utah, including the governorship, federal judges, and the United States marshal and attorney, the Mormons occupied many local offices such as probate judgeships, justices of the peace, mayorships and sheriff's offices. Church members who had complaints against Mormon civil officers often looked to the church courts for resolutions. For example, in an 1867 Salt Lake High Council case, a member charged George W. Bean and William B. Pace, probate judge and sheriff of Utah County, respectively, for "exacting unlawful fees" and "for unlawfully selling at a sacrifice property on execution" (1867, Fd. 4; file incomplete). And in an 1859 case the Provo High Council rebuked the Utah County Probate Court officials for attaching a defendant's property without a hearing, and for selling the property without an accounting (1859, Fd. 7). The case went to the First Presidency on appeal, where it was affirmed. Brigham Young added his own opinion of the court officials' conduct:

We cannot look upon the transaction but as reflecting upon that character of fair, honorable, and equal administration of justice which should be the pride of every officer who holds position in this kingdom to maintain. There is one great truth, which those who have not learned will have yet to learn. The kingdom of God guarantees and protects all men in their rights, religious, civil and personal, irrespective of their opinions.

Similarly, in an 1869 case, the Salt Lake High Council held that the county court had exceeded its authority in granting a fishing monopoly on Utah Lake. The council's decision not only resolved the particular conflict, it also provided the county court with a rule about water rights. The judge apparently did not feel that the high council court was interfering inappropriately in civil matters.

Judge Elias Smith, probate judge of Salt Lake County, often testified before the Salt Lake High Council when the high councils reviewed his decisions. For example, in 1866 the high council had Judge Smith testify regarding a divorce case in which he had awarded the husband the house and ordered the wife to leave. The wife asked the high council to review the case. The council reviewed the matter and agreed that she had no legal claim to the house, but granted her an award of $300 and allowed her to stay until her husband paid her. The First Presidency unanimously sustained the decision on 2 October 1866 (1866, Fd. 2). Elias Smith testified in other church court cases regarding civil dispositions in his court. In some cases the church courts followed Judge Smith's disposition, while in others the decisions were modified (see, e.g., 1870, Fd. 16; 1872, Fd. 3[2]).

In at least some areas, and for at least the first two decades of Mormon residence, civil officials sought the assistance of the church courts in bringing recalcitrant citizens into line. For example, in 1861, the assessor and collector of taxes for Salt Lake City complained to the Salt Lake High Council that certain members had failed "to pay according to tax ordinances in common with their brethren and others." The high council ordered the offending members to pay the tax or be excommunicated (1861, Fd. 5). But in another case, the Salt Lake High Council refused to compel the payment of an assessed school tax where the school district had not complied with the applicable law. Thus church courts instructed both civil officers and citizens in their civic responsibilities.

Church courts did not hesitate to modify civil court decisions, even those made by non-Mormon judges. For example, in an 1873 case the Salt Lake High Council increased a judgment awarded by the Third District Court from $14,000 to $15,001.55 (1873, Fd. 9). The high council also recommended that the prevailing party "extend the hand of leniency and mercy toward [the loser]" and compromise the matter, thereby demonstrating a difference in orientation between an ecclesiastical and a civil judgment. In 1889, the bishop of Smithfield Ward, Cache Valley Stake, ordered a recently divorced wife to give back certain properties that had been awarded her by the judge of the First District or be disfellowshipped (1889, Fd. 1). These typical cases illustrate that any civil judgment between church members was subject to modification by a church court.

As part of exclusive jurisdiction, church courts held that any litigation before them was final, except for appeals, and that any review of a church decision in the civil courts would subject the complainant to church sanctions. The Bear Lake High Council in Idaho heard a claim for assault and battery in 1897. It specifically instructed the parties, in making its decision, that the church proceedings were a bar to any further litigation,

> thus discouraging further litigation before the civil courts, and at the same time respecting the rights of the injured for remedy. Since in this case there was no civil suit pending . . . it was understood that this action of the church be a bar against any proceeding in the civil court, and [the plaintiff] would have been held as in contempt of the Bishop's Court had he sued [the defendant] for damages at law.

Even more interesting was an 1889 case heard by the Beaver Stake High Council (1889, Fd. 6). The high council decided to entertain a charge that a church member had criminally assaulted another member's ten-year-old daughter, even though the state was prosecuting the case in the civil courts. The high council voted not to postpone the action because the controversy over the assault charge had caused family hardship and continuing embarrassment. The criminal action had been continually delayed, "and there is no telling when the matter will be adjudicated in the courts." By hearing the case, despite the pending criminal action, the church court expedited a resolution of the incident in the community, while permitting the criminal action to proceed so that if the defendant were found guilty a penalty could be imposed.

In these and other cases, the church courts, by exercising an exclusive-jurisdiction rule, created Mormon-style justice in disputes about real property, natural resources, domestic relationships, contractual arrangements, and tort claims. Their decisions supported a vision of society markedly at variance with the social environment prevailing in nineteenth-century America.

10

Refinements in the Mormon
Judiciary

Although the church relied on the bishop's court, the high council court, and the First Presidency court established during the lifetime of Joseph Smith, alternative forums were also developed whenever ecclesiastical leaders believed they would be helpful. While no procedure or forum became uniform during the nineteenth century, a review of the files provides a rare glimpse into the day-to-day workings of a church court system used extensively by the priesthood to create a unified religious community.

THE ROLE OF TEACHERS

The duty of teachers was described in a revelation announced by Joseph Smith in April 1830: "The teacher's duty is to watch over the church always, and be with and strengthen them/and see that there is no iniquity in the church, neither hardness with each other, neither lying, backbiting, nor evil speaking; and see that the church meet together often, and also see that all the members do their duty" (D&C 20:53–55).

The teacher's role as an investigator of misconduct, feelings, and community conflict became routine in the Great Basin. In a formal circular distributed to the bishops for public reading to ward members on 11 July 1877, the First Presidency encouraged the teachers to serve as mediators of conflict at the ward level:

> Many persons have claimed fellowship in the church who have not lived according to the requirements of the gospel; but this should no longer be permitted. The laws of the Lord must be more strictly enforced, and such persons must repent and bring forth the fruits of righteousness in their lives, or be severed from the church. If persons professing to be members of the church be guilty of lying, drunkenness, sabbath-breaking, profanity, defrauding or backbiting their neighbors, or any

other kind of wickedness or unrighteous dealing, they should persist in their wrong-doing, then their cases should be brought before the bishops and his counselors, and they should be cited to appear to answer the charges made against them. If, upon proper and sufficient testimony, it should appear that they have been guilty of acts which are in violation of the law of God, and they will not repent, then they should be expelled from the church, and their names be no longer numbered among the Saints. If teachers, priests and bishops, or other officers, suffer iniquity to exist in the church, in districts where they preside, without taking action, against it, they become partakers of other men's sins and they are unworthy of their positions. (Clark 2:284)

President John Taylor, on 14 October 1877 at his first meeting with the Saints following the death of Brigham Young, reiterated: "Where there may be difficulties to settle and it is not within the power of the teachers to satisfactorily adjust them, report them to the bishop, who sits as a common judge in Israel, and to adjudicate all such matters" (JD, 14:42).

Thus the involvement of the teachers in ecclesiastical proceedings grew naturally out of their more general religious duties of rooting out iniquity in the church. They were soon filing complaints against errant members for apostasy, as well as arbitrating conflict between members as the first stage in the church court process.

The persistence of this role is illustrated by an 1885 case in which the bishop read and explained the empowering verses in section 20 of the Doctrine and Covenants, then explained: "We have made a solemn covenant to see that the laws of God are enforced. We are here for the purpose. The teachers are appointed to go through the church and see that no iniquity exists, and when it exists they report it to the Bishop; and we are obliged to sit on these cases, or we would be neglecting our duty." (Ecclesiastical Court Cases, Disfellowship Records, are hereinafter cited by year, file designation, and folder number; 1885, Disfellowship File, Fd. 2.) James Dunn Stirling's Letterbook (1886–90), which includes high council proceedings, reveals that the high council sent back an 1886 case that had been brought before them because the member "did not proceed according to the order of the Church, by first submitting his case to the Teachers" (Stirling, 15). In 1887, the Salt Lake High Council sent back another case for failure to comply with the preliminary procedure of a teacher's arbitration hearing: "If the teachers fail to effect a reconciliation between the brethren, the complained of and the aggrieved party, then they are liable to be brought before their respective Bishops in the form of a Bishop's court. This course should be pursued before this High Council is appealed to" (Stirling, 90).

The teachers were therefore the first to hear the cases. If they failed at reconciliation efforts, proceedings would then be commenced in the bishop's court. Although the teachers' involvement in dispute resolution may have occasionally exacerbated an already sensitive problem, it institutionalized neighborhood responsibility for maintaining good feelings and cooperation. Even if the conflict could not be settled, the teachers helped discover the facts and identify the issues for the bishop's trial. Thus the teachers held a sort of pretrial or preliminary hearing. The teachers' involvement also reminded members that their religious commitments were reflected in their social relations.

In addition, the teachers often were considered responsible if they were unable to resolve a case before it reached the bishop. In an 1875 case the bishop implied that the case would not have come before him in the first place if the teachers had been spiritually prepared: "The teachers did not have a particle of the spirit of the Lord and they [the teachers] had better dismiss and go home and pray to get the spirit of the Lord before they came together to settle difficulty."

ARBITRATION PROCEEDINGS

After their arrival in Utah, the Saints frequently relied on arbitration to resolve difficulties. Each party would select a referee, and the referees would select a tie-breaking referee. The referees would investigate the matter and then meet together for an arbitrated resolution. Occasionally the arbitrators simply served as expert witnesses in church court proceedings. Like the use of ward teachers, the use of arbitration probably strengthened social bonds by involving more of the community in conflict resolution.

Arbitration was especially useful in cases requiring extensive accounting analysis, such as construction contract disputes. For example in 1869 the Salt Lake High Council assigned arbitrators to a case involving a complex set of contracts extending over a number of years. The high council authorized the arbitrators to make a recommendation "subject to the superior wisdom of the council," rather than to make a final decision.

Bishops and stake presidents occasionally used arbitration where a hearing before the regular court raised a conflict of interest. For example, when a party had a contractual claim against the church and sought redress in the church courts, arbitration provided a solution that would prevent a conflict of interest (1878, Fd. 9). Church officials also used arbitration in suits against political subdivisions (1866, Fd. 6) and city councils (1864, Fd. 7).

It is apparent that church tribunals gave substantial deference to the findings of arbitrators even though their recommendations were not binding. A bishop in San Bernadino on 16 August 1856 counseled that the bishopric "honor the decision of the Referees," which had been appealed, giving as a reason, "otherwise the arbitrators would not give a decision" (1856, Fd. 6; 1878, Fd. 14). Where arbitrators could not agree, at least two church courts split the difference between their respective recommendations (1870, Fd. 10; 1878, Fd. 9).

Church courts might require the parties to post bonds before assigning arbitrators to ensure compliance. In one case, the bond was the staggering sum of $10,000, apparently because the complainant was not Mormon (1858, Fd. 2, no. 7).

PRIESTHOOD QUORUMS

Priesthood quorums occasionally attempted to resolve disputes before the parties resorted to the bishop. The quorums apparently enforced their decisions by threatening disfellowshipping from the quorum. It is unclear what this enforcement actually consisted of, since it probably did not affect a man's church membership or his ability to exercise his priesthood. Nevertheless, being cut off from the quorum could have a powerful social impact in the close-knit Mormon communities. Moreover, a bishop's court often followed so the offending brother could be cut off from the church (1858, Fds. 4–6; 1856, Fd. 9, Disfellowship File, Fd. 1).

OTHER CHURCH FORUMS

Church court records also preserve the actions of ad hoc bodies organized for cases that could not be properly decided using ordinary procedures. On at least one occasion, a domestic conflict was resolved through arbitration by the wife's bishop and the husband's bishop (1864, Fd. 2). Where a bishop was being sued, occasionally an apostle or a committee of three bishops was assigned to hear the case (1860, Fd. 2; 1864, Fd. 12). An apostle also might be assigned to the case where the high council was unfairly biased (1886, Fd. 5).

Between the death of Brigham Young in 1877 and the sustaining of John Taylor as president of the church in 1880, the Quorum of the Twelve presided as the highest court of appeal (1878, Fd. 10; 1879–80 Fd. 2, 3; 1889, Fd. 10). Apostles also were occasionally assigned to hear cases being appealed to the First Presidency. For example, in 1892 three apostles were assigned to take care of a backlog of twelve cases (1895, Fd. 2; 1892, Fd. 1).

In all of these cases, the ad hoc nature of the forum does not seem to have been an issue. The parties seemed willing to accept the judgment of the particular forum, and the forums themselves seemed to serve the community by resolving conflict and restoring good feelings.

RULES OF EVIDENCE IN CHURCH COURTS

Evidentiary rules in the church courts grew out of experience and priesthood directives. Procedure varied from court to court, but most church courts admitted all relevant evidence and largely ignored common-law exclusionary rules such as the rule against hearsay.

The courts preferred but did not require that witnesses appear in person to testify. Ward and stake clerks issued orders requiring members to appear and testify if their testimony was necessary, and if they otherwise refused to appear voluntarily. When distance, illness, or expense made it difficult for a witness to appear personally, the courts normally accepted written statements. At least one court refused to admit written testimony when the witness was readily available (1892, Fd. 2). In another case, a court required an unavailable witness to answer specific questions by affidavit (1882, Fd. 7). Nonmember witnesses were generally excluded because the penalty for perjury, disfellowshipping, could have no effect on them.

Although a church court usually did not administer an oath before hearing testimony, the witness was expected to tell the truth. In one case a bishop warned that the "consequences are probably greater, and it is just as binding upon us, and more so if possible, to tell the truth before the Priesthood as it is before any court or tribunal in the land." The bishop then added that "the spirit of the Lord has also born witness to us: that some had given 'crooked testimony.' " Although he was prepared to render a decision, he encouraged the party to confess, warning that "the time will come when we will have to pass the angels and the Gods and they cannot be deceived. Tell the truth and we will be as lenient as possible." The party in question broke down and admitted, "Yes, Bishop there was crookedness, all I ask is what mercy you can extend" (1889, Fd. 2).

JURISDICTIONAL PROBLEMS

As the church court began functioning on a regular basis in Utah, jurisdictional disputes cropped up but were never resolved in any definitive manner. In 1851, the Salt Lake High Council considered whether appellate courts could also exercise original jurisdiction.

David Fullmer, a member of the stake presidency, felt that "the Brethren would do honor to the Bishop to refer these small charges to the Bishop first, and if there is difficulty to appeal to the High Council." The high council decided to hear the case anyway "on account of [its] complex nature." Later that year the high council again considered the question of jurisdiction. This time, one speaker counseled "that if it was likely to come before the high council eventually, particularly where the witnesses or parties lived a great distance away, then it should originally be heard by the high council." President Daniel Spencer agreed: "If the case will come before this council in the end, he thought it wisdom to admit it here at first" (1851, Fd. 11).

In an 1892 case, one bishop referred the case to the high council because of a conflict of interest; one of the parties was his counselor's brother (1892, Fd. 1). In comparison, when the bishop of a St. George ward in an 1872 case referred a land controversy to the high council because of an apparent conflict of interest, the high council referred it back, "advising me as Bishop of the Ward to go right along advising, dividing, and giving such decisions as my best wisdom dictates, so that the putting in of crops and general business of the settlement will not be interrupted" (1872, Fd. 2).

In another case, the Salt Lake High Council in 1897 refused to excuse a bishop from hearing a paternity case filed against his son. President Cannon "held that he was not only eligible, but that it was his duty to so act" (1897, Disfellowship File, Fd. 12). Although such rulings are consistent with the high standards of integrity the church expected of its officers, the challenging parties still must have wondered about the property of interested priesthood leaders hearing cases. In any event they submitted to church court jurisdiction.

Some litigants critized the church's involvement in certain types of cases. Some claimants denied that the church had jurisdiction to hear real property cases, claims for debts that had been discharged by civil bankruptcy proceedings, cases involving criminal conduct, and cases involving probate matters already determined by the probate courts. The church tribunals, however, generally recognized jurisdiction of any matter in which all of the interested parties were Latter-day Saints and a Mormon resolution would further the cause of Zion.

Occasionally, a problem of jurisdiction arose when one of the parties in a complaint was a corporation. In one 1882 case the Weber High Council was unsure whether they ought to take jurisdiction over a dispute involving ZCMI. The stake president met with President John Taylor who instructed the council to take jurisdiction because ZCMI was church owned (1982–83, Fd. 1). In an 1890 Salt Lake Stake case, however, a high councillor noted that the high council "will not entertain a case in which a company against an individual are complainants for the reason that it places the individual at a disadvantage, in this: a Council would be loath to disfellowship a whole company for what it might, comparatively without much ado, nip off an individual. Again, part of a company might be willing to abide the Council's decision and part not; part might be in the Church and part non-members, thus rendering it impossible for the Council to enforce its decision" (1890, Fd. 5).

Normally, a case was brought before the bishop in the defendant's ward or in the ward where the subject matter of the dispute was located. The litigants sometimes voluntarily transferred venue to a more convenient location but the courts rarely mandated a change of venue. For example, when a bishop was suspended from his office for misconduct in one stake, the case for his fellowship was heard in the stake to which he and the witnesses had since moved (Stirling, 28). But when a case involving fishing rights in Utah Lake came before the Salt Lake High Council, it insisted on hearing the case over the objections of one party that the Provo High Council was the proper jurisdiction and further objections that neither the teachers nor any bishop had heard the matter prior to the filing before the high council (1864, Fd. 3[d]). Similarly the Salt Lake High Council heard a dispute between Ogden and its city attorney, Aurelius Miner, even though Odgen's Mayor Lester Herrick protested that the case should have been heard by the Weber High Council (1870, Fd. 15).

The courts were not unsympathetic to procedural issues, but in general, they were less concerned with consistency than with equity. Once a court decided a particular procedural or evidentiary issue on appeal, it would tend to use the same rule in similar cases in the future as long as the personnel of the court remained the same. Since no court published any decision, however, other courts might and did handle similar problems differently.

APPELLATE PROCEDURES

It was assumed that the men hearing cases in church courts would have spiritual insight and that their decisions would be correct and just. One high councillor remarked during a case, that "inasmuch as the church was built upon the rock of Revelation, they [the parties] need not be under any fears that an unrighteous decision would be given" (1853, Disfellowship File, Fd. 1). This feeling and the prevailing value attached to harmonious community living probably worked together to persuade quarreling parties to accept decisions even when they were not completely satisfactory.

However, the Doctrine and Covenants authorized a right to "appeal to the high council of the seat of the First Presidency of the church, and have a rehearing, which case shall there be conducted, . . . as though no such decision had been made" (D&C 102:27, 30–31). The church courts universally accepted the right of each member to appeal from a bishop's decision to a high council court and from there to the First Presidency.

On the other hand, the bishop in one case told the parties, "I want you both to feel satisfied with this decision. I don't want to hear of one word being said that injustice has been done; that is the reason I said appeal if you want to. This is a lower tribunal" (1889, Fd. 5). The Salt Lake High Council had noted the year before that "they have the right of appeal to the High Council, but those desiring an appeal must ask for it, and also set forth sufficient reasons for doing so before the Council will entertain the case" (Stirling, 198).

There were also some practical limitations on this theoretical right of unlimited appeal. In one 1853 case involving a $30 assessment for fencing a portion of Salt Lake City's "big field," the high council chastised AN for being unwilling to accept his bishop's judgment: "This is, a small matter to bring before 12 or 15 men. . . . He should have honored the decision of the Bishop and not bothered the High Council" (1853, Fd. 4). The high council affirmed.

A court of appeals could reverse or modify any decision of a lower court, despite the aura of inspiration associated with church court decisions. In 1887, the Salt Lake High Council remanded a case back to the bishop and suggested that he change his decision regarding a land controversy (Sterling, 112). In another 1880 case President John Taylor and the Council of the Twelve Apostles prefaced their opinion with: "In the judgment given by McQuarrel [of the Weber High Council] and confirmed by the High Council in above case and stake, we respectfully do not concur" (1880, Fd. 10). In one case where the majority of the high council would not confirm the stake president's decision—a rare occurrence—compromise was created (1884, Fd. 23). In another case heard in 1891, President Smith of Davis Stake, after "a great deal of thought on this matter" and prayer, asked the First Presidency what to do "if at the close of the rehearing the views of the president and the majority of the Council differed." The First Presidency advised President Smith to "formulate his decision in accordance with the majority of the Council" since "it takes a majority of the Council to pass a decision" (1891, Fd. 5).

The scriptural injunction that a hearing should be treated "as though no such [former] decision had been made" was one of the clearer appellate rules. When the Salt Lake High Council excluded evidence that had not been presented at the bishop's trial, President John Taylor, after reviewing the file on appeal, directed the high council to rehear the case "as though it had not been heard, and without reference to previous trials." Specifically, Taylor explained:

> We infer, from his [the stake president's] statement, that the High Council seemed to consider itself merely an appellate court, as the lawyers would call it, and declined to go outside the record brought from the Bishop's trial. We do not know what rule had prevailed in this respect in High Council, but can see no impropriety in that body hearing new evidence that will throw light upon a case, especially when the other party is in a position to bring forward any rebutting testimony.
>
> The object of all trials in the Church is to get at the equities of the cases to be tried; and no evidence should be rejected upon mere technicality that will throw light upon the subject before the Council. The 102 section of the Book of D & C says, expressly, that the appointment of the high council is for the purposes of settling difficulties which cannot be settled by the Church or the Bishop's Council to the satisfaction of the parties. (1884–86, Disfellowship File, Fd. 6)

When high council decisions were appealed to the First Presidency, it dealt with the written record only. If someone wished to add more evidence, the First Presidency remanded that case to the high council (1852, Fd. 4[2]; 1878–80, Fd. 1).

Once the three-level appeal process was exhausted, a member either had to comply with the final decision or face disfellowship or excommunication.

SANCTIONS AND COURT REMEDIES

The church court system relied on the voluntary submission of church members to its decision. While the state courts enforced decisions with fines, imprisonment, and even death, church courts could only disfellowship or excommunicate recalcitrant church members. Doctrine and Covenant 134:10 provides:

> We believe that all religious societies have a right to deal with their members for disorderly conduct, according to the rules and regulations of such societies; provided that such dealings be for fellowship and good standing; but we do not believe that any religious society has authority to try men on the right of property or life, to take from them this world's

goods, or to put them in jeopardy of either life or limb, or to inflict any physical punishment upon them. They can only excommunicate them from their society, and withdraw from them their fellowship.

Between 1846 when the Municipal High Council exercised criminal jurisdiction in Winter Quarters, until 1849 when the State of Deseret was established, church courts applied coercive as well as spiritual sanctions. With the exception of this brief period, however, church courts relied solely on disfellowshipping or excommunication. A disfellowshipped member could not exercise his priesthood, take the sacrament (communion), or otherwise actively participate. Excommunication removed a person from membership in the church. His or her records were destroyed. Although such persons were still considered legally married and their children legitimate, no other relationship to the church was allowed. It simultaneously removed the offender from the body of the church and passed upon him or her a kind of sentence of spiritual death. It could be reversed only by retracing the path of a new member: repentance acceptable to the relevant ecclesiastical authorities, baptism (which was recorded as a first-time ordinance), confirmation, and the specific restoration of priesthood blessings. Church leader B. H. Roberts stressed the spiritual consequences of these sanctions:

> To those who hold lightly their standing in the church, suspension of fellowship, or excommunication has no special terror; but to the man of faith, whose full hopes of eternal life with all its advantages stand or fall with his standing in the church of Christ, no greater punishment can threaten him, and since man in his imperfect state is influenced to righteousness by his fear of punishment, as well as by his hope of reward, the punishment of suspended fellowship and of excommunication has a salutary effect in preserving the discipline of the church. (CHC 2:376–77)

In addition, sanctioned members often suffered economic privation because Saints usually did business only with other church members.

Anthropologist Paul Dredge observed that excommunication or disfellowshipping "effectively denied [a member] his full ritual participation and the feeling of solidarity that participation in ritual imparts." He further notes, however, that the church did not encourage shunning or the ignoring of the disciplined person, but instead encouraged members to be "understanding and helpful" in order to lead the individual back into full fellowship (Dredge, 203).

To achieve the twin objectives of social harmony and personal righteousness among the Saints, ecclesiastical leaders wielded sanctions with some acuity. The key concept was repentance, which usually included asking forgiveness of the person or persons wronged.

Church leaders extolled the virtues of voluntary reconciliation, encouraging members to freely request and extend forgiveness to other community members. Voluntary reconciliation, even if the threat of sanctions hovered in the background, enhanced social harmony by increasing the chances of a permanent solution. According to one stake president:

> The cold, matter of fact decision of this council, however just, is likely to be viewed by one of the parties at least as unfair, whereas if they could come together each being willing to concede a little and if needs be a great deal in order to amicably settle this difficulty, the spirit of the Lord would warm their hearts, brotherly feeling would be restored and these complex difficulties would vanish like dew before the sun. In this digression I have only performed an important part of our duty which is to explain and bring to bear the spirit of the gospel that if possible we may be able to restore good feelings between brethren which this case particularly seems to demand. (1884–86, Disfellowship File, Fd. 1)

A bishop in an 1883 case similarly "expressed his regret at the necessity of having to sit in judgment on his brethren. Said he has always endeavored to bring about a reconciliation among the parties before proceeding to trial" (1883, Disfellowship File, Fd. 1).

Despite conciliatory efforts, however, church courts used their powers to ensure they would be taken seriously. Members who refused to appear at the hearing were disfellowshipped for "contempt of the priesthood" and were restored only after willingly submitting to the court's jurisdiction.

Church courts required that the guilty party confess errors and ask forgiveness of those wronged, which sometimes included the entire ward. This forced the wrongdoer to accept responsibility for misconduct, but without unnecessary humiliation. Although one bishop advised a defendant "to humble himself before God, said a few dollars was nothing compared with his standing in the Church" (1881, Fd. 7), John Taylor admonished another bishop not to be too "strenuous about the required acknowledgement [of error] . . . as it is not our desire to degrade any of our brethren" (1885, Fd. 4[2]). The church also expected the injured person to forgive and forget. Apostle Orson Hyde reminded a congregation reviewing the alleged misconduct of a bishop that "if we are not generous to forgive, we need not expect God will be generous to save us" (1861, Fd. 6). Of course, not all church members were so charitable. One defendant, after the high council "received his acknowledgement and fully forgave him," asked forgiveness from the ward as well. All forgave him except one couple who did not believe his acknowledgement was "sufficiently definite" (1854, Fd. 4).

The court also considered the sincerity of the wrongdoer in making its decision. In one case the Salt Lake High Council unanimously rejected the defendant's confession as insincere. He then made another "partial acknowledgement" that the council also rejected as incomplete. President Spencer urged him to make a more complete acknowledgment of his errors at the hearing; he complied, and the council finally accepted his repentance as full and sincere (1852, Fd. 12).

DECISIONAL STANDARDS

Transgressions against basic social standards, including adultery, theft, murder, and lying posed no special problems for church courts. But where the case involved property, contracts, torts, or domestic disputes, the appropriate decisional standard was less clear. The courts justified whatever decisions they made less on arguments of formal justice than the inspired "higher law" of Zion.

One scholar who investigated the ecclesiastical courts of a single Mormon stake in Arizona between 1884 and 1896 argued that these "processes predisposed Mormons to adjust, adapt, and continually change the meanings and definitions that they applied to the whole of life . . . By not using precedent, or not considering the context of any past event used as a citation, or not having lawyers . . . a government that used sanctity to rule forgot its own history" (Leone, 117).

This observation is empirically inaccurate. Mormon communities, comprised largely of members from widely varying backgrounds, accepted the need to adapt to their new community, and church court rules often reflected these changes. But past events were critical in the process of adaptation. High councils did not make ad hoc decisions in each case. Instead, they relied extensively on scripture and instructions from church leaders, which were soon embodied in local customs. In fact, the decisions are remarkably uniform, whether in land and water disputes, contracts, sexual morality, or plural marriages. Although any customary rule or past experience was subject to adjustment through inspiration, aberrations could always be appealed. In short, though precedent never controlled church court decisions, and canon law never developed as a limitation on the discretion of local leaders, church court decisions were broadly consistent throughout the period.

TRYING PRIESTHOOD LEADERS

Ecclesiastical trials against church leaders did not disappear during the Utah period even though the trek west constituted a ferocious sifting out of the less committed. The Council of the Twelve excommunicated Apostle Amasa M. Lyman 6 May 1867 for denying that the atonement of Jesus Christ was necessary for salvation (CHC 5:270–71). Several members of the Salt Lake City School of the Prophets were disfellowshipped in 1869 for attacking Brigham Young's "dictatorial practices." The Godbeite movement, named after W. S. Godbe, was reminiscent of the Far West dissension that denied priesthood authority in temporal affairs. Apostle Albert Carrington was excommunicated on 1 November 1885, for "lewd and lascivious conduct and adultery" (Jenson 1899, 125). In short, false doctrine, dissension over temporal as well as spiritual matters, and personal immorality mobilized the church courts to defend Zion.

Toward the end of the century, the church's political influence created sharp divisions among the "General Authorities." In June 1891, the church dissolved the exclusively Mormon "People's Party" and encouraged members to align themselves with national parties of their choice in an attempt to gain statehood. In the same month the First Presidency stated that the "church will not assert any right to control the political actions of its members" (CHC 6:303).

Five years later, however, when Apostle Moses Thatcher accepted the Democratic nomination to the Senate, the First Presidency asked that he sign a "political manifesto" acknowledging that any "General Authority" should first consult with priesthood authorities before accepting political office (*Deseret News*, 11 April 1896). Thatcher refused. The church insisted that the "manifesto" was intended to preserve proper order and discipline in the church, but Thatcher argued that it violated the separation of church and state. When he refused to appear before the Council of the Twelve on 19 November 1896, he was "deprived of his apostleship and other offices in the priesthood" (CHC 6:335). The Salt Lake Stake High Council investigated on 30 July 1898 and required Thatcher to publish a declaration that he had been mistaken in his earlier position or be disfellowshipped. Reluctantly, Thatcher complied (CHC 6:336).

The Manifesto discontinuing polygamy also caused dissension among church leaders that resulted in church court actions against apostles John W. Taylor and Matthias F. Cowley. Taylor and Cowley, perhaps under the direction of the First Presidency (Quinn, 1985), understood the manifesto to apply in the United States only. They continued to encourage and perform plural marriages in Mexico. When President Joseph F. Smith in 1904 issued a "Second Manifesto" disclaiming the continued practice of polygamy in any jurisdiction, Taylor and Cowley resigned their positions as apostles. In 1911 the Quorum of the Twelve tried them for encouraging polygamy. Taylor was excommunicated, but a repentant Cowley was merely dropped from the Quorum (Collier and Black, 12, 18).

11

Mormon Land Policy and Church Courts

The control exerted by Mormon leadership over the acquisition and transfer of land in the Great Basin played a pivotal role in the effort to establish a literal land of Zion. The church's innovative land distribution policy permitted the systematic and relatively harmonious colonization of the Great Basin, encouraged cooperative fencing and irrigation, and reinforced the role of church courts in resolving economic conflicts.

The Mormons, of course, were not the only settlers in the Great Basin, so they soon reinforced the ecclesiastical land policy with territorial legislation. Unfortunately, the Saints had no legal authority to legitimize land grants, and in 1869 when the first land office opened, the federal government insisted on applying its own homestead and preemption rules. The ownership of Utah lands represents a complex dynamic of Mormon attempts to subvert the federal regulations through legislation, "paper" compliance, and the use of church courts to mediate land conflicts between members.

MORMON AND FEDERAL METHODS OF ALLOCATING LAND

When the Mormons arrived in the Great Basin in 1847 the land was legally part of Mexico, though that country never exercised control over the area.[1] Had Mexico retained title, the Mormons surely would have sought political independence to establish the "kingdom of God and his laws."[2] With the signing of the Treaty of Guadalupe Hidalgo on 2 February 1848, all of the land became United States property, but the federal government did not extend its land laws to the Great Basin until 1869. Between 1847 and 1869 Mormon settlers could not obtain legal title to lands they had settled. They were, in effect, squatters on the public domain.

The absence of a federal land law proved both boon and bane, jeopardizing Mormon efforts to solidify their early claim on settled lands but giving them time to implement a distinctive allocational policy.

On 25 July 1847, the day following his arrival in the Salt Lake Valley, Brigham Young announced: "No man should buy or sell land. Every man should have his land measured off to him for city and farming purposes, what he could till. He might till it as he pleased, but he should be industrious and take care of it."[3] As applied the policy meant: (1) the early settlers could not acquire vast lands and speculate, as some Saints had in Kirtland, on land appreciation with the impending migration; (2) priesthood leaders would allocate both city and farming lots on some equitable basis; (3) ownership would be predicated on actual use; and (4) agrarian households would constitute the primary social unit in the Great Basin.

The Great Salt Lake High Council on 18 October 1847 established a committee "to receive the claims on the plowed land and adjust them."[4] On 26 December 1847 it began to provide legislation "in the absence of any organized jurisdiction of any territory, for the peace, welfare and good order of our community . . . for the government and regulation of the inhabitants of this city and valley for the time being, subject to the approval of the people."[5] The next fall, an ordinance was passed on 30 September 1848 providing for "a land record and fees for the surveyor and clerk."[6] These legislative responsibilities shifted to the State of Deseret in March 1849 and then to the territorial government in 1851. The Mormon-dominated legislative bodies essentially ratified the high council's earlier practice. They had no authority to grant patents to federal lands, but they could and did establish priority among land claims. Territorial legislation in 1852 provided that any seller of land was to quitclaim any interest he might have to the buyer, the buyer being responsible to register the quitclaim deed with the county recorder. An 1861 statute "provided that any person who enclosed a portion of unclaimed government land should be regarded as the rightful owner of that land and any buildings and improvements he had placed upon it."[7] This "enclosure law" legitimized the Mormon practice of limiting claims on the basis of the claimant's ability to fence (and presumably to use beneficially) the land enclosed.

The territorial legislature also repeatedly petitioned Congress to create federal land laws that would cover Mormon practices. An 1858 memorial, for example, requested:

> To Congress for the preemption of Irrigated lands. To the Honorable, the Senate and House of Representatives, in Congress assembled:
> Your memorialists, the Governor and Legislative Assembly of the Ter-

ritory of Utah, would respectfully represent, that in the settlement of this wild and desert country, it was found necessary against the savages, and to enable the settlers to irrigate the lands, they were under the necessity of surveying and enclosing small tracts of from one to forty acres each; very few, however, exceed twenty acres. By this means, in locating almost every settlement, from fifty to one hundred farmers cultivate the same section, which is watered by a canal owned by each agriculturist, in proportion to the area of his farm, meadow or garden; the waters of said canal being distributed to each man in separate water ditch; a hundred or more of these streams water every section cultivated.

Your memorialists would therefore respectfully pray your honorable body, to pass a law enabling the occupants of such portions of land, to appoint one of their number an agent, who shall be authorized to preempt and enter said lands in a body, and distribute the same by giving titles to proper claimants.[8]

The federal government acted slowly. When in 1869 it did act, it refused to frame special land laws for the Great Basin, but merely applied the existing homestead and preemption laws. These laws, developed in other climates and under other social conditions, represented a compromise between an eastern and a frontier perspective on territorial lands. From an eastern perspective, the frontier was a source of revenue: settlers should pay for land grants. To the frontiersman the frontier represented an unclaimed section of the state of nature: possession justified entitlement. The conflict between these contradictory objectives resulted first in the Preemption Act of 1841[9] and then in the Homestead Act of 1862.[10] Triggered by interest in the frontier settlement of Oregon, the Preemption Act permitted a settler to acquire 160 acres at $1.25 per acre provided he or she resided on the land for fourteen months. The later Homestead Act, reflecting more of a frontier perspective, permitted the free entry of 80 to 160 acres of land upon proof of five years' residence. In an effort to acknowledge the climatic differences of the Great Basin, the Desert Land Act of 1877 allowed the acquisition of 640 acres of desert land at $1.25 per acre provided the claimant could prove that crops could only be produced through irrigation.[11]

Although each of these statutes provided relatively inexpensive ways to acquire title to federal lands, none were well suited to the Mormon situation. The Mormon settlement pattern clustered the farmers in villages with farms on the outskirts. This permitted community interaction and security, but made it more difficult to prove residence under the act. In addition, Brigham Young had made the first principle of his land policy that "no man should hold more land than he could cultivate; and if a man would not till his land, it should be taken from him" (CHC 3:55, 269). This policy suited the arid climate of the Great Basin where arable land was at a premium, achieved relative equality in land holdings, and prevented the land speculation and waste that had proven disastrous in Kirtland. In the Great Basin, a nineteenth-century family could intensively cultivate a maximum of forty acres, with the average farm size being about fifteen acres (Hunter, 154–57). Irrigation and fencing requirements also provided practical limitations on the size of land holdings. The 160 acres allowed by preemption and homestead laws was designed to encourage settlement in the Pacific Northwest or the fertile Midwest, but was not practical for Mormon settlers in the desert Great Basin.

The law also required that an applicant anywhere in Utah territory had to present himself or herself at the land office in Salt Lake City and offer proof of residence and cultivation. After filing, the settler had to wait for an ownership patent, a sometimes lengthy process over which the settler had little control. Although most applicants had no recourse against the delays and inconveniences associated with land filings, Thomas McBride of Grantsville in 1877 brought a successful but rare suit of mandamus against the Secretary of the Interior, Carl Schurz, in the U.S. Supreme Court to compel the granting of his patent application. The Court ordered Schurz to issue the patent for the claim McBride had proven in 1874 (*United States v. McBride*, 102 US 378 [1877]).

Although the federal government refused to acknowledge Mormon peculiarities in fashioning Utah's land policy and instead imposed the standard homestead and preemption solution, the Mormons followed their own priesthood-directed distributional pattern. Local priesthood leaders appointed "trustees" who would secure patents in compliance with federal land laws, then transfer portions of their legally acquired land to claimants with LDS-recognized titles. This procedure allowed the Mormons to affirm their previous practice and was probably an equitable way to ensure that people were not defrauded for the improvements they had already made on the land.

But the system did not go unchallenged. A Mormon farmer in Bountiful, L. S. Burnham, testified in 1879 before the Public Lands Commission that under Mormon customary practices individuals could claim tracts of no more than twenty acres and only with the permission of the bishop. He also "testified that a number of fraudulent entries had been made, including some for which the church was responsible" (Rollins 245). Several years later, in 1886, Williams A. J. Sparks, commissioner of the General Land Office, alleged in his annual report that the church had fraudulently produced lands under the preemption laws (Rollins 246). The evidence does not permit an evaluation of the merits of these accusations, but there is little doubt that Mormons viewed technical land-title claims as obstacles that could be legitimately superseded by Mormon customary practices. Milton R. Hunter, quotes George Thomas, author of *The Development of Institutions under Irrigation*, who observed:

> The only thing to be said for the violation of the land laws of the United States was that it was done with the full knowledge and at least the connivance of the United States officials and not with the idea of speculation or fraud against the government but to secure title to the soil that the pioneers had reclaimed and made productive by irrigation. (Hunter, 163)

In laying out Salt Lake City and other towns, Brigham Young generally relied on the pattern Joseph Smith had established for the city of Zion in Jackson County, Missouri (Hunter, 149). The center of Salt Lake City was given over to a block of ten acres for ecclesiastical structures. Each city block contained eight lots, ten by twenty rods, with streets eight rods wide. One house was to be built in the middle of each lot, twenty feet back from the street. Brigham Young and Heber C. Kimball assigned lots the first year; thereafter allocation was made by drawing lots. Called "inheritances," they were free, but the church required settlers to pay one dollar to the surveyor and fifty cents to the recorder. The farming lands were located in a joint enclosure outside Salt Lake City called the Big Field, with each farmer responsible for a section of the fence. As new settlers arrived, land claimants applied to the local bishop for an inheritance of unclaimed city and farming land. This precedent influenced settlement patterns in the early Mormon communities. Although the lot assignment and joint-enclosure practice surely were not uniform throughout the Great Basin for an extended period, respect for priesthood direction and entitlement based on prior occupancy seems to have been pervasive.

The objective of Mormon land policy was to establish self-sufficient and harmonious communities where the resources were distributed in an equitable, if not equal, fashion. Immediate control of the land facilitated cooperative efforts in fencing, irrigation, the building of schools and churches, and other community projects. Lowry reasonably suggests that Brigham Young's city-of-Zion plan both reflected and enhanced the "development of extraordinary group solidarity" and gave the groups a fighting chance to establish themselves in the hostile "environment of the Great Basin" (Hunter, 157).

The church courts after 1869 adjudicated many land disputes between members. Examining church courts record gives a unique glimpse into Mormon land practices. Although an attempt to understand these practices through the lenses of Church court proceedings suffers from incompleteness, it offers significant evidence refuting contemporary theories of early Utah history. Michael Raber argues that the imposition of federal land laws in 1869, not the arrival of the railroad in the same year, marked the real transition in Mormon history. He claims it ended the "regional institutional attempts to guarantee minimum sets of rights in land to individual families" (1978, 89), and that the Latter-day Saints had no particular purpose in continuing their peculiar custom beyond the point when "secure title to land could be achieved" (1978, 38–39).

There seems to be no question that Raber is mistaken. He assumes, wrongly, that Brigham Young's control of land distribution was equivalent to the situation described in Gluckman's paradigm for tribal societies that he cites. Brigham Young was not a tribal king. He did not dispense land grants to tribal members as a matter of individual status. Nor did the grantees owe tribal duties to him because of the land grants. In fact, there is little evidence to indicate that Young was personally involved in land allocation decisions after the initial distribution of land in Salt Lake City in 1847–48. Thereafter the rules became Mormon customary practice administered by local priesthood authority. By legislation, these rules applied to Mormons and non-Mormons alike, awarding land to settlers on the basis of ability to use it beneficially, not upon their relationship with Young. The church courts even deferred to these customary rules over direct priesthood grant. Moreover, it is difficult to find evidence that Young's authority diminished markedly after 1869. He remained the spiritual head of Zion and could override legal rights in favor of Mormon entitlements through the operation of the church courts.

Furthermore, the principle of beneficial use continued after the land office opened in 1869. The church courts acted as a vehicle for adjusting disputes created by the two conflicting systems so that the civil/Mormon views of ownership could be simultaneously satisfied. Existing church court records report land conflict cases from as early as 1848 (1848, Fd. 15). and as late as 1920 (1920, Fd. 1). Although accommodating civil law became increasingly important in the 1890s, the early-established customary rules continued to be operative in church court cases into the twentieth century.

EARLY LAND DISTRIBUTION CASES

The centralization of authority—both in distributing land and in adjudicating disputes—is shown in two early cases heard before the Salt Lake High Council.

In the first case, the Salt Lake High Council sorted through the rights of prior occupancy and officially assigned land (1849, Fd. 12). LH established that her husband had, without approval of priesthood leaders, built a house on certain land located near Cottonwood Creek. He left for California during the gold rush, and LH temporarily abandoned the house. JM, the claimant, showed that the local bishop had received instructions from Brigham Young to grant inheritances in the area as long as an individual or family did not take more land than they could fence and farm. Pursuant to this instruction the bishop had granted JM an inheritance that conflicted with LH's earlier occupancy, but since LH had apparently abandoned the premises no initial conflict arose. Thereafter, JM fenced the land and began to farm it. The controversy ensued when LH returned and claimed entitlement based on prior occupancy. Angered by JM's presence, she tore up his vines and vegetables. JM filed a complaint in the bishop's court and the bishop's decision was thereafter appealed to the Salt Lake High Council.

The council censured LH "for pulling up the vines as she was not activated by the Spirit of God when she did it." Furthermore, her husband should not have gone "on his own to Cottonwood Creek before the Presidency arrived to give us our inheritances." Still, the equities of the earliest claims required that "each man's claim shall be his own and we will recognize each other's claims." The stake president rebuked JM for his unreasonable and unChristian decision "to root and drive her out of there," saying, with some irritation, "I don't believe all this that we are contending for is worth 2 cents." The decision required LH to either pay JM for the fencing if she wanted to keep the property or sell JM the house her husband had built and relinquish her claim to the property.

Another land dispute case was heard by the Salt Lake High Council on 5 October 1849. Thomas Grover, a former member of the high council at Far West and later at Council Bluffs, complained that he had been the first to "stake out" certain lands upon his arrival in 1847, but had left them and gone to his farm outside the valley. Meanwhile, two other members, AB and AR, had arrived, found the land unoccupied, and begun to work it. When Grover returned the dispute over ownership arose.

The Salt Lake High Council acknowledged Grover's prior claim, but required him to compensate AB and AR for the improvements they had made. They also encouraged Grover to assist his neighbors: "When you have all the land you want let others gather round to join your farm. Should Aunt Mary Smith [probably the widow of Hyrum

Smith] wish to tarry near you accommodate her the best you can as she is striving hard for a livelihood" (1849, Fd. 10). The court action thus confirmed the equities of prior occupancy, sought an equitable recognition of the later settlers' labor, and encouraged the parties to look after the disadvantaged.

Whereas Mormon land rules necessarily controlled the disposition of early land conflicts, after Congress extended federal land laws to Utah in 1869, the Saints could rely on separate rules to establish legal entitlement. But very little seems to have changed after 1869: Mormon customary rules continued to supersede legal entitlement. Mormons were directed to use federal land law only to legitimize established holdings. Disputes nonetheless arose as to how to best use federal land laws and as to which laws were to be preferred.

The Salt Lake High Council heard a case on 19 August 1870 brought by Bishop Andrew Cahoon against SA for failing to abide by his counsel legitimizing prior land holdings (1870, Fd. 7[2]). Bishop Cahoon had told members that in acquiring land from the government they "should adopt the Homestead Laws [free land but five years of residency required], because there was not sufficient money in the ward to preempt it [$1.25 per acre with fourteen months residency]." Pursuant to this advice Bishop Cahoon selected representatives to "enter the land" in accordance with the homestead law. SA had instead preempted certain lands as recommended by the School of the Prophets. Upon establishing legal title he asked prior claimants to pay him his proportional costs ($1.25 per acre plus costs in proving the claim). Bishop Cahoon viewed this as contempt for his direction, and ordered SA to grant the land to the prior occupants at homestead rates or face disfellowshipping. Hosea Stout and J. C. Little, prominent Mormon lawyers, intervened on behalf of the School of the Prophets, and testified in SA's favor against Bishop Cahoon.

Little and Stout testified that under the direction of the First Presidency the School had studied the homestead and preemption laws and determined that preemption was preferable wherever possible to ensure that prior claimants would get their deeds. Bishop Cahoon charged that "the school had trampelled [sic] upon his priesthood authority by giving counsel contrary to his views" to ward members. President Wallace decided that Bishop Cahoon was wrong because he ignored the school. Its assignment to "study legal problems and advise bishops who did not understand all the points of the law," should have been appreciated by Bishop Cahoon who had threatened "he would see that his principle [homesteading preferred over preemption] was carried out if he lost his office." The court legitimized SA's action in preempting contrary to the bishop's advice. SA would have to transfer portions of the land to the previous LDS occupants, and they would be required to pay the preemption price per acre plus ten percent interest and a proportional share of the surveying expenses.

Some members did, however, rely on legal claims to defeat church land policies. For example, in 1884, the Box Elder High Council heard a complaint filed by JZ that RH had taken advantage of federal land laws to defraud "some unknown Indians" of certain lands (1884, Fd. 25). The land in question had been enclosed by the Brigham City Co-operative, which later transferred it to the church "in favor of the Indians." RH had nonetheless entered the Indian land under the Desert Land Act. A high councillor speaking for the cooperative spelled out the grounds of the court's involvement: "We are here as men interested in the welfare of the Kingdom of God. The law of the land may suffer a person to do certain things that justice and equity will not support and that is the position [RH] occupies. He has taken advantage of the law to defraud the Indians of the land inside the enclosure."

The high councillor assigned to speak for RH could only say that "as an American citizen [RH] had a right to claim that land, but as a brother in the church . . . he should have consulted [the bishop]. "The court decided that RH should "relinquish all claims" to the "Indian farm." RH appealed to the First Presidency, but received short shrift from John Taylor who "had no fellowship for Brethren that would hedge up the way of the Indians."

These and similar cases leave little support for Raber's claim that the Mormon apparatus for allocating land disintegrated in 1869. They also evidence harsh treatment of members who asserted legal rights over church directives.

The available land cases reveal an impressive willingness on the part of members to give up legal rights in accordance with church policy. When SA challenged Bishop Cahoon's direction in acquiring land, for example, he (and his wife) did not claim that their legal entitlement by preemption extinguished the rights of prior occupants, but only that they were entitled to the costs they had incurred in acquiring the land (1870, Fd. 6). Since the only disputed cases are recorded in court records, it is impossible to establish what percentage of these doubly claimed lands were transferred amicably. Without the benefit of researching the church court records, Hunter suggests, "It was almost an unheard of thing for the holder of the patent to fail to transfer the land to the occupants" (Hunter, 163).

The most interesting land cases, however, are those in which disagreements tested the application of community values in land cases.

The Weber High Council heard an interesting case on 17 March 1881 (1881, Fd. 12). A witness testified that when the land initially came on the market, AE "secured all he could by Homestead and Pre-Emption, and got some Soldier Warrants and covered about 600 acres." After securing title in 1876 he reportedly announced at church that those with interests in any of the property should "come and settle with me in a reasonable time, and they shall have their land. But I do not want to wait 7 or 8 years." AE felt that he had fulfilled his religious obligations to prior claimants through this formal invitation. By the time AM heard AE had secured title, however, AE had sold the land to EF. AM complained, "It has been customary for any person entering land to make the neighbors acquainted with it. I knew nothing about this land being in the hands of [AE]. As soon as I learned that he had a patent for the land, I went to him about it." The court agreed and informed AE and EF, the subsequent purchaser, that AM still owned the land if he paid proportional costs. EF, the subsequent purchaser, in turn, was entitled to reimbursement from AE.

Another interesting case began in a bishop's court in Juab Stake in 1884 and ultimately reached the First Presidency (1884, Fd. 2). AM initially filed a preemption entry on May 1883 on a certain piece of land. AR thereafter mistakenly fenced six acres of it. When the mistake was called to his attention, he agreed to move the fence. He still had not done so, however, when he sold the land to AB the next year. Am asked AB to move the fence; AB delayed. AM threatened to haul the fence away and make AB pay the costs. In retaliation, AB in April of 1884 filed an entry under the Desert Land Act upon eighty acres that covered in part, the disputed land, even though he knew AM had pre-empted it the year before and had plowed and cultivated the land. The bishop stopped AB "from taking any further steps to claim that land until [AM] has had a good opportunity to perfect his title," ordered him to "ask forgiveness for the wrong he had done," and gave him two weeks to comply before he was disfellowshipped.

AB appealed to the Juab High Council where he argued that AM's preemption was "a second filing and consequently illegal." Furthermore, AM's plural wives also had each secured quarter sections. AB had thus felt justified in filing, "considering that it would save him the expense of moving 136 rods of 'Bull' fence, and not deprive [AM] of any just or legal right." The comments of the high councillors focused primarily on the breach of community harmony. One speaker for AM observed that AB "should have went to [AM] and ascertained if there was not some way of settling the matter without making an entry over the entry of [AM]. That if [AB] had acted the part of a latter-day Saint he would have sought [AM] and endeavored to settle the difficulty in a brotherly manner." Another speaker for AM protested that he "had done nothing wrong in allowing his wives to enter land, but that it was the right and duty of every Latter-day Saint to take up and occupy as much Government land as would be consistent with law and right." A councillor speaking for AB disagreed: "It was not the right of any Latter-day Saint to take or hold any more land than he could use with profit." President Paxman decided that AM was not entitled to all of the land covered by his preemption filing and therefore held that AB "be allowed to perfect his title" to the land he had entered under the Desert Act. He nonetheless required that AB deed back to AM a portion of the disputed land, with AM paying the filing costs.

AM appealed to the First Presidency, protesting first that the high council had been biased in favor of AB because he was a counselor in a bishopric and second that the land in AM's wives' names was not relevant to the case. In forwarding the records, the high council added a comment justifying their examining the legitimacy of AM's wives' property:

> In considering the matter, in endeavoring to adjust matters, we could see no other way than a thorough examination of the subject in all its bearings, and with a prayerful spirit sought to fully learn the causes of all the trouble, and in righteousness of spirit to adjust matters by a decision that, not only embraced the grounds of the original complaint, but would go sufficiently far beyond, to completely adjust matters.

The high council also reported that the land office had already declared AM's filing void and AB's valid. Permitting AB to complete his filing, then granting a portion of it to AM, would be equitable for all parties.

The high council's decision that AM's family already had enough land prompted a written protest from AM to the First Presidency:

> After being stripped of almost every right I held as a citizen of the United States I must strenuously object to being robbed of what little I have left in the name of God and under the cloak of this holy priesthood, not for the sake of property but for the sake of those principles which I value high above any other consideration.

The First Presidency heard the case on 28 May 1885, a full year after the bishop's court. It disposed of the issue of AM's wives and their quarter sections by observing that "it is right under law for women to make entries of land in their own name where they are the heads of families. There appears to be no reason why [AM] should be punished for his wives having entered this land." The bishop's decision was affirmed and the high council's reversed.

Nevertheless, the story was not ended. The high council filed charges against AM for his "contempt of the honor and dignity of the Holy Priesthood," because AM had criticized the high council in his appeal petition (1885, Fd. 4). AB also asked for a rehearing, pointing out that we had a legal entry upon the land, but a Decree has been made that notwithstanding that fact . . . . I must abandon it, and it is to go to AM whose filing is illegal and could not be completed." Because ecclesiastical directives overrode legal determinations, the First Presidency denied AB's request for a rehearing. In this case church court jurisdiction seemed to rankle both parties but both apparently complied anyway.

While cases like these established the preeminence of priesthood authority in legal disputes, other cases worked at refining the "Mormon way" of acquiring land. In a case filed in Smithfield on 10 May 1884, JS claimed that PN and NT had entered claims in the land office for "lands which we have claimed and occupied and cultivated for a number of years." The bishop decided that JS had not done enough work on the land to give him a priority of claim. The stake president for the Logan High Council reversed this decision, deciding that according to "common custom" JS had the best claim to the land. The high council, by a vote of seven to five, refused to sustain the decision, and the parties compromised. PN and NT gave JS ten acres free of expense and JS relinquished his legal claim (1884, Fd. 23).

Another interesting and difficult case occurred in 1885 in Clarkston Ward in the Cache Valley Stake (1885, Fd. 8). AG filed a preemption on a forty-acre tract, then hauled in materials to build a house. But he moved off before completing it. DB had built a house on an adjacent forty acres, and then filed a homestead claim on his own forty acres as well as on AG's forty acres, even though he knew AG had filed a preemption claim. The bishop decided in favor of DB because AG had abandoned the premises before perfecting his claim.

The ecclesiastical courts also heard cases involving other natural resources. In 1870 the Manti High Council granted JP and JR the "sole privilege of working coal" in a disputed mine they had discovered, opened up, and built a road to, against GB's claim that they had abandoned it for eight years and had thereby relinquished any claim (1870, Fd. 4). The church courts also considered exclusive claims to timber (1873, Fd. 6; 1878, Fd. 6).

Discrepancies between federal and Mormon surveys also generated land disputes. Orson Pratt and Henry G. Sherwood began the first survey in Salt Lake City on 31 July 1847. Known as plat A, it covered 114 blocks and was completed 20 August. Other surveys of outlying townsites were carried out between 1851 and 1854. The earliest federal surveys, however, were run in conjunction with the extension of federal land laws to Utah in 1869. Thus, each federal land grant not only was a potential trouble spot between the federal claimant and prior Mormon claimants but also raised potential conflicts with adjoining landowners who may have established their boundaries following the Mormon surveys.

By custom, the lines established by the Mormon survey were given priority in the church courts in every instance where the issue was raised. In one 1884 case in Smithfield, for example, TH appealed an unfavorable bishop's decision regarding boundaries to the Logan High Council. The parties disputed the validity of an 1875 government survey line in comparison with the Jessie Fox survey of 1868 that had been relied upon by Mormon settlers. The difference amounted to twenty-six acres. TH testified that "at the time he bought his claim he supposed that it would go to government lines. But on learning of the church regulation he was willing to be governed by the old lines, though it was to his disadvantage." TW in response "thought he had a right to the land by the rule of the church and according to law." The high council concluded "that all parties concerned in the entries of land before us today shall abide by the old lines."

This resolution was relatively simple. In Cache Valley, however, the conflict between old and new survey lines became so heated that the Cache Valley Stake Presidency had called a mass meeting and publicly announced that "the old lines would prevail over governmental survey lines." Apparently most members complied voluntarily, but TD filed a suit in federal district court to enforce his legal title to the land based on governmental survey lines. The high council court disfellowshipped TD "for failing to adhere to the old lines," but later he "retraced his steps, asked forgiveness of the brethren and was restored."

As a result, the Cache Valley High Council, with President Card presiding, on 23 March 1885 applied the then well-established rule that "in order for a man to retain his standing in this church he must respect the Local Claims" (1885, Fd. 1). The priority given to local lines, however, was not peculiar to Cache Valley. In a letter dated 20 June 1900 to A. M. Cannon, President of the Salt Lake Stake, the First Presidency affirmed the bishop's and the high council's decisions, despite public criticism against the church taking jurisdiction over land disputes, that the newer federal surveys established no legitimate claims against boundaries established by older lines "generally accepted." Any other disposition "would change every piece of land in the neighborhood" (1890, Fd. 1).

Although there is no indication that the church courts considered civil rules in deferring to the older survey lines, that position was not without legal support. The issue was litigated in 1887 before Alexander C. Pyper, Justice of the Peace, who decided that a claim based on old lines had acquired legal validity by adverse possession. On appeal, the United States District Court affirmed the decision (1887, Fd. 9).

In 1891, this new convergence of legal and Mormon rules was used in an interesting case before the Salt Lake High Council, where Salt Lake City attempted to widen a street in the Twentieth Ward and an old settler objected on the grounds that it would upset the boundary line established by Sherwood in the original 1847 survey. The city argued that the 1867 Fox survey was more accurate and official, a point upheld by Fox himself who testified that Sherwood had used a "common compass and chain" that he had dragged "over sage brush and other obstacles."

A high council speaker observed that the Sherwood survey established the earliest lines, regardless of its accuracy, and that old settlers were entitled to rely on it. He added that "in making their decisions they might take into consideration the civil law, and the actions of the civil courts if it seemed proper to do so." The civil case cited was *Odell v. Rose*, heard just that spring before T. J. Anderson of the Third Judicial District Court, 2 May 1891, wherein the judge instructed the jury "that the exterior boundaries of a lot or block are to be determined when wanting, by ascertaining where the lines and corners were originally established, when it was first surveyed, if that can be done." The high council court reviewed the customary rule versus the legal rule and decided that the city could not widen the street to correspond to the "correct" survey line when it conflicted with the earlier survey line (1891, Fd. 20).

Church courts always encouraged informal compromise and rendered decisions only as a last resort. For example, the Salt Lake High Council heard a case on 29 July 1864 between brothers who had divided property between themselves. LP owned a corral on EP's property and a dispute arose over the right of way. The high council suggested a compromise: the ward teachers would help move the corral to LP's property, and he would sell the right-of-way property to EP for $50. The brothers accepted this cooperative resolution, which kept peace in the family as well as the neighborhood (1864, Fd. 15).

In another case, GG had purchased some land from JB's polyga-mous wife fourteen years earlier while JB was on a mission, but JB felt she had been cheated and refused to deliver the deed. Brigham Young, who was present for the hearing, urged the parties to com-promise rather than let such a minor matter cause hostility between brethren. GG responded by offering an additional $500 for the land, JB accepted, and they left reconciled to one another (1869, Fd. 1).

If one party was willing to compromise but the other was not, the courts were likely to decide against the stubborn one. For example, AS filed an appeal against JD to the Weber High Council on 16 November 1878. AS had previously filed a claim on railroad land on which he had built a house, but when the land came up for sale, he did not buy it. JD did—from the railroad—but would not pay AS for his improvements. The bishop had decided that each party was to select an arbitrator to value the house "according to the present existing circumstances and not by what it may have cost when it was built." JD was willing to pay AS the arbitrated value of the house but AS refused the settlement; he appealed the proposed resolution to the Weber High Council. AS complained to the high council: "Now I am poor, and have no place to set my foot. I want you to give me instructions how I am to get a piece of land, if this land is taken from me." Since JD was younger, a high councilor asked him if he would let AS buy part of the land so he wouldn't have to move. JD responded: "I will give [AS] five acres of the land to occupy as long as he lives provided that he will it me when he dies. If he is not satisfied with that, I am willing to turn the whole thing over to him, if he will pay me $125 and complete the balance of the payments on it."

AS refused. He wanted JD to deed him the five acres without any limitations attached. JD then offered AS a different five acres and vol-unteered to help him move the house. AS again refused. President David Peery decided: "My desire was to have this matter compro-mised. Brother [JD] has made a good proposition. I do not think that I would make any fairer. But as Brother [AS] will not accept that propo-sition, and the case is submitted to us, my decision is that we confirm the decision of the Bishop's Court." President Peery's decision, requir-ing JD to pay AS the arbitrated amount for the value of the house, was unanimously sustained (1879–80, Fd. 3).

In a property case in the Twenty-first Ward in Salt Lake City, the bishop decided that AG had been deceived about the boundaries of land he had purchased from a third party. EB, the adjoining land-owner, argued that his deed covered some of the same property. The bishop encouraged EB, the true owner, to compromise. EB offered to sell the disputed parcel to AG for $150 or purchase AG's adjoining property for $150. AG refused both offers, and the bishops decided that EB owned the disputed land free and clear (1887, Fd. 2).

These cases, however unconventional from a legal perspective, illustrate the emphasis on compromise. The courts were mindful that these disputes were between neighbors, so they deliberately downplayed adversarial relations and insisted that members treat each other fairly and respectfully. The decisions surely did not always remove the conflict, but the records indicate that most courts had reconciliation as their ultimate purpose.

An excellent example of compelled "concern" appears in a land case the Sevier High Council heard 5 March 1894 (1893–94, Fd. 1). PQ had cultivated a two-acre parcel for fifteen years and had acquired water rights for it but didn't have enough money to obtain legal title. A neighbor, JW, subsequently obtained legal title to eighty acres, including PQ's plot, and ordered him to leave. PQ offered him $50 for the land, but JW refused, countering with an offer of $75 for the water rights. The bishop on 2 February 1893 decided JW ought to pay PQ $125 for the water rights or accept PQ's offer of $50 for the disputed two acres. JW appealed. After the high council had heard both sides, George W. Bean, who was presiding as first counselor in the stake presidency, stated that he was "sorry to see [JW] a man of his age, to take such decided stand and be so narrowed up selfish to take the little all there is from his brother because he has a legal right." The high council affirmed the bishop's decision that JW had to accept PQ's offer of $50 for the land or pay $125 to PQ for the water rights.

In another interesting case, JJ came to Bishop Kesler of the Salt Lake Sixteenth Ward on 8 February 1889 complaining that a group of neighbors had conspired to keep a certain piece of property out of his hands even though he was the rightful owner (1888, Fd. 13). The dispute arose initially over a will contest. Certain property passed to CJ by will when her husband died. Her son, JJ, claimed that he had been inadvertently left out of the will. Rather than fight a will contest, CJ agreed to deed the disputed property to JJ if he did not contest the will in the probate court. But CJ later refused to deed the land to JJ as previously promised. Bishop Kesler ordered CJ to deed over the land to JJ, and JJ to take care of CJ if she ever suffered "for the necessaries of life." The Salt Lake High Council affirmed and disfellowshipped CJ for refusing to comply. The decision was also affirmed on appeal to the Quorum of the Apostles. Instead of complying with priesthood directives, CJ transferred the property to a dummy third party who in turn sold it to WT. WT, who owned property adjoining the disputed parcel, wanted to keep the land from falling into JJ's hands because JJ planned to cut down the trees on the property once he took possession. WT had threatened JJ to be "Porter Rockwell to him and follow him to the ends of the earth" if he brought a Church action against him on the disputed land. WT initially denied his complicity with CJ, but the bishop stated that "the spirit of the Lord had born witness to us" that WT was lying, and the defendants admitted their unbrotherly conduct. WT was ordered to execute a warranty deed in JJ's favor within thirty days (1889, Fd. 2).

This regard for brotherly feelings was quite clearly intended to promote community harmony. In one 1870 case, heard before the Salt Lake High Council, ET was chastised for refusing JW access to his pond for fishing: "I wish to say to Brother [ET] that if he allowed those feeling to exist, that canker worm to gnaw into his breast it will eventually carry him out of the church and to hell, therefore I would say to [ET] to strangle it right here and not let it live another moment." He was also chastised for being willing to sell his land "to anyone that came along Mormon, Jew, or Gentile, Enemy or friend if he could not have it as he wanted. I am sorry he manifests such a spirit" (1882, Fd. 6).

As these land cases show, legal considerations were less important than the perceived fairness of a situation. In an 1864 case the Salt Lake High Council interpreted a lease that provided that rent was to be paid from a percentage of the sales of a match-splitting factory. When a key piece of machinery proved defective, the tenant used the building for another business but refused to hand over to the lessor the agreed-upon percentage of his earnings. The high council decided that the defect voided the rent clause but that "a reasonable rent" was just. It ordered the tenant to pay $40 a month for the time he had occupied the building and to be out within three months (1854, Fd. 10).

In another case, the Sevier High Council decided that FG had taken unfair advantage of the mother and child who owned the property legally but were not thought "fully competent to attend their business." The high council ordered FG to pay them the fair market value of the land (1882, Fd. 6). Similarly, another bishop voided a land transaction as being "one-sided" because the seller had not really understood the transaction (1889, Fd. 10).

Another group of cases, however, suggested that members should be held responsible for their freely accepted obligations. In one case the plaintiff, RP, had given a lot between Main Street and West Temple and First and Second South to a destitute friend with permission to use an alley from Main Street for access to the lot. The friend later sold the lot, including the right-of-way claim as well, which was specified in the deed. Now RP wanted to refuse further use of the alley to the subsequent purchaser. Speakers on the Salt Lake High Council assigned to speak for the defendant pointed out that RP had made a bona fide grant to his friend, AM, and that WJ (the subsequent purchaser) certainly had a right to rely on the legal title he had acquired in the purchase, which included the right-of-way. The speakers for RP agreed that WJ should be able to rely on the legal description given of the subject property, even in situations where the seller had received the property as a gift. RP was held bound to his grant to AM even though AM had abused RP's generosity (1878, Fd. 10).

In an 1892 case, LS complained that JS had misrepresented a piece of farmland LS had purchased from JS. The Sevier High Council reviewed the facts and stated that since LS, an experienced farmer, had "passed upon the land himself," he should have been able to evaluate it. Nevertheless, to avoid hard feelings, JS agreed to take the land back for the amount of purchase (1892, Fd. 17).

Since the colonization pattern involved bishops and stake presidents in land distribution, it was important that the courts provide a forum for redress against the abuses of ecclesiastical officers. In Cache County in 1872, some members filed an action against a local bishop for misappropriating funds in connection with land distribution. Brigham Young personally investigated the charges with two apostles, but the file does not contain the outcome (1872, Fd. 13). The fact that members looked to the church courts for satisfaction against local officials who had misused the public trust, nonetheless demonstrates the respect afforded these courts in Mormon communities.

The next year in Bishop Hunter's court in Salt Lake City, PL complained that DB, a bishop in another ward, had torn down his fence and had built the Big Cottonwood Cooperative Society Store on PL's property without his consent. Bishop Hunter roundly condemned "the disgraceful conduct of each, in giving way to the devilish spirit of fighting and abusing one another." He disfellowshipped both parties and directed that DB's ward "be governed henceforth by the Councilors until further action by President Brigham Young." After the bishop's decision was sustained by the Salt Lake High Council, DB appealed to the First Presidency. Brigham Young and Daniel H. Wells sustained the bishop and high council's decision stating that PL "has rights and they should be held sacred, and no one should infringe upon them one hairs breadth" (1873, Fd. 1).

THE END OF EXCLUSIVE JURISDICTION

Mark P. Leone concluded in his study of Mormon ecclesiastical courts in Arizona that their "real florescence occurred in the Utah period of the church and ceased when the United States set up fully operative civil courts in all Western territories by the turn of the century" (1979, 118). The federal court system was fully operational in Utah by 1852; yet, as we have demonstrated, the church courts routinely heard land cases through the 1890s. The use of federal courts for dispute resolution was disapproved throughout this period. For instance, in 1864 TH protested to the Salt Lake High Council that his brother FH had attempted by "the quibbles of law" to deprive him of five acres that TH held under local custom. The high council agreed and ruled that "the expenses of the Court according to the rule of this Council must be paid by [FH] seeing that he plainted the suit" (1864, Fd. 13).

In an 1879 suit, a widow and her daughter complained to the Salt Lake High Council that JM was trying to take the land "by means forbidden in the church and dragging us in common with our company into the district court." They also charged AA's Mormon attorney, John B. Milner, for "being defiant of all [Church] instruction and prosecuting us willfully, maliciously and unnecessarily" (1879, Fd. 6). The file is incomplete on the outcome.

The conflict between church courts and civil courts over land dispute jurisdiction was not one-sided. The federal courts also had an interest in reducing the power of the ecclesiastical courts over property claims. Opposition became increasingly vocal during the 1880s and 1890s as federal pressure on the church intensified in other ways. In 1886, for example, an attorney, S. W. Darke, questioned the legality of a church court decision in a land controversy between WP and WD. WP had filed a complaint against WD in a federal district court but had withdrawn it when WD brought charges before the Wasatch High Council that WP was suing him at law. Darke, who was representing WP's co-complainant against WD, advised WP by letter that the high council could not settle the case because "the settlement of differences of this nature by arbitration is prohibited by the Territorial Law Section 1135 page 355 of the Laws passed in 1884—as follows: 'Persons capable of contracting may submit to arbitration any controversy which might be the subject of a civil action between them, except a question of title to real property in fee or for life'" (1886, Fd. 13). Unfortunately, the file is incomplete, and it is not known whether WD was convinced by the legal citation.

The federal courts had the whole range of legal sanctions to enforce compliance. The church had only the right to withhold fellowship from someone it deemed behaving inappropriately as a Latter-day Saint. As a result, the inherent conflict between the two systems and the differing degrees to which they could enforce their decrees led to some interesting inconsistencies between public statements and actual practice.

In Salt Lake City's Fifteenth Ward, EC brought a complaint against WJ. EC had farmed a certain forty-acre plot for thirty years when WJ filed an 1877 claim under the Desert Land Act to land that included EC's forty acres. EC had filed a protest in the land office, but in 1884, WJ had obtained title. When personal attempts to settle the matter failed, EC came to the bishop's court.

During those proceedings, WJ tried to introduce the patent; but the bishop would not consider it because "they were not trying the law but the equity of the case." The bishop ordered WJ to deed EC the forty acres and ordered EC to pay WJ the proportional cost of filing of $1.25 an acre plus $1.75 an acre that WJ had incurred in proving title against other claimants.

Although both parties complied, WJ appealed to the stake high council six years later in 1896. He presented a *Deseret News* editorial dated 25 January 1896 that differentiated between land controversies and other disputes with regard to the propriety of church court intervention:

> In cases of title to lands, water and others of like character, the Church courts would not consider them if requested to do so, as the Church discipline is such that it will not attempt the adjustment of any controversy where there might be a possibility of conflict with the laws of the land. The Church courts are virtually tribunals of friendly arbitration, and no more. In civil cases such as proceedings for debt, disputed account etc., outside of the exceptions noted, members of the Church are expected to have recourse to the Church arbiters or courts, so that the dispute may be settled in the amicable feeling that should exist between brethren, and without expense to either party, before proceeding to litigation which is always attended with ill feelings and an outlay of money.

Both the high council and the First Presidency, which rendered decisions on appeal on 20 June 1900, disregarded this editorial point of view and sustained the bishop's decision (1890, Fd. 1). Here a clear disparity existed between public pronouncement and actual practice.

The same editorial was cited in a similar case brought in Manassa Ward Colorado in 1900. SS had acquired a patent of the disputed land and sought to exclude LC, a prior occupant, from any ownership interest. When LC availed himself of the Mormon rule giving priority to earlier occupants, SS quoted this editorial as representing the church's policy that "we should not be a law unto ourselves but governed by the laws of the commonwealth." The high council, however, simply returned to its old rule of equity. Although SS had legal title, "we are not dealing with the laws of the land but the laws of the church." The bishop's decision, which was affirmed on appeal, was that SS was to grant LC legal title to the land he had previously occupied, with LC responsible to pay SS the money he had expended in acquiring the property.

A string of cases up through 1901 not only shows that the church courts were hearing land cases, but that they vigorously defended their right to do so when members complained that land should be considered only in the civil courts (1880, Fd. 7; 1896, Fds. 2, 4; 1898, Fds. 3, 10, 11; 1900, Fd. 9; 1901, Fd. 1; Stirling 1886–87, 47, 96, 112; 1894, Fd. 7; 1899, Fd. 10).

Although the historical end of the church's claims to exclusive jurisdiction in land disputes lies beyond the limits of this study, it is clear that church courts, as long as they decided land disputes, applied a distinctively Mormon approach to landownership issues. Beneficial use, prior occupancy, and community harmony, not legal rights, were the guiding principles. In addition to modifying the substantive rules on land distribution, church courts encouraged compromise, made settlements on the basis of equity, emphasized collective concerns over private interests, and reminded members that Zion had a higher law than the surrounding society. Although nonmembers and dissidents resisted the exclusive jurisdiction of church courts, the church's actual withdrawal from those cases came long after federal courts were in place. Church courts finally stepped back from land disputes as part of the church's redefinition of Zion.

12

Mormon Water Law and
Dispute Resolution

The distinctive water law system Mormon settlers fashioned when they arrived in the Great Basin was the product of climatic, economic, social, and religious factors.

The religious convictions of the Mormons helped them accept this new system and motivated them to seek resolution of disputes in the ecclesiastical courts. Although the church-enunciated doctrine of water rights was applied to non-Mormons through duly enacted legislation, members relied almost completely on the ecclesiastical courts to resolve water disputes with other members.

The common-law doctrine of riparian rights treated water law as incidental to the law of real property. Proprietors of land adjoining streams had the "natural" right to use water in its natural flow, subject only to the correlative right of other riparians to coequal use. This right required no affirmative action by the property owner to legitimize use.[1]

But the Southwest lacked the abundant rainfall, extensive rivers, and numerous streams of the East. Instead, the limited spring runoff of canyon rivers and streams had to be captured in reservoirs and transported many miles to its final destination. Miners in California and Colorado therefore rejected the doctrine of riparian rights and substituted a customary rule of prior appropriation.[2] State supreme courts in New Mexico and Arizona also upheld the doctrine of prior appropriation, apparently influenced by earlier Spanish and Indian settlements.[3] These systems of appropriation developed along lines similar to Mormon water law but borrowed their forms from customary practices. In contrast, Mormon water law was part of a broader social effort, its extensive irrigation projects requiring more cooperation than other frontier communities. Various Mormons have claimed with some pride that the "Mormons were the first among the Anglo-Saxon peoples to practice the art of irrigation on an extensive scale"

(Hunter, 165). Hunter concludes that "in the utilization of the limited supply of water found in the Great Basin, Brigham Young and his co-religionists developed a definite water policy which was distinctly Mormon."

Irrigation was one of the first acts of the vanguard company that arrived in the Salt Lake valley 23 July 1847. Orson Pratt recorded in his journal that day "in about two hours after our arrival we began to plow, and the same afternoon built a dam to irrigate the soil; which at the spot where we were plowing was exceedingly dry." Brigham Young appointed Edson Whipple as watermaster or "ditch-rider" to "attend to the distribution of water over the plowed land," and the Mormon irrigation system was born (Arrington, Fox, and May 1976, 49).

Soon after the Saints entered the Salt Lake Valley, Brigham Young announced three basic principles that were to control Mormon water law. First the principle of public ownership of natural resources: "There shall be no private ownership of the streams that come out of the canyons, nor the timber that grows on the hills. These belong to the people; all the people" (CHC 3:269). With 20,000 Mormons en route and the anticipation that thousands would follow, it was obvious that a first-come, first-served policy would seriously jeopardize a co-operative community effort. By ignoring riparian landowner entitlements, the church was able to control the distribution of a limited water supply and increase the habitability of land that did not abut rivers and streams. If settlers miles away from the water source could obtain water for domestic and agricultural purposes by public grant, then entire valleys could be settled rather than just the river banks. This policy, therefore, was an important alternative to the common-law principle of riparian rights.

The second principle of Mormon water law involved priesthood-directed entitlement rules. Initially equal distribution was applied. Soon priesthood rules of priority and beneficial use emerged. Priority provided a standard for mediating between claims of equivalent beneficial use, while beneficial use limited water claims to those based on need and use rather than property rights. These principles provided a standard for evaluating public applications and mediating conflicts. They also prevented monopoly control, speculation, and hoarding of water supplies.

The third principle of Mormon water law, cooperative irrigation, was followed by communities throughout the Great Basin. Early high councils directed the construction of canals and ditches to carry water from canyon rivers and streams to the various wards in the valleys.

The bishops then directed the division of these ditches to each block in their wards, and ultimately to each user. The users were responsible for maintaining part of the ditch, depending on the acreage held and the intended use. A watermaster, originally the bishop but later a full-time officer, regulated the use and maintenance of the local irrigation system. Eventually the irrigation cooperatives were organized into self-contained companies and then nonprofit corporations. In this way, independent farmer control replaced church control of these cooperative enterprises. Ultimately all of these irrigation companies "were built by the farmers, owned by the farmers, and operated by the farmers. In fact they constitute one of the greatest and most successful community or cooperative undertakings in the history of America" (Arrington, 53).

The Mormon view of water as a public resource appears in a statute passed by the first territorial legislature in 1852:

> The county court shall have control of all timber, water privileges, or any water course or creek, to grant mill sites, and exercise such powers as in their judgments shall best preserve the timber and subserve the interest of the settlement in the distribution of water for irrigation or other purposes. Grants of rights held under legislative authority shall not be interfered with. (1852, Utah Laws, § 38)

One scholar observes that by establishing the public ownership of such natural resources as "the streams and canyons, as in the land, and requiring the permission of the Council [later the county court] for the erection of mills, the laying out and fencing of land, and the cutting of wood in the canyons and creek bottoms, the Mormons made a substantial contribution to the legal theory of the West" (Morgan 1940, 73).

CHURCH COURT JURISDICTION

The exclusive jurisdiction rule prevailed in water law as in other areas. For example, in an 1869 case PM was chastised for proceeding to the secular court instead of taking the case to the priesthood when a conflict arose as to the validity of an exclusive fishery grant on the Utah Lake. The Salt Lake High Council required PM to withdraw the civil action, pay all the defendent's costs, and refile before the church courts (1869, Fd. 3). In an 1872 case, AC and GW complained that IH and JB had sued them "before Judge Clinton" in regard to rights to certain "water from the west canal over Jordan River, which belongs to us by right of early survey and grant by City Council" (1872, Fd. 6). The file is incomplete on the disposition of the matter.

The Salt Lake High Council insisted on exclusive jurisdiction in several actions filed in the 1880s. One dispute continued for almost a decade. The Summit High Council had allocated water one-third to WA and two-thirds to NP. NP later moved into Salt Lake Stake, possibly "to avoid the decision being enforced as we believe." When WA tried to exercise his water rights, NP sued him before the Third District Court. In response WA preferred charges against NP "for unchristian-like conduct in suing me before the Third District Court of Utah." The high council ordered NP "to withdraw the suit and if [WA] had damaged him proceed against him by church law." The council also ordered NP to pay WA $50 for the costs WA had incurred defending the civil suit (1884, Fd. 14[27]). In 1884, the Salt Lake High Council heard a case brought by thirteen complainants, including a nonmember who agreed to abide the church court's rule. They stated that "they do not approve the course pursued by [defendants] as members of the church, in bringing suit against them unjustly and forcing them to defend their rights to water in the courts and putting them to unnecessary trouble and costs . . . they ask that they be required to desist from further prosecuting and make restitution." The high council agreed and ordered the defendants to pay $130 as "the expense which they had put the plaintiffs to in the case before the Third District Court" (1884, Fd. 19).

PUBLIC WATER RESOURCES

The public granting of water rights usually meant that local church officers controlled water privileges. Men who received water privileges were often called upon to construct "public" works such as mills and canals. Brigham Young, for example, was granted "the privilege and control" of City Creek and Canyon for the nominal sum of $500, by the General Assembly of the State of Deseret in December 1850; previously, in 1847, he had been granted the privilege of building a mill on city creek by the Salt Lake High Council (Morgan 1940, 106). On the same day, the assembly granted Apostle E. T. Benson "waters in Tooele County for mills and irrigating purposes," leaving him, as Morgan has observed, "in rather complete control of the economic resources of that county" (Morgan, 106). To outsiders these extensive grants to church leaders established abusive control over public resources.

Church leaders answered the criticisms by explaining that many of these investments required substantial capital only men of means could provide. The grants also legitimized the customary practice of priesthood leaders controlling the distribution of resources in the community. Thus, Brigham Young in Salt Lake and Apostle Benson in Tooele oversaw the orderly distribution of water resources.

Often the grants served as public subsidies or incentives to public works. The Salt Lake High Council heard a dispute on 30 December 1869 that illustrates the relation between the private development of public works and community benefit. The Davis County Court had granted JW rights to use stream water to operate a mill. He spent $1,419 to bring streams together and went to the high council, seeking partial reimbursement from downstream water users who benefited from the increased water flow; he also sought a right-of-way to the mill over their land.

The high council decided that "it would be just" to allow JW the road if he paid the property owners a proportion of the cost of their land patents. It ordered "all parties using the water brought together by the labor of [JW], to pay one half of the cost of bringing those streams together to [JW]. To the end that the said water shall be free to the people of the settlement for the developing of every mechanical interest which shall advance the growth of the same." This result, which seemingly favored JW, contributed to water development for the entire community (1869, Fds. 9, 10).

The church courts also instructed public bodies on the propriety of certain grants. Thus, the Cache Valley High Council in 1876 acknowledged that a "Charter granted to the City of Smithfield by the Territorial Legislature confers upon the City Council the control of the water and water courses leading to the city. Provided that such control shall not be exercised to the injury of any right already acquired by actual settlers thereon." However, Smithfield had granted water rights that threatened injury to TM's grist mill. Accordingly, the council ordered that

> the City Council of the City of Smithfield shall grant at their next regular meeting to [TM] a water privilege sufficient to run his grist mill. Said water to be brought through a newly contemplated head race which shall within ten days from the date hereof be surveyed and permanently located by a competent engineer . . . and until this shall be fully accomplished he shall continue to hold control of his present water course, but thereafter, as a water course, he shall have no claim thereto, unless in the construction of the contemplated race it may be found necessary to use a part of the location occupied by the present race. (1876, Fd. 4)

BENEFICIAL USE

The limiting principles of priority and beneficial use determined the initial water use grants and provided the rationale for ecclesiastical decisions in water disputes. Thus in 1868 the Salt Lake High Council held that Tooele retained jurisdiction of certain surplus waters not beneficially used by a bishop who previously had been granted the water rights to benefit the community (1868–69, Fd. 1).

In an 1897 case a bishop's court specifically recognized that "L & G did acquire a water right by making use of unappropriated water and such water is theirs by virtue of its use" (1897, Fd. 5). This case implies almost a common-law theory of entitlement based on use, representing yet another decisional standard relied on in the church courts. It is consistent with common-law development in western states generally, and the doctrine of appropriation that developed in the West as an alternative to riparian rights. The Utah Supreme Court, for example, in *Monroe v. Ivie* had decided in 1880 that the free appropriation of water on the basis of beneficial use was open to all (Utah 2:535, 1880).

COOPERATIVE IRRIGATION

The success of the Mormon cooperative irrigation systems depended on the cohesiveness of the religious communities. As Arrington, Fox, and May summarize:

> the Mormon failure to make distinctions between secular and religious affairs encouraged a degree of cooperation not readily obtained in communities where a common religious commitment was less pronounced. Mormon leaders often made a secular pursuit, such as the settling of a new area, a religious obligation. Many Mormons cheerfully obeyed the advice of church leaders even when it was clearly not in their own material interests to do so. Given this tendency to see compliance with the advice of church authorities as a moral obligation, whether the advice touched upon religious or secular concerns it is not surprising that the frequency and intensity of disputes over water were kept at a relatively low level. (1976, 56)

When irrigation conflicts arose, church courts encouraged the parties to compromise their claims. One 1869 case heard by the Salt Lake High Council raised an issue of the respective responsibility of mill owners and farmers to repair irrigation ditches used to bring water from the canyons. Brigham Young, present for the hearing, decided "that those who use the water and have the advantage of it shall pay for keeping the ditch in repair, mill machines and people in proportion to the use thereof and that the water master shall see this decision is carried into effect and also that the former expenses that have been incurred on the ditch be settled according to this decision" (1869, Fd. 3)

The Juab High Council in 1881 also heard a dispute between old and new settlers. The early settlers of Levan claimed priority on the basis of their earlier efforts and continued use. Later settlers worked the canyon to increase the water flow, helped to repair the existing system, and paid the water master for their turn. As a result they argued that they were entitled to a proportional share of the water. The bishop appointed a special committee to effect a compromise. When compromise proved impossible, the high council chastised the parties, and ordered that the older settlers be given 75 acres of thin (divided) water rights, rather than the 150 acres they claimed. The parties appealed the decision to the First Presidency and John Taylor affirmed the high council decision (1881, Fd. 14). In another case filed in 1885, parties who were in dispute over the use of water "originally given by the priesthood" were gently rebuked by the stake president, who in compromising the dispute stated he "was very sorry to hear the feeling between the brothers, it was Laman and Lemuel again" (1885–87, Fd. 1).

Water companies had their own internal methods for handling disputes, but occasionally their decisions had to be confirmed by ecclesiastical authority. When JQ refused to abide the decision of the Logan Cow Pasture Company, it filed a complaint in the bishop's court on 18 June 1891. The bishop decided that JQ, a member of his ward, must "comply with the decision of the Board of the above said company and that he make a public confession of what he has done, also that he use the water no more until this case is settled." The high council sustained the decision by a 7 to 5 vote but rebuked the bishop, also a director of the water company, "for some hard words used in his court" (1881, Fd. 17).

These mild urgings toward compromise were backed up with authority. The bishop of Granite Ward in Salt Lake City in 1885, for example, heard a dispute between brothers who had purchased land and water shares together in the Brown and Sanford ditch. AG claimed a right to all the water shares transferred with the land since the ditch was on his divided portion, but the bishop decided that he should deed half of the water to his brother. When AG refused, the bishop disfellowshipped him (1886, Fd. 6). In another proceeding, JR, on behalf of the East Jordan Canal Company on March 1, 1889, filed a claim against NN for "interfering with the gates on the East Jordan Canal, and taking more water than belongs to him." When asked to confess and repent, NN refused and was disfellowshipped (1889, Fd. 3).

In an 1890 case, the Weber High Council enforced a water tax on the Wilson Irrigation Company. It quoted the compiled laws of Utah that made the improper appropriation of water a misdemeanor and required owners to pay or work for their percentage of expenses in keeping and constructing the irrigation canal (1892, Fd. 3). The church courts heard varied types of disputes, ranging from damaged water ditches to loss of entitlement from disuse (1875, Fd. 7; 1898, Fd. 10; 1848, Fd. 6; 1881, Fd. 14).

The importance of the ecclesiastical court system cannot be overemphasized. Through these courts, a policy of public control over water resources was substituted for the common-law doctrine of riparian rights. The Mormons applied an innovative doctrine of beneficial use and assisted cooperative irrigation companies in working for the more efficient and equitable distribution of limited water resources. The church courts enforced each of these policy objectives for many years, despite the availability of alternative civil forums.

13

Domestic Conflict and
Church Courts

Mormon theology teaches that marriages and families are potentially eternal relationships and that a man and a woman cannot achieve an exalted state without each other. The principle of polygamy, however, introduced a potential source of conflict that increased the likelihood of domestic disputes. It is not surprising that Mormons preferred to resolve domestic disputes, polygamous or otherwise, before ecclesiastical rather than civil courts. This emphasis was consistent with their efforts at self-sufficiency, safeguarded their felt need for privacy, and in troubled relationships promoted reconciliation over divorce. Theologically, a marriage sealed by priesthood authority could not be dissolved by civil means. Practically, since civil courts refused to recognize polygamy, church courts were the only forum available to polygamous spouses or their children. For all of these reasons, church courts played an important role in resolving domestic conflicts in nineteenth-century Mormon communities. That function still survives in the bishop's pastoral role as counselor to troubled couples and the First Presidency's role in canceling temple sealings.

Brigham Young initially heard all marriage disputes. For example, when a husband was brought before the Municipal High Council in Winter Quarters on 7 September 1847 for "putting away his wife," the council deferred to the authority of Brigham Young and Heber C. Kimball. They stayed the proceedings until Young and Kimball returned from the West (1847, Fd. 1). When the church courts were set up in the Great Basin, bishops or high councils heard the divorce cases and sent recommended decisions to Brigham Young for his approval. A $10 fee for divorce was the only fee regularly charged in the church courts. The husband generally paid the fee directly to the President. It is not clear whether the fee was instituted as a deterrent to filing for divorce, as an indicator of seriousness, or simply as a means for paying the prophet for an inordinate amount of time divorce filings required of him. As formality developed during the succeeding years, the courts made out divorce bills in triplicate; the parties each received a copy and Brigham Young retained the original.

Young soon realized that he could not reconcile every family dispute and began relying on the existing church court system for assistance. He personally sent a divorce case to the Salt Lake High Council in 1852, explaining: "My object in bringing it here is to get rid of such cases, as I am continually annoyed with such business, and to have a decision that will remain." The council heard the evidence, recommended a divorce, and forwarded a suggested property settlement to Brigham Young for final approval (1852, Fd. 10).

Priesthood leaders stressed reconciliation as the ideal solution to domestic disputes. In 1854, President Young assigned a divorce petition to Apostle Orson Hyde, who reconciled the parties, admonishing each "to make it work" (1854, Fd. 5). When President Young received an 1857 request for divorce from a plural wife, he referred the case back to her bishop for his recommendation. The bishop had the teachers investigate the matter, and they determined that the problem was hostility between the wives. Since the husband opposed the divorce and there were no grounds, the bishop recommended that the divorce be denied and the plural wife humble herself in the plural family relationship (1857, Fd. 1).

For the Saints, preserving marital harmony was a community, as well as a personal, goal. One bishop, for example, assigned teachers in a case to visit a polygamous wife who wanted a divorce. Their instructions were to make her "acknowledge her abusive nature" and "to honor and respect her husband" (1866, Fed. 11). In another case involving conflict within a polygamous marriage, the husband, BH, asked a bishop's court to persuade HH, his first wife, to let another wife and her children live in part of their house. After unsuccessful efforts by the teachers and the bishops, the parties presented their grievances to the Salt Lake High Council. President Wallace expressed sorrow that husband and wives could not be voluntarily reconciled: "These cases that come before the authorities of the Church, are the most difficult ones, and whenever a person comes to me with family difficulties, I advise them to settle them themselves, and thus keep them from the council as much as possible." After hearing the testimony of the parties, one speaker admonished the uncooperating wife, HH, to "humble herself before God and her brethren and undo the evil she has done as much as possible, and not do so anymore, but seek to do good, be a wife in every deed unto her husband, failing this I can see no other way of their being reconciled." The President decided that HH should "accept the terms [BH] has to offer, take the house he offers, make it clean as possible, do all she can to make her husband happy and comfortable, and [BH] shall treat her kindly, provide for her and be to her a husband" (1870, Fd. 16[4]).

While these particular cases were decided in accordance with the wishes of the husband, the cases are not always one-sided. Women filing for divorce were much more likely than men to have the petition granted. Brigham Young, for example, in an 1852 case condemned a husband for abusing and defaming his wife: "I treat my wives' feelings with reverence and they honor and obey me in return. If this people knew the Lord's feelings . . . I tell you they would be willing to cover each other's faults" (1852, Fd. 7). In another case, the combined authority of the Council of Seventy, the Twelve, and the First Presidency united on behalf of a runaway but repentant wife to compel the unforgiving husband to take her back and forgive her for any past acts (1868, Fd. 2).

The courts often compelled husbands to provide adequate economic support. When a plural wife in 1853 complained to Salt Lake High Council that her husband had driven her from the home, the council told her to "go back and so long as she acted as a wife, he must take care of her" (1853, Fd. 6). To the same effect, Brigham Young in an 1864 case assigned two bishops to judge a plural wife's claim that her husband had deserted her and her children. MA admitted he had abandoned them because he could not support his entire family. Both bishops criticized him for not asking his bishop for assistance. One bishop concluded "that no man is justified in deserting his family under any circumstances," since church resources were available to maintain families intact.

In another desertion case filed by a plural wife, HC, before the Weber High Council in 1878, the stake presidency met with the parties and helped them to arrive at an amicable adjustment of their grievances. The husband later stated the agreement before the high council: "We would drop the past, and let it go for what it was worth. She wanted a house built on the farm. I left it to the President and his councillors, and was willing to do what they said about it. They came to the conclusion that I should build her a house of four rooms on the farm, and make her as comfortable as I could. I am willing to carry this out, as well as possible" (1878, Fd. 2).

Similarly, in a "support" dispute filed before a high council in 1891—seven months after the Manifesto—the parties received counsel, "asked each other for forgiveness and each forgave the other and both thanked the Council for its patience and counsel" (1891, Fd. 9).

Efforts to achieve reconciliation were not always successful. In 1856, Brigham Young approved a divorce the bishop recommended "on the ground that [JL] don't know enough to keep a wife—too big a fool. He is not fit to have a wife—for three years I caution all the girls against him. He had no just cause to put away his wife" (1856, Fd. 3). Moreover, in at least two cases where the parties were initially reconciled they ultimately returned for divorces (1885–86, Fd. 1; 1851, Fd. 9). Anthropologist and scholar of the church courts Paul Dredge argues that "unless there was constant physical abuse or complete abandonment, the thought of divorce or separation did not even enter the minds of most Mormons of the nineteenth century" (1979, 19–32). Although the cases belie this conclusion, the Saints surely felt obliged to make their marriages work, an obligation reinforced by the church courts.

DIVORCE IN CHURCH COURTS

The emphasis placed on reconciliation, however, did not preclude divorce, and polygamy increased its likelihood. Though for Mormons divorce had grave consequences, if the couple insisted, the brethren did not stand in the way; the courts usually granted a divorce when the parties insisted.

Early divorce legislation in Utah Territory was more liberal than most domestic law of the period. "The Act in Relation to Bills of Divorce," 1851, allowed divorce if "the parties cannot live in peace and union together, and that their welfare requires a separation." The 1851 legislature, which was dominated by priesthood leaders, recognized the real possibility of family conflict under polygamy, but probably anticipated that most divorce decisions for members would be handled by the church courts. A liberal statute provided the means for a simple confirmation of a previous church court action if legal action subsequently became necessary. Furthermore, they probably believed that an unsuccessful marriage would not be patched up by strict divorce laws. Church courts sought to resolve the underlying causes of the marital disharmony rather than assume that formal rules of law could avoid the problem entirely.

Expediency required that members look to the civil courts and the liberal divorce statutes to legitimize divorces to nonmembers (or to confirm church divorces to avoid subsequent polygamy prosecution), but the church regularly enforced the "exclusive jurisdiction" rule in other domestic cases. Leonard Arrington's biography of Brigham Young, benefiting from research of "literally thousands of letters" on domestic disputes, concludes that, although not an advocate of divorce, Brigham was nevertheless fairly liberal in granting it, especially in cases of plural marriages (Arrington 1985, 318). Arrington suggests that Brigham personally decided divorce cases during the early years, but beginning in 1870 he "referred people to the probate courts" (Arrington 1985, 320). This is only partially true. The probate courts served important, but only limited functions for the Saints. Church courts continued to hear divorce cases well after 1870. For example, in 1877 the Salt Lake High Council condemned a husband, JL, for filing a divorce petition in a civil court. Noting that "there was a way to dissolve the marriage without going to the gentile law," the council ordered JL to withdraw his complaint from the Third Judicial Court, accept the high council's decree as final, and have the probate court affirm the church court's decision so as to make it legal (1877, Fd. 6). Other church courts disfellowshipped at least three men for refusing to withdraw civil divorce suits (1875, Disfellowship Files, Fd. 2; 1885, Fd. 18; 1887, Fd. 16).

Church leaders allowed—even advised—divorce for adultery, even if the parties later reconciled. A bishop in one case recommended a wife's divorce petition be granted when she established that her husband had had sexual relations with a woman while he was serving on a mission to England, even though upon his return to the Great Basin, he had married the woman as his second wife. The husband, JM, tried to defend himself by introducing a point of "gentile law." The bishop refused to consider it explaining that "we had nothing to do with gentile law. It was the laws of this church we had to do with" (1878, Fd. 2).

In an 1881 case, a husband, SB, wrote Apostle Wilford Woodruff for counsel when he discovered that his wife had committed adultery. Elder Woodruff responded: "You are entirely free from that woman and inasmuch as she has committed adultery you are entitled to a bill of divorce . . . get you another wife, and have nothing to do with her." When he began divorce proceedings, however, the ward teachers, assigned by the bishop to investigate, surprised SB by reporting that "considerable censure was due to her husband for not taking more than ordinary care of his wife when her mental condition was considered, she not being as bright in intellect as the ordinary woman." The bishop recommended a divorce, but admonished SB to take care of her because she

> is not aware of the enormity of the crime she has committed . . . we
> recommend her husband to take care of her and look to her support, but

have no sexual intercourse with her. . . . We are aware it is his privilege to put her away, but how much more God like to put forth the helping hand to help save even the transgressor. If her husband does not see to her support, we call upon her father to take her to his home and hearth and see that she does not suffer the necessaries and comforts of life. (1881, Fd. 1)

In another case a church court "cut off" a member "for . . . [civilly] divorcing his wife through falsely accusing her of adultery and then marrying another outside the church." Since the divorce had been civil, his second marriage was considered adulterous. President Smith of Cache Valley in explaining the decision of the high council, stated: "I do not know of a single instance where a man who has had his endowments has married a gentile woman and been justified, or married another woman by a justice of the peace and been justified" (1893, Disfellowship File, Fd. 2).

Church courts also readily granted divorce petitions on grounds such as "licentious conduct," habitual drunkenness, desertion for more than a year, or brutality (1885, Fd. 27; Disfellowship Files: 1885, Fd. 2; 1897, Fd. 14, 1891, Fd. 3; 1893, Fd. 5). And if the parties could not be reconciled, church leaders recommended divorce even in the absence of other legitimate grounds, a practice consistent with the "irreconcilable differences" of the 1851 statute. In an 1880 divorce case, the bishop concluded that though "the evidence brought forward was not sufficient to justify a divorce," the wife expressed such a spirit of hostility that he would recommend a divorce and "leave the matter to the judgment of President [John] Taylor" (1880, Fd. 6).

Similarly, a bishop in Fillmore recommended a divorce for a wife in 1883 even though she could not establish any grounds other than personal dislike for her husband: "We consider in our opinion that it would not be wise to compel [MH] although her grounds are not just, to continue to be the wife of [CH] inasmuch as she claims that she does not now nor never did have any affections for him" (1883, Fd. 6; also 1886, Fd. 8).

Some church courts used a printed form to expedite uncontested divorces. The following form used in a divorce action at St. George is illustrative (1875, Fd. 6):

Know all Persons by these presents: that we the undersigned [*MAM*] and [*MAK*] his wife, before her marriage to him [*MAK*], do hereby mutually covenant, Promise and agree to Dissolve all the relations which have hitherto existed between us as Husband and Wife, and to keep ourselves Separate and Apart from each other, from this time forth.

In Witness Whereof, We have hereunto set out hands at *St. George, Utah,* this *1st* day of *June* A.D. 1876.

Signed in the Presence of ———   ———   ———   ———

The same form was also used in St. George in 1879 (Fd. 3) and Salt Lake in 1886 (Fd. 7) for uncontested divorces.

In addition to dissolving marriages, church courts often became involved in property disposition and supervising child custody disputes. They retained a supervisory role even after a divorce, to ensure that the children would be raised by a responsible parent. Refusing to comply with the court's property settlement was itself grounds for disfellowshipping (1853, Disfellowship File, Fd. 1).

In one uncontested divorce filed in the Pleasant Grove Ward in 1877, the bishop awarded the wife the husband's "interest [$145.00] in one threshing machine, one cow, one calf, and five bushels of wheat. The said [husband] to retain and have the custody and control of the three children. And all property both real and personal, except as above awarded to his wife" (1877, Fd. 4; 1879, Fd. 4). In another case, the bishop awarded the wife "a certain house and lot . . . one cow, one sack of flour, one load of wood, one bedstand table, two chairs, bake oven, and allow her to take those things in the house that belong to her such as her clothing and bedding and some dishes and some other cooking utensils" (1879, Fd. 3). Another bishop ordered FC to give his wife, EC, "one cow not to be sold, for the benefit of the children, three pigs, chickens she calls hers, the stove, furniture, bedding and clothing and $52 per year for child support until the minor children are over 9 years old" (1885, Fd. 9).

Sometimes the parties agreed to arbitrate property and custody issues. RG and MG, for example, executed the following arbitration agreement:

> Holding ourselves each and severally bound, in good faith and in actual practice, to abide by the decision of such Board of Arbitrators both as regards property and children, covenanting and agreeing each for ourselves to accept the judgment of said Board as a final decision putting an end to controversy between us.

The bishop and stake president as the appointed arbitrators distributed the property, granted the wife custody so long as she retained her church membership, and required the husband to support her as long as she remained unmarried (1879, Fd. 1). In 1879, a wife was held in contempt for refusing to abide by an arbitration committee's decision regarding the distribution of property (1879, Fd. 2).

In most cases, church courts departed from the common-law rule of *patria potestas*[1] and awarded the mother custody of small children. Brigham Young, in a case filed before the Salt Lake High Council, counseled in 1861, "I do not believe in a man getting children," and recommended in one case that the wife retain custody and the husband pay support (1861, Fd. 1). Daniel Spencer, president of the Salt Lake High Council, noted in an 1852 case that "it was general counsel from the Presidency that women are more competent to take care of little children than a man." Accordingly, the council awarded the younger children to the mother and the older children to the father (1852, Fd. 3). Similarly, a Manti bishop's court in 1870 recommended that the father be given custody of the older children, aged twelve and ten, while the bishop agreed to act as guardian for the mother and the younger children, aged seven and four (1870, Fd. 9). The husband was also ordered to pay alimony "so long as she remains unmarried." An 1887 church court in Tooele awarded custody to a mother of a six-year-old until he turned eight and permanent custody of a four-year-old (1885 Fd. 3). Also, in at least one paternity action, the mother retained custody and the father was "required to make public confession before the Saints of the Ward, and also to furnish means . . . to support her child" (1890, Fd. 10).

INTERACTION WITH CIVIL DIVORCE COURTS

Although church courts were an inexpensive forum for obtaining a divorce and the only means for dissolving a marriage-sealing, occasionally members obtained civil divorce decrees from the probate courts. The probate courts retained concurrent jurisdiction with the federal courts over divorce even after the Poland Act of 1874 substantially limited their jurisdiction over other matters. It was only with the Edmunds-Tucker Act of 1887 that the federal government vested civil jurisdiction over divorce exclusively in the federal courts.

A civil divorce, however, had only a limited effect on temple sealings. In an 1885 case in Logan, the bishop advised a wife who had obtained a probate decree of divorce that "she did not get a bill from president Young" and was, therefore, still sealed to her husband for the eternities (1885, Fd. 19). In another case, a wife followed her bishop's advice and asked for a divorce from the bishop's court for the Smithfield Ward even though she had received a decree of divorce from the Logan Probate Court three years earlier (1885, Fd. 14).

As early as 1875, couples had been instructed to formalize ecclesiastical divorces by applying to Judge Elias Smith of the Salt Lake

Probate Court for a civil decree (1875, Disfellowship File, Fd. 1). After the *Reynolds* decision in 1879 denied First Amendment protection to polygamy, it became increasingly important for church court divorce decrees to be legalized by a civil decree. Until 1888 it was a simple matter for ecclesiastical leaders, who were often officers of the probate courts, to have church court decrees legally affirmed by probate decrees.

In one case a church court decree granting the wife a divorce, custody of the minor children, and child support was formalized into a probate decree, which the Mormon judge signed (1881, Fd. 13). Four years later, another bishop recommended that the parties "mutually apply to the Probate Court for a divorce as the law requires so that when the husband and wife separate that neither can use the law on each other afterward, also to get a writing of divorce from President Taylor to dissolve as far as that will their eternity marriage" (1885, Fd. 24).

President Wilford Woodruff announced the same policy recommendation in a case referred to him from a bishop's court in 1889:

> If the first wife is to be divorced by this action, she should procure a divorce from the courts to be entirely free . . . after which, if an ecclesiastical divorce is desired, that can then be attended to. If the parties are agreed, by judicious action there need not be much difficulty in obtaining a divorce and having the property described in [the bishop's decision] awarded to her by the courts. By consulting with one of our brethren who is an attorney, the proper way to proceed will be known. (1889, Fd. 11)

These cases illustrate an active and cooperative interaction between the Mormon-controlled probate courts and the church courts, particularly as polygamy prosecutions became an ever-present threat to Mormon families.

The need for a civil decree, however, proved only a limited exception to the exclusive jurisdiction rule. In one 1877 case, JL, the husband, originally filed a divorce petition in the probate court and then moved the case to district court when BL obtained a continuance from the probate judge to let her petition in the church courts. BL then preferred charges before the Salt Lake Council on the ground that JL's filing for divorce in the civil courts was "contrary to the law of the church." Angus M. Cannon, President of the Salt Lake Stake, counseled JL that "there was a way to dissolve the marriage without going to gentile law," and asked him to "make a generous proposition, setting forth how much he would allow his wife." When JL was unwilling to offer a reasonable amount in settlement, the council ordered him to place $5,000 in trust for BL, who was to receive the interest. JL also was to withdraw his complaint from the district court and petition the probate judge for a "legal" divorce for "incompatibility of temper" (1877, Fd. 6).

DIVORCE PROCEEDINGS INVOLVING THE DEAD

Occasionally a wife wished to reconsider her eternal marriage after the husband's death. These cases constituted a unique body of actions for ecclesiastical courts.

When MR filed a divorce action against her deceased husband, WR, the bishop of WR's ward was asked to represent the interests of the deceased. MR, a plural wife, charged that her deceased husband had forced himself upon her three weeks before their marriage and had never repented of that transgression. After several people testified about WR's good character, the case was referred to the First Presidency for a decision (1881, Fd. 15).

Seven years later, another widow sought a cancellation of her sealing because her husband had committed adultery but not repented, causing her to "fear she will be left alone in the hereafter" (1888, Fd. 11). In a similar case filed in 1884 President John Taylor referred EH's request for cancellation of sealing from her deceased husband to the Logan High Council to hear testimony on "the deceased's fitness, lest he be wronged by the cancellation of the sealing" (1884, Fd. 10).

In a third case, filed in 1883, a polygamous wife, EF, had been separated from her husband, AF, for more than a year. Before her divorce petition was processed, AF died. Nevertheless, EF petitioned again for the divorce, "for it is one that concerns my eternal welfare." After the bishop recommended the divorce, the stake president forwarded the recommendation to President Taylor, who responded:

> Cases of the kind of Brother [AF] and Sister [EF] pertaining to the dead are very complicated, and it becomes quite a question if they should be disturbed, as the parties are out of our reach and not in a position to defend themselves. It is stated that Brother [AF] was not in good standing in the hearts of the people; if he was not, it became the duty of the Bishop to deal with him as a delinquent; and as this was not attended to he died in the faith and fellowship of the gospel. It is stated that it was believed that he would have made any confession or concession rather than be deprived of his fellowship, which concessions had they been called for would probably have been received and acted upon. However, inasmuch as an application for divorce was made during his lifetime

although not carried out and completed you are at liberty to release her from him, as it appears there is a complete alienation; but the children and all the Temple records must remain as they are. (1885, Fd. 11)

As peculiar as these cases seem, they do not exhaust the possibilities for unique divorce proceedings. In an 1878 case HP, who was married civilly to TP, requested that she be sealed to WD because her husband "treated her poorly and was not in good standing with the Church." WD consented to the sealing, provided that HP would stay with her husband during his life. When TP died, HP requested that WD either furnish her a home or agree to the cancellation of the sealing so that she could be sealed to yet another party, JS, who insisted on the sealing as a condition for providing her with basic necessities. WD responded: "I am not in circumstances financially to comply with her request, but would have felt glad to have done it if it had been in my power, and if she feels desirous to be sealed to Brother [JS] under these circumstances if it can be done to be unsealed I am willing to relinquish my claim" (1878, Fd. 3).

CHURCH COURTS AND POLYGAMOUS DISPUTES

The Church courts provided the only forum for the complaints of polygamous wives and children. Thus the bishop of Salt Lake City's Seventh Ward noted that a plural wife "has been to the Gentile law herself to get a divorce and they told her that she does not need one" (1885, Fd. 26). The church court emphasis on arbitration, fairness, and compromise was nowhere more important than in dealing with the complexities of plural marriage.

One Salt Lake bishop's judgment in an 1880 case illustrates the level of wrangling possible when plural households shared one roof:

> We feel that it is our duty to condemn in the strongest terms, the conduct of an elder in Israel who will threaten his wife with violence, insult her womanhood . . . and we consider that justice would demand a retraction and an apology for those accusations, both to her and to her children.
>
> In regard to the division of the house, we consider it only just that she should have, in connection with the rooms she already occupies, the room now occupied as a kitchen by the first family, together with the room now used as a bathroom. These being really necessary, in our opinion, to the ordinary comfort of herself and her children; this still leaving the much larger, and by far the better part of the house for the use of the other part of the family.
>
> And we hereby enjoin upon each portion of the family that they shall

hereafter scrupulously avoid performing any act that will tend in any way to unnecessarily harass or annoy the other portion. (1880, Fd. 3)

Another typical problem of plural marriage involved the equitable distribution of property. For example, in one case the bishop dealt with the property distribution by appointing

> three polygamists to ascertain the number of persons in his family and the amount of means he has on hand and report the amount [the wife] shall have, how many children she shall keep and then make a report to the Presidency of the Stake for their approval of what is done. The Presidency of the Stake shall select a man that [the husband] will approve of, who shall hold the property in trust for her and her children, and at her death or marriage the property so held shall go to her children in equal shares.

The bishop forwarded the decision for approval to President John Taylor on 31 January 1881, with the notation, "We got her to wait almost a year with no reconciliation, therefore, we recommend she have one" (1881, Fd. 21).

Neglect arguments presented special problems in polygamy cases. Since many polygamous families lived in separate homes or even different towns, a husband's capacity for time, energy, and interest was strained. FA sued for divorce against her husband in the Rexburg Ward because, though she believed "in the principle of Celestial Order of Marriage . . . it just has not worked here," for "he has not paid that attention to me that he might have done, or that he paid to his other wife" (1887, Fd. 21).

During the 1880s, husbands occasionally succumbed to threats of prosecution and repudiated their plural wives. Repudiating polygamy was strongly disapproved of because it often required the ward to support the abandoned plural families and betrayed the cause of Zion by placing human law above God's law. Thus when Bishop JS avoided a jail sentence by agreeing to repudiate polygamy, a church court was held to decide whether he should continue as bishop. Joseph Taylor presided and noted that Bishop JS's conduct set a bad precedent:

> If Bishop [JS] is justified in the course he has taken then every other bishop in Israel would be justified in taking a similar course; presidents of the stakes would be justified. The President of this Stake (Brother Angus M. Cannon) is now suffering imprisonment for doing exactly the opposite to that which the Bishop has done, and we justify him for acting the opposite to Bishop [JS].

Bishop JS protested that his wives were past childbearing years and that he intended to support them, but the council argued that JS's example would still affect brethren with younger wives and that if JS "possesses physical vitality [he] ought to take another wife and thus continue the labor." The court applied a revelation that had been announced following the passage of the Edmunds Act that "it is not meet that men who will not abide my law shall preside over my priesthood" to release Bishop JS from his office. The First Presidency affirmed on 15 October 1885 (1885, Fds. 22–23).

The temptation to repudiate polygamy became especially strong when the federal government offered amnesty oaths. EM, a plural wife, was able to obtain a divorce from FK when he "took the [following] oath to receive amnesty of the President . . . for bigamy":

Territory of Utah
County of

I, [FK] being first duly sworn do depose and say: That I have not been in the practice of bigamy or polygamy since the 15 day of *December* 1884, that I am not now a bigamist or polygamist, that I have not since the 15 day of *December* 1884, nor do I now believe in, advocate, or in any way uphold or countenance the practice of bigamy or polygamy, and that in the future I will do all I can to oppose the Mormon Church in its efforts to oppose the laws, and obstruct the due course of justice, and that I will not violate any law of the United States.

/S/ [FK]

Subscribed and sworn to before me, this
_____ /S/ (notary public)

We recommend the above named   [FK]   as a proper person to receive amnesty under the sixth section of the act entitled: 'An Act to amend section 5352 of the Revised Statutes' in reference to bigamy, and for other purposes.

/S/ Eli H. Murry   (Governor)
C. J. Zane
J. S. Boreman
Judges of the Supreme Court.
(1886, Fd. 1)

Members were also punished for testifying against polygamists. For example, in an 1882 case CN was charged with betraying, through his testimony, a polygamist "into the hands of the enemies and talking lightly about the principles of the Church." CN acknowledged his error, asked for forgiveness, and offered to do all that he could to make it up to FH (1882, Fd. 11).

Of course, church courts could only be effective against those willing to submit to the priesthood. In one case, AC brought a complaint against JC, her husband, because he had refused to comply with an earlier bishop's order to support her children. JC, an attorney, had explained to AC that even if the bishop's court excommunicated him, "that would not benefit her any, as the moment that was done, I would be under no obligation to do anything for her and she would only injure herself in a financial sense and I fail to see how she will be benefitted by my excommunication." Unimpressed, the high council declared JC to be in contempt of the priesthood and told him he could be forced to pay support as Brigham Young's *Ann Eliza* case demonstrated.

JC scoffed at such "scare tactics" and lectured them on the law of the matter:

> Judge McKean did give Ann Eliza alimony and upon President Young's refusal to pay was sent to the Pen for contempt and in 48 hours afterwards I think Judge McKean was removed and his successor reversed that ruling. In the *Senior* case Judge Zane ruled that a polygamous wife had no right to any portion of her husband's estate; although the second wife in this case had lived with her husband over a year before he died, and although she was the only living wife he had, the first wife dying a year before the husband. In the *Eardley* habeas corpus case Judge Zane decided that polygamous children born after January 1, 1883 had no claim upon their father for support.
>
> Judge Zane will do what I want done, adjudge the child to my care and keeping as no one else in the sight of the law had any right to the child but myself and therefore I have no objection to [AC] going to the law. I want the children and if I can get them in that way it will be much easier and better. I don't think any U.S. Judge will rule the way [AC] would like because the Government is not ready yet to legalize our plural marriages. Remember that I am not saying anything about the righteousness of the law in these matters . . . I don't want any law as I have had a great deal more than I like so I leave it alone as much as I possibly can but I will not be bulldogged by her threatenings of the law.

The perplexed high council condemned his bad spirit, affirmed the divorce decree and custody order over JC's objections, and upon JC's refusal to comply with the decision, disfellowshipped him from the church (1887, Fd. 6).

The Manifesto, read in general conference 4 October 1890, forbade new plural marriages, but the church courts continued to condemn husbands who did not support their polygamous families. A bishopric counselor in an 1891 case commented that since the "law will not allow you to give [the plural wife] your companionship . . . I think that the wife who is deprived of the company of her husband should have a little more kindness and care than the one who has the company of her husband all the time." The bishop further added that "these wives are equal in the sight of God, you are expected to do the square thing by each of them, and a man who makes a distinction is doing wrong." He concluded that "it is cases of this kind that bring the principle into disrepute among the young people" (1891, Fd. 13). One 1892 court disfellowshipped a member for refusing to support his polygamous wife: "Our duty is to support our families now (meaning our plural wives) as before but we cannot live with them" (1892, Disfellowship File, Fd. 2).

When JR petitioned the president of Payson Stake for a divorce from his plural wife "because he desires to obey the law of the land which prohibits their sustaining the relationship of husband and wife," the high council granted the divorce but required JR to continue to support his plural wife (1894, Fd. 3).

When a polygamous father or husband died, a plural wife and her children could only look to the church courts for a share of the inheritance; the courts, then, became critical to both estate planning and the security of polygamous families. For example, in one case the will left the entire estate to the

> wives together, but if they cannot live together to be divided equally by brethren in the Church but by no means to be sold out of the Church, and in case my second wife Sarah should marry again she is to leave the property to my first wife Catherine so that she may not be left destitute in her aged and decrepid [sic] condition, but in case of the death of my wife Catherine before that of Sarah, I wish Sarah to enjoy the whole property after her death. . . . In case my second wife Sarah should marry out of the Church the property after the death of Catherine is go to the Church. (1874, Fd. 2)

When a father died intestate, the polygamous children shared equally with legitimate children. When CL died intestate, for example, the arbitrators ordered that the four wives each receive $600 and the 54 children $375 each. They permitted one wife to retain property previously deeded to her "in consideration of the large number of minor children she has to rear and educate" (1879, Fd. 6).

Clearly, the availability of church courts allowed polygamists to more effectively resolve their problems. Local church leaders often reconciled the parties by appealing to their sense of religious duty. Where there were irreconcilable differences or more serious grounds for divorce, church courts were inexpensive and continued to express Mormon social values.

14

Contract Disputes and
Church Courts

Contract disputes raised special theological and historical problems for church courts. Doctrinally the Mormon liturgy of covenants bears close resemblance to contract. Baptism, sacrament, and temple ordinances, for example, all specify reciprocal blessings in exchange for obedience. Accountability for covenants teaches moral responsibility while reinforcing human agency. In temporal affairs, enforcing contracts likewise teaches responsibility while respecting the freedom of the contracting parties. Nevertheless, Mormon theology also teaches an ethic of responsibility for others, freely accepted by covenant at the time of baptism. The familiar antinomies of justice and mercy represented by these opposing views raised difficult issues for Mormon adjudicators considering contractual disputes.

The law of consecration afforded priesthood leaders some direction during the nineteenth century. Announced by Joseph Smith on 9 February 1831 in Kirtland, Ohio (D&C 42:32; 119), it accommodated both individual agency and community responsibility. Members demonstrated social responsibility and exercised free agency by "consecrating" their worldly goods to the bishop and by managing the goods returned to them as their "stewardship." Although experiments with consecration in the East were short-lived due to persecution and dissension, Brigham Young reinstituted a variety of cooperatives, "united orders," and other collectives in Utah. However, internal strife, pressures from the market economy, and the financial and leadership drain resulting from polygamy persecutions prevented the establishment of a stable alternative system (Arrington, Fox, and May 1976; Arrington 1953). But the principles embedded in consecration and stewardship remained to undergird economic affairs in Mormon communities: individual rights had to be reconciled with community needs. The church courts helped achieve this norm by enforcing freely assumed contractual obligations while encouraging members to forego some of their potential contractual advantages. Thus, church courts applied civil rules in contract cases more often than in other substantive law areas, but also mitigated by appealing to a sense of mercy.

EXCLUSIVE JURISDICTION IN CONTRACTS

Here as elsewhere, church courts asserted exclusive jurisdiction. For example, in 1858 the Salt Lake High Council chastised BL for suing JB on a note before the civil courts and required him to pay the costs of the action (1858, Disfellowship File, Fd. 2[5]). Indeed, several contract cases filed in the 1880s demonstrate a continued claim to exclusive jurisdiction long past the time when economic assimilation had become inevitable. DB, for example, brought an action against SS before the Weber High Council in 1885 for "suing me at law and making me pay expense" in defending the suit. The high council heard both parties, then decided that DB really owed SS the money claimed but that SS had nonetheless erred in suing DB in civil court. Accordingly, the high council awarded DB his court costs and attorney's fees of $46 (1885, Fd. 25).

In a second 1885 case, FC complained against HW for suing at law on a note. HW defended himself on the ground that the bank had been the party that foreclosed on the note, forcing the sale of JC's property. Despite the obvious problems in overriding a civil judgment, the bishop decided that HW "did wrong and acted contrary to the law of the church," and ordered HW to "restore to [JC] as far as possible in reason all the property and machinery that was attached . . . . [so] that [JC will] be placed financially as far as the property is concerned on as good a footing as before the attachment." The bishop also requested "the brethren who have bought any portion to be reasonable in their charges and let [HW] have said property back on as easy terms as possible without actual loss" (1885, Fd. 29). This sweeping judgment not only required the creditor to restore property the courts had legally granted him but also asked nonparties to cooperate (1885–89, Fd. 1).

In a third example, Horace S. Eldredge and S. W. Sears, superintendents of Zion's Cooperative Merchantile Association (ZCMI), the largest church-owned cooperative, sued WP in the Third Judicial Court in Salt Lake City on 20 March 1880 for judgment on a note of $2,100. The court awarded judgment. Subsequently a U.S. marshal sold at public auction WP's hay land, and the merchandise in WP's Ogden Store. In February 1882 WP filed a complaint before the Weber High Council against these ZCMI superintendents, claiming that their actions "violated the order of the Church," and had "financially ruined me, destroyed my business credit, both at home and abroad, and injured my character, and reduced my family to want."

The high council hesitated to hear the case since the real defendant was ZCMI, a corporation. But the First Presidency instructed the council "to go on with the case." In defense, the ZCMI attorney, Nathan Tanner, testified that WP had consistently refused to pay anything on the debt even though he was making an effort to pay off other creditors. The suit had been filed, Tanner explained, because "the process of Teachers [was] slow, and [WP's] other creditors [were] crowding him." Tanner testified that ZCMI had delayed execution of the judgment until it became apparent that WP was selling his assets to avoid paying the judgment. WP explained that he had paid on the account "as long as I could, without falling on the Bishop's hands for support" and that he had "never connived with any man to cheat my creditors."

The Weber High Council decided that even though WP owed a substantial debt to ZCMI, ZCMI had improperly "sued him before the ungodly." The high council then assigned a committee of its members "to ascertain how many dollars of costs he has been put to, and how much trouble and annoyance he had been caused, and the amount he has sustained through being sued in the Third District Court."

The committee determined that the sale of WP's assets had yielded $1,000 on the $2,100 debt and concluded that WP "is entitled to the cancellation of all claims held against him in the Courts or otherwise by the Institution." The committee may have been swayed by the terms of the underlying debt that made it difficult for him to earn any profit. WP further suggested that had he "done as other men had done and suffered myself to be cut off from the Church rather than not trade with the Institution, some would have taken their hats off to me today." The high council excused WP from any further obligation to ZCMI on the note (1882–83, Fd. 1).

ZCMI was a corporation that had to compete with non-Mormon establishments. Imposing religious standards that, in this case, resulted in an $1,100 loss to ZCMI vividly demonstrates the primacy of the exclusive jurisdiction rule in economic cases heard before church courts.

CIVIL LAW IN CONTRACT CASES

Church courts in contract cases recognized civil rules as relevant, though not necessarily binding. The civil rules were considered helpful because they reflected normal commercial practices and would help make business practices in the Great Basin more consistent. A claimant, however, who felt he had contract law on his side could not be absolutely sure that a church court would see it the same way. This was especially true when a point of contractual law contained technicalities or subtleties that might offend an ecclesiastical court's sense of substantive justice.

One 1883 case provides an excellent example of the complexities of contract litigation in the church courts. AT of Logan contracted with GH to construct a house for the agreed-upon price of $2,850. He paid GH $1,000 in advance. GH employed several subcontractors to do the work and then left town without paying them. They completed the house even though they had no contract with AT and demanded payment from him.

AT argued that he owed them nothing. First, the house had not been completed according to the terms of the contract. Second, he had never agreed to pay the subcontractors. The subcontractors tried to compromise. They had the house appraised and asked reimbursement only for the amount of material and labor that exceeded the amount AT had paid GH. The home was appraised at $1,515 so the subcontractors claimed only $515, about sixty-four cents on each dollar they had invested. When AT offered $375 as his top figure, the subcontractors filed before a bishop's court.

The decision went against AT and he appealed to the Logan High Council in October 1883. AT's first point on appeal was that the church officials had served in the legislature that passed the "Mechanics and Laborer's Lien Law of 1869," and therefore must have intended that the law be binding on church courts. AT then introduced a copy of the statute:

> Any subcontractor, journeyman, or laborer, employed in the construction of repairing of any building or other improvement or in purchasing any material for the same, may give the owner notice thereof in writing, particularly setting forth the amount of his claim and the services rendered for which his employer is indebted to him, and that he holds the owner responsible for the same, and the owner of the building or other improvement shall be liable for such claim *if indebted to the employer to the amount; if not then for the amount due from him to the said employer at the time such notice was served,* which claim or amount may be recovered by an action against the owner if brought within one year after the completion of the building or other improvement, or the repairs thereon [italics in original].

AT argued that he had not received such written notice and that the subcontractors had not commenced an action within a year of completing the building.

Then he cited several Mormon scriptures about obeying the law of the land: a bishop, as a judge in Israel, should decide "according to the law" (D&C 107:72); "Let no man break the laws of the land, for he that keepeth the laws of God hath no need to break the laws of the land" (D&C 58:21); "Wherefore, be subject to the powers that be, until he reigns whose right it is to reign, and subdues all enemies under his feet" (D&C 58:22); "Therefore, I the Lord, justify you, and your brethren of my church, in befriending that law which is the constitutional law of the land" (D&C 98:6); and, finally, "For this purpose have I established the Constitution of this land, by the hands of wise men whom I raised up unto this very purpose, and redeemed the land by the shedding of blood" (D&C 101:80).

AT's third argument was that "the Constitution of the United States given by inspiration provides against impairing the validity of contracts," a reference to Section 10, clause 1, "prohibiting any law impairing the obligation of contracts."

One high councillor agreed that "this Council could not afford to ignore and nullify contracts as they were on an old and well established rule and usage in business transactions"; he recommended that the subcontractors learn from their mistakes. Still, the high council rejected AT's sophisticated argument: "technically the plaintiffs could not claim anything from the defendant, but in justice to each party we think each should sustain a portion of the losses," and awarded the subcontractors $445, a compromise between the $515 they claimed and the $375 AT offered (1883, Fd. 15).

Other church court decisions mirror the principle implicit in this case—that people who in good faith provide money, services, or materials to other members ought not to be disappointed in payment regardless of the applicable civil law. As it was explained in an 1887 case, for Mormons "an honest debt is never outlawed in the eyes of justice" (1887, Disfellowship File, Fd. 10).

This principle is illustrated in an 1879 case. AF had loaned LC 100 pounds in London to be repaid in two months. LC used the money to help his family and others to emigrate; those he assisted gave LC notes for their share of the expenses. LC died shortly after reaching Utah, and AF asked LC's widow, JC, to pay the debt. JC offered to assign the emigration notes to AF, but AF insisted on cash. JC protested that she had no cash. Her husband had left no estate, and she had already mortgaged her home to pay for funeral expenses.

The bishop's court ordered JC to pay AF $50 and to assign him the emigration notes for the balance of the debt. AF appealed, and the stake president, after reviewing JC's finances, ordered payment in full, explaining, "I believe that [JC] is amply able to meet this note and take up the obligation of her husband, and make him honorable and [AF] glad that he trusted an honest man in Utah. . . . Still I would ask [AF] not to be harsh or in a hurry, but give [JC] time." The Quorum of the Twelve affirmed the decision (1879–80, Fd. 2). Thus, the church court system on all three levels affirmed the importance of meeting contractual obligations, even though a civil court could not have enforced such a claim against the debtor's widow when the deceased debtor lacked an estate.

In an earlier 1873 case, President George Wallace of the Salt Lake Stake rejected another contractual arrangement that seemed to compromise justice. JV had agreed to bale some hay for JW; after JV performed, JW refused to pay because he had not made a written agreement. JV brought his case before the high council; President Wallace stated that "if there was a bargain made . . . and it is proved it is just the same as though it was put on paper, for when it is put on paper it is only evidence that such a contract was made." He ordered JW to pay JC. The First Presidency affirmed the decision (1873, Fed. 16). In comparison, more than twenty years later, JW complained before the Bear Lake High Council that DD had hired him to build a home for $294.86 but afterward had left on a mission without paying. The high council held that the contract was unenforceable because it was orally given and too "indefinite" (1898, Fd. 9).

Latter-day Saints who pled bankruptcy posed a special problem. Legally a member who complied with the bankruptcy laws was immune from subsequent suits by creditors; the church courts however, regularly insisted that bankruptcy did not bar the obligation. A bankruptcy case during the presidency of Brigham Young first raised the issue of civil bankruptcy as a defense. Three partners, JP, BP, and JB had organized the Pioneer Mining and Smelting Company in St. George. The business failed and the partners filed bankruptcy. They later went before the St. George High Council for a determination of respective obligation in March 1876. President Gardner asked Apostle Erastus Snow to give the decision. Snow found JB liable for half the company's liabilities, and JP and BP liable for the other half. JB said he would not pay. He felt that bankruptcy extinguished "any and all claims."

President Gardner notified JB of the seriousness of his noncompliance: "As a member of the Church, you of course understand that if you persist in neglecting to comply with the decision of the Council and do not take any action by way of appeal or otherwise, your fellowship will be called in question and dealt with by the High Council." JB persisted in taking advantage of the bankruptcy laws contrary to priesthood direction, and the high council excommunicated him on 11 August 1877. "The clerk was instructed to forward a notice of the action to the *Deseret News* for publication" (1878, Fd. 12).

Another interesting case was heard in 1889. JS borrowed $500 from TD in 1873 at 24 percent annual interest. When JS filed for bankruptcy, TD brought the case before the Weber Stake High Council because his claim would soon be "outlawed." The high council was reluctant to hear the case and initially asked the parties to settle it without a trial "on account of their prominent positions that they hold in the church." TD challenged the high council's jurisdiction to hear a claim pending before the bankruptcy court:

> Has any court or tribunal in this church the right or authority to say obligations remaining unpaid in the shape of notes or accounts in cases like mine of assignment or bankruptcy that they shall follow the delinquent; or in other words, if a brother is forced into bankruptcy and he fails owing to the forced sell [*sic*] of his property, by which he is made to sacrifice on the value thereof thousands of dollars, and he is thereby unable to redeem his liabilities, can, or will the Church assume, or take that position that it has the right to impose on the unfortunate victim of such untoward circumstances the payment of all notes and accounts remaining unpaid?

The high council asserted that its jurisdiction included claims "outlawed" by bankruptcy proceedings. The council ordered TD to renew the note to JS, excused the accrued interest and directed TD to pay the debt as soon as possible. TD appealed to the Twelve Apostles, who upheld the decision. The Quorum of the Twelve thereby clearly established the priority of church policy over civil disposition of bankruptcy claims.

The policy on bankruptcy did not change until 1908, when the tension between civil and church courts over contractual matters prompted President Joseph F. Smith to refer the matter to a committee of apostles. A report of 15 October 1908 from a committee of the Council of Twelve Apostles made the following recommendations:

> First: We recommend that church courts be not used as agencies for the collection of ordinary debts. Such debts should be collected as provided by civil law, but if a member of the church shall unjustly, and in an unchristianlike manner, bring his brother before the civil courts, or if there be an element of fraud or dishonesty on the part of a member who owes a debt, which he refused to pay, either would be liable to trial for his fellowship in the church by the Bishops Court or High Council.
>
> Second: Where church members have been adjudged by the civil courts to be bankrupt, and after having made settlement with their credi-

tors, as provided by law, become financially able, at a later date to meet their former obligations, or any part of them, they should do so. Moral suasion should be used, and every consistent effort made to persuade them to settle with their former creditors, but if they still claim the exemption which the civil law guarantees, the Church Courts shall not be used to enforce compliance with this moral obligation.

Third: The recommendation made in regard to bankrupts applies also to church members whose notes or accounts have become outlawed, it being always understood that if there be an element of fraud or dishonesty on the part of a member who becomes bankrupt, or whose notes or accounts have become outlawed he would be liable for his fellowship before the courts of the church.

This policy statement was a watershed. By withdrawing the exclusive jurisdiction of church courts in contractual matters, the church abandoned a significant aspect of the effort to establish Zion. The church retained its jurisdiction in cases of fraud, however, indicating a distinction between spiritual and temporal offenses in business matters.

These changes are, of course, symptoms of more fundamental accommodations the church made during this period as it assimilated mainstream America's economic and social values. What is surprising is not that a change of policy came, but that it came so late.

RELIGIOUS PRINCIPLES AND CONTRACTS

The overwhelming majority of contract cases argued before church courts underscored a strong presumption in favor of enforcing contracts. However, the courts usually justified their decision in religious terms, not by legal principles. For example, the courts argued that individuals could and should be held accountable for their freely chosen actions. They also stressed strict adherence to the principle of honesty.

When the Salt Lake High Council, in an 1870 case, found that one member was ambivalent about repaying money he had borrowed from another member, the stake president not only required repayment, but added 10 percent interest and criticized the debtor's attitude: "It shows that we as brethren are not as punctual as we ought to be in settling our indebtedness. We think[,] well so and so is a Brother and he can wait for his pay—that we are not as punctual in settling our debts with a brother as we are with gentiles" (1870, Fd. 22).

Obedience to priesthood authority was another community value stressed by the church courts. In one interesting case in 1863, TG hired JM to teach his children in exchange for a certain number of bushels of wheat. He actually paid the debt in cash, claiming that he did not have enough wheat. JM wanted the wheat as agreed upon, and brought the case before a bishop's court showing that TG had been selling large quantities of wheat to non-Mormon speculators. The bishop had specifically counseled against such practices and "did not think that a man who will refuse wheat to his brother under these circumstances is worthy of fellowship." He disfellowshipped TG until "he makes restitution," not only by paying JM in wheat but also for trafficking with nonmembers. On appeal the Salt Lake High Council, with Brigham Young in attendance, affirmed (1863, Disfellowship File, Fd. 1; 1863, Fd. 1).

Obedience to priesthood directives was also the underlying issue in a case the Weber High Council heard in May 1878. JP was charged with a debt of $51.75, representing an assessment on all the stockholders of the Ogden Publishing Company for its outstanding debts. JP denied any ownership interest in the company. He explained that President Richards and Bishop Herrick had asked him to pay $100 to support the failing publishing company. JP had told them that he could not afford it, but that if they insisted he would pay $50. Bishop Herrick borrowed the $100 in JP's name with JP's reluctant consent. Although he contributed the money, he insisted, "I never applied, either directly or indirectly, to become a member of the company, and never considered myself a stockholder therein."

David H. Peery, president of Weber Stake, decided that it was in the community's best interests for JP to pay the assessment: "I sympathize with [JP] and believe that his intention is to do right. But there is only one way to get around this matter—the debts of the company have to be paid. I hope in all these trials you will feel that the decisions have been based on principle, and inspired by the best of motives." JP, who questioned both the inspiration and the fairness of the decision, appealed to the First Presidency, arguing that ten members of the high council were stockholders of the Ogden Publishing Company, and therefore, interested parties; that he never was a stockholder; and "that I have good grounds for believing that this matter is being pressed against me from vindictive feelings, originating in matters of difference in regard to public policy and secular measures of minor importance." No decision from the First Presidency appears in the file. Since JP's standing in the church depended on his acceptance of this directive by his ecclesiastical leaders, it was clear that they were subordinating his legal rights to broader social interests (1878, Fd. 11). Moreover, JP's response demonstrates possible friction arising from priesthood leaders' use of the church courts to further parochial interests.

Similarly, the exact terms of the contract were less important than an ecclesiastical principle in an 1884 case. AR leased his flock of 1,425 sheep to WB in 1876 with a contract specifying annual payment in lambs, wool, and mutton. WB secured the contract by taking out a mortgage on his property of $2,850. When a bitter first winter killed all but 285 sheep, AR gave WB five years to make up the losses; seven years later, in 1884, AR brought an action in a bishop's court against WB for $536.50 in wool that had not been delivered.

The bishop acknowledged that WB owed the money but refused to order payment:

> We have this to say, [1880] was our year of jubilee, the Church by unanimous vote at the general conference in April 1880 empowered its Trustee-in-Trust to cancel *honest debts* to the amount of thousands of dollars, the people were advised through the Presidency of the Church and the Apostles to take the same course one towards another; and brother [AR] shall extend mercy to Brother [WB] so shall God have mercy upon and bless him and his posterity after him.

AR, not in a merciful mood, appealed to the stake. The high council agreed with the bishop that the harsh winter of 1876–77 and the jubilee year were good reasons to have AR cancel the debt (1884, Fd. 1).

Several other cases show the willingness of ecclesiastical courts to override the letter of a contract to achieve justice. For example, in an 1854 case, AS complained that she had not fully understood a contract that she had signed with DK and now felt that he was treating her unjustly. The bishop declared the contract invalid and reprimanded DK for attempting to "swindle a poor person in the ward." DK asked forgiveness and promised to do better in the future, after which the court "received his acknowledgement and fully forgave him" (1854, Fd. 4).

In one case, a widow, AD, and her son, JD, of Sevier County contracted with FG to file on eighty acres of land they wished to homestead in Beaver. AD and JD had signed an agreement to transfer forty acres to FG for a nominal fee as his wage for the service, but now protested that they had not understood the contract, that they had trusted FG to treat them fairly—which did not mean taking half the land—and asked the Sevier Stake High Council to rescind the decree FG had already received in probate court.

The stake president and high council decided that the mother and son were "not . . . fully competent to attend [to] their business" and hence recommended that FG pay them the full value of the land transferred to him minus the expenses he had incurred in going to Beaver to file on the land for them (1882, Fd. 6).

In an 1891 case in Paris, Idaho, the bishop acknowledged that "legally and technically the memorandum of agreement . . . conveyed to [WP] the entire mill, but from a moral and equitable standpoint we claim that the memorandum referred to did not . . . contain or express the real intent of the vendor." The bishop ruled that WP should receive three-fifths of the mill while the seller was entitled to retain two-fifths (1891, Fd. 22).

The Salt Lake High Council also sliced through a tangle of legal complication to reach a "fair" settlement in a case that one high councillor described as "sometimes in accordance with law, at others based upon the relationship of brotherhood, and at other times [with] a little astrology mixed with it." Three associates who believed they had "struck a bonanza" invested in a mining company "for the development of their hidden treasure." Debts continued to exceed profits until the property was sold in 1877 by a U.S. marshal to satisfy the wage claims of employees. WJ, one of the shareholders, bought the mine, with the company holding a three-month redemption option that it did not exercise. Thus, the mine legally belonged to WJ.

SR, another shareholder, filed a protest before the high council, claiming that WJ had agreed to redeem the mine on behalf of all the shareholders. JW denied it but offered to sell the mine to the other shareholders for the sum of his total investment in the company. SR argued that WJ had been acting as a trustee and hence was entitled only to be reimbursed for his expenses in redeeming the mine.

The stake president agreed that WJ legally owned the mine but that he should give the other two shareholders an additional three months to pay WJ's redemption expenses to restore the status quo (1880–83, Fd. 1).

ENFORCING CONTRACTS

Although the courts regularly set aside civil law where it was felt equity would not be served, they also recognized that individuals acting as free agents must be accountable for their actions.

In an early case heard by the Salt Lake High Council in October 1847, AS, who was representing a wagon company, complained that JT had agreed to do the company's blacksmithing in return for having the company haul his tools, burn the coal, set up his forge, and take his guarding and herding turns while he worked. The company performed the services, but JT also demanded pay, so the company hired another blacksmith. JT argued that the company had failed to do his chores as agreed. The high council decided that JT had violated the terms of the contract and ordered him to pay damages equal to the amount of money paid the other smithy (1847, Fd. 29). In an 1868 case, the Salt Lake High Council refused to excuse the interest owed on a note even though the debtor's business had been severely damaged because of Indian difficulties (1868, Fd. 2[2]).

Utah's barter economy during the first several decades of settlement made it difficult to determine honesty precisely. Wheat was a popular cash substitute, but its volatile price made timely payments critical. One 1864 court held that Bishop BC, who had contracted to exchange wheat for horses on a specified date, owed the horse owner $453.60— the difference in value of the wheat between the agreed-upon date of delivery and the actual transfer date (1864, Fd. 8).

In 1868 WG sold JM a train of mules and wagons in exchange for flour to be delivered in Montana on a specified date. JM delivered half the flour on time but waited eighteen months on the other half. By that time the value of flour had dropped from approximately $14 to $7.50 a sack. WG brought his complaint before the Salt Lake High Council in August 1868, and it required JM to pay the amount of the loss ($2,000). It also instructed WG to disregard a judgment for $3,000 he had received on the same claim against JM in a civil action filed in Montana (1868, Fd. 10).

Church courts also ruled on the enforceability of notes, despite their sometimes complicated terms. In several cases an ecclesiastical court required payment of a note and threatened or actually disfellow-shipped individuals for refusing to pay what were considered just debts (1867, Fd. 1; 1884, Disfellowship File, Fd. 6; 1889, Disfellowship File, Fd. 5; 1900, Disfellowship File, Fd. 3). A fairly typical case was brought before the Salt Lake High Council in 1876. JW and JB filed a complaint against PS for defaulting on a note for $1,369. The council denied PS's defenses and ordered payment in full. PS resisted; he would not pay or renew the note even "if the whole conference decided he should." The high council, after "faithfully labor[ing] with him," cut him off from the Church and gave JW and JB permission to "file in civil court to avoid having the note outlawed" (1876, Fd. 7).

An interesting and important case involved the proper computation of interest. RG purchased a tannery from Bishop AR, agreeing to pay for it over a two-year period in leather at 20 percent interest per annum. After collection RG felt that AR had computed the interest improperly and asked him to return $1,109.43. AR refused and RG filed his complaint before the Salt Lake High Council in April 1873.

In an unusual move, the high council allowed both parties to have attorneys represent them because commercial necessity required some uniformity in assessing interest rates. President Wallace urged the high councillors to consider their actions carefully, "for this case is something new to the Council and we should not get over it in a hurry, but weigh the subject well and arrive at conclusions that will be just and that will be a precedent for the Council to go by."

RG's attorney, Aurelius Miner, cited common-law authority showing that AR's computation of interest had been unjust because he had calculated interest on the full amount of the debt for the entire two years even though RG had reduced the principal through periodic payments. He urged that the previous settlement be set aside upon the "principles of justice and equity."

AR's attorney, E. D. Hoge, cited other common-law authorities establishing that once an account had been settled, it could only be set aside for fraud or mistake of fact, not for mistake of law.

After the presentations of the attorneys and the traditional comments of assigned high councillors, President Wallace decided that usual commercial practice should be followed in computing interest and ordered Bishop AR to refund any overpayments that had been made. On appeal, the First Presidency agreed that the case should be decided strictly by "the commercial rule of computing interest when partial payments are made" (1873, Fd. 10). Although this case was never cited as precedent, most church courts conformed to accepted business practices in computing interest (1896, Fd. 4; 1897, Fds. 10, 11; 1898, Fd. 1).

In several interesting cases, church courts acknowledged the legitimacy of the contract interest rate but urged the claimant to apply a lower rate anyway. For example, in an 1894 case, the Logan High Council successfully urged the complainant to forgive the accrued interest and accept a lower interest rate for the balance owing (1894, Fd. 10). In another case, the creditor followed a church court's recommendation to excuse half the accrued interest on a note and compromise the balance. In that case, President Lorenzo Snow personally paid the claimant, and the defendant later paid Snow when he was financially able, thus demonstrating the flexibility of a system that accommodated both justice and mercy (1899, Fd. 2).

Another interesting example of the nice balance between justice and mercy occurred in an 1870 case heard before the Salt Lake Stake High Council. PM had agreed to help KS, a widow, and her family emigrate to Utah. KS paid PM $77, but PM did not follow through. She came on her own nonetheless. Eleven years later, she found herself destitute and brought the complaint against PM for breach of contract. PM admitted that he had provided no assistance to KS in crossing the plains but claimed the money had been a gift, not wages, and that he was destitute himself. The bishop determined that PM was obligated to KS in the amount of $100 and ordered him to pay it in $10 monthly installments. PM protested that he could not pay, but the bishop reassured him that "he would put him in a way to earn it." The widow and her debtor then "shook hands and agreed to bury the hatchet" (1870, Fd. 18). This creative solution achieved justice and helped resolve the financial problems of a destitute widow without grinding down a poor man in the process.

If a complainant refused to compromise or forgive part of a legally contracted debt, church courts generally enforced the contract rather than compelling the member to forgive the debt. In one 1888 action for $25 representing unpaid interest on a note, the bishop counseled: "We see from the face of the note that it calls for interest, but Brother [JG] seems very poor and broken down and if Brother [CC] would forgive him the remainder of the debt he would not lose very much by doing so." CC insisted on payment and the bishop ordered JG to pay in full within the week or be disfellowshipped (1888, Fd. 9).

As the nineteenth century moved to its close, church courts generally insisted more strictly on the enforcement of contracts. In one 1893 case, the high council found that a member cheated a widow in purchasing a right-of-way but enforced the contract nonetheless. The stake president noted, "It is a rule with this Council never to interfere with contracts." The high council ordered the widow to deliver the right-of-way for the agreed-upon sum of $1, and the First Presidency affirmed the decision on appeal (1893, Fd. 2). In four additional cases heard in that decade, the contracts were enforced, one on pain of disfellowshipping (1890, Fd. 6; 1898, Fds. 4, 5).

ARBITRATING CONTRACTUAL CLAIMS

As in other areas, church courts in contract cases preferred that the parties resolve conflict privately. Not only would the parties feel more committed to the decision, they would also help perpetuate community harmony. Thus in a case before the Salt Lake High Council in 1862, one speaker commented that "if [the parties] had the Spirit of God they should not have come before this High Council but settled it themselves" (1862, Fd. 1). In another case, the stake president said, "I do not like the spirit of the thing, the time of this body of men ought not to have been wasted today." The parties subsequently compromised (1863, Disfellowship File, Fd. 2; see also 1864, Fd. 14).

Church courts used arbitration in complicated contract disputes, especially where accounting procedures required interpretation. Typically, each party selected an accountant as his arbitrator, and the two arbitrators selected a third. Unlike the "teachers' arbitration" used widely on disputes at the local level, accountants' arbitration was intended to be binding on the parties. The terms were often incorporated in a written agreement, and a copy was filed with the probate court.

An example of an arbitration agreement from 1867 is typical:

> [GJ and PJ] do hereby mutually covenant and agree to, and with each other that [three arbitrators] or any two of them shall arbitrate and determine of and concerning all, and all manner of action and actions, cause and causes of actions, suits, controversies, claims, and demands whatsoever now pending, existing or held by and between us, the parties aforesaid, and we do further mutually covenant and agree, to and with each other, that the award to be made by the said arbitrators or any two of them shall in all things by us, and each of us be well and faithfully kept and observed . . . . That in case either party or both shall formally oppose or object to the conditions of the decision, that a copy thereof with the necessary paper be filed with the Probate Clerk, for Record and the same enforced according to law (1867, Fd. 1)

In 1878, Thomas Taylor, the church emigration agent in the East, brought a claim in the church courts to recover compensation for his services. Since Taylor, while acting as emigration agent, had profited by selling goods at a church store in Wyoming, the parties agreed to an accountants' arbitration. They agreed to each choose a bookkeeper to go over the records and render a written decision; if the bookkeepers could not agree, the two would select a third accountant, and the majority opinion would be binding. Unfortunately, the records themselves were not complete. Both parties made unsubstantiated claims and offered extrinsic evidence. Unable to reach a compromise, the two accountants appointed a third arbitrator, who recommended that Thomas Taylor be awarded the very substantial sum of $12, 797.41. The other arbitrators did not concur and John Taylor refused to pay since "outside matters have been introduced, accounts acknowledged without vouchers and no majority decision has been arrived at." The parties met again and arrived at a much more modest figure of $4,373.06, which John Taylor as trustee-in-trust agreed to pay (1878, Fd. 9).

Even when the parties refused to arbitrate, a church court often appointed arbitrators to shorten the long evidentiary process. For example, in 1868, WJ filed an action against WW for "damage sustained in waiting for freight at Austin in November of 1867, the damage being expense in feeding mules and men, and men's wages during the detention." The high council appointed three arbitrators to determine WJ's actual losses, and then ordered WW to pay the arbitrators' recommended sum.

In another example two years later, CA, a builder, claimed that he had been hired by F to construct a building in Salt Lake City, and that he had done so, but that F had not paid the balance of the unpaid contract price. F contended that CA's work was unsatisfactory and refused to pay. The Salt Lake High Council appointed three arbitrators to investigate the respective claims. They established that F had paid $14,758.50 on a contract of $17,832.21. From the balance owing they subtracted $353.90 for work that CA had either omitted or completed defectively. The high council ordered F to pay the final balance of $2,719.81 (1870, Fd. 1).

The work of arbitrators was generally respected by church adjudicators. In 1856, in an early case involving arbitration, the bishop of San Bernardino Ward recommended that his counselors accept an arbitrator's decision so that arbitrators "would continue to hear such complicated cases" (1856, Fd. 6). In an 1870 case where the Weber High Council had incorporated an arbitrators' decision in its judgment, the defendant appealed to the First Presidency. Brigham Young ordered a rehearing before the Salt Lake High Council that affirmed the arbitration and the previous decision as fair (1870, Fd. 2; 1884, Fd. 12; 1886, Fd. 16).

Church courts in other contract cases ordered shareholders in corporations to pay their outstanding stock subscriptions when their corporations became insolvent (1893, Fd. 12); required employers to pay agreed-upon wages (1872, Fd. 6); compelled leasee sheepherders to pay their lessors in wool, mutton, and increase of lambs as agreed upon (1896, Fd. 3; 1897, Fd. 3); and ordered merchants to obey the terms of their contracts with other merchants (1867, Fd. 3; 1868, Fd. 4).

A review of the contract cases heard by church courts reinforces the image of Zion as a community controlled by religious norms even in strictly commercial disputes. Although the Latter-day Saints tried to do business according to accepted commercial practices, they rarely allowed those practices to disrupt social harmony. Many of these cases had a uniquely Mormon solution, with religious considerations modifying and shaping commercial needs. Some of the principles of consecration, even in areas where a cooperative system was not functioning, provided a set of reference points for decision.

By accepting contract law as relevant, the church courts made the LDS economy efficient and responsive to the national economy; by retaining the power to go beyond legal technicalities, they continued to affirm the overriding importance of building the Kingdom of God. By providing a forum without court costs, legal fees, or the divisive influence of "gentile" lawyers, the Latter-day Saints effectively maintained a separate community throughout the nineteenth century.

15

Tortious Conduct and
Church Courts

Tort is derived from the Latin *torquere*, "to twist," or *tortus*, "twisted."
In law, the term usually applies to "conduct which is crooked, not
straight" (Chapin 1917, 1–2). This definition, which makes the tor-
tiousness of an act depend on the morality of the community, is particularly applicable to nineteenth century Mormons. As members of
a religious community, they had distinctive moral standards, which
they defined and refined through their own court system. They did
not use the terminology of tort law, but their decisions paralleled the
development of tort law in late nineteenth-century American courts.[1]

INTENTIONAL MISCONDUCT

Intentional misconduct is objectionable in any society and especially
so in Zion. Church leaders acted through the courts to punish intentional wrongdoers, to recompense the injured, and to signal to the
community at large that such conduct would not be tolerated. By exercising jurisdiction over these tort cases, church leaders drove home
the doctrinal point that building Zion entailed broad social commitments as well as beliefs and spiritual responsibilities.

Conventional civil offenses like assault and battery, defamation,
sexual misconduct, fraud, and theft often came before church courts.
So did such distinctively religious offenses as exercising "unrighteous
dominion" and such social acts of discourtesy as swearing, drinking,
and disturbing the peace. Of course, sanctioning discourtesy increases
the oppressiveness of the community. It promotes community peace
and unity, but at the expense of individual nonconformity.

In some ways, this situation parallels the period in the development
of the common law when serious breaches of the king's peace were
treated as semi-criminal offenses. In church courts intentional misconduct was treated as a public, quasi-criminal offense, not as the strictly

private injury it would have been considered in the civil courts. From 1848 to 1850, the church courts actually applied the nonecclesiastical remedies of fines and physical punishment. After federal courts were introduced in 1851 and territorial legislation expanded probate court jurisdiction to include criminal actions, the church courts limited their sanctions to disfellowshipping and excommunication.

Assault and Battery

During the nineteenth century, assault and battery cases heard in church courts exhibited a steady pattern of public censure and private remedies. An assault and battery case highlighting the public nature of such cases involved a long-standing dispute between Bishop TJ of the Fourth Ward and SB, a high priest in the Eighth Ward. At one point, a teachers' hearing attempted to reconcile differences between TJ and SB; they each agreed to stay away from each other. TJ believed that he had not received justice at the previous teachers' hearing and continued to hold a grudge against SB. Several years later, when they encountered each other in the Eighth Ward corral, TJ threatened SB with personal violence.

As a result, the ward teachers filed a complaint in the Eighth Ward bishop's court against both men for unChristianlike conduct. By so doing, they transformed a private controversy into a public affair; one in which the religious community asserted an interest in the behavior of the quarreling members. Bishop Hunter "deprecated the idea of holding hard feelings year after year without trying to reconcile them." One of his counselors further

> expatiated on the purity and dignity of the priesthood, and how low and degrading a course [Bishop TJ] had stooped to by an unprovoked attack upon Brother [SB] while he was peaceably prosecuting his business. A man that has revenge is a coward and cannot nor will not be tolerated by men holding the priesthood. We ought to lay a foundation of integrity before our wards and offspring. He called upon [Bishop TJ] to humble himself before God and his brethren, and exhorted men to act as Men of God.

The sanction in this case was limited to chastising the parties for unChristianlike conduct (1866, Fd. 5).

In an 1897 case, JW, a church member and an editor of a local newspaper, had published a series of articles criticizing county officials for excessive public expenditures. When JN, also a church member, was elected deputy sheriff, JW published another editorial claiming that JN was best known as a local loafer and would be a terrible sheriff. JN thereupon came to JW's office, broke up his furniture and "whipped him for it." A few days later, JN quietly confessed judgment in probate court and was fined $10.

Unsatisfied with the probate judgment, JW filed a complaint against JN before the bishop's court of Paris Ward. The bishop reproved JN for his cowardly conduct and ordered him to pay $40 in damages. JN bought one of JW's notes to pay the fine but JW refused to accept it when JN tendered it. JN consequently was disfellowshipped.

JN appealed to the high council. The stake president "sharply reproved [JW] for publishing the offensive article," but told JN that he should obtain redress "in a lawful manner . . . instead of breaking the law by a criminal assault upon his brother." The council ordered JN to confess his guilt publicly on Sunday, 14 November 1897 and censured the Mormon probate judge for collaborating to minimize the seriousness of JN's offense (1897–99, Fd. 1).

These two cases are typical of the assault cases in the records of this survey. The courts recognized that each party contributed to the hostility, but still disapproved the violence without qualification. In both these cases, the parties complied. In at least one other case an unrepentant assailant was disfellowshipped (1850, Disfellowship File, Fd. 1).

Defamation

Defamation was definitely actionable in church courts. Such actions threatened the unity of the community and demonstrated the defamer's lack of spirituality and good feeling. Church courts required offending parties to compensate those injured by their statements and to apologize publicly, usually at the weekly sacrament meeting of the ward congregation.

Church courts regularly punished members who defamed the church or its leaders. Among such cases was an 1852 case where an individual "defam[ed] the church regarding polygamy" (Fd. 19); an 1856 case where an individual had told some emigrants that church leaders "upheld cheating and abusing the emigrants" (Fd. 8); an 1866 case where an individual had written a defamatory letter about his bishop to his stake president—even though the offense was private the apology was public (Fd. 10); and another case where an individual had ridiculed the church courts (1885–86, Disfellowship File, Fd. 1). One member who called his bishop a liar refused to repent and was disfellowshipped (1866, Fd. 10). When Bishop JT of Pleasant Grove's First Ward was running for mayor, a couple accused him and his clerk of having stolen wheat from the tithing office some thirteen years earlier. The bishop's court, the high council, and ultimately, in April 1893, the First Presidency, required the accusers to admit their wrong publicly. The First Presidency insisted upon an urgent public acknowledgment because of the mayoral campaign in which JT's reputation was being damaged (1892, Fd. 4).

While the courts did not impose criminal penalties such as fines, the wrongdoer occasionally was ordered to pay damages to the injured party. For example, when in 1889 WT accused SE of having worked at a house of "ill fame," the Granite Ward Bishop's court ordered WT to acknowledge his error publicly and pay SE $200 damages. When he refused, he was disfellowshipped (1889, Fd. 7). And in an 1884 case, a bishop imposed $25 in damages for slander (1884, Disfellowship File, Fd. 17). In most cases, however, the penalty was limited to a public apology. In an 1887 case where one Salt Lake policeman slandered another, contributing to the other's suspension from the force, the Salt Lake High Council required the accuser to acknowledge his wrong to their superior and "to effect a reconciliation with the fellow officer himself or be disfellowshipped" (Stirling 1887, 141).

The courts allowed the defense of truth if the statements were also justifiable. In an 1887 case, Dr. EF (a female physician) came to a bishop's court in Spanish Fork in February 1884 complaining that ES, a member of the Board of Directors for the Deseret Hospital, had slandered her, resulting in her dismissal as house surgeon for the Deseret Hospital. ES introduced testimony from hospital personnel that EF's irresponsible use of drugs had caused the death of one patient, that she had dominated the hospital staff in an arbitrary way, and that she had refused to allow elders to minister to patients without her approval. The court dismissed the case (1884, Fd. 8).

If the plaintiff could not prove his case, the courts usually required him to acknowledge culpability for bringing the case. In 1892 NT complained before Bishop Robert McQuarrie of Ogden that JP had given evidence that resulted in NT's arrest and conviction for unlawful cohabitation. Since NT could not prove that "JP had been involved in securing his conviction," the bishop ordered NP to acknowledge his wrong before the ward and ask for JP's forgiveness. Although NT did confess and ask for forgiveness, the bishop felt that this statement did not satisfactorily acknowledge the falsity of the accusation and refused to issue NT a temple recommend. On appeal, the high council ruled that substantial compliance had been sufficient in this case and that the bishop should extend his forgiveness (1892, Fd. 5).

Sexual Offenses

The Latter-day Saints required strict premarital chastity and post-marital fidelity. Although most outsiders saw polygamy as a form of licensed adultery, church court records show that authorized polygamy was viewed as a sacramental marriage; sexual relations outside this relationship were strictly forbidden. Sexual misconduct was considered a direct threat to the personal and institutional purity of Zion, especially because of the religious nature of polygamy. In fact the most common grounds for disfellowshipping during this period were adultery, seduction, rape, and other sexual offenses.

Many critics of the Mormon practice of plural marriage would be surprised to learn that unauthorized polygamy constituted sexual misconduct. In two 1883 cases, Bishop Despain of the Granite Ward disfellowshipped one man for "having a girl married to him by a justice of the peace while he was living with a wife whom he married in the Endowment House" and disfellowshipped another for the same offense of having "married a wife by Gentile law while he was living with a wife whom he married in the House of the Lord" (1883, Disfellowship File, Fd. 4 [3 and 4]). At least five other similar cases are recorded (Disfellowship Files: 1884, Fd. 2; 1886, Fd. 3; 1893, Fd. 3; 1898, Fds. 10 and 11; Stirling 1889, 242).

Seduction also came under severe condemnation. In an 1891 case, JG was condemned for seducing AA by promising to marry her when he had no intention of doing so. The bishop ordered JG to make public confession (1891, Fd. 11).

Usually courts acknowledged the weaknesses of the flesh even though they did not condone lapses. Courting couples whose relationships became improper were usually disfellowshipped and required to confess their fault publicly, but generally were allowed full church participation upon compliance (1885, Fd. 12).

Church courts also punished couples for courting without parental permission. In one case, the parents and ward teachers agreed to let a young man "keep company" with the daughter as soon as "he could get the Priesthood and a recommend from the bishop." The girl did not insist on the same conditions, however, and was of age, so they continued to court. As a result, the parents and ward teachers complained to the bishop, who chastised the young couple for claiming that "her being of age" made a difference and instructed the young couple that "it was not right for her to disobey her parents." The bishop disfellowshipped JC but later authorized his rebaptism at the express wish of the parents (Disfellowship File, 1883, Fd. 3). In another case, when JH married IM, a minor, without her parents' permission, the bishop ordered JH to seek the parents' forgiveness, which presumably they were required to grant in order to restore good relationships (1881, Fd. 7).

To nineteenth-century priesthood leaders, adultery constituted an automatic dissolution of the marriage even without legal action. The innocent spouse had little discretion to forgive such misconduct. A church court, for example, disfellowshipped WP because he continued living with his wife after she admitted to adultery. "According to the laws of God and the Church," a bishop explained in this 1882 case, "she ceased to be his wife as soon as she had committed adultery and as the matter stood he also was guilty of the same crime" (1882–83, Disfellowship File, Fd. 1).

Similarly, in 1884 the bishop of the Logan Fifth Ward disfellowshipped FB "for having had sexual intercourse with his wife after knowing that she was in the family way with another man." Although the stake president called FB's offense adultery, President John Taylor later corrected this term, but was no less severe in condemning the husband:

> A professed Latter-Day Saint must have but little conception of the purity of the marriage relation and of the obligation which a people, such as we profess to be under, who can be guilty of such conduct as that attributed to this man. A man who could take an adulteress back to his bosom as a wife must have a very low view of morality and the ordinary decencies of life; and the Saints did quite right in saying to him that they could not fellowship such conduct in one of their number. Such conduct sets a bad example and should not be permitted to go unrebuked. Yet while we cannot express too strongly our condemnation of such conduct, it cannot properly be called adultery. It is immoral, low and degrading, and utterly unworthy of a man calling himself a Latter-Day Saint. (1884, Disfellowship File, Fd. 5)

These cases imply that an innocent spouse would have to seek a divorce unless the transgressor repented of the sin and was forgiven by the church. In an 1886 case, the husband was ordered not to have sexual intercourse with his adulterous wife until she had repented and been rebaptized (1885, Disfellowship File, Fd. 8). In an 1895 case, eight of the twelve high councillors objected when a stake president characterized the husband of an adulterous wife as an adulterer himself for continuing to have sexual relations with her, but no one felt such conduct was entirely blameless (1895, Disfellowship File, Fd. 4). Other examples of disfellowshippings for adultery, all in the Disfellowship files, are: 1883, Fds. 13 and 14; 1884, Fd. 8; 1885, Fd. 12, 16, and 17; 1886, Fd. 13; 1887, Fd. 9; 1888, Fds. 1, 2, 3, and 10; 1892, Fds. 1, 3, 4; 1893, Fd. 1; 1895, Fds. 1 and 5; 1897, Fds. 12, 13, and 17; 1898, Fds. 3, 8, and 9; 1899, Fd. 1; and 1900, Fd. 1.

There are no reported cases accusing women of prostitution. But there are three cases of men tried for associating with women "of ill repute." In an 1881 case, a man was disfellowshipped for "harboring a woman of immoral character 'not a member of the church' and affording her shelter as his wife and refusing to put her away, knowing her immoral practices" (1881, Disfellowship File, Fd. 3). In 1883, another man was disfellowshipped for associating with prostitutes (1883, Disfellowship File, Fd. 1). And in 1897, a church court disfellowshipped another man for "lewd and lascivious conduct with a woman of ill repute in a public saloon" (1897, Disfellowship File, Fd. 5).

Rape presented a special problem since it was also a criminal offense. In one case, a bishopric counselor opposed exercising jurisdiction in a rape case since the territorial courts had already taken jurisdiction. The bishop countered that "a civil court of justice is no criterion for us, for female virtue is there trampled under foot." The accused man, FB, denied any misconduct; but the bishop found him "guilty from the spirit he manifested" and disfellowshipped him (1881, Disfellowship File, Fd. 1).

In an 1884 case, a church court disfellowshipped a married man for the attempted rape of a woman and required him to live separately from his wife and children for two years to demonstrate his repentance (1884, Disfellowship File, Fd. 14). At the end of the two years, he was rebaptized and allowed to live with his family again. The same penalty was followed in an 1886 case that also ended with the rebaptism of the repentant sinner (1886, Disfellowship File, Fd. 2).

Church courts also took action in paternity actions. In 1890 a bishop's court refused to dismiss a paternity claim brought by the mother's father even though criminal proceedings were also pending. Although the defendant denied responsibility, the court required him to make public confession before the members of the ward and to provide support for the woman and child (1890, Fd. 10). Nine years earlier, in a similar case, a church court required the father of an illegitimate child to keep the woman "in clothing, fuel, provisions and furnish her with a house for the next twelve months," but he was "to keep away from the woman and to send through his Bishop what she needed" (1881, Fd. 5). In another case in the 1890s, the Oneida Stake High Council in Idaho ordered the father to marry the pregnant woman or be cut off from the church (1897–98, Fd. 1).

Fraud or Theft

Church courts exercised both civil and ecclesiastical jurisdiction in fraud and theft cases from the Nauvoo exodus in 1847 to the establishment of territorial law in 1850. Brigham Young had instructed the transplanted Municipal High Council of Nauvoo near Council Bluffs on 17 August 1846 to "serve as a City and High Council to decide in matters of difference between all members of the church, that some had already transgressed or trampled on the rights of the Priesthood and should be brought to justice, that he was not so much afraid of going into the wilderness alone but offenders go unpunished for such or like offenses" (1846, Fd. 1).

Presumably in compliance with Brigham Young's directive, the Municipal High Council on 30 July 1847 gave the police captain in Winter Quarters authority to bring in all disorderly characters (1847, Fd. 19).

In 17 January 1848, a bishop's court ordered the marshal to give one individual "39 lashes on his bare back" for horse stealing (1848, Fd. 30). Some cattle rustlers in 1848 were sentenced by the high council "to work 100 days for the public" (1848, Fd. 32). In an 1849 case, a thief who had stolen some iron was ordered by a bishop's court to pay the owner four times the value plus a $10 fine and court costs. He was also disfellowshipped. Even after the territorial courts had taken over criminal cases, one member guilty of stealing tithing funds was required to pay back four times the amount stolen (1857, Fd. 2 [4]).

After the church courts abandoned criminal penalties, they continued to exercise concurrent jurisdiction over criminal conduct. For instance, in an 1852 case heard before the Salt Lake High Council, the defendant was found guilty of stealing a cow. He was ordered to confess his wrongdoing and pay the plaintiff $35 as the fair market value of the cow (1852, Fd. 12).

If the church courts found the defendant guilty, then the church proceedings simply added an ecclesiastical sanction. But if a church court found a defendant innocent, pursuing a criminal action in the civil courts created special problems. In 1861, IE charged that several members of his priesthood quorum had disregarded a quorum decision. IE and others had been cleared of grand larceny in a quorum investigation almost a year earlier, but the case had been brought up again before a grand jury impaneled in Provo. The minutes do not give the result of the grand jury investigation or the consequences of the action brought before the quorum (1891, Fd. 4). Most church courts, however, delayed hearing such cases until the criminal courts had rendered a judgment, unless special circumstances created an urgent need for a hearing.

Church courts also relied on inspiration and the spiritual gift of discernment. In one 1852 case the Salt Lake High Council heard evidence concerning the disputed ownership of an ox. One of the high councillors said: "There is strong evidence on both sides to prove the ox is owned by both. But it cannot be so. I feel to submit the case to the President and that his decision will be full of light according to the office upon him." The high council unanimously sustained the president's decision.

One church court case demonstrates the scrupulous honesty required of Saints who found lost property. CC complained in 1850 before the Salt Lake High Council that AB had been guilty of un-Christianlike conduct in keeping saddlebags he had found on the road. Since he had reason to believe that they belonged to CC, he had, CC charged, disregarded the revelation that "if thou findest anything belonging to thy Brother thou shalt diligently seek till thou shalt deliver it to him again." The high council ordered AB to return the saddlebags and to pay CC for the property they had contained (1850, Fd. 1).

Fraud was an elastic charge involving more than disputes over the ownership of personal property. Any breach of trust that damaged social relationships in Zion was considered actionable. In 1885, the Salt Lake Stake High Council considered a breach of trust in an ecclesiastical stewardship. WS persuaded AJ, a ninety-three-year-old widow, to make him her trustee. When he got into financial difficulties, he used some of her property for his own benefit, and AT subsequently complained to her ecclesiastical leaders. Stake President Angus M. Cannon stated: "It is our judgment that Brother [WS] used his Priesthood to subserve his own purposes to relieve immediate necessities." The court "suspended [WS] from the priesthood" and required him to return all of the widow's property within ten days (1885, Fd. 22[2]).

Obedience to Priesthood Directives and
Cases of Unrighteous Dominion

While bishops and stake presidents were not considered infallible, their priesthood decisions were presumed valid, and leaders were only sanctioned for clearly overbearing behavior.

For example, when one high priest in Lehi in 1858 condemned his bishop for urging the Saints to "lie to deceive the enemy in favoring of the Brethren" (presumably in connection with trouble with the gentiles that had prompted the so-called Utah war), his priesthood quorum leadership required a public confession of the bishop's condemnor. The Lehi High Priest Quorum deemed the bishop's "protective" counsel to be within his priesthood prerogative.

In another case, SE was "disfellowshipped for insulting and abusing the priesthood and treating the bishop's court with contempt." SE had charged that the teachers' arbitration decision "was a plan laid to rob him" and the bishop's decision "no better." When he refused to appeal to the high council because it too was unfriendly and "he could not expect to be justly dealt with by the high council," he was promptly cut off (1885, Disfellowship File, Fd. 9).

A bishop or stake president however, could not automatically expect his superiors to support him in every action. A revelation received by Joseph Smith in 1839 about the nature and responsibilities of the priesthood had warned against the priesthood exercising "unrighteous dominion" (D&C 121:39).

Because bishops and stake presidents occupied sensitive and important positions in the community, trying them occasionally prompted special procedures. It was not uncommon for the president of the church to assign members of the Quorum of the Twelve to conduct the investigation when local leaders were charged. For example, a Nephi bishop's refusal to follow Brigham Young's standing counsel that all communities should have a fort for Indian protection prompted investigation in 1854. Many members had complained that the bishop's slothfulness had operated to their disadvantage. Brigham Young assigned Apostle Wilford Woodruff to investigate the charges. Woodruff invited all male members of the ward to the hearing, where he reassured them that "the Presidency of the Church has a fatherly care for the people and will not let any President of a branch tyrannize over the people." After hearing complaints from both the bishop and the ward members, Woodruff persuaded everyone to forgive each other and to work together, presumably in building the fort (1854, Fd. 3).

Seven years later Brigham Young sent Apostles John Taylor, George A. Smith, and Joseph A. Young, who was president of the First Quorum of the Seventy, to hear a controversy involving another Nephi bishop. In his opening remarks, John Taylor made it clear that if the bishop had misbehaved, "his Priesthood should not shield him." Some of the local members in a public meeting presented evidence that Bishop JB had been "overbearing and abusive to those he presides over." When this question was presented to the congregation, the great majority sustained the bishop against the charges. Joseph Young "spoke at length on the philosophy of unity and the necessity of its observance by those who wish to build up the kingdom of God" and exonerated the bishop (1861, Fd. 2).

An interesting 1861 case was brought against Bishop WJ and his counselor GP in connection with the theft of cattle from the U.S. Army herd. GP apparently alleged that Bishop WJ authorized him to steal the cattle, but the evidence was unclear, though WJ had suggested the gentiles ought to pay "tithing."

Because of this action and other alleged misconduct, WJ's congregation voted to no longer sustain him as bishop. Brigham Young appointed Apostles Orson Hyde and Isaac Morley to hear evidence on the controversy. Brigham Young instructed them: "The people have taken a vote upon the head of Bishop [WJ]—let the vote remain: but I want to know the facts in the case. Let the people come together and pour out their complaints . . . keep a faithful record, give a righteous decision, and forward the facts to me." Orson Hyde presided over a public meeting in which members were invited to air their grievances. Hyde encouraged the bishop and GP to confess fully, promising, "I am bound to extend the hand of kindness and mercy." Bishop WP responded:

> Brethren and Sisters . . . I do not wish to try to justify myself. I feel that I know I have done wrong in many things. I know this is the Kingdom of God, and I know what it takes to obtain salvation and I know I cannot obtain it without that one thing—and wherein I have done wrong in thought, word or deed, I humbly ask your forgiveness. Wherein I have done wrong in my "deals" I am now willing to make all things right . . . . I throw myself on the mercies of my brethren, and I will try to comply with their decision. I have got to get on the right track, and regain the confidence I have lost—I ask for forgiveness.

Hyde replied, "And you shall not ask in vain!" Apostle Hyde made a motion to forgive the bishop that was carried unanimously by the congregation. His counselor GP did not fare as well. Apostle Hyde, after hearing his testimony, said he did not feel he was "a man of truth." GP wept at the criticism. Undaunted, Hyde responded: "Weeping does not disarm me unless I see a disposition to repent." GP was disfellowshipped for a "lying spirit" and associated wrongs (1861, Fd. 6).

Cases against bishops were also heard in the regular high council courts, especially in later years. For example, in 1873 in the Big Cottonwood area of Salt Lake City, PL complained that his bishop coercively appropriated his land for a cooperative store. The high council found that the bishop had exercised unrighteous dominion and suspended him from acting. PL was also condemned for his contentious attitude. He too was temporarily disfellowshipped to give him a chance for "reflection and repentance." The two counselors were given responsibility for governing the ward. The stake president further admonished Bishop DB that "Brother [PL] had rights and they should be held sacred, and no one should infringe upon them one hair's breadth." The First Presidency approved the decision.

Social Misconduct

The Mormons believed a community of the righteous should follow the norms of the larger society, if they did not conflict with specific religious teachings. Misconduct was considered socially irresponsible and religiously suspicious. As a result, church courts often brought ecclesiastical pressure to bear on nonconformists.

Frontier humor lightened even the most weighty matter of church discipline. An obvious parody of more serious cases was this mock charge to Orrin Porter Rockwell, at Pioneer Camp on 26 May 1847:

> Sir, you are hereby commanded to bring, wherever found, the body of Col. [GM] before the Right Reverend Bishop Whipple at his quarters, there to answer to the following charge, viz:—"That of emitting a sound (in a meeting on Sunday last) *a posteriorari* (from the seat of honor) somewhat resembling the rumble of distant thunder, or the heavy discharge of artillery, thereby endangering the . . . nerves of those present, as well as disturbing their minds from the discourse of the speaker. (1847, Fd. 24)

A more typical charge involved unauthorized alcohol. Although Mormons did not strictly prohibit the use of alcohol during the nineteenth century, the easy availability of liquor was not approved. JT, for example, was charged in September 1886 with "building a brewery and selling beer against counsel." JT argued that he had not been counseled against the endeavor until after the brewery had been built, and could not drop it now because he had too much invested. The bishop gave him six weeks to sell or be disfellowshipped. JT appealed to the stake high council, where he argued that since the "people wanted beer he had the right to make it and keep the money at home instead of sending the money out of the country." The court was unrelenting: "If we put temptation before the young we would have something to answer for as it was generally the poor who indulged in drink and take away the means the children needed." The bishop's decision was sustained. When JT refused to comply he was disfellowshipped (1886, Fd. 12). In parallel cases during the 1880s, one man was disfellowshipped for "selling whiskey and doing other things unbecoming a Latter-day Saint," and three were disfellowshipped in separate cases for "keeping a liquor saloon contrary to counsel" (1883, Disfellowship File, Fds. 9 and 15; 1884, Fd. 16; 1886, Fd. 12).

Other cases were heard over a wide range of offenses. One young man in 1866 was charged "with being a member of the Young Men's Social Club" contrary to his bishop's counsel and for "further conduct unworthy of a Saint of God"; other cases heard charges on disorderly behavior at parties, teaching false doctrines, publishing incorrect information about church practices, and using "language . . . calculated to destroy [the influence of priesthood leaders] with the young people of the various ecclesiastical organizations of the ward" (1866, Fds. 8 and 12; 1876, Fd. 1; 1891, Fds. 8 and 17; 1900, Fd. 4). There are at least nine cases on drunkenness and associated fighting and profanity (Disfellowship Files: 1859, Fd. 2; 1880, Fd. 2; 1883, Fd. 8; 1885, Fds. 3 and 14; 1886, Fds. 4 and 6; 1898, Fd. 1; 1893, Fd. 3). Failing to pay tithe, working on Sunday, and making public statements that "prophets should stay out of temporal matters" also led to court action (Disfellowship Files: 1882, Fd. 4; 1885, Fds. 6, 8, and 19; 1897, Fds. 10 and 19; 1898, Fd. 4). Publicly condemning polygamy was itself grounds for excommunication, and threatening to turn a polygamous spouse over to civil authorities could result in disfellowshipping (Disfellowship Files: 1885, Fd. 19; 1886, Fd. 9; 1887, Fds. 11, 19).

UNINTENTIONAL MISCONDUCT

Church courts also heard cases involving two main forms of unintentional transgression: damages caused by trespassing animals and personal injuries caused by negligence. Although these problems were not as divisive as intentional misconduct, they nonetheless threatened social harmony.

Trespassing Animals

The need to pasture animals and the rapid increase in the size of herds created severe aggravation among neighbors, especially since fencing entire farms was difficult and expensive. Furthermore, in the early days of many settlements, the enclosed "Big Field," encompassed the property of many individuals. This communal system required special rules, which were enforced by the church courts.

At common law the owner of trespassing animals was completely liable for any damages regardless of whether the landowner had fenced his property. In frontier America, where fencing vast fields was impractical, common-law rules changed to require the landowner to fence his property. In Mormon communities a farmer might help fence the Big Field but his own property within it would not be enclosed. Thus, neither common-law rule resolved the problem of trespass and the church courts fashioned their own rules.

For example, in an 1852 case, AT was accused of allowing his cattle to graze in the common wheat and corn fields, contrary to the community rule that animals were excluded until after harvest. When AB threatened to take AT before the bishop's court, AT assaulted him. The bishop lectured AT for his unChristianlike conduct, fined him $25 for misconduct, ordered him to pay AB $20 for the damage caused by his animals and for the assault, and instructed him to obey the communal rule about keeping animals out of the fenced field. The stake high council affirmed the decision, though it substituted public confession for the fine (1852, Fd. 13).

In an 1855 action, AP presented a complaint before a court conducted by a seventy's quorum that LE had damaged his crops by letting cows trespass in the Big Field. AP, in a conciliatory mood, offered to forego damages if LE would promise to keep his cattle out of the field. Both parties asked the other's pardon for harsh words, promised to do better in the future, and "shook hand of fellowship" (1855, Fd. 3).

Even where a cooperative field was not involved, church courts required livestock owners to bear the responsibility for their animal's behavior. In one 1874 case, a man put up a fence so he could pasture his horses, then tried to extract half the cost of the fence from the neighboring property owner. The stake president ruled that "everyone should take care of their own, whether it is cattle, horses, or mules, and keep their property from damaging another" (1874, Fd. 3).

In two other cases that spanned the settlement period, a church court in 1852 directed AL to pay AG damages to his crops caused by a trespassing ox. It also criticized AG for keeping the trespassing ox until the damages were paid (1852, Fd. 4). In the second case, this one in 1894, the Granger Bishop's Court ordered WO to give WS two tons of lucerne to compensate for the damage caused by WO's trespassing horses (1894, Fd. 4).

The civil pound law designated a pound-keeper who had authority to keep strays until their owner paid for the damages they had caused plus a fee for their interim keep. If no one claimed the animals or paid the damages, the pound-keeper could sell them. These minor civil functionaries in Mormon communities were nearly always Latter-day Saints and empowered to act by LDS town councils, however, members were sanctioned for using the pound laws rather than the church courts to resolve problems with trespassing animals.

Church courts enforced the exclusive jurisdiction rule even when only the pound laws were violated. For example, in 1886, WD took thirty trespassing sheep to the pound. After holding them for the required period, the pound-keeper sold them to pay for the damages. The owner of the sheep, WG, had previously informed WD that if damages occurred he would pay. WG complained in a Tooele bishop's court that WD's reliance on pound laws rather than on a brotherly discussion of the problem, was unChristianlike conduct. The bishop agreed: "We do not justify taking our trouble to law anymore in a case of trespass than for any other debt; we hold that Brother [WD] should have exhausted the laws of the church first." Since both had been wrong, the bishop ordered WD to give WG half of the $17.75 he had received from the sale (1886, Fd. 14).

A more pointed example of the exclusive jurisdiction rule occurred when JB successfully sued TK in civil court for the damages caused by his livestock and was awarded $38.75. TK responded by suing JB in the church courts for unChristianlike conduct. The high council condemned JB for suing a fellow member in civil court. One speaker in JB's defense argued that trespass was essentially a criminal matter and hence an exception to the jurisdiction of church courts, but President Orson Smith insisted that "going to the law, if becoming prevalent would hinder our progress as Latter-day Saints." Not only did the high council instruct JB to disregard the civil judgment, it also denied that damage had been done on the grounds that the land was not fit to grow hay. President Smith counseled in summary: "I hope, Brother [JB], if anything like this should occur again, you will exhaust every effort to have the matter settled according to the law of the Church" (1893, Fd. 3).

Negligence

Negligence cases raised special conceptual problems for church courts, and here the common law was no guide. The idea that everyone has a general duty of care even when a special or contractual relationship does not exist emerged only in the late nineteenth century. As late as 1881, Oliver Wendell Holmes wrote in his famous *The Common Law*: "The general principle of law is that loss from accident must lie where it falls. . . . 'No case or principle can be found . . . subjecting an individual to liability for an act done without fault on his part'" (1881, 94–95). Tort actions were seen as "very largely a matter of some specific relation, by reason of which the defendant may be regarded as having undertaken a duty to act" (Prosser, 1941, 171).

In the few church court cases involving negligence claims, the courts generally took the position that a person could not be held culpable for accidental injuries, except in the case of intentional misconduct. At the same time, however, these cases invoked the sympathetic action appropriate in a Christian community toward the victims of negligence.

Church courts generally punished members who willfully misbehaved in ways that caused unintentional injuries. Thus, in 1849 when the church courts exercised criminal jurisdiction, a Salt Lake bishop fined two men $25 for improperly running their horses in the street and accidentally running over a boy. It also awarded the injured boy $5 plus any other medical fees necessary as a result of the injury (1849, Fd. 7).

In 1877 a four-year-old boy wandered onto a streetcar track and lost his right leg when he was struck by the streetcar. The father brought charges against the Street Railroad Company before the Salt Lake High Council. Brigham Young appeared as president of the railroad company and claimed that it "did not owe the first red cent from a business point of view." The streetcar had been driven within the speed limit authorized by the city, and there was no evidence of misconduct on the driver's part. Nevertheless, Brigham Young personally offered charitable assistance to the maimed boy. President Angus M. Cannon echoed Brigham Young's attitude on both policy and personal involvement, offering to contribute to the boy's aid himself. President David O. Calder, a counselor in the stake presidency, concurred. He pointed out the Scottish rule protected pedestrians only within railroad crossings and against reckless driving. He warned that making the railroad liable would encourage parents to be less attentive to the care of their children. The other counselor, J. E. Taylor, urging the father to accept the charitable offer, also agreed that "he could not feel to establish a precedent in making the railroad company pay any damages." He felt the "railroad company had the right to the road, not the children." The father was willing to leave the issue to the "brethren" for their just disposition (1877–83, Fd. 1 [2]).

It is impossible to say, of course, how much Brigham Young influenced the decision of the stake presidency. Nevertheless, a civil court would probably have come to a similar conclusion, given the state of common-law development at that time.

In one case where a complainant demonstrated the existence of a special duty, she was able to receive damages. In 1894 AB was injured when a defective seat caused her to fall out of MB's mail wagon en route from Paris to Montpelier, Idaho. She filed an action against MB in the Paris Bishop's Court. The bishop rebuked AB for threatening to take MB to civil court but basically upheld her claim for $50 in damages on the grounds that MB's business as a common carrier owed its passengers a duty of care which it breached by failing to maintain the seat.

In some cases the courts asked the parties to share responsibility. For example, in 1878 five boys, four of whom were CS's children, were gleaning wheat in the Big Field for the Relief Society. CS's nine-year-old lit a match to smoke a cigarette and caused a fire that burned 100 bushels of wheat. JW, who owned the land, filed an action in the bishop's court. CS explained that he had not wanted his boys to go into the Big Field but allowed them to do so after repeated calls from the bishop "for all idle persons to go and glean wheat for the purpose of laying up bread stuffs."

The bishop agreed that the father's intention was commendable and decided that, since the loss was accidental, the parties should share the loss. He ordered CS to pay JW fifty bushels of wheat within three months. In effect, the bishop compromised damages because he could not find culpable negligence (1878, Fd. 8).

An early case heard before the Tooele bishop's court in July 1863 also compromised a negligence complaint. EK charged that his sheep had been killed by the dogs of AS and TA and claimed he was entitled to damages. The bishop reviewed the evidence and concluded EK had not proven that those particular dogs were involved in the killing, or that the defendants had been careless in controlling their dogs. However, because AS and TG's dogs might have been involved, he ordered them each to give EK a sheep to help cover some of the losses. EK suffered the balance of the loss because he had left his sheep unprotected within the settlement (1863, Fd. 5).

Tort claims in Mormon courts exhibit the close relationship between religious duties and social obligations. By requiring members to bring these claims to church courts rather than civil courts, the ecclesiastical structure could accommodate both of these standards. Members were encouraged to seek amicable settlement, but failing that they could bring complaints to the church courts, where they would be heard in a religious environment of shared rights and duties.

Similarly, if a local leader exercised unrighteous dominion, or if a member refused to obey a court's decision, the church courts provided a means for returning the errant member to social conformity. In each area, the church courts promoted reconciliation, afforded members recompense for just losses, and held the authority to expel unrepentant wrongdoers.

Epilogue

For the Mormon today, Zion is not dead, even though many of the institutions of nineteenth-century Mormonism are gone or have been modified beyond recognition. Polygamy is not practiced, although the concept of the continuity of marriage and the family unit through mortality into the hereafter is central to Mormon belief and temple ceremony. The United Order did not survive the nineteenth century though Mormon cooperatives did, and Mormon institutions thrive today whose origins were in those idealistic beginnings. Consecration of self and possessions continues in theory and temple ceremony and, in daily life, to the level of a member's commitment.

A central feature of nineteenth-century Mormon experience was its concept of Zion, a community of Saints where God and his people could dwell together in harmony. As long as Mormons retained this central social concept they remained a gathered and a peculiar people. Only when this vision faded into an indeterminate future did Mormon social institutions, including the court system, wither. Church courts in fact continue, though they now perform only the traditional functions of church discipline, with secular courts and government institutions playing roles within the Mormon community not unlike their functions within non-Mormon communities.

From the beginning the unique Mormon social institutions demanded a legal system of their own. To the extent that Mormon doctrine espoused a distinctive and clearly articulated set of goals and standards for this community, its courts flourished. As political, economic, and social circumstances forced the Latter-day Saints to abandon their most distinctive practices, the involvement of church courts in temporal matters became increasingly anachronistic. Although others have noted that the Mormon economy merged with the national economy after 1869, the church courts continued to handle essentially temporal disputes between members for the remainder of the century. The gradual acceptance of American political pluralism in place of the

Mormon concept of Zion marked the end of an era for the Mormon ecclesiastical court system.

The importance that Latter-day Saints attached to their own courts during the nineteenth century explains a great deal about the nature of early Mormon communities and doctrines.

The Mormon legal experience suggests that a subculture's judicial systems often arise from its efforts to create and maintain a separate identity. The Mormon ecclesiastical court system emerged during the early years of the church's existence to delineate the boundaries of what it meant to be Mormon. At this stage, the court system paralleled the traditional use of ecclesiastical courts in other churches for judging strictly religious offenses. If a member did not believe a certain doctrine or would not accept a specific religious obligation, the church courts provided a means of severing him or her from the community. Thus, church courts provided a forum for setting the doctrinal bounds of Mormonism and regulating divergent views or conduct. Nonconforming members were exiled from the community, while those who remained learned the limits of accepted beliefs and the seriousness of being committed to the legitimized norms.

The Mormon experience with church courts also implies that the range of cases for an established legal system reflects the reach of that community's aspirations. Jurisdiction expands as the community's power grows; it decreases as the community accepts a more limited sphere of influence. The Mormon court system did not hold itself out to church members simply as an alternative to the civil system. Instead it actively competed with the civil system as Mormonism transcended the place usually accorded religion and became an all-encompassing social regulator.

For many Mormons, ultimate allegiance, present even in our time, is reserved for that which is most vital, most central to their lives, the church. Their willingness to sacrifice for the Kingdom is impressive. They support their church with the payment of a tithe, or ten percent of their income. Mormons staff, entirely, a church without professional clergy in one of the most intricate and effective ecclesiastical governments to be found. Mormon youth regularly accept mission calls in which two years are devoted, at their own expense and without compensation, to proselytizing and the work of the church. From home teachers who visit every Mormon home monthly, to officers and teachers in wards (parishes) and stakes (dioceses), Mormons donate a significant portion of their lives to church service. The effective and seemingly omnipresent nature of Mormon church governance is experienced by active Mormons without particular thought since it exists almost as if such were the nature of things. But immediate and effective response to a supervening event, perhaps a natural or man-made disaster, demonstrates to members and nonmembers alike the efficiency and power of Mormon government, based almost entirely on volunteer, nonprofessional labor.

In the development of Mormon communities in the nineteenth century, the religious duty to support and build Zion came to mean a commitment to distinctive economic, political, domestic, and social practices. As long as the scope of Mormonism included such temporal concerns, the jurisdiction of the church courts in temporal matters was inevitable. Insofar as temporal matters affected the quality and purposes of the community's spirituality, they became a proper subject for religious control.

For example, where Mormon land distribution policies differed from those of the federal government, the church courts intervened to legitimize the church's position. Where views of appropriate marital relationships conflicted with those of the nation, church courts provided a forum for supporting and regulating distinctive Mormon practices. Where theological considerations of equity conflicted with the demands of formal justice, the church courts resolved disputes more flexibly than civil courts. Where social behavior was morally offensive though not illegal, the church courts acted to uphold community norms without violating the right of the accused to depart from the community if he wished. And where the community's interest conflicted with the rights and interests of an individual, the church courts encouraged him to forego those rights for the sake of Zion.

For Latter-day Saints in the nineteenth century, the civil courts, lawyers, and law represented an inadequate and frequently corrupt system that worked against the establishment of Zion. For non-Mormons, such peculiar Mormon practices as polygamy and communal economic practices were so threatening to the larger community that suspending the normal operation of the law seemed justified. Mobs, frequently headed by respectable members of their communities, often law enforcement officials acting outside of the law, forcibly expelled Mormons from legally purchased homes and lands. The federal government restructured the concepts of due process and religious freedom to compel Mormon conformity with the larger community. When legal pressures threatened the survival of the church, church leaders yielded and accepted a more limited role.

The changed relationships between Mormons and non-Mormons since the turn of the century demonstrate that with assimilation comes a reversal of behavior in some of the members of the competing communities. Non-Mormons became more tolerant of Mormon religious beliefs as soon as Mormons relegated religion to a limited sphere of belief and conformed to more traditional conduct. Mormons came to appreciate lawyers and the law, although they remained wary of possible corruption in each. Political and social pluralism came to be seen as the flowering of the doctrine of free agency.

This particular history, of course, explains why a Mormon community today will express, in religious concepts and terms, those issues that in other communities are considered secular. The division between church and state is balanced differently, in favor of the church, in the Mormon community. A recent and intense religiously motivated colonization would hardly be expected to produce a different situation. But then, colonization of the West produced the Mormons' own vision of society—Zion. This assured profound effects on the nature of that society far into its future.

In western history generally, the treaties of Westphalia and Utrecht are taken to represent a changing paradigm, a fundamental shifting of primary allegiance from religious affiliation and feudal structure to the modern secular and territorial nation-state. But for the Mormons the older paradigm remains vital still.

However, that paradigm's dynamic communal strengths possess a shadow as surely as does the individual's ego. Allegiance to the Kingdom, while perhaps avoiding a form of secular state idolatry, carries within it the possibility that allegiance to church may supplant allegiance to God. Obedience to ecclesiastical leaders, if placed near the top of the ladder of moral virtues, may stultify normal growth toward moral maturity and replace it with perpetual spiritual adolescence and dependency. The warmth of the Mormon community can become uncomfortably hot, not only to the dissenter or the nonmember, but to the believer with individualistic tendencies as well. The status quo within the religious community can be elevated, without critical thought, to be a reflection of God's will, when in reality it may simply be the status quo. Isolation from hostile neighbors was almost surely necessary for particular Mormon institutions to evolve and survive. But refusal today to engage in inter-faith cooperation and dialogue would reflect a trivialization of the role of God in all history.

The Mormons were from the beginning a gathered people. Identifying powerfully with ancient Israel of the Old Testament, Mormons "gathered" first to Kirtland, Ohio; later to Jackson County, Missouri; and then Nauvoo, Illinois. They finally found sanctuary in the Great Basin. Protected by the Rocky Mountains, their society followed a unique path of development until the world caught up with and then swallowed and assimilated them.

Mormonism survived by projecting Zion into the millennial future. The nineteenth-century Mormon legal experience provides a rare insight into a community whose aspirations exceeded its grasp. What is remarkable, nevertheless, is not that they failed but that they succeeded against great internal and external odds for such an extended period of time.

For the Mormon in the twentieth century—indeed, for the religiously committed person of any tradition—the question still remains whether intense religious experience can be had outside community. If indeed the Mormons of the nineteenth century were right, then the pilgrim's path continues, searching with St. Paul and St. Augustine— and with Joseph and Brigham—for the City of God.

Abbreviations

A.L.R.	*American Law Reports Annotated.*
Amer. Dec.	*American Decisions: Cases decided in the courts of the several states.*
Ariz.	*Arizona: Reports of cases argued and determined in the Supreme Court of the State of Arizona.*
Cal. App.	*California Appeals: Reports of cases determined in the District Courts of Appeal of the State of California.*
Cal. Rptr.	*California Reporter: Reports of cases determined in the Supreme Court of the State of California.*
Cal.2d.	*California Reports, 2d Series: Reports of cases determined in the Supreme Court of the State of California.*
CCR	Nauvoo City Council Records.
CHC	Roberts, B. H. *Comprehensive History of the Church of Jesus Christ of Latter-day Saints.*
C.J.S.	*Corpus Juris Secundum: A Complete Restatement of the Entire American Law as Developed by All Reported Cases.*
Comp. Laws	*The Compiled Laws of the Territory of Utah.*
D&C	*Doctrine and Covenants of the Church of Jesus Christ of Latter-day Saints.*
F.2d	*Federal Reporter, Second Series: Cases argued and determined in the United States Courts of Appeals, United States Court of Claims, and United States Court of Customs and Patents.*
F. Cas.	*Federal Cases: Comprising cases argued and determined in the Circuit and District Courts of the United States.*
F. Supp.	*Federal Supplement: Comprising cases argued and determined in the District Courts of the United States.*
HC	Smith, Joseph, Jr. *History of the Church of Jesus Christ of Latter-day Saints.*
Ill.	*Illinois: Reports of cases at common law and in chancery, argued and determined in the Supreme Court of the State of Illinois.*
JD	*Journal of Discourses.*
JH	Journal History of the Church of Jesus Christ of Latter-day Saints.

Mass.	*Massachusetts Reports: Cases argued and determined in the Supreme Judicial Court of Massachusetts.*
Minn.	*Minnesota: Cases argued and determined in the Supreme Court of Minnesota.*
Mo.	*Missouri: Reports of cases argued and determined in the Supreme Court of the State of Missouri.*
NE	*Northeastern Reporter: Cases argued and determined in the courts of Illinois, Indiana, Massachusetts, New York, and Ohio.*
Nev.	*Nevada: Reports of decisions of the Supreme Court of the State of Nevada.*
N.M.	*New Mexico: Reports of cases argued and determined in the Supreme Court of the Territory of New Mexico.*
NW	*Northwestern Reporter: Cases argued and determined in the courts of Iowa, Michigan, Minnesota, Nebraska, North Dakota, South Dakota, and Wisconsin.*
N.Y.	*New York: Reports of cases argued and determined in the Court of Appeals of the State of New York.*
P.	*Pacific Reporter: Cases argued and determined in the courts of Arizona, California, Colorado, Idaho, Kansas, Montana, Nevada, New Mexico, Oklahoma, Oregon, Utah, Washington, and Wyoming.*
P.2d.	*Pacific Reporter, Second Series: Cases argued and determined in the courts of Arizona, California, Colorado, Idaho, Kansas, Montana, Nevada, New Mexico, Oklahoma, Oregon, Utah, Washington, and Wyoming.*
Pa.	*Pennsylvania State Reports: Containing Cases Adjudged in the Supreme Court.*
Report	*Report: Made to the Senate and House of Representatives of the State of Illinois, December 2, 1844.*
Stat.	*Statutes at Large of the United States of America, 1789–.*
SW	*Southwestern Reporter: Containing all the current decisions of the Supreme Courts of Missouri, Arkansas, and Tennessee, Court of Appeals of Kentucky, and Supreme Court and Court of Appeals/Criminal Cases of Texas.*
US	*United States Reports: Cases adjudged in the Supreme Court.*
Utah	*Utah Supreme Court: Reports of cases decided in the Supreme Court of the State of Utah.*
Utah Code Ann.	*Utah Code Annotated, 1953.*
Utah Laws	*Utah (Ter.). Laws, memorials and resolutions of the Territory of Utah, 1851–1894. Also Laws of the State of Utah, 1896–.*

Notes

Introduction

1. Recent studies of Mormonism reflect an increased interest in the church's early history and major transformations. Since the mid-1970s, several excellent general histories have appeared, including Jan Shipps, *Mormonism: The Story of a New Religious Tradition* (1985); Klaus J. Hansen, *Mormonism and the American Experience* (1981); Leonard J. Arrington and Davis Bitton, *The Mormon Experience: A History of the Latter-day Saints* (1979); Mark P. Leone, *Roots of Modern Mormonism* (1979); Leonard J. Arrington, Feramorz Y. Fox, and Dean May, *Building the City of God: Community and Cooperation among the Mormons* (1976); James B. Allen and Glen M. Leonard, *The Story of the Latter-day Saints* (1976); and Richard S. Van Wagoner, *Mormon Polygamy: A History* (1986). Richard L. Bushman, *Joseph Smith and the Beginnings of Mormonism* (1984); Leonard Arrington, *Brigham Young* (1985); and Linda King Newell and Valeen Tippetts Avery, *Mormon Enigma: Emma Hale Smith* (1985), although biographical in nature, offer substantial insights into Mormon history. Each general history highlights such radical Mormon concepts of the past century as plural marriage, economic communitarianism, and the political kingdom of God; each also notes, sometimes with regret, Mormonism's metamorphosis into a conservative religion that supports the social and economic values of modern American society.

These works also present theories to account for Mormonism's ability to change strategies and yet survive institutionally. Shipps explains this continuity amidst change by noting how church leaders focused on the authority of revelation to justify institutional adjustments. Leone claims Mormons were able to adapt easily because they were ahistorical or "without a collective memory" (Leone 1979, 146). Hansen views the changes as a pragmatic capitulation to outside pressure and an "internal response to modernization," leaving aside the larger question of why the either occurred in the first place (Hansen 1981, 205, 176). Arrington and Bitton (1979, 129, 242) locate the change in the shift from communitarian economics to the ethic of capitalism; however they see Mormon distinctiveness persisting in the current preference for large families that follow traditional roles.

Most analyses follow contemporary historiography in stressing the pivotal role of economic factors while minimizing intellectual or theological influences. In general, they argue that Mormons began to give up the theocratic Kingdom of God in 1869, when the railroad reached the Great Basin and federal land laws were applied there. As communitarian economic systems were absorbed into the national economy of laissez-faire capitalism, Mormon distinctiveness eroded rather quickly. Polygamy and political exceptions were aftershocks following the economic quake. Jan Shipps locates the change in the early twentieth century and focuses more on theological ideas rather than economic factors alone. Her alternative view is somewhat closer to our own.

1. Zion and the State: Peaceful Coexistence

1. The Mormon view on civil disobedience is consistent with contemporary philosophical analysis of the subject (Mangrum 1988). Ronald Dworkin argues that civil disobedience is morally as well as legally justified where laws do not afford the citizens equal concern and respect, as required by the political morality of the regime (Dworkin, 206–22). John Rawls also states that civil disobedience is morally justified when it aims to move the society to an increased appreciation of individual rights. He defines "civil disobedience as a public, nonviolent, conscientious yet political act contrary to law usually done with the aim of bringing about a change in the law or policies of government. By acting in this way one addresses the sense of justice of the majority of the community and declares that in one's considered opinion the principles of social cooperation among free and equal men are not being respected" (Rawls, 364). Rawls distinguishes conscientious refusal as an act required by conscience that is contrary to law. It is public but does not have the purpose of causing change.

2. "Honestus" is commonly thought to be Benjamin Austin, a Boston politician. The articles were published as a pamphlet in 1819 and republished in *American J. Legal History* 13 (1969): 244–302. See also Grant (1982, 68:580).

3. Klaus J. Hansen, in *Quest for Empire* (1967), maintains this separation thesis arguing that the Council of Fifty would preserve the constitutional rights of each. His thesis is consistent with the reverence in which Joseph Smith held the principles embodied in the United States Constitution qualified by his distrust of the civil government's ability to preserve them.

2. The Mormon Ecclesiastical Court System

1. E.g., Far West Record, "The Conference Minutes and Record Book of Christ's Church of Latter-day Saints," 21.

2. E.g., ibid., 9.

3. E.g., the trial of Chancery Cole on 24 September 1831 at Amherst, Ohio, was before three elders. In comparison, several cases were heard before nine elders at one elders' conference held on 6 December 1831 at Randolph County, Ohio (ibid., 20). Apparently all the noninterested elders present at

the conference would sit together in council. No cases were heard by a single elder.

4. D&C 42:80. Nonmembers were generally thought to be incompetent to testify in church proceedings. They were considered not spiritually in tune with Mormon beliefs and less trustworthy, and ecclesiastical sanctions for giving perjured testimony were unavailable.

5. E.g., Far West Record, 24.

6. E.g., ibid.

7. Ibid., 6.

8. D&C 42:89. Anthropologist Paul Dredge interprets this confidentiality requirement as follows: "Here is the first reference to the excluding of gentiles totally and members not directly concerned with a case from church courts: the dirty linen of the church was to be kept in the closet so that non-Mormons might not feel that Mormons were contentious; that therefore, proselytizing efforts with them would not be hindered; and that the developing faith of the young or new converts would not be shaken by dissension within the church" (Dredge, 193–215).

9. Far West Record, 21–23.

10. Ibid., 23.

11. Keeler, 5.

12. See D&C 58:17, 18 for the role of the bishop as a judge in Israel.

13. Far West Record, 32.

14. Ibid.

15. HC 1:359. The bishop apparently was accepted as a moderator in the early high priest councils, in his capacity as presiding high priest over the local congregation. Far West Record, 36.

16. Far West Record, 36.

17. Ibid., 43.

18. The prophet called David Whitmer as president, W. W. Phelps and John Whitmar as assistants, and Oliver Cowdery as clerk of the Far West High Council. After serving faithfully for several years, this presidency fell into transgression. The council removed and eventually excommunicated its entire presidency. Some individuals later rejoined the church but none ever again held leadership positions in the church.

19. Far West Record, 48.

20. Ibid., 59–60.

21. D&C 102:30, 31. Joseph Smith amended D&C 102 prior to the publication of the Doctrine and Covenants to include the Quorum of the Twelve as an alternate court of final appeal.

22. The power of the First Presidency to call twelve high priests to assist as counselors in these courts, almost on the same pattern as the high council, was given on 28 March 1835 at Kirtland by revelation (D&C 107:78, 84). The practice of having twelve high priests assist, however, was discontinued over time.

23. Far West Record, 72, 94–95; HC 2:483–84.

24. Far West Record, 107.
25. Far West Record, 132–33.
26. Far West Record, 118–19. See also Gunn, 154–55.
27. Far West Record, 26.
28. Gentry, 421–50.
29. HC 3:284; HC 3:345. Frederick G. Williams had served as a counselor in the First Presidency from 1832, but on 7 November 1837 he was rejected as a counselor by the Saints gathered at a general assembly at Far West (HC 2:522–23). Accordingly, his excommunication here was lawful because he was not then a member of the First Presidency. On 8 April 1840 at a conference held at Nauvoo, Williams confessed his sins in Missouri, asked for forgiveness, and was received back into the fellowship of the church (HC 4:110).

3. Early Trials in New York and Ohio

1. Dr. Purple's account suggests that Smith was discharged. The trial record indicates Smith was found guilty but mentions no sentence. Noble's letter and Benton's article agree that Smith was condemned, but Noble suggests Smith jumped bail and left. Benton, however, suggests that the court took into account Smith's age and hoped his conduct might be reformed, and therefore "he was designedly allowed to escape." In any case, it seems no sanction was imposed, and the court did not pursue the matter any further.

2. D&C 32. For the early history of the church in Ohio, see Fielding, 21–68; Backman, 346; Anderson 1974, 474. For a larger perspective on the beginnings of the Ohio period see Layton, 423.

3. In December 1830 Joseph Smith received a commandment to move the church to Ohio (CHC 1:240; HC; D&C 37). On January 2, 1831, at a conference in Fayette, New York, the commandment to gather in Ohio was repeated (CHC 1:241; HC 1:140–43; D&C 38). During the later part of January 1831, Joseph Smith, Emma Smith, Sidney Rigdon, and Edward Partridge moved to Kirtland, arriving February 1, 1831 (CHC 1:242; HC 1:141). In May 1831 the main body of New York Saints began coming to Ohio (HC 1:145).

4. HC 1:352, 355. Newspapers of the day carried accounts of Dr. Hurlburt's theories on the Spalding manuscript and the Book of Mormon. *Guerney Times*, January 18, 1834; *The Ohio Repository*, February 28, 1834.

5. HC 2:47. See also *Chardon Spectator & Geauga Gazette*, April 12, 1834; *The Ohio Repository*, April 18, 1834. Judge Birchard presided at the trial.

6. *Chardon Spectator & Geauga Gazette*, April 12, 1834.

7. *Chardon Spectator & Geauga Gazette*, October 30, 1835.

8. CHC 1:358–60, 370–71; HC 2:61–134.

9. *Painesville Telegraph*, December 5, 1934.

10. Hill, Rooker, and Wimmer, 81. Joseph Smith was represented on appeal by Benjamin Bissell.

11. *Chardon Spectator & Geauga Gazette*, October 30, 1834.

12. *Painesville Telegraph*, April 24, 1835; June 26, 1835. This edition contains

a rough transcript of the trial proceedings. Lucy Mack Smith testified that she saw some of the fray from upstairs and heard Stoddard talking loud, calling Joseph Smith "a d—d false prophet, [and] a d—d one thing and another." She stated that she saw Joseph slap him but did not hear Stoddard say he would flog him and did not see Stoddard attempt to strike him.

William Smith testified that he saw Stoddard coming along cursing and swearing. Joseph went out, and Stoddard said he would whip him and drew his cane on him. Joseph backed the cane off and struck him with a flat hand. "Burgess," identified only as a friend of Joseph Smith and a member of the church, testified that Stoddard struck at Smith first and raised his cane in a threatening manner.

13. CHC 1:400–403; HC 2:467–68. For a discussion of the organization of the Kirtland Safety Society see Sampson and Wimmer, 427–36. The "Kirtland Safety Society Anti-Banking Company" was organized as a "stock industrial company" under which it "proposed the management of their respective occupations," consisting of "agriculture, mechanical arts and merchandising." See HC 2:470–73.

14. See Hanson, 158–59.

15. E.g., *Painesville Telegraph*, January 20, 1837: "A new revolution—Mormon [*sic*] Money. During the past two days an emission of bills from the society of Mormons, has been showered upon us. As far as we can learn there is no property bound for their redemption, no coin in hand to redeem them with, and no responsible individuals whose honor or whose honesty is pledged for their payment. They seem to rest upon a spiritual basis.—Aside from the violation of the statute rendering them void, and of course the notes given from them, we look upon the whole as a most reprehensible fraud on the public, and cannot conceal our surprise that they should circulate at all."

Painesville Telegraph, February 24, March 31, 1837; *Painesville Republican*, February 9, 1837; *Cleveland Herald and Gazette*, May 6, July 15, and September 8, 1837; *Cleveland Weekly Gazette*, January 18, and 25, and February 1 and 8, 1837; *Cleveland Daily Gazette*, January 12, 1837; *Painesville Republican*, January 12, 1837; *Western Reserve Chronicle*, February 7, 1837.

16. CHC 1:402. For a discussion of the causes of the failure of the Kirtland Safety Society see Hill, Rooker, and Wimmer, 81; S. H. Partridge, 437–52.

17. *Painesville Republican*, June 5, 1937; *The Ohio Statesman*, July 5, 1837; *Painesville Telegraph*, June 3, 1834; *Cleveland Herald and Gazette*, June 2, 1837; *Ohio Repository*, June 22, 1837; *Painesville Republican*, July 6, 1837; *Painesville Telegraph*, May 26 and June 9, 1837. Solomon Denton, as his testimony was reported by the newspaper, claimed to have first met Joseph Smith in New York in 1830; from there he came to Kirtland in 1831 and "embraced" the religion. Subsequently he moved to Missouri and then returned to Kirtland in 1833 or 1834, where he worked in the printing business with Davis, Rigdon, Cowdery, and Smith. Sidney Rigdon testified Denton had been excommunicated two or three months prior to the trial.

The only information known about Davis is that Solomon Denton claimed he was engaged in a printing business with him in Kirtland. Sidney Rigdon also testified that Davis had "never been strictly subservient to the rules of the society."

Luke Johnson testified that Joseph Smith had said that if Newell or any other man should head a mob against the Mormons, he "ought to be put out of the way, and it would be our duty to do so."

Mr. Whitney testified that he had heard Grandison Newell's name mentioned often at the bank but had never heard Joseph Smith threaten his life. Warren Parrish, a clerk at the Kirtland Safety Society Bank, testified only that he heard Grandison Newell's name mentioned several times at the bank. B. H. Roberts states that "much reliance had been placed on Parrish's testimony by Grandison Newell, but when put on the stand and asked 'whether he knew anything in the character or conduct of Mr. Smith which is unworthy of his profession as a man of God,' he answered—'I do not' " (CHC 1:405 n.32).

Mr. Hyde testified that he had been at the Kirtland Safety Society Bank one day and had heard people speculating that suit might be brought against the bank, and Mr. Newell might be the person to do it. At that time, Joseph Smith said Mr. Newell should be "put out of the way" and that "destroying" Grandison Newell would be justifiable before God, but later apologized for using such language.

Denton testified that in April or May, Davis came to him and told him that Joseph Smith wanted them to kill Grandison Newell. He subsequently borrowed a pistol from Sidney Rigdon. Later, Joseph Smith told him, "I know where you are going and what your business is." Denton also testified that Smith "said that he had seen Davis and told him I would be a good hand to go with him, said this was a good work, and we must be very wise; then spoke of Newell, said he had injured the society, and that it was better for one man to suffer than to have a whole community disturbed; that it was the will of Heaven that Newell should be put out of the way."

Hyrum Smith testified that he had heard Denton was plotting on Grandison Newell's life, and when he confronted Denton, he denied it.

Mr. Cahoun testified as did Mr. Rigdon. The newspaper account reported the witness's name was "Mr. Cahoun." It is not clear whether this was a reference to Reynolds Cahoun, a prominent Mormon leader of the day. Sidney Rigdon testified that about two years previously he had heard that Davis and Denton were conspiring against Grandison Newell, but had no indication that Joseph Smith instigated or approved of the conspiracy (*Painesville Telegraph*, June 9, 1837).

18. CHC 1:405 n.32.

19. *Painesville Telegraph*, May 26, 1837.

20. Court records from October term of Geauga County Court of Common Pleas, 359, 362 (LDS Church Archives). See also CHC 1:402–3; *Painesville Republican*, January 19, 1837.

One commentator has stated that at this point Joseph Smith knew that unless the case could be won, there was no chance for survival of the bank. When Joseph Smith's demurrer to the plaintiff was overruled by the court in

June, even though the case was continued by jury trial, he must have known the bank was finished.

21. CHC 1:403. Joseph Smith and Sidney Rigdon entered the bill of exceptions, appealing on five points: (1) To prove the existence of the association of the Kirtland Safety Society the plaintiff introduced the written articles of association. Defendants "objected to proof without first showing notice to said society to produce said articles"; (2) The court allowed the plaintiffs to prove that the Kirtland Safety Society had loaned their bills without requiring them to produce the actual bills that had been loaned; (3) The statute under which the plaintiff was prosecuting was not in force; (4) Even if it was in force, the Kirtland Safety Society was not loaning paper within the meaning of the statute; and (5) There was insufficient evidence for the jury to find the defendants guilty. See Geauga County Court of Common Pleas, 359, 362.

22. Geauga County Court of Common Pleas, 399. See also Hill, Rooker, and Wimmer, 81. Plaintiff's attorney in this action was Ira C. Paine.

23. *Cleveland Herald and Gazette*, July 17, 1837 (*Herald*, vol. 19, no. 9; *Gazette*, vol. 1, no. 80).

24. HC 2:502.

25. Court records from October term of Geauga County Court of Common Pleas, 351 (LDS Church Archives).

26. HC 2:528.

27. See Geauga County Court of Common Pleas, execution docket G.

28. See ibid.

29. E.g., mortgage foreclosure notice in mortgage foreclosure by Chauncey Calkins against Jared Carter (*Painesville Republican*, January 4, 1838; *Painesville Telegraph*, January 11, 1838); mortgage foreclosure notice in mortgage foreclosure by John Johnson and Christopher Quinn against John F. Boyton and Lyman E. Johnson (*Painesville Telegraph*, January 11, 1838).

30. Hill, Rooker, and Wimmer, 29.

4. Persecution in Missouri

1. The Mormons sympathized with the abolitionist movement but apparently conducted no illegal abolitionist activities. An article entitled "Free People of Color," in the *Evening and the Morning Star*, of July 1833 (HC 1:377–78), primarily quoted the laws of Missouri on slavery. When it was interpreted as abolitionist, an "Extra," printed on 16 July 1833 in the form of a handbill (HC 1:378–79), denied any abolitionist intentions, but the disclaimer went unheeded. Mob violence began a few days later.

2. The mob justified its attack on the printing office by claiming the Mormons were printing materials that considered Indians and blacks to be spiritual brothers of whites and therefore entitled to respect. These ideas were viewed as dangerous to a frontier community that included slaveowners among its more prominent members. An interesting parallel would develop in Nauvoo when the Mormons destroyed a non-Mormon press after the city

council had declared it a public nuisance. In Jackson County, the community's racist values justified holding free speech in abeyance; in Nauvoo non-Mormons found it reprehensible that church leaders presumed community peace should override the right of the press.

3. HC 3:175. The entire order was rescinded on 25 June 1976 by Governor Christopher S. Bond as part of Missouri's bicentennial events.

4. On 24 January 1839 Joseph Smith petitioned the Missouri legislature for a change of venue, providing information respecting King's impropriety:

We know that much of that prejudice against us is not so much to be attributed to a want of honest motives amongst the citizens as it is to misrepresentation.

It is a difficult task to change opinions once formed. The other obstacle which we candidly consider one of the most weighty, is the feeling which we believe is entertained by Hon. Austin A. King against us, and his consequent inability to do us impartial justice. It is from no disposition to speak disrespectfully of that high officer, that we lay before your honorable body the facts we do; but simply that the legislature may be apprised of our real condition. We look upon Judge King as like all other mere men, liable to be influenced by his feelings, his prejudices, and his previously formed opinions. From his reputation we consider him as being partially, if not entirely, committed against us. He has written much upon the subject of our late difficulties, in which he has placed us in the wrong. These letters have been published to the world. He has also presided at an excited public meeting as chairman, and no doubt sanctioned all the proceedings. We do not complain of the citizens who held the meeting, they were entitled to that privilege. But for the judge before whom the very men were to be tried for a capital offense to participate in an expression of condemnation of these same individuals, is to us, at least, apparently wrong; and we cannot think that we should, after such a course on the part of the judge, have the same chance of a fair and impartial trial as all admit we ought to have.

We believe that the foundation of the feeling against us, which we have reason to think Judge King entertains, may be traced to the unfortunate troubles which occurred in Jackson County some few years ago; in a battle between the "Mormons" and a portion of the citizens of that county, Mr. Brazeale, the brother-in-law of Judge King, was killed. It is natural that the judge should have some feelings against us, whether we were right or wrong in that controversy.

We mention these facts, not to disparage Judge King; we believe that from the relation he bears to us, he would himself prefer that our trials should be had in a different circuit, before a different court" (HC 3:247–48).

5. In the Saints' petition to the U.S. Congress a year later, the church alleged that the Missouri captors purposefully permitted the prisoners to escape to avoid the exposure of wrongdoing at trial: "That they were suffered

to escape admits of no doubt. The truth is the state of Missouri had become ashamed of their proceedings against the "Mormons," and as the best means of getting out of the scrape, gave the prisoners an opportunity to escape. In proof of this, the prisoners have ever since been living publicly in the state of Illinois, and the executive of Missouri has made no demand upon the executive of Illinois. Can it be supposed that the people of Missouri would thus tamely submit to the commission of treason by a portion of their citizens, and make no effort to punish the guilty, when they were thus publicly living in an adjoining state? Is not this passiveness evidence? They knew the "Mormons" were innocent, and the citizens of Missouri wrong?" (HC 4:35–36).

5. The Illinois Period

1. This position of nonjusticiability of the guarantee clause was first declared in *Luther v. Borden* (US 48:1 [1849]) and powerfully reaffirmed in *Baker v. Carr* (US 369:186 [1962]).

2. Since the passage of the Fourteenth Amendment following the Civil War, that amendment's due process clause, directed against state government, has been held, over a century's time, to include within its meaning nearly all of the basic rights of the Bill of Rights (Firmage 1975, 594, 614–15). Joseph Smith intuitively looked beyond the incorporation doctrine, by which the provisions of the Bill of Rights came to apply against the states, when he expressed himself on the Constitution in Nauvoo, one year before his murder:

> It is one of the first principles of my life, and one that I have cultivated from my childhood, having been taught it by my father, to allow every one the liberty of conscience. I am the greatest advocate of the Constitution of the United States there is on the earth. In my feelings I am always ready to die for the protection of the weak and oppressed in their just rights. The only fault I find with the Constitution is, it is not broad enough to cover the whole ground.
>
> Although it provides that all men shall enjoy religious freedom, yet it does not provide the manner by which that freedom can be preserved, nor for the punishment of Government officers who refuse to protect the people in their religious rights, or punish these mobs, states, or communities who interfere with the rights of the people on account of their religion. Its sentiments are good, but it provides no means of enforcing them. It has but this one fault. Under its provision, a man or a people who are able to protect themselves can get along well enough; but those who have the misfortune to be weak or unpopular are left to the merciless rage of popular fury (HC 6:56–57).

3. Mr. *Linn*, said he hardly knew what should be done with a memorial like this. A sovereign state seemed about to be put on its trial before the senate of the United States, and he was entirely opposed to the jurisdiction. The memorial and documents were wholly *ex parte*, and,

if these papers were depended on *alone*, they could not fail to make impressions unjust and injurious to the state and people of Missouri. . . . He was entirely unwilling to believe that, amid such a population [as Missouri's] there was not a sufficient number of persons to prevent such flagrant acts of wrong and oppression as were complained of by the memorialists. At all events, he would not consent that a black mark should be placed here upon the character of the state or people without giving them an opportunity of being heard; and *if* these papers should be referred to a committee, he would move that it have power to send for persons and papers, that the investigation might be searching and thorough. Mr. L. said this was truly an extraordinary state of things, when an independent state should be arrainged [*sic*] at this bar for a violation of her own municipal laws. . . .

Mr. *Linn* said that he could not believe that an order from the governor, which was in violation of every law of God and man, would be executed by the people. In the absence of all testimony to the contrary, he was bound to believe that the governor and other authorities had done their duty. . . .

Mr. L said, from his absence from home, here and elsewhere, he had not an opportunity to learn all the particulars of their disturbance, and the causes that led to such serious results. But the Mormons were accused of committing the first aggressions, by burning houses, plundering and destroying property and other acts of violence, saying that they were within the limits of the New Jerusalem, which had been given to them *exclusively* by the Lord. If these charges were correct, the Mormons were the aggressors, and brought upon themselves the punishment which followed. . . . He said he was very unwilling to believe that either the legislature or judiciary would do injustice or aid or even countenance oppression, and he wished that, if the parties implicated by the Mormons were to be tried at the bar of the senate, they might have an opportunity to be heard.

Young responded that

he did not regard the whole state of Missouri as implicated; but he thought the memorialists had made out a hard case against some of her people. In addition to the violence and destruction of improvements, these Mormons had three hundred certificates from the land office for land purchased by them in Missouri, from which they had been driven not only by the people, but by an order from the governor. (*Niles National Register*, 57:364)

4. Norvell had originally proposed that the matter be laid on the table "that it may lie there forever." Henry Clay of Kentucky said that he was "indifferent as to the motion" but felt that "the subject ought to be made by the committee whether it is a matter of grievance, and, if it is, whether congress has any power of redress" (*Niles National Register*, 57:364). With William C. Preston of South Carolina and Missouri's own Thomas Hart Benton also calling for

"a proper investigation," Norvell modified his motion, and the matter was tabled only temporarily.

5. Some scholars suggest that the provision for a militia was Bennett's contribution (Flanders 1965, 110; Kimball 1966, 6). Unlike Smith, Bennett had some experience in military affairs, and was commissioned as brigadier general in the Invincible Dragoons by Governor Carlin of Illinois under the Act to Incorporate the Invincible Dragoons of the 2nd Division of Illinois Militia in 1839 (Chamberlin, 577). Many officers in the legion used their positions to rise to power in the church, according to Flanders (1965, 111).

6. A year before his death, according to William Clayton, Smith told Douglas: "Judge, you will aspire to the presidency of the United States; and if ever you turn your hand against me or the Latter-day Saints, you will feel the weight of the hand of Almighty upon you" (HC 5:394). Mormons attributed Douglas's loss to Abraham Lincoln in the 1860 presidential election and his premature death the following year at the age of forty-eight to this prophecy and a speech by Douglas in 1857 in which he denounced conditions in the the territory of Utah and called for repeal of the organic law of the territory (HC 5:395–98).

7. In a letter to the Nauvoo City Council after the destruction of the *Nauvoo Expositor* in June 1844, Governor Thomas Ford, Carlin's successor, expressed similar views:

> You have also assumed to yourselves more power than you are entitled to in relation to writs of *habeas* under your charter. . . .
>
> For the purpose of insuring more speedy relief to such persons [those breaking Nauvoo ordinances], authority was given to the Municipal Court to issue writs of *habeas corpus* in all cases arising under the ordinances of the city.
>
> It was never supposed by the Legislature, nor can the language of your charter be tortured to mean that a jurisdiction was intended to be conferred which would apply to all cases of imprisonment under the general laws of the state or of the United States, as well as the city ordinances. (HC 6:535)

8. Joseph Smith said, "The lawyers themselves acknowledge that we have all power granted us in our charters that we could ask for—that we had more power than any other court in the state; for all other courts were restricted, while ours was not" (HC 5:473). Ford and others have attributed such advice to the lawyers' desire to curry favor with the Saints in their efforts to win political offices (Ford to the Mayor and Council of the City of Nauvoo, 22 June 1844, in HC 6:535; HC 6:xxxi–xxxii). Smith may have encouraged such self-serving counsel, for he introduced Cyrus Walker, a candidate for Congress, to a Nauvoo audience with these words: "I have converted this candidate . . . [to the idea] that the right of habeas corpus is included in our charter. If he continues converted, I will vote for him" (HC 5:467–68).

9. One of Smith's lawyers was Cyrus Walker, whom Smith considered "the greatest criminal lawyer in that part of Illinois." Walker was campaigning

for Congress at the time and agreed to represent Smith in exchange for Smith's promise to vote for him. He then exulted, "I am now sure of my election, as Joseph Smith has promised me his vote" (HC 5:444).

10. The Nauvoo Municipal Court used the writ of habeas corpus to free persons in connection with at least two other civil actions–to secure the release of John M. Finch in an action brought by Amos Davis (HC 6:80), and to release John P. Greene, Andrew Lytle, and John Lytle in a suit brought by Chauncey Higbee (HC 6:286).

The Smiths' candidacies may have hastened their martyrdom. They "put the two major parties [Whigs and Democrats] on notice that neither could hope to win the decisive Mormon vote [in Illinois], thus removing any moderating influence either party might previously have exerted" (Oaks 1965b, 863).

11. Interestingly, the Illinois Supreme Court itself later relied on this case and Blackstone to support a municipality action in another nuisance-abatement case (*King v. Davenport*, Ill. 98:305, 311 [1881]; see also *Sings v. City of Joliet*, Ill. 237:300; NE 86:663 [1908]). In each of those cases, the municipality had acted under its charter or statutory authority to abate nuisances, which was nearly identical to that of Nauvoo.

12. Compare *Earp v. Lee* (Ill. 71:193), an 1873 Illinois case that sustained a saloonkeeper's action for damages where his saloon had been destroyed on the grounds that it was a public nuisance. Joseph Smith acknowledged that the city council would be liable for damages if it had acted wrongly and expressed his willingness to abide by a court decision on the matter (HC 6:538, 585).

13. The Illinois Senate Committee on the Judiciary reported to the legislature:

> The act incorporating the city of Nauvoo, being a public act, and creating, as it does, a municipal incorporation, your committee has no hesitation in arriving at the conclusion that it is legitimately within the power of the Legislature to repeal the same, but they readily admit, and feel, that that power should in all cases be exercised with great caution. It is the duty of the Legislature to guard the interests of all the people legislated for against abuse. . . . But the history of the times furnishes your committee with abundance of evidence of not only flagrant abuses of the powers conferred by said act on the city of Nauvoo, and those oft repeated, but a disposition on the part of the citizens to continue those abuses in defiance of all law, and with an utter disregard of the rights of their fellow citizens. Those abuses of their chartered privileges not only furnish cause for uneasiness among their neighbors, but also the theme of public animadversion at home and abroad.

The committee cited as examples of these "abuses" the municipal court's use of habeas corpus and the destruction of the *Nauvoo Expositor*. It concluded that the Mormons had

> by their many and flagrant abuses of their incorporation, kindled the flames of civil war within our hitherto peaceful and happy State, profess-

ing, as they do, the Mohometan faith under a name but little varied from the original, the tendency of which strikes at the very foundation of our society.

We would be remiss in the discharge of our duty to the people were we not to withdraw from them all pretence in future to re-enact again those deeds so recently the cause of just alarm to our citizens throughout the State. (Report 1:139–40)

14. At least some Mormons may have had standing to challenge the composition of the grand jury since the same grand jury that indicted the accused assassins of Joseph Smith also returned an indictment against eleven Mormons for riot in the destruction of the *Nauvoo Expositor* (Oaks and Hill, 51). Only Jesse P. Harmon and John Lytle—law enforcement officers in Nauvoo— ever stood trial for the destruction of the *Expositor*, and they were acquitted, in October 1845 (Oaks and Hill, 199–201).

15. The authority the defense cited—Blackstone's *Commentaries*—applied only to cases where the officials charged with selecting potential jurors were parties to the action or related to one of the parties (Oaks and Hill, 98–99, 109 n.11).

16. The Butterfield-Penrose correspondence, as well as other original documents concerning Smith's bankruptcy, are part of the records of the solicitor of the Treasury, Record Group 206, Part I (1841–52) at the National Archives, Washington, D.C. (Oaks and Bentley, 738 n.10).

17. Under Illinois law, the judgment attached as a lien to the judgment debtor's real property (Oaks and Bentley, 743 n.35). See also *Jones v. Guthrie* (Ill. 23:367 [1860])—a judgment of a federal circuit court becomes a lien on the real property of the judgment debtor as provided by local law; *Reynolds v. Henderson* (Ill. 7:111, 118 [1845])—once a lien attaches to property by reason of a judgment, it continues in effect till satisfied; and *Rogers v. Dickey* (Ill. 6:637, 644–45 [1844]).

18. See also *St. Peter's Roman Catholic Congregation v. Germain* (Ill. 104:440, 446 [1882]), in which the Illinois Supreme Court, in construing a similar statute, concluded that "any amount in excess of [ten acres] is expressly forbidden by the statute, and it follows that all conveyances, deeds or other contracts made in violation of this prohibition, are absolutely void." The consequence of Pope's decision was that those who had purchased the property from the church before its removal to Utah had defective titles, which embarrassed the church and cost the subsequent purchasers thousands of dollars (Oaks and Bentley, 780–81).

6. The Early Attack on Polygamy

1. Although the church officially renounced the practice of polygamy in 1890, plural marriages continued to be performed with church authority until 1904 (Quinn 1985, 56–59).

2. Two leading Mormon scholars estimate that, in fact, "no more than 5 percent of married Mormon men had more than one wife; and since the great

majority of these had only two wives, it seems reasonable to suppose that about 12 percent of Mormon married women were involved in the principle" (Arrington and Bitton, 199).

3. Eight years after the passage of the Morrill Act, the appeal for patience was repeated in Congress. Representative Thomas Fitch of Nevada suggested that the eventual natural demise of polygamy was imminent:

> I believe polygamy has run its course. I believe that the railroad which deprived the Mormons of their isolation has struck it a mortal blow. . . . I do not believe that a practice which is at war with the interests of society, hostile to the spirit of the age, and opposed to the instincts of human nature, can, even when sustained by religious convictions, maintain itself against the silent, insidious, persistent, restless assaults of the social forces arrayed against it. . . . Adventurous miners find precious metals in the vicinage, and another wave rolls in from East or West and makes a chasm in the family circle. Thus the elements of destruction are busy about it (*Congressional Globe*, 1870, 1518).

But by then a full-scale attack on Mormonism was well under way.

4. The district and supreme courts, however, were not courts of the United States, deriving their powers from Article III of the Constitution. Rather, they were courts created by Congress under its power to regulate the territories (U.S. Const. Art. IV, § 3, ¶ 2) and were granted jurisdiction similar to courts of the United States (*Clinton v. Englebrecht*, US 80:434, 447 [1871]).

5. Although the *Cast* decision (*Cast v. Cast*, Utah 1:112 [1873]), limiting the jurisdiction of probate courts, was rendered subsequent to *Englebrecht*'s broad reading of territorial powers, the Utah court in *Cast* refused to consider *Englebrecht* as relevant and dismissed its applicability curtly: "The supreme court of the United States have, in the late case, but upon a totally different subject, given some dicta, which, by some, is supposed to bear upon the question involved in this case. Upon a fair and candid examination, however, of such dicta, we do not think that such will be found to be the case" (Utah 1:127). In affirming the *Cast* view in *Ferris v. Higley* (US 87:384 [1874]), the United States Supreme Court made no reference to *Englebrecht*.

6. Grant further suggested that Congress might adopt legislation clarifying the status of plural wives and children so that the campaign against polygamy would not punish innocents. However, Congress did not attach as great a priority to this suggestion as it did to the president's other recommendations.

7. The mysteries of the Endowment House continued to intrigue the nation, with publicists eager to imagine the most ghastly sorts of rituals occurring there. In 1889, a district court was even persuaded to hold hearings on the question of whether the Mormons exacted a blood oath from immigrants in the Endowment House to wreak vengeance on the United States for the murder of Joseph Smith (Dwyer, 245–46). The Mormons finally resolved the problem by razing the house in 1889 (Allen and Leonard, 406).

8. The United States Supreme Court recently denied certiorari in *Potter v. Murray City* (US 474:849), and thereby avoided an opportunity to reconsider *Reynolds*. Potter, a police officer for Murray City, Utah, was dismissed because

of his religiously motivated practice of polygamy. He sued the city and state in federal district court for the district of Utah, alleging that his constitutional rights had been violated (F. Supp. 585:1126 [1984]). The trial court, relying on *Yoder* and *Sherbert*, held that the state had to show a compelling interest to justify infringing on Potter's religious practices. Although the state failed to present any empirical or testimonial evidence of such a compelling interest, the trial court took judicial notice of the state's interest in maintaining the social order now based on monogamy, and held that sufficient to meet the state's burden. Potter was unable to prevail even though the state conceded that it had "never asserted that polygamy is inherently or demonstrably a moral evil with direct consequences of a negative nature to its participants or to its neighbors."

The Tenth Circuit Court of Appeals, relying mainly on *Reynolds*, denied Potter's appeal (F.2d 760:1065). His petition for a writ of certiorari to the Supreme Court was denied. For a more thorough explanation of the *Potter* case, see Note, Utah L. Rev. 1986:345.

7. The Decisive Attack on Polygamy

1. The state, in presenting its case, had introduced evidence suggesting that Cannon had sexual relations with his plural wives. While Powers agreed with the court's interpretation of the Edmunds Act and concluded that cohabitation did not necessarily require proof of intercourse, he thought Cannon should have been permitted to introduce evidence demonstrating the absence of intercourse, even though it would not have constituted a defense to the charge (P. 7:385–86).

2. According to Tribe,

As a matter of due process, a law is void on its face if it is so vague that persons "of common intelligence must necessarily guess at its meaning and differ as to its application. . . ." This indefiniteness runs afoul of due process concepts which require that persons be given fair notice of what to avoid, and that the discretion of law enforcement officials, with the attendant dangers of arbitrary and discriminatory enforcement, be limited by explicit legislative standards" (Tribe, 718).

3. Stat. 18:254, § 3 (1874). The United States Supreme Court greatly reduced the usefulness of this appeal provision in *Clawson v. United States* (US 113:143 [1885]). Rudger Clawson was charged and convicted of both polygamy and cohabitation and sentenced to three years and six months and a $500 fine for polygamy and six months and a $300 fine for cohabitation. While the appeal to the territorial supreme court was pending, he petitioned the trial court to be released on bail. Both it and the territorial supreme court denied bail.

Clawson appealed that refusal to the United States Supreme Court. Under Utah law, the Court noted, an appeal to the territorial supreme court automatically stayed the execution of a sentence only if the trial court certified that probable cause existed for the appeal (US 113:147). If such a certificate was filed, Utah law further provided that "the sheriff must, if the defendant be in his custody, upon being served with a copy thereof, keep the defendant in his custody without executing the judgment, and detain him to abide the judgment on appeal" (Utah Laws, 1878, 138). An admission to bail where a defendant had been sentenced to imprisonment lay within the discretion of the court.

Thus, by certifying Clawson's appeal but denying him bail, the trial court created a situation where Clawson was remanded to the Utah penitentiary during the course of his appeal, but apparently without that period of incarceration being counted toward completion of his sentence, inasmuch as "it is not claimed that he is treated as a convict in the penitentiary undergoing the sentence pronounced in pursuance of the judgment appealed from, but only that the officer uses that institution as a place for the confinement of the accused while the latter is in his custody" (US 113:149).

Clawson's appeal before the United States Supreme Court raised only the question of whether he was entitled to be released on bail as a matter of right. On this issue the Court held that he had been deprived of no right since the granting of bail was a matter of discretion. The Court declined to reach the question of whether the Utah courts had abused their discretion in denying Clawson bail or whether the marshal's action in placing Clawson in the state penitentiary pending his appeal was legal.

Such a ruling, thus, made the appeal of polygamy convictions a potentially very costly privilege for convicted polygamists. By staying execution of an appellant's sentence and denying bail, further years could, in effect, be added to his sentence. Mormon attempts to resist polygamy prosecutions by raising all legal defenses and appealing all decisions thus became a more costly practice that might result only in greater punishment being inflicted on those who resisted.

4. The two *Eldredge* decisions arose from the case of George Q. Cannon. Cannon was arrested for cohabitation and required to post $10,000 bail. The money was provided by Horace S. Eldredge and Francis Armstrong. When Cannon went into hiding, the United States instituted an action to recover on Eldredge's bond. Eldredge asserted a number of defenses based on alleged defects in the indictment brought against Cannon, including the argument that two cohabitation charges had been brought against Cannon, contrary to the Supreme Court's ruling in *In re Snow*. Thus, two separate judgments were levied against the sureties, one for each cohabitation indictment (P. 14:46). While conceding that one of Cannon's indictments must necessarily be invalid, the Utah Supreme Court refused to release Eldredge from either bond. According to the court: "It is an anomalous situation, but one of the accused's and his sureties' own making; for this double responsibility could have been avoided by the accused having been produced in court at the appointed time. Trial and judgment upon one of the charges or indictments would thus have been reached. The accused then could not have been called to trial upon the other" (P. 14:46).

8. The War against Mormon Society

1. Construction of a "pioneer iron mission" at Cedar City began in late 1851. By 1858, the Mormons had expended approximately $150,000 but had been unable to overcome the technical problems in producing usable iron. The result of nearly ten years' labor was "nothing more than a few hand-irons, kitchen utensils, flat irons, wagon wheels, molasses rolls, and machine castings" (Arrington 1958, 127).

Wool manufacturing equipment purchased in England in 1853 did not arrive in Salt Lake until 1862. The industry was never successful because of the scarcity of sheep. A large cotton mission established in southern Utah had a greater, though temporary, success. During the Civil War, Utah was even able to ship some cotton east. The drop in cotton prices after the Civil War, labor shortages, and inhospitable soil and climate all conspired to strangle this fledgling industry by the end of the century (Arrington 1958, 121–22, 216–22).

Mormon farmers were successful in raising sugar beets, but the Mormons were unable to process the beets successfully into sugar. They used equipment purchased in Europe which was laboriously hauled across the prairies in wagons. All told, the church and private investors lost nearly $150,000 in this venture. In the 1890s, however, Mormons established a successful sugar factory (Arrington 1958, 116–20).

Thomas Howard, a skilled English papermaker and convert to the church, established the first successful paper mill west of the Mississippi in Utah, and a church-sponsored pottery works became operational after an expenditure of $12,000. In 1856, a successful pottery business was established without church support (Arrington 1958, 114–16).

Mormon leaders sponsored the construction of trunk railroad lines connecting the Mormon settlements in Utah and Idaho with the transcontinental railroad. Soon after completion, the more important lines were sold to the Union Pacific Railroad, achieving the church's principal goal of improving transportation among the Mormon settlements.

2. Utah's present law, like that of many states, similarly provides that an illegitimate child may inherit from his father if he has been acknowledged by his father, if the natural parents participated in a marriage ceremony before or after the birth, or if paternity has been otherwise satisfactorily established (Utah Code Ann. § 75-2-109b [1953]).

3. See, e.g., *Pratt v. Young*, Utah 1:347 (1876); *Cain Heirs v. Young*, Utah 1:361 (1876); and *Cooke v. Young*, Utah 2:253 (1876). The Young involved in this last suit was Brigham's grantee, Hyrum S. These cases involve disputes over possession and ownership of real property.

11. Mormon Land Policy and Church Courts

1. The Great Salt Lake High Council purchased lands in the Ogden region from Miles Goodyear, an Indian trader, which he claimed he held on a Mexican grant. Most historians, however, have concluded that Goodyear

fabricated the grant since it appears that no Spanish or Mexican grants were ever made in the intermountain region (Morgan 1940, 66, 73 n.20).

2. Hansen 1967, 125.

3. CHC 3:269. This same policy was first announced in Garden Grove, Iowa, on 25 April 1846, when Brigham Young had advised that "if a man would not till his land, it should be taken from him," and "No man shall hold more land than he can cultivate" (see ibid., 54–55). Roberts correctly states that "these views he had of land ownership . . . governed him throughout his colony-planting career. . . ."

4. Morgan 1940, 66, 73.

5. Ibid., 75.

6. Ibid., 77, 78. Morgan notes that exclusive mill sites and timber grants were granted by the High Council as early as October 1847 (78 n.39).

7. Rollins, 239, 244.

8. Hunter, 162.

9. Preemption Act, ch. 16, *Stat.* 6, 453–58 (1841).

10. Homestead Act, ch. 75, *Stat.* 12, 392–93 (1862).

11. Desert Land Act, ch. 108, *Stat.* 19, 377–80 (1877).

12. Mormon Water Law and Dispute Resolution

1. The common-law doctrine that the riparian landowner had a vested right to make reasonable use of water in its streamflow was commonly accepted in the eastern states. See, e.g., *Ingraham v. Hutchinson*, Conn. 2:584, 590, 1818; *Tyler v. Wilkenson*, F. Cas. 14:312, F. Cas. 24:474 (D.R.I. 1827).

2. The earliest judicial acceptance of the doctrine of prior appropriation as a customary substitute for the common law of riparian rights is *Irwin v. Phillips*, Cal. 5:140, Am. Dec. 63:113, 1855.

3. In *Clough v. Wing*, Ariz. 2:371, P. 17:453, 1888, and in *United States v. Rio Grande Dam Irrigation Co.*, N.M. 9:292, P. 51:674, 1898, the respective supreme courts for Arizona and New Mexico recognized the law of prior appropriation as settled by legislation, judicial decision, and custom antedating American sovereignty of the area.

13. Domestic Conflict and Church Courts

1. Blackstone stated the common-law rule of patriarchal preference as follows: "The legal power of a father (for a mother, as such, is entitled to no power, but only to reverence and respect,) the power of a father, I say, over the persons of his children ceases at the age of twenty-one. . . . Yet, till that age arrives, this empire of the father continues even after his death; for he may by his will appoint a guardian to his children" (*Blackstone*, 2:452–53). Justice Joseph Story (in this country) acknowledged the "right of the father to have the care and custody of his children. That right in a general sense is not to be disputed" (*Story*, 3:377–78). Similarly, Kent stated the rule as follows:

"The father (and on his death, the mother) is generally entitled to the custody of the infant children" (*Kent,* 2:218).

It is true that a "tender years" presumption giving preference to the mother in the case of a young child, particularly a daughter, began to emerge in some jurisdictions in the mid-nineteenth century (Roth 1976–77, 432–34 n.38). Thus the Mormon position may be viewed as one of the earliest systems of developing a preference for the mother. For a general discussion of this area, see Mangrum 1981–82.

15. Tortious Conduct and Church Courts

1. Torts as a separate branch of law was given little attention in American legal history until the late nineteenth century. Legal historian Edward White notes that "the first American treatise on torts appeared in 1859, torts was first taught as a separate law school subject in 1870, the first torts casebook was published in 1874" (White, "The Intellectual Origins of Tort Law in America," *Yale L.J.* 86:671 [1977]). White adds that while courses in contract and property were regular subjects at Litchfield and Harvard Law School, at these, "the primary centers of formal legal education in the early nineteenth century . . . no courses in Torts were offered . . . and almost no attention was given to individual actions in tort, such as assault, battery, defamation, deceit, or false imprisonment. . . . Moreover, the great treatise writers of the early nineteenth century, James Kent and Joseph Story, did not perceive Torts as a discrete legal subject" (ibid.). This is not to suggest that the civil courts were not hearing tortious claims during this period, but only to point out that common-law actions in tort were undergoing a formative transition during this period. The availability of the ecclesiastical forums for tort disputes allowed the Saints to control their own development of tort principles.

Bibliography

Aaron, Richard I. "Mormon Divorce and the Statute of 1852: Questions for Divorce in the 1980's." *Journal of Contemporary Law* 8 (1982):5–45.

Ahlstrom, Sidney E. *A Religious History of the American People.* 2 vols. Garden City, N.Y.: Image Books, 1975.

Alexander, Thomas Glen. "The Utah Federal Courts and the Areas of Conflict, 1850–96." M.A. thesis, Utah State University, 1961.

Allen, James B. "The Development of County Government in the Territory of Utah, 1850–1896." M.A. thesis, Brigham Young University, 1956.

———. "The Unusual Jurisdiction of County Probate Courts in the Territory of Utah." *Utah Historical Quarterly* 36 (Spring 1968):132–42.

———., and Glen M. Leonard. *The Story of the Latter-day Saints.* Salt Lake City: Deseret Book Co., 1976.

American Decisions (Select Cases). San Francisco: Bancroft-Whitney Co., 1910–.

American Law Reports Annotated. 175 vols.; 2d series, 100 vols.; 3d series, 100 vols.; 4th series, 37 vols. to date. Rochester, N.Y.: Lawyers Co-operative Publishing Co.; San Francisco, Cal.: Bancroft-Whitney Co., 1919–.

Anderson, Mark H. "The Efficient Use of Utah's Irrigation Water: Increased Transferability of Water Rights." *Utah Law Review* 1975 (1975):158–78.

Anderson, Richard Lloyd. "The Impact of the First Preaching in Ohio." *BYU Studies* 11 (Summer 1971):474–96.

Andrew, Laurel B. *The Early Temples of the Mormons: The Architecture of the Millennial Kingdom in the American West.* Albany: State University of New York Press, 1978.

Andrus, Hyrum L. *Doctrinal Themes of the Doctrine and Covenants.* Provo, Utah: Brigham Young University Press, 1970.

———. *Doctrines of the Kingdom.* Salt Lake City: Bookcraft, Inc., 1973.

———. *Joseph Smith and World Government.* Salt Lake City: Deseret Book Co., 1958.

Arizona: Reports of cases argued and determined in the Supreme Court of the State of Arizona. St. Paul, Minn.: West Publishing Co., 1866–.

Arrington, Leonard J. *Brigham Young.* New York: Alfred A. Knopf, 1985.

———. "Early Mormon Communitarianism: The Law of Consecration and Stewardship." *Western Humanities Review* 7 (Autumn 1953):341–69.

———. *Great Basin Kingdom: An Economic History of the Latter-day Saints.* Cambridge, Mass.: Harvard University Press, 1958.

————, ed. "Crusade against Theocracy: The Reminiscences of Judge Jacob Smith Boreman of Utah, 1872–1877." *Huntington Library Quarterly* 24 (November 1960):1–45.

————, and Davis Bitton. *The Mormon Experience: A History of the Latter-day Saints.* New York: Alfred A. Knopf, 1979.

————., Feramorz Y. Fox, and Dean May. *Building the City of God: Community and Cooperation among the Mormons.* Salt Lake City: Deseret Book Co., 1976.

Bachman, Daniel W. "A Study of the Mormon Practice of Plural Marriage before the Death of Joseph Smith." M.A. thesis, Purdue University, 1975.

Backman, Milton V., Jr. *American Religions and the Rise of Mormonism.* Salt Lake City: Bookcraft, Inc., 1965.

————. *The Heavens Resound: The History of the Latter-day Saints in Ohio, 1830–1838.* Salt Lake City: Deseret Book Co., 1983.

————. "The Quest for a Restoration: The Birth of Mormonism in Ohio." *BYU Studies* 12 (Summer 1972):346–64.

Bancroft, Hubert Howe. *History of Utah: 1540–1887.* San Francisco: The History Company, 1890.

Barrett, Ivan J. *Joseph Smith and the Restoration.* Provo, Utah: Brigham Young University Press, 1974.

Bates, Irene M., "William Smith, 1811–1893: Problematic Patriarch." *Dialogue* 16 (Summer 1983):11–23.

Bedell, George C., Leo Sandon, Jr., and Charles Wellborn. *Religion in America.* New York: Macmillan, 1975.

Bennett, John C. *The History of the Saints or an Expose of Joe Smith and Mormonism.* Boston: Leland & Whitney, 1842.

Benton, Abram W. "Mormonites." *Evangelistical Magazine and Gospel Advocate* (Utica, N.Y.) 2 (April 9, 1831):120.

Bestor, Authur E., Jr. *Backwoods Utopias: The Sectarian Origins and the Overnite Phase of Communitarian Socialism in America: 1663–1829.* Philadelphia: University of Pennsylvania Press, 1950.

Bitton, Davis. "The Waning of Mormon Kirtland." *BYU Studies* 12 (Summer 1972):455–64.

Black, Barbara A. "The Constitution of Empire: The Case for the Colonists." *University of Pennsylvania Law Review* 124 (May 1976):1157–1211.

Blackstone, William. *Commentaries on the Laws of England.* 17th ed., 4 vols. London: Richard Taylor, 1830.

Blakely, Thomas A. "Utah's Runaway Government Officials of 1851." *Utah Forum* 2 (Winter 1983):13–27.

Bloomfield, Maxwell. "Lawyers and Public Criticism: Challenge and Response in Nineteenth-Century America." *American Journal of Legal History* 15 (1971):269–277.

Book of Commandments. Independence, Mo.: W. W. Phelps & Co., 1833.

Book of Mormon. Salt Lake City: Church of Jesus Christ of Latter-day Saints, 1986 printing.

Braden, George D., and Rubin G. Cohn. *The Illinois Constitution: An Annotated and Comparative Analysis*. Urbana: University of Illinois, Institute of Government and Public Affairs, 1969.

Brodie, Fawn M. *No Man Knows My History: The Life of Joseph Smith, the Mormon Prophet*. 2d ed., rev. and enl. New York: Alfred A. Knopf, 1972.

Brooks, Juanita. *The Mountain Meadows Massacre*. New ed. Norman: University of Oklahoma Press, 1962.

————, ed. *On the Mormon Frontier: The Diary of Hosea Stout, 1844–1861*. 2 vols. Salt Lake City: University of Utah Press, 1964.

Buerger, David John. "The Fullness of the Priesthood: The Second Anointing in Latter-day Saint Theology and Practice." *Dialogue* 16 (Spring 1983):10–46.

Bush, Lester E., Jr. "The Word of Wisdom in Early Nineteenth-Century Perspective." *Dialogue* 14 (Autumn 1981):46–65.

Bushman, Richard L. *Joseph Smith and the Beginnings of Mormonism*. Urbana: University of Illinois Press, 1984.

California Appeals: Reports of cases determined in the District Courts of Appeal of the State of California. San Francisco: Bancroft-Whitney Co., 1906–.

California Reporter: Reports of cases determined in the Supreme Court of the State of California. 209 vols. to date. St. Paul, Minn.: West Publishing Co., 1960–.

California: Reports of the cases determined in the Supreme Court, State of California. San Francisco: Bancroft-Whitney Co., 1872–.

California Reports, Second Series: Reports of cases determined in the Supreme Court of the State of California. San Francisco: Bancroft-Whitney Co., 1935.

Cannon, Donald Q., and Lyndon W. Cook, eds. *Far West Record: Minutes of the Church of Jesus Christ of Latter-day Saints, 1830–1844*. Salt Lake City: Deseret Book Co., 1983.

Cannon, Kenneth L. II. "'Mountain Common Law': The Extralegal Punishment of Seducers in Early Utah." *Utah Historical Quarterly* 51 (Fall 1983):308–27.

Cannon, M. Hamlin, ed. "Documents: Bankruptcy Proceedings against Joseph Smith in Illinois." *Pacific Historical Review* 14 (December 1945):425–33.

Chamberlin, Ralph V. *The University of Utah: A History of Its First Hundred Years: 1850 to 1950*. Salt Lake City: University of Utah Press, 1960.

Chapin, H. Gerald. *Handbook of the Law of Torts*. St. Paul, Minn.: West Publishing Co., 1917.

Clark, J. *Messages of the First Presidency of the Church of Jesus Christ of Latter-day Saints, 1833–1964*. 6 vols. Salt Lake City: Bookcraft, Inc., 1965.

C. M. "The Original Prophet by a Visitor to Salt Lake City." *Fraser's Magazine* 87 (n.s. vol. 7, no. 38, 1873):225.

Collier, Fred C., and Robert R. Black, comps. *The Trials for the Membership of John W. Taylor and Mathaias [sic] F. Cowley*. 2d printing, n.p., 1976.

The Compiled Laws of the Territory of Utah. Salt Lake City: Deseret News Steam Printing Establishment, 1876.

Congressional Globe. Washington, D.C.: Government Printing Office, 1835–73.

Congressional Record. Washington, D.C.: Government Printing Office, 1873–.

Cook, Lyndon W. *The Revelations of the Prophet Joseph Smith*. Provo, Utah: Seventies' Mission Bookstore, 1981.

Corpus Juris Secundum: A Complete Restatement of the Entire American Law as Developed by All Reported Cases. St. Paul, Minn.: West Publishing Co., 1936–.

Creer, Leland Hargrave. *Utah and the Nation*. University of Washington Publications in the Social Sciences, vol. 7. Seattle: University of Washington Press, 1929.

Davis, Ray Jay. "Plural Marriage and Religious Freedom: The Impact of Reynolds v. United States." *Arizona Law Review* 15 (1973):287–306.

———. "The Polygamous Prelude." *American Journal of Legal History* 6 (1962): 1–27.

Davies, W. D. "Israel, the Mormons and the Land." In *Reflections on Mormonism*, ed. Truman Madsen. Provo, Utah: Religious Studies Center Monograph Series, 1978.

Dobbs, Dan B. *Handbook on the Law of Remedies: Damages–Equity–Restitution*. St. Paul, Minn.: West Publishing Co., 1973.

Doctrine and Covenants of the Church of Jesus Christ of Latter-day Saints. Salt Lake City: Church of Jesus Christ of Latter-day Saints, 1981 printing.

Document Containing the Correspondence, Orders, &c in Relations to the Disturbances with the Mormons; and the Evidence Given before the Hon. Austin A. King, . . . November 12, 1838, on the Trial of Joseph Smith, Jr., and Others, for High Treason and Other Crimes against the State. Fayette: Missouri General Assembly, 1841.

Dredge, C. Paul. "Dispute Settlement in the Mormon Community: The Operation of Ecclesiastical Courts in Utah." In *Access to Justice*, vol. 4: *The Anthropological Perspective: Patterns of Conflict Management: Essays in the Ethnography of Law*, ed. Klaus-Friedrich Koch. Alphen aan den Rijn, Neth.: Sijthoff and Noordhoff; Milan: Dott. A. Giuffre Editore, 1979.

Durham, Reed C., Jr. "The Election Day Battle at Gallatin." *BYU Studies* 13 (Autumn 1972):36–61.

Dworkin, Ronald. *Taking Rights Seriously*. Cambridge, Mass.: Harvard University Press, 1977.

Dwyer, Robert Joseph. *The Gentile Comes to Utah: A Study in Religious and Social Conflict (1862–1890)*. Rev. 2d ed. Salt Lake City: Western Epics, 1971.

Ecclesiastical Court Cases Collection, General Court Trials, 1832–1963. LDS Church Archives.

Ecclesiastical Court Cases, Disfellowship Records, 1839–1965. LDS Church Archives.

Egan, Howard R. *Pioneering the West, 1846 to 1878*. Ed. William M. Egan. Richmond, Utah: Howard R. Egan Estate, 1917.

Egbert, Donald Drew, and Stow Persons, eds. *Socialism and American Life*. 2 vols. Princeton: Princeton University Press, 1952.

Ehat, Andrew F. " 'It Seems Like Heaven Began on Earth': Joseph Smith and the Constitution of the Kingdom of God." *BYU Studies* 20 (Spring 1980):253–80.

———. "Joseph Smith's Introduction of Temple Ordinances and the 1844 Mormon Succession Question." M.A. thesis, Brigham Young University, 1982.

———., and Lyndon W. Cook. *The Words of Joseph Smith*. Provo, Utah: Religious Studies Center Monograph Series, 1980.

Eliade, Mircea. *Patterns in Comparative Religion*. New York: New American Library, 1974.

Ericksen, Ephraim Edward. *The Psychological and Ethical Aspects of Mormon Group Life*. Salt Lake City: University of Utah Press, 1922.

Far West Record. "The Conference Minutes and Record Book of Christ's Church of Latter-day Saints, Belonging to the High Council of Said Church or Other Successors in Office of Caldwell County, Missouri." *Far West* (April 6, 1838).

Federal Cases: Comprising cases argued and determined in the Circuit and District Courts of the United States. 30 vols. St. Paul, Minn.: West Publishing Co., 1894–97.

Federal Reporter, Second Series: Cases argued and determined in the United States Courts of Appeals, United States Court of Claims, and United States Court of Customs and Patents. St. Paul, Minn.: West Publishing Co., 1925–.

Federal Rules of Evidence. St. Paul, Minn.: West Publishing Co., 1987.

Federal Supplement: Comprising cases argued and determined in the District Courts of the United States. St. Paul, Minn.: West Publishing Co., 1933–.

Fiedler, George. *The Illinois Law Courts in Three Centuries, 1673–1973: A Documentary History*. Berwyn, Ill.: Physicians' Record Co., 1973.

Fielding, Robert Kent. "The Growth of the Mormon Church in Kirtland, Ohio." Ph.D. diss., Indiana University, 1957.

Firmage, Edwin Brown. "The Church in Politics? A Church Cannot Stand Silent in the Midst of Moral Decay." *Sunstone* 6 (July/August 1981):37–39.

———. "Eternal Principles of Government: A Theological Approach." *Ensign* 6 (June 1976):11–16.

———. "Jesus the Christ." *Ensign* 1 (November 1971):22–27.

———. "The Utah Supreme Court and the Rule of Law: Phillips and the Bill of Rights in Utah." *Utah Law Review* 1975 (1975):593–627.

Flanders, Robert Bruce. *Nauvoo: Kingdom on the Mississippi*. Urbana: University of Illinois Press, 1965.

Flynn, John J. "Federalism and Viable State Government—the History of Utah's Constitution." *Utah Law Review* 1966 (1966):311–25.

Ford, Thomas. *A History of Illinois, from Its Commencement as a State in 1818 to 1847*. Chicago: S. C. Griggs & Co., 1854.

Foster, Lawrence. *Religion and Sexuality: The Shakers, the Mormons and the Oneida Community*. Urbana: University of Illinois Press, 1984.

Freeman, Harrop A. "A Remonstrance for Conscience." *University of Pennsylvania Law Review* 106 (1958):806–30.

Fried, Charles. *Contract as Promise: A Theory of Contractual Obligation.* Cambridge, Mass.: Harvard University Press, 1981.

Gager, John G. "Early Mormonism and Early Christianity: Some Parallels and Their Consequences for the Study of New Religions." *Journal of Mormon History* 9 (1982):53–60.

Gayler, George R. "Attempts by the State of Missouri to Extradite Joseph Smith, 1841–1843." *Missouri Historical Review* 58 (October 1963):21–36.

Geauga [Ohio: County] Court of Common Pleas, [Extracts from Record Book U], October Term 1837. LDS Church Archives.

Gee, Elizabeth D. "Justice for All or for the 'Elect'? The Utah County Probate Court, 1855–72." *Utah Historical Quarterly* 48 (Spring 1980):129–47.

Gentry, Leland H. "The Danite Band of 1838." *BYU Studies* 14 (Summer 1974):421–50.

———. "A History of the Latter-day Saints in Northern Missouri from 1836 to 1839." Ph.D. diss., Brigham Young University, 1965.

Godfrey, W. Kenneth. "Causes of Mormon–Non-Mormon Conflict in Hancock County." Ph.D. diss., Brigham Young University, 1967.

Goodwin, C. C. *History of the Bench and Bar.* Salt Lake City: Interstate Press Assoc. Publishers, 1913.

Grant, Frederic, Jr. "Observations on the Pernicious Practice of the Law." *American Bar Association Journal* 68 (May 1982):580–82.

Gunn, Stanley R. *Oliver Cowdery: Second Elder and Scribe.* Salt Lake City: Bookcraft, Inc., 1962.

Hansen, Klaus J. *Mormonism and the American Experience.* Chicago: University of Chicago Press, 1981.

———. *Quest for Empire: The Political Kingdom of God and the Council of Fifty in Mormon History.* East Lansing: Michigan State University Press, 1967.

Hanson, Earl. "Money of the Mountains." *Improvement Era* 64 (March 1961):158.

Harrow, Joan Ray. "Joseph L. Rawlins, Father of Utah Statehood." *Utah Historical Quarterly* 44 (Winter 1976):59–75.

Hill, Marvin S. "Joseph Smith and the 1826 Trial: New Evidence and New Difficulties." *BYU Studies* 12 (Winter 1972):223–33.

———. "Secular or Sectarian History? A Critique of 'No Man Knows My History'." *Church History* 43 (March 1974):78–96.

———., C. Keith Rooker, and Larry T. Wimmer. *The Kirtland Economy Revisited: A Market Critique of Sectarian Economics.* Studies in Mormon History, vol. 3. Provo, Utah: Brigham Young University Press, 1977.

History of Jackson County, Missouri. Kansas City, Mo.: Union Historical Co., 1881.

Holmes, Oliver Wendell, Jr. *The Common Law.* 1881. Reprint, Boston: Little, Brown, 1944.

Hunter, Milton R. *Brigham Young the Colonizer.* Salt Lake City: Deseret News Press, 1941.

Illinois: Reports of cases at common law and in chancery, argued and determined in the Supreme Court of the State of Illinois. Chicago: Callaghan & Co., 1877–.

Jennings, Warren A. "Zion Is Fled: The Expulsion of the Mormons from Jackson County, Missouri." Ph.D. diss., University of Florida, 1962.

Jenson, Andrew. *Latter-day Saint Biographical Encyclopedia.* 4 vols. Salt Lake City: Andrew Jenson History Co., Andrew Jenson Memorial Association, 1901–36.

———, comp. *Church Chronology: A Record of Important Events Pertaining to the Church of Jesus Christ of Latter-day Saints.* 2d ed., rev. and enl. Salt Lake City: Deseret News Press, 1899.

Jensen, Therald N. "Mormon Theory of Church and State." Ph.D. diss., University of Chicago, 1938.

Journal History of the Church of Jesus Christ of Latter-day Saints. Microfilm in LDS Church Archives.

Journal of Discourses. 26 vols. 1855–86. Reprint, n.p., 1966.

Journal of the House of Representatives of the Twelfth General Assembly of the State of Illinois, 1840–41. Springfield: William Walters, 1840.

Journal of the Senate of the Twelfth General Assembly of the State of Illinois, Held in the City of Springfield, November 23, 1840. Springfield: William Walters, 1840.

Keeler, Joseph B. "The Bishop's Court, Its History and Proceedings." Lecture delivered before the High Council of the Utah State of Zion, 1902.

Kent, James W. *Commentaries on American Law.* 11th ed., 4 vols. Boston: Little, Brown, 1867.

Kilts, Clair T. "A History of the Federal and Territorial Court Conflicts in Utah, 1851–1874." M.A. thesis, Brigham Young University, 1959.

Kimball, James L., Jr. "The Nauvoo Charter: A Reinterpretation." *Journal of the Illinois State Historical Society* 64 (Spring 1971):66–78.

———. "A Study of the Nauvoo Charter, 1840–1845." M.A. thesis, University of Iowa, 1966.

———. "A Wall to Defend Zion: The Nauvoo Charter." *BYU Studies* 15 (1975):491–97.

[Knight, Newel.] *Newel Knight's Journal.* In *Scraps of Biography.* Faith-promoting Series, no. 10. Salt Lake City: Juvenile Instructor Office, 1883.

Kurland, Philip B., and Gerhard Casper, eds. *Landmark Briefs and Arguments of the Supreme Court of the United States: Constitutional Law.* 142 vols. to date. Washington, D.C.: University Publications of America, 1978–.

LaFave, Wayne R., and Jerold H. Israel. *Criminal Procedure.* Hornbook Series, student ed. St. Paul, Minn.: West Publishing Co., 1985.

Larsen, Herbert Ray. " 'Familism' in Mormon Social Structure." Ph.D. diss., University of Utah, 1954.

Larson, Gustive O. *The "Americanization" of Utah for Statehood.* San Marino, Cal.: Huntington Library, 1971.

———. "The Crusade and the Manifesto." In *Utah's History,* ed. Richard D. Poll. Provo, Utah: Brigham Young University Press, 1978a.

———. "Government, Politics, and Conflict." In *Utah's History,* ed. Richard D. Poll. Provo, Utah: Brigham Young University Press, 1978b.

Laws of the State of Utah. Salt Lake City: 1896–.

Layton, Robert L. "Kirtland: A Perspective on Time and Place." *BYU Studies* 11 (Summer 1971):423–38.

LDS Church Archives. Historical Department, Church of Jesus Christ of Latter-day Saints, 50 East North Temple Street, Salt Lake City, Utah 84150.

LDS Church Library. Historical Department, Church of Jesus Christ of Latter-day Saints, 50 East North Temple Street, Salt Lake City, Utah 84150.

Leone, Mark P. *Roots of Modern Mormonism.* Cambridge, Mass.: Harvard University Press, 1979.

LeSueur, Stephen C. "The Mormon War: The Struggle to Maintain Civil Order in Northwestern Missouri in 1838." M.A. thesis, George Mason University, 1981.

Linford, Lawrence L. "Establishing and Maintaining Land Ownership in Utah prior to 1869." *Utah Historical Quarterly* 42 (Spring 1974):126–43.

Linford, Orma. "The Mormons and the Law: The Polygamy Cases: Part I." *Utah Law Review* 9 (1964):308–70.

———. "The Mormons and the Law: The Polygamy Cases: Part II." *Utah Law Review* 9 (1965):543–91.

———. "The Mormons, the Law, and the Territory of Utah." *American Journal of Legal History* 23 (July 1979):213–35.

Linn, William Alexander. *The Story of the Mormons: From the Date of Their Origin to the Year 1901.* New York: Macmillan, 1923.

Lyman, Edward Leo. "Isaac Trumbo and the Politics of Utah Statehood." *Utah Historical Quarterly* 41 (Spring 1973):128–49.

Lyon, T. Edgar. "Doctrinal Development of the Church during the Nauvoo Sojourn." *BYU Studies* 15 (Winter 1975):4.

McMurrin, Sterling M. Critique of William Mulder, "The Mormons in American History" (unpublished ms., 20 pp.).

Mangrum, R. Collin. "Exclusive Reliance on Best Interest May Be Unconstitutional: Religion as a Factor in Child Custody Cases." *Creighton Law Review* 15 (1981–82):25–82.

———. "Mormonism, Philosophical Liberalism and the Constitution." *BYU Studies* 27 (Summer 1987), in press.

———. "The Revolution That Never Was." Paper Presented at the Mormon History Association Conference, 1985.

Massachusetts Reports: Cases argued and determined in Supreme Judicial Court of Massachusetts. Boston: Little, Brown, 1875–.

Miller, Perry. "The Half-Way Covenant." *New England Quarterly* 6 (December 1933):676–715.

———. *The New England Mind: The Seventeenth Century.* New York: Macmillan, 1939.

———, and Thomas H. Johnson, eds. *The Puritans: A Sourcebook of Their Writings.* New York: Harper & Row, 1963.

Millet, Robert L. "The Development of the Concept of Zion in Mormon Theology." Ph.D. diss., Florida State University, 1983.

Minnesota: Cases argued and determined in the Supreme Court of Minnesota. St. Paul, Minn.: West Publishing Co., 1877–1977.

Missouri: Reports of cases argued and determined in the Supreme Court of the State of Missouri. St. Louis, Mo.: Gilbert Book Co., 1890–1956.

Morgan, Dale L. "The State of Deseret." *Utah Historical Quarterly* 8 (April, July, October 1940):67–239.

Mulder, William. "Immigration and the 'Mormon Question': An International Episode." *Western Political Quarterly* 9 (June 1956):416–33.

———. "Mormonism's Gathering: An American Doctrine with a Difference." *Church History* 23 (September 1954):3–18.

Nauvoo City Council Records. LDS Church Archives.

Nebeker, John. "Early Justice in Utah." Ms, 1884, reprinted in *Utah Historical Quarterly* 3 (January 1930):87–89.

Nelson, Lowry. *The Mormon Village: A Pattern and Technique of Land Settlement.* Salt Lake City: University of Utah Press, 1952.

Nevada: Reports of decisions of the Supreme Court of the State of Nevada. 1865–82. San Francisco: Bancroft-Whitney Co., 1877–.

Newell, Linda King, and Avery, Valeen Tippetts. *Mormon Enigma: Emma Hale Smith.* New York: Doubleday, 1985.

New Mexico: Reports of cases argued and determined in the Supreme Court of the Territory of New Mexico, 1852–83. 2 vols. Chicago: Callaghan & Co., 1897.

New York: Reports of cases argued and determined in the Court of Appeals of the State of New York. New York and Albany: Banks & Brothers, 1888–.

Nibley, Hugh. "The Hierocentric State." *Western Political Quarterly* 4 (June 1951):226–53.

———. *The Mythmakers.* Salt Lake City: Bookcraft, Inc., 1961.

———. "What Is Zion? A Distant View." In *What Is Zion?,* Joseph Smith Lecture Series 1972–73. N.p., n.d.

Nordhoff, Charles. *The Communistic Societies of the United States.* New York: Harper & Bros., 1875.

Northeastern Reporter: Cases argued and determined in the courts of Illinois, Indiana, Massachusetts, New York, and Ohio. St. Paul, Minn.: West Publishing Co., 1885–.

Northwestern Reporter: Cases argued and determined in the courts of Iowa, Michigan, Minnesota, Nebraska, North Dakota, South Dakota, and Wisconsin. St. Paul, Minn.: West Publishing Co., 1933–.

Note. "Potter v. Murray City. Another Interpretation of Polygamy and the First Amendment." *Utah Law Review* 1986 (1986):345.

Oaks, Dallin H. "Habeas Corpus in the State—1776–1865." *University of Chicago Law Review* 32 (1965a):243–88.

———. "The Suppression of the *Nauvoo Expositor.*" *Utah Law Review* 9 (1965b): 862–903.

———., and Joseph I. Bentley. "Joseph Smith and Legal Process: In the Wake of the Steamboat *Nauvoo.*" *BYU Law Review* 1976 (1976):735–82.

———., and Marvin S. Hill. *Carthage Conspiracy: The Trial of the Accused Assassins of Joseph Smith.* Urbana: University of Illinois Press, 1975.

Olsen, Steven L. "Zion: The Structure of a Theological Revolution." *Sunstone* 6 (November/December 1981):21–26.

Ostler, Blake T. "The Idea of Pre-Existence in the Development of Mormon Thought." *Dialogue* 15 (Spring 1982):59–78.

Pacific Reporter: Cases argued and determined in the courts of Arizona, California, Colorado, Idaho, Kansas, Montana, Nevada, New Mexico, Oklahoma, Oregon, Utah, Washington, and Wyoming. St. Paul, Minn.: West Publishing Co., 1931– .

Pacific Reporter, Second Series: Cases argued and determined in the courts of Arizona, California, Colorado, Idaho, Kansas, Montana, Nevada, New Mexico, Oklahoma, Oregon, Utah, Washington, and Wyoming. St. Paul, Minn.: West Publishing Co., 1931–.

Parkin, Max H. "Conflict at Kirtland: A Study of the Nature and Causes of External and Internal Conflict of the Mormons in Ohio between 1830 and 1838." M.A. thesis, Brigham Young University, 1966.

Partridge, Edward. "Extracts from an Affidavit Filed before Congress on May 15, 1839, at Quincy, Illinois." Original in National Archives, Mss 1942 #9, p. 5. Copies in possession of Max Parkin, Institute of Religion, Church of Jesus Christ of Latter-day Saints, Salt Lake City.

Pennsylvania State Reports: Containing Cases Adjudged in the Supreme Court. Philadelphia: T. & J. W. Johnson, 1846–.

Porter, Larry C. "I Have a Question: How Did the U.S. Press React When Joseph and Hyrum Were Murdered?" *Ensign* 14 (April 1984):22–23.

Powell, Jay E. "Fairness in the Salt Lake County Probate Court." *Utah Historical Quarterly* 38 (Summer 1970):256–62.

Pratt, Orson. *The Orson Pratt Journals.* Comp. Elden J. Watson. Salt Lake City: Elden J. Watson, 1975.

Pratt, Parley P. *Autobiography of Parley Parker Pratt.* Salt Lake City: Deseret Book Co., 1938.

Prosser, William L. *Handbook of the Law of Torts.* St. Paul, Minn.: West Publishing Co., 1941.

Quinn, D. Michael. "The Council of Fifty and Its Members, 1844 to 1945." *BYU Studies* 20 (Winter 1980):163–97.

———. *Early Mormonism and the Magic World View.* Salt Lake City: Signature Books, 1987.

———. "LDS Church Authority and New Plural Marriages, 1890–1904." *Dialogue* 18 (Spring 1985):9–105.

———. "The Mormon Succession Crises of 1844." *BYU Studies* 16 (Winter 1976):187–233.

Raber, Michael Scott. "Religious Polity and Local Production: The Origins of a Mormon Town." Ph.D. diss., Yale University, 1978.

Rawls, John. *A Theory of Justice.* Cambridge, Mass.: Belknap Press of Harvard University Press, 1971.

Ray County Circuit Court Records, July Term 1836. Original in Ray County Clerk's Office, Mo. Copies in possession of Max Parkin, Institute of Religion, Church of Jesus Christ of Latter-day Saints, Salt Lake City.

Report: Made to the Senate and House of Representatives of the State of Illinois, December 2, 1844, 14th Illinois Gen. Assembly, Senate Judiciary Committee, 1st Sess., 1844–45, 1:139–40.

Report of Mssrs. Brandebury, Brocchus, and Harris to the President of the United States, Washington, 19 Dec. 1851. House Executive Document 25, 1852.

Revised Statutes of Utah. Salt Lake City: Deseret News Publishing Co., 1898.

Richardson, James D., comp. *A Compilation of the Messages and Papers of the Presidents, 1789–1897.* 10 vols. Washington, D.C.: Government Printing Office, 1896–99.

Ritchie, John, Neill H. Alford, Jr., and Richard W. Effland. *Cases and Materials on Decedents' Estates and Trusts.* 5th ed. Mineola, N.Y.: Foundation Press, 1977.

Roberts, B. H. *Comprehensive History of the Church of Jesus Christ of Latter-day Saints.* 6 vols. Salt Lake City: Deseret Book Co., 1930.

——. *The Missouri Persecutions.* 1900. Reprint, Salt Lake City: Bookcraft, Inc., 1965a.

——. *The Rise and Fall of Nauvoo.* 1900. Reprint, Salt Lake City: Bookcraft, Inc., 1965b.

Rollins, George W. "Land Policies of the United States as Applied to Utah to 1910." *Utah Historical Quarterly* 20 (July 1952):239–51.

Roth, Allan. "The Tender Years Presumption in Child Custody Disputes." *Journal of Family Law* 15 (1976–77):423–62.

Rourke, Constance. "The Shakers." In *The Roots of American Culture and Other Essays,* ed. Van Wyck Brooks. New York: Harcourt, Brace, 1942.

Sampson, D. Paul, and Larry T. Wimmer. "The Kirtland Safety Society: The Stock Ledger Book and the Bank Failure." *BYU Studies* 12 (Summer 1972):427–36.

Senate Judiciary Committee. *Report on the Memorial of the Delegation of the Latter-day Saints.* Sen. Doc., 26th Cong., 1st Sess., 5 (1840).

Shipps, Jan. *Mormonism: The Story of a New Religious Tradition.* Urbana: University of Illinois Press, 1985.

Simpson, Alan. "The Covenant Community." In *Religion in America,* ed. John M. Mulder and John E. Wilson. Englewood Cliffs, N.J.: Prentice-Hall, 1978.

Smith, E. Gary. "The Patriarchal Crisis of 1845." *Dialogue* 16 (Summer 1983): 24–56.

Smith, Joseph, Jr. *History of the Church of Jesus Christ of Latter-day Saints.* 7 vols. Ed. B. H. Roberts. 2d ed. rev. Salt Lake City: Deseret Book Co., 1978.

——. *The Pearl of Great Price.* Salt Lake City: Church of Jesus Christ of Latter-day Saints, 1978 printing.

Smith, Joseph Fielding, comp. *Teachings of the Prophet Joseph Smith.* 2d ed. Salt Lake City: Deseret News Press, 1940.

Southwestern Reporter: Containing all the current decisions of the Supreme Courts of Missouri, Arkansas, and Tennessee, Court of Appeals of Kentucky, and Supreme Court and Court of Appeals (Criminal Cases) of Texas. 300 vols. St. Paul, Minn.: West Publishing Co., 1887–1928.

Statutes at Large of the United States of America. Boston: Little, Brown, 1789–.

Stenhouse, T. B. H. *The Rocky Mountain Saints: A Full and Complete History of the Mormons, from the First Vision of Joseph Smith to the Last Courtship of Brigham Young*. New York: D. Appleton and Co., 1873.

Stevens, Frank E. "Life of Stephen A. Douglas." *Journal of the Illinois State Historical Society* 16 (Oct. 1923–Jan. 1924):247–673.

Stirling, James Dunn. Letterbook, 1886–1890, Salt Lake Stake High Council Proceedings. LDS Church Archives.

Story, Joseph. *Commentaries on Equity Jurisprudence*. 14th ed., 4 vols. Boston: Little, Brown, 1918.

Swenson, Raymond T. "Resolution of Civil Disputes by Mormon Ecclesiastical Courts." *Utah Law Review* 1978 (1978):573–95.

Tanner, Jerald and Sandra. *Joseph Smith and Money Digging*. Salt Lake City: Modern Microfilm Co., 1970.

———. "Joseph Smith's 1826 Trial." Salt Lake City: Modern Microfilm Co., 1971.

Thomas, George. *The Development of Institutions under Irrigation: With Special Reference to Early Utah Conditions*. New York: Macmillan, 1920.

Tribe, Laurence H. *American Constitutional Law*. Mineola, N.Y.: Foundation Press, 1978.

Tullidge, Edward W. *Life of Brigham Young; or Utah and Her Founders*. New York: n.p., 1876.

United States Reports: Cases adjudged in the Supreme Court. Decisions of the United States Supreme Court before 1875 were compiled and printed under the names of the various official court reporters and were titled *Reports of Cases Argued and Adjudged in the Supreme Court of the United States*.

Urch, Erwin J. "The Public Career of William Barton Warren." *Journal of the Illinois State Historical Society* 21 (1928):93–110.

Utah Code Annotated, 1953. Containing the general and permanent laws of the state in force at the close of the twenty-ninth legislature, 1951. Indianapolis, Ind.: P. Smith Co., 1952.

Utah Supreme Court: Reports of cases decided in the Supreme Court of the State of Utah. Salt Lake City: Arrow Press, 1855–.

Utah (Ter.) Laws, memorials and resolutions of the Territory of Utah, 1851–1894. Salt Lake City: Star Print Co., [1851]–94.

Van Wagoner, Richard S. *Mormon Polygamy: A History*. Salt Lake City: Signature Books, 1986.

Wakolee, Beulah H. "A Comparison of the Original Springfield Charter and the Nauvoo City Charter." Unpublished ms, 1971. Photocopy in LDS Church Archives.

Wallace, Foster. "The Mormons in Hancock County." *The Review* (Dallas City, Hancock County, Ill.) March 20, April 10, 1902. Microfilm in LDS Historical Department Library, Salt Lake City.

Walters, Wesley P. "From Occult to Cult with Joseph Smith, Jr." *Journal of Pastoral Practice* 1 (Summer 1977):121–37.

————. "Joseph Smith's Bainbridge, N.Y., Court Trials." *Westminster Theological Journal* 36 (Winter 1974):123–55.

Warren, Charles. *Bankruptcy in United States History.* Cambridge, Mass.: Harvard University Press, 1935.

Weisbrod, Carol, and P. Sheingorn. "*Reynolds v. United States*: Nineteenth-Century Forms of Marriage and the Status of Women." *Connecticut Law Review* 10 (1978):828–58.

Wells, Merle W. *Anti-Mormonism in Idaho, 1872–92.* Studies in Mormon History, vol. 4. Provo, Utah: Brigham Young University Press, 1978.

Wendell, John L. *Reports of Cases Argued and Determined in the Supreme Court of Judicature, and in the Court for the Trial of Impeachments and the Correction of Errors of the State of New York.* Albany, N.Y.: Banks & Brothers, 1883.

Whitney, Orson F. *History of Utah.* 4 vols. Salt Lake City: George Q. Cannon & Sons Co., 1892–1904.

Widtsoe, John A. *The Principles of Irrigation Practice.* Rural Text-Book Series. New York: Macmillan, 1914.

Wilson, John F. "Some Comparative Perspectives on the Early Mormon Movement and the Church-State Question." *Journal of Mormon History* 8 (1981): 63–78.

Yeates, Jasper. *Reports of cases Adjudged in the Supreme Court of Pennsylvania, with Some Select Cases at nisi prius, and in the Circuit Courts, [1791–1808].* Philadelphia, reprinted by J. Campbell; St. Louis: W. J. Gilbers, 1871. (Originally published 1817–19.)

NEWSPAPERS

Burlington Hawkeye. LDS Church Archives.

Chardon Spectator & Geauga Gazette. Special Collections, Harold B. Lee Library, Brigham Young University, Provo, Utah.

Chattanooga Gazette. LDS Church Archives.

Chenango Union. Norwich, N.Y. Special Collections, Harold B. Lee Library, Brigham Young University, Provo, Utah.

Cleveland Daily Gazette. Bachman Ohio Research Files, LDS Church Archives.

Cleveland Herald and Gazette. Special Collections, Harold B. Lee Library, Brigham Young University, Provo, Utah.

Cleveland Weekly Gazette. Special Collections, Harold B. Lee Library, Brigham Young University, Provo, Utah.

Deseret News. LDS Church Library.

Evening and the Morning Star. LDS Church Archives.

Guerney Times. Bachman Ohio Research File, LDS Church Archives.

Nashville Daily News. LDS Church Archives.

Niles National Register. Bachman Ohio Research File, LDS Church Archives.

Ohio Repository. Bachman Ohio Research File, LDS Church Archives.

Ohio Star. LDS Church Archives.

Ohio Statesman. Bachman Ohio Research File, LDS Church Archives.

Painesville Republican. Bachman Ohio Research File, LDS Church Archives.

Painesville Telegraph. Special Collections, Harold B. Lee Library, Brigham Young University, Provo, Utah.

Times and Seasons. LDS Church Library.

Western Reserve Chronicle. Bachman Ohio Research File, LDS Church Archives.

Index

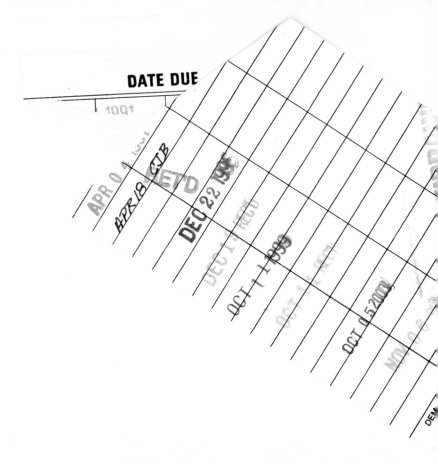